CARRIER CLASH

Books by Eric Hammel

76 Hours: The Invasion of Tarawa (with John E. Lane)
Chosin: Heroic Ordeal of the Korean War
The Root: The Marines in Beirut
Ace!: A Marine Night-Fighter Pilot in World War II
(with R. Bruce Porter)
Duel for the Golan (with Jerry Asher)
Guadalcanal: Starvation Island
Guadalcanal: The Carrier Battles
Guadalcanal: Decision at Sea
Munda Trail: The New Georgia Campaign
The Jolly Rogers (with Tom Blackburn)
Khe Sanh: Siege in the Clouds
First Across the Rhine (with David E. Pergrin)
Lima-6: A Marine Company Commander in Vietnam
(with Richard D. Camp)
Ambush Valley
Aces Against Japan
Aces Against Japan II
Aces Against Germany
Air War Europa: Chronology

CARRIER CLASH

THE INVASION OF GUADALCANAL &
THE BATTLE OF THE EASTERN SOLOMONS
AUGUST 1942

ERIC HAMMEL

ZENITH
PRESS

Books by Eric Hammel

76 Hours: *The invasion of Tarawa*

Chosin: *Heroic Ordeal of the Korean War*

The Root: *The Marines in Beirut*

Ace!: *A Marine Night-Fighter Pilot in World War II (with R. Bruce Porter)*

Duel for the Golan *(with Jerry Asher)*

Guadalcanal: *Starvation Island*

Guadalcanal: *The Carrier Battles*

Guadalcanal: *Decision at Sea*

Munda Trail: *The New Georgia Campaign*

The Jolly Rogers *(with Tom Blackburn)*

Khe Sanh: *Siege in the Clouds*

First Across the Rhine: *(with David E. Pergrin)*

Lima 6: *A Marine Company Commander in Vietnam (with Richard D. Camp)*

Ambush Valley

Fire in the Streets: *The Battle for Hue*

Six Days in June

Aces Against Japan

Aces Against Japan II

Aces Against Germany

Air war Europa: *Chronology*

Carrier Clash

Aces at War

Air War Pacific: *Chronology*

Aces in Combat

Bloody Tarawa

Marines at War

Carrier Strike

This edition published by Zenith Press, an imprint of MBI Publishing Company, Galtier Plaza, Suite 200, 380 Jackson Street, St. Paul, MN, 55101-3885 USA.

Published by arrangement with Pacifica Military History.

MBI Publishing Company Books are also available at discounts for in bulk quantities for industrial or sale-promotional use. For details write to Special Sales Manager at MBI Publishing Company, Galtier Plaza, Suite 200, 380 Jackson Street, St. Paul, MN, 55101-3885 USA

Cover design by Tom Heffron

ISBN: 0-7603-2052-7

Printed in the United States

For Barbara

Glossary and Guide to Abbreviations

A6M IJN Mitsubishi "Zero" fighter
A6M2-N IJN Nakajima "Zero" floatplane fighter
ACRM Aviation chief radioman
ACTG Advanced carrier training group
Adm Admiral
Airacobra USAAF Bell P-39 fighter
AirSoPac Aircraft, South Pacific Force
AM1 Aviation metalsmith 1st class
AMM3 Aviation machinist's mate 3d class
Angels Altitude expressed in thousands of feet
AOM2 Aviation ordnanceman 2d class
AP1 Aviation pilot 1st class
ARM2 Aviation radioman 2d class
AvCad Naval aviation cadet
Avenger USN Grumman TBF light/torpedo bomber
B5N IJN Nakajima "Kate" attack/torpedo bomber
BAR Browning automatic rifle
BB Battleship
Betty IJN Mitsubishi G4M twin-engine attack bomber

Bf-109 German Messerschmitt fighter

BM1 Boatswain's mate 1st class

Buntaicho IJN unit leader

Buster Radio code for "immediate"

Butai Unit

CA Heavy cruiser

CAP Chief aviation pilot

Capt Captain

Carp Warrant Carpenter

Catalina USN Consolidated PBY twin-engine amphibian patrol bomber

Cdr Commander

CEM Chief electrician's mate

ChElec Chief warrant electrician

ChMach Chief warrant machinist

Chutai IJN flight, usually six to nine planes

CinC Commander in chief

CL Light cruiser

CLAA Light antiaircraft cruiser

CMM Chief machinist's mate

CO Commanding officer

Col Colonel

ComAirSoPac Commander, Aircraft, South Pacific

Cox Coxswain

Cpl Corporal

CQM Chief quartermaster

CSF Chief ship fitter

CV Fleet aircraft carrier

CVE Escort aircraft carrier

CVL Light aircraft carrier

CWT Chief watertender

CXAM RCA experimental air-search radar

CY Chief yeoman

D3A IJN Aichi "Val" dive-bomber

Dauntless USN/USMC Douglas SBD dive-bomber

DD Destroyer

Devastator USN Douglas TBD light/torpedo bomber
E13A IJN Aichi "Jake" reconnaissance floatplane
EM3 Electrician's mate 3d class
Emily IJN Kawanishi H8K four-engine amphibian patrol bomber
Ens Ensign
Exec Executive officer
(F) Flagship
(FF) Fleet flagship
F1M IJN Mitsubishi "Pete" reconnaissance floatplane
F3 Fireman 3d class
F4F USN/USMC Grumman "Wildcat" fighter
FC3 Fire controlman 3d class
FDO Fighter direction officer
1stLt First lieutenant
1stSgt First sergeant
Fulmite Chemical fire retardant
G4M IJN Mitsubishi "Betty" twin-engine attack bomber
Gen General
GM2 Gunner's mate 2d class
Gun Warrant gunner
GySgt Gunnery sergeant
H6K IJN Kawanishi "Mavis" four-engine amphibian patrol bomber
H8K IJN Kawanishi "Emily" four-engine amphibian patrol bomber
HIJMS His Imperial Japanese Majesty's Ship
Hikokitai IJN carrier air group
Hikotaicho IJN air group leader
IFF Identification, friend or foe
IJN Imperial Japanese Navy
Jake IJN Aichi E13A reconnaissance floatplane
(jg) Junior grade
Kate IJN Nakajima B5N attack/torpedo bomber
LCdr Lieutenant commander
LSO Landing signal officer
Lt Lieutenant
Lt(jg) Lieutenant junior grade

LtCol Lieutenant colonel

Mach Warrant machinist

Maj Major

MajGen Major general

Maru Japanese transport or cargo ship

Mavis IJN Kawanishi H6K four-engine amphibian patrol bomber

MG Warrant marine gunner

mm Millimeter

MM1 Machinist's mate 1st class

MoMM2 Motor machinist's mate 2d class

NAP Naval aviation (enlisted) pilot

OS2U USN Vought "Kingfisher" observation scout floatplane

P-400 USAAF Bell Airacobra fighter (export model)

Pancake Radio code for "land immediately"

PB Patrol boat

PBY USN Consolidated "Catalina" twin-engine amphibian patrol bomber

Pete IJN Mitsubishi F1M reconnaissance floatplane

Pfc Private first class

PhM1 Pharmacist's mate 1st class

PhoM3 Photographer's mate 3d class

PO1 Petty officer 1st class

Pvt Private

RAdm Rear admiral

RAN Royal Australian Navy

RBA Rescue breathing apparatus

RE Warrant radio electrician

Rikusentai IJN special naval landing unit

RM3 Radioman 3d class

RN Royal Navy

S1 Seaman 1st class

SBD USN/USMC Douglas "Dauntless" dive-bomber

2dLt Second lieutenant

Sgt Sergeant

SgtMaj Sergeant Major

Shotai IJN fighter/bomber element, usually three planes

SM2 Signalman 2d class
SOC USN Curtiss observation scout floatplane
SoPac South Pacific Area/Force
Sub-Lt Sub-Lieutenant (as in Royal Australian Navy)
TBD USN Douglas "Devastator" light/torpedo bomber
TBF USN Grumman "Avenger" light/torpedo bomber
TBS "Talk Between Ships" voice radio
TSgt Technical sergeant
VAdm Vice admiral
Val IJN Aichi D3A dive-bomber
VB USN bombing squadron
VF USN fighting squadron
VMF USMC fighting squadron
VMO USMC observation squadron
VMSB USMC scout-bomber squadron
VP USN patrol squadron
VS USN scouting squadron
VT USN torpedo squadron
Wildcat USN/USMC Grumman F4F fighter
WO Warrant officer
WT1 Watertender 1st class
Y2 Yeoman 2d class
Zero IJN Mitsubishi A6M fighter

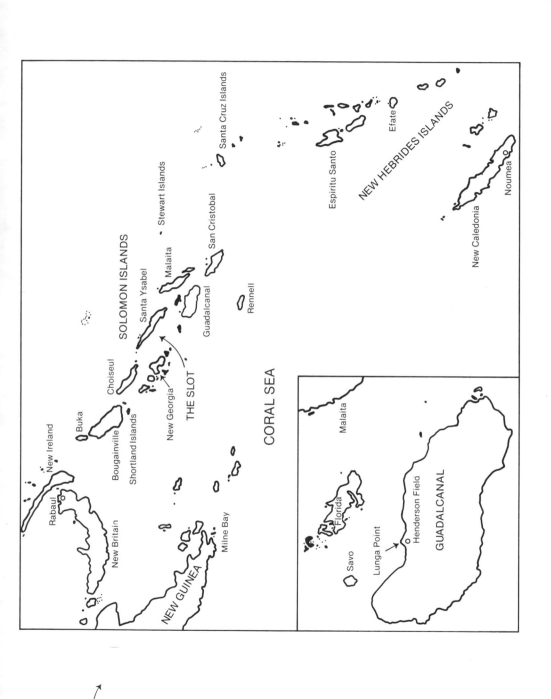

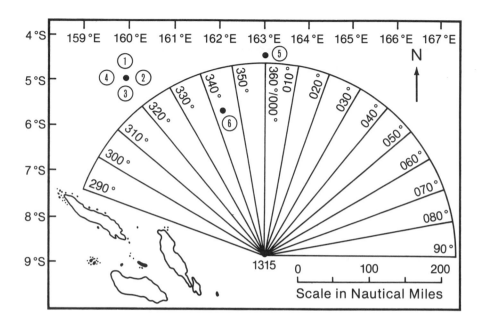

BATTLE OF THE EASTERN SOLOMONS
Air Group 6 Search
August 24, 1942

Sector	Pilots
290-300	Weissenborn
	Mears
300-310	Myers
	Corl
310-320	Jorgenson
	Bingaman
320-330	Jett
	Bye
330-340	Strong
	Richey
340-350	Davis
	Shaw
350-360	Lowe
	Gibson
360-010	Horenburger

CONTACTS WITH JAPANESE SHIPS
by Air Group 6 Searchers

1. Jett and Bye find **Ryujo**, 1440
2. Myers and Corl find **Ryujo**, 1500
3. Jorgenson and Bingaman find **Ryujo**, 1510
4. Strong and Richey find **Ryujo**, 1510
5. Lowe and Gibson find Abe's cruisers, 1510
6. Davis and Shaw find **Shokaku** and **Zuikaku**, 1545

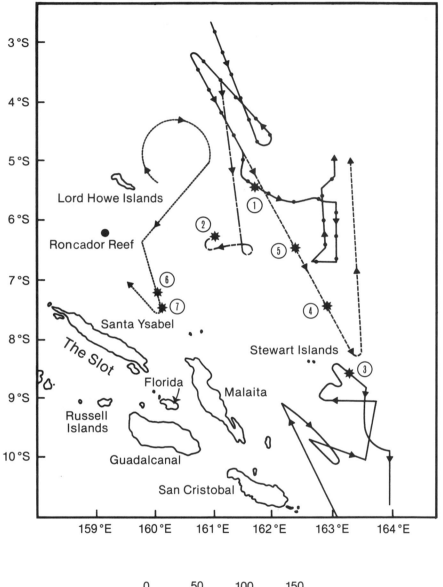

3 °S

4 °S

5 °S

6 °S

Lord Howe Islands

Roncador Reef

7 °S

8 °S

Santa Ysabel

The Slot

Florida

Malaita

Russell
Islands

Guadalcanal

San Cristobal

Stewart Islands

① ② ③ ④ ⑤ ⑥ ⑦

9 °S

10 °S

159 °E   160 °E   161 °E   162 °E   163 °E   164 °E

0   50   100   150

Scale in Nautical Miles

BATTLE OF THE EASTERN SOLOMONS
August 23-25, 1942

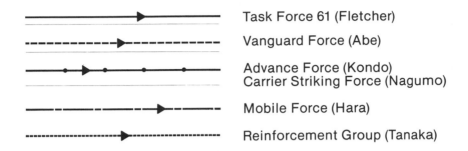

Task Force 61 (Fletcher)

Vanguard Force (Abe)

Advance Force (Kondo)
Carrier Striking Force (Nagumo)

Mobile Force (Hara)

Reinforcement Group (Tanaka)

August 24
1   1545 — Davis and Shaw find Nagumo.
2   1605 — Air Group 3 attacks **Ryujo.**
3   1712 — Japanese attack **Enterprise.**
4   1820 — U.S. torpedo bombers attack Kondo and Abe.
5   1820 — Elder and Gordon attack **Chitose.**
August 25
6   0835 — Cactus dive-bombers hit **Kinryu Maru** and **Jintsu.**
7   1015 — B-17s sink **Mutsuki.**

BOW

Port Bow Starboard Bow

Port Beam Starboard Beam

Port Quarter Starboard Quarter

STERN

Part I

★

Carrier Operations

Chapter 1

The world's first true aircraft carrier, HMS *Furious*, launched the world's first carrier air strike against German zeppelin sheds in northern Germany on July 19, 1918.

America's first true aircraft carrier, a converted collier, was recommissioned USS *Langley* on March 20, 1922, and designated CV-1 (*C* for carrier and *V* for heavier-than-air, a common designator for non—gas-filled flying machines). During the six years it took the United States to build two additional carriers, the *Langley* served as the test bed for the development of carrier-based air operations. Most of the techniques employed in launching and recovering carrier aircraft were developed and refined during the *Langley's* watch as the U.S. Navy's only operational flattop.

While the *Langley* pilots and aircrewmen were developing and learning their trade, the U.S. Navy was building two new fleet carriers. Both were converted from the newly built hulls of huge battlecruisers that were proscribed at the Naval Disarmament Conference held in Washington, D.C., in 1922. The first of the new electric-powered carriers to be launched was the *Saratoga* (CV-3), which was commissioned on November 16, 1927. Less than a month later, on December 15, the *Lexington* (CV-2) joined the United States Fleet. Both of the huge carriers were powered like the swift battlecruisers they were originally intended to be; both could run at nearly 35 knots (more than double the *Langley's* top speed of 14 knots). Moreover, both of the new carriers were large enough to operate at least seventy-five warplanes from their 800-foot-long, 160-foot-wide armored steel flight decks, and both were capable of sailing vast distances between refuelings. Both were considered strategic weapons of the first order, and their appearance on the high seas carried the potential for U.S. naval aviation well into the late first half of the twentieth century.

Only two years after the *Lexington* and *Saratoga* joined the United States Fleet, the U.S. Navy authorized construction of a small fourth carrier, the *Ranger* (CV-4), which was to be the namesake of a line of inexpensive but numerous new constructions. Though the *Ranger,* which was commissioned in 1934, was the first American carrier to be designed as such from the keel up, her marginal performance (top speed of 29 knots, deficient arresting gear, and elevators between the flight and hangar decks that did not quite fit the bill) forced naval strategists to opt for larger, more expensive carriers that could do the job required of them.

The designers amassed all the information that could be gleaned from the four previous efforts, and in 1932 the Navy requested two swift new 20,000-ton carriers. Though the original request was turned down by the Congress, the 1933 naval appropriations budget contained authorization for two slightly smaller but thoroughly modern fleet carriers.

The new ships, the *Yorktown* (CV-5) and the *Enterprise* (CV-6), were to be the prototypes for most of the fleet-type aircraft carriers that eventually carried the U.S. Navy through World War II. There were numerous changes made along the way, but the *Yorktown*-class carriers set the pace.

Each of the new carrier decks was constructed of teak or Douglas fir laid over a steel frame (similar to the *Langley's* and the *Ranger's,* but unlike the *Lexington's* and the *Saratoga's* steel platform flight decks). Both could get up to operational speeds of 32 knots, and both had plenty of built-in underwater anti-torpedo protection. The underwater protection was considered crucial for avoiding and defeating submarine- or air-launched torpedoes, and the high speed would aid in the launch and recovery of airplanes as well as in the avoidance of torpedoes and bombs. Each new carrier had three built-in elevators to speed the stowing and readying of airplanes between the flight and hangar decks. And both were fitted out with numerous antiaircraft weapons—up to 5-inch guns—mounted in gun galleries edging the flight deck. Each of the new carriers was capable of operating approximately seventy-five warplanes.

The *Langley* was downgraded to tender status in 1934, which allowed the United States to replace her within the 135,000-ton allocation provided for fleet carriers under the 1922 arms-control treaties. The lobby that had brought forth the *Ranger* as a precursor of small, inexpensive carriers got another chance. Thus the seventh U.S. carrier, the *Wasp* (CV-7), was something of a throwback. She was a vastly improved *Ranger*-type carrier, capable of operating a full seventy-five–plane air group (the standard of the day) as efficiently as her larger sisters. Numerous delays and ongoing upgrades prevented the *Wasp* from joining the United States Fleet until 1940.

The 1922 Washington Naval Disarmament Treaty lapsed at the end of 1936, but the U.S. Congress did not authorize any new carrier constructions until 1938, when a third *Yorktown*-class carrier, dubbed the *Hornet* (CV-8), was more or less forced upon a Navy that, strangely, desired no new carriers. The *Hornet* was commissioned on the eve of the Pacific War. A much-improved ninth fleet carrier, the *Essex* (CV-9), was authorized in 1938, but because of ongoing design changes, she and the rest of her new class would not begin appearing until 1943.

The need for other types of carriers besides standard fleet carriers was seen, but little was done before the outbreak of the Pacific War to get the new types into service. A number of cruiser hulls were set aside for a makeshift breed of light carriers (CVLs), but none of the new type would be operational until 1943. Also, a breed of small auxiliary carriers to be used as aircraft ferries or convoy escorts was authorized, and the first of these, a converted merchant ship recommissioned the USS *Long Island,* was commissioned in June 1941. Eventually dubbed escort carriers (CVEs), the auxiliary carriers would have been useful on all the war-torn oceans from the first day of the war. However, the numerous delays commonly associated with ironing out bugs in a new system and establishing a doctrine resulted in a slow start on new constructions.

Other world powers experimented with aircraft carriers during the interwar years. The Royal Navy, which was the first to employ carrier air power, built just three carriers between the wars but had four modern carriers under construction when war broke out in Europe in 1939. The Germans built just one carrier, and it had no impact upon the course of the war in Europe.

The U.S. Navy's only real competitor in the field of carrier-based aerial operations was Japan, a maritime nation whose position in the world depended utterly upon the strength of her Imperial Navy. Shackled like the U.S. Navy with the fruits of the 1922 naval disarmament accords, Japan was allotted tonnage in each category of warship at a rate only 60 percent that allotted the United States. Thus, the Japanese concentrated on getting more bang for the ton than did the Americans.

Japan's first true carrier, tiny *Hosho,* which weighed in at only 7,470 tons, was commissioned in 1922. Like the *Langley,* she served as the test bed for future constructions and the proving ground for Japanese carrier flight operations.

Japan's next two carriers—*Akagi* and *Kaga* (commissioned in March 1927 and March 1928, respectively)—were built upon the incomplete hulls of proscribed battlecruisers, just like the *Lexington* and the *Yorktown.* The *Kaga* weighed in at 38,200 tons, and the *Akagi* displaced 36,500 tons. (The *Lexington* and *Yorktown* were each rated at 36,000 tons.) The Japanese announced, however, that each of the new carriers was rated at 26,900 tons, thus saving the Imperial Navy 21,000 tons in its overall carrier construction allotment.

Neither of the big Japanese carriers had a superstructure, which was a familiar feature of all the American fleet carriers. Both also featured innovative upper and lower flight decks, which allowed for more rapid or simultaneous launch and recovery of airplanes. On the negative side, the two giant Japanese carriers could each operate air groups of only sixty warplanes, as compared to the American standard of seventy-five warplanes per carrier air group. (The *Kaga* and the *Akagi* were both extensively remodeled between 1935 and 1937 to increase their capacities to ninety warplanes each.)

The fourth Japanese carrier, the *Ryujo,* was completed in 1931. At 10,600 tons, she was rated a "light" carrier (CVL in U.S. naval parlance). She was capable of operating forty-six warplanes.

The *Soryu* and the *Hiryu* were authorized at 10,050 tons each when their keels were laid, but they wound up weighing in at 15,900 and 17,300 tons, respectively, when they were launched in December 1937 and July 1939, respectively, long after the expiration of the terms of the 1922 naval disarmament accords. They were similar in many ways to their contemporaries, the American *Yorktown*-class carriers.

Following the termination of the naval construction accords, Japan went into the business of building floating gunnery platforms—battleships and large cruisers. She did so pretty much at the expense of new carrier constructions. While geared up to almost manic levels, the Japanese shipbuilding industry was severely limited in its ability to churn out new ships. Rather late in the game, when some spare capacity became available, the Imperial Navy placed orders for a pair of thoroughly modern new carriers. These were the *Shokaku* and the *Zuikaku*, both rated at 26,675 tons, about 5,000 tons larger than the American *Yorktown*-class carriers. Each of the new Japanese carriers could steam at 34 knots (versus 32 for the *Yorktown*) and could operate ninety-six warplanes (versus seventy-five for all the American fleet carriers). The *Shokaku* was commissioned on August 8, 1941, and the *Zuikaku* was commissioned on September 25—just months before their air groups participated in the Pearl Harbor attack along with the air groups from the *Kaga, Akagi, Hiryu*, and *Soryu*.

Smaller Japanese carriers available on December 7, 1941, included the light carriers *Hosho* and *Ryujo* and the escort carrier (CVE) *Taiyo*. Light carriers *Shoho* and *Zuiho* were nearly ready for a wartime role.

The United States began the war with six operational fleet carriers (not counting the marginal *Ranger*) and one operational auxiliary carrier—plus several hybrid conversions used exclusively for ferrying work. Japan opened the war with six fleet carriers, four light carriers, and one escort. The opponents traded the light carrier *Shoho* for the fleet carrier *Lexington* at the Coral Sea on May 7–8, 1942. That trade accrued some additional advantage to the Japanese side in relative numbers of carrier decks, tonnage, and numbers of operational carrier warplanes. Midway more than redressed the imbalance. There, the U.S. Navy lost the *Yorktown*, but Japan lost the fleet carriers *Kaga, Akagi, Hiryu*, and *Soryu*.

By the end of the first week of June 1942, the United States Navy was left with four operational fleet carriers and their air groups, and Japan was

left with two fleet carriers, three light carriers, and one escort. Two new
Japanese fleet carriers were about to be commissioned, but neither would
be fully operational for some months. Similarly, several American light and
auxiliary carriers under construction or about to be launched could not be
operational before the end of 1942 or by mid-1943.

Chapter 2

U.S. Navy and Imperial Navy fleet carrier air groups in mid-1942 each were composed of three basic warplane types: torpedo/horizontal bombers, scout/dive-bombers, and fighters. The mix of airplanes within a fleet carrier air group reflected the similar—but not identical—offensive and defensive doctrines employed by the two warring powers.

The U.S. Navy's standard fighter of the period was the Grumman F4F-4 Wildcat. First employed at Midway as a replacement for the underpowered four-gun F4F-3 variant, the F4F-4 featured six .50-caliber wing-mounted machine guns, a fairly modern gunsight, improved performance characteristics, and, as important as anything else, folding wings. It had a top speed of 318 miles per hour at 19,400 feet and a combat radius (quite a bit less than half the 770-mile maximum range) of well under 300 miles. While the enhanced performance and fighting characteristics improved the chances of individual fighters to triumph and survive in aerial combat, the innovative folding wings allowed the U.S. Navy to pack more Wildcats aboard the fleet carriers of the day—an extremely significant development. In July 1942, the typical fleet carrier fighter squadron carried thirty-six Wildcats on its roster.

Basically a defensive weapon—an interceptor—the carrier-based Wildcat was marginally designed to accompany carrier-launched bombers to their targets in order to fend off enemy fighters. The real function of the carrier-based F4F was to patrol above friendly carriers and other ships to fend off enemy bombers and fighters. A distinctly tertiary role—after bomber escort—was the provision of ground strafing during hit-and-run raids of the type that had characterized U.S. Navy carrier operations very early in the war. And there was an as-yet nascent role in the field of support for forces ashore.

The Wildcat fighter was a mixed blessing, but the full extent of the mixture was still not completely known, even after the type had weathered a fair number of fighter-versus-fighter engagements during its second carrier battle, at Midway in June 1942. For example, there was an unperceived weakness arising from the placement of oil coolers in either wing. As were all U.S. Navy aircraft throughout World War II, the Wildcat was powered by an air-cooled engine; but oil was vitally important as a lubricant, and so oil coolers were vital, too. There was no place to put them except in the wings, but the wings were big targets in an aerial engagement, and so the coolers were vulnerable. If one was shot full of holes, the engine would eventually seize for lack of oil. Another mixed blessing was the F4F-4's six wing guns. The four guns in the F4F-3 had not had sufficient killing power, whereas the six guns in the F4F-4 certainly did. But the added weight and space requirements of the two extra guns meant that each gun was armed with fewer bullets, which translated to less time that the guns could be fired, which of course influenced the airplane's overall killing power. On balance, six guns with fewer bullets were probably better than four guns that could fire longer, but it was a very close call.

On the other hand, every Wildcat in the U.S. Navy inventory had a reasonably modern two-way radio. This was a terrific boon, for individual fighters could be precisely controlled from afar, and fighter pilots could warn one another about impending danger. Also, the Wildcat could absorb a terrific beating. Some performance was sacrificed to the likes of radios, self-sealing fuel tanks, and heavy armor plate behind the pilot's seat, but all these things added appreciably to the overall effectiveness of the fighter and the longevity of the pilot, so the sacrifices in performance were seen as trade-offs that by far favored the Wildcat's overall ability to fight and survive.

The U.S. Navy's standard scout/dive-bomber of the day was the Douglas SBD-3 Dauntless. Earlier versions had entered active service with the U.S. Marine Corps in mid-1940 and become operational aboard U.S. Navy carriers in March 1941. The SBD-3 had a top speed of only 250 miles per hour (actually quite speedy for a dive-bomber of the day), and its combat radious, fully loaded, was only 250 to 300 miles; but it boasted a substantial search range—up to 1,750 miles under ideal conditions. Its payload was usually a 500-pound bomb or 500-pound depth charge on patrol, and a 1,000-pound bomb on a strike mission. The extremely maneuverable SBD-3 was well adapted to defending itself with two forward-firing, cowl-mounted .50-caliber machine guns fired by the pilot, and two .30-caliber machine guns mounted on a free-moving ("flexible") frame fired by the rear-facing radioman-gunner.

Designed as an offensive dive-bomber and a long-range scout, the SBD was also typically employed close to a friendly carrier deck for antisubmarine defense or, in extreme cases, as a last line of defense against low-flying torpedo bombers. The SBD was a fine airplane.

The third and newest U.S. carrier type was the Grumman TBF-1 Avenger torpedo bomber. The Avenger was just coming into operational service in early June 1942, so only a handful appeared at Midway, and they had all been land-based. By far the largest carrier-based airplane type of mid-1942 and, indeed, of the Pacific War, the TBF was sturdy and long-ranged. The first carrier pilots to fly the Avenger operationally loved it for its ability to get into the air fully loaded long before running out of flight deck. The crew of three had adequate, if not ample, defensive firepower; the pilot could fire one cowl-mounted .30-caliber machine gun through the propeller disc, the radioman could fire a single power–turret-mounted .50-caliber machine gun, and the bombardier could fire a single tunnel-mounted .30-caliber stinger across the lower rear quadrant.

Used offensively, the Avenger could carry one aerial torpedo or up to four 500-pound bombs in the first internal bomb bay featured by any carrier bomber in the world. The TBF was also designed to fill in as a long-range scout and was often employed in tandem with SBDs. The TBF's only reasonable defensive role was on patrol against submarines, in which case it could carry up to four 500-pound aerial depth charges.

The Japanese fleet fighter of the day was the Mitsubishi A6M2 Model 21 Zero. This fast but very small and lightly built long-range airplane was, in its early career, simply the finest fighter available to any of the world's military powers. Its edge was its extreme maneuverability and exceptionally high rate of climb. Simply stated, in a one-on-one fight anytime in 1942, a well-flown Zero could almost always get away from nearly any adversary in the skies.

The Zero was armed with a pair of wing-mounted 20mm cannon and a pair of cowl-mounted 7.7mm machine guns. The two sets of guns could be fired separately or together. Usually, the 20mm cannon were used sparingly because of limitations in the number of 20mm rounds that could be carried (sixty) and because of the weapon's relatively low rate of fire and low muzzle velocity. The 7.7mm machine guns were used at longer ranges, mainly to get on target, whereas the 20mm cannon were usually used only for killing blows. In general, the carrier-based Zeros were used the same way as their American counterparts, for escorting bombers and to defend friendly warships under attack by enemy aircraft. However, because the Zero was longer ranged than the Wildcat, it almost always accompanied carrier-launched bombers; the Wildcat did so far less frequently.

Many Imperial Navy land-based fighter units were also equipped with A6M2 Model 21s, but there was also a new shorter-legged version that began appearing in mid-1942: the A6M3 Model 32. This airplane, with its shorter wingspan (for denser stowage aboard carriers), turned out unsuitable for long-range operations and was thus to be used mainly in a point-defense interceptor role in proximity to friendly bases.

The Zero's maneuverability was its best and, at times, only defense. The Japanese designers had sacrificed all manner of ruggedness and pilot amenities to the concepts of range and maneuverability. Land-based Zeros were not equipped with radios, because radios weighed too much. And the added weight of self-sealing tanks was avoided. When asked if they would like to have radios and other amenities, Zero pilots were quick and unanimous in saying *no!* They wanted nothing that would sacrifice a scintilla of maneuverability.

The Japanese counterpart to the American SBD was the Aichi D3A1 Type 99 Val "carrier bomber." (Name designations such as *Val* were not widely employed until late 1942, but they are used in this volume for convenience and familiarity.) The Val, which became operational in 1939, could lug up to 370 kilograms (816 pounds) of payload. For convoluted doctrinal reasons, however, carrier-based Vals usually flew with one 250-kilogram bomb, and land-based Vals were usually armed with only two 60-kilogram bombs. Vals could fly up to 1,250 miles at a cruising speed of just under 250 miles per hour. Unlike its newer American counterpart, the Val featured old-fashioned spatted fixed landing gear. Its usual combat dive was undertaken at an angle no greater than 60 degrees (as opposed to the SBD's steeper, faster 70-degree dive).

Crewed by a pilot and observer-gunner, the Val's defensive armaments consisted of a pair of cowl-mounted 7.7mm machine guns and a single rear-facing flexible 7.7mm machine gun. Like the SBD, the Val was employed on scouting, dive-bombing, and antisubmarine missions.

The Nakajima B5N2 Type 97 Kate "carrier attack" bomber was accepted for fleet operations in 1937 and was thus a full generation older than its American counterpart, the TBF Avenger. A highly innovative model when first introduced, the Kate was a low-wing monoplane with retractable landing gear capable of lugging the superb 800-kilogram (1,764-pound) Type 91 21-inch aerial torpedo at the relatively high attack speed of 160 miles per hour. It had a 300-mile-plus combat radius. In addition to its primary role as a torpedo bomber, the Kate had proven itself in China and even at Pearl Harbor as an effective light horizontal bomber. In this role, it could carry up to 800 kilograms of bombs.

The Kate's three-man flight crew occupied a single cockpit covered with a distinctive, very long greenhouse canopy. The Kate's only defensive armament was a single 7.7mm flexible machine gun manned by the rear-facing observer-gunner. Neither the pilot nor the man in the middle, the bombardier, had anything with which to contribute to the defense of the airplane.

Other naval aircraft types that might be available to either side were land-based scouts, bombers, and patrol bombers.

The American surface-ship–based scout of the day was the flimsy, underpowered Curtiss SOC scout-observation floatplane. The SOC's main function was observing naval gunfire against land targets. Constructed mainly of fabric and wire, and impeded in all but level flight by its bulky pontoon, the lightly armed SOC was in no way qualified to defend itself against any form of aerial opposition.

The Consolidated PBY-5A Catalina amphibian patrol bomber, powered by a pair of powerful engines mounted on a distinctive "parasol" wing, had been successful thus far in the war—up to a point. This tender- or land-based patrol bomber could stay aloft at a cruising speed of 117 miles per hour over distances of more than 2,000 miles. The PBY-5A was marginally capable of defending itself in a fight with its pair of .30-caliber bow-turret guns, a single rear-firing .30-caliber stinger, and single .50-caliber machine guns mounted in each of two waist blister turrets. If nothing else, the Catalina had proven itself to be extremely rugged in the face of enemy attack, and it most often carried its crew—and vital information—home. When on patrol, the Catalina could carry up to 4,000 pounds of payload, such as a pair of wing-mounted 500- or 1,000-pound bombs, a pair of wing-mounted 500-pound depth charges, or a pair of wing-mounted aerial torpedoes. (At the time, the U.S. Navy was also operating the faster but less-well-armed PBY-5.)

The Japanese fielded a somewhat larger array of scouts, bombers, and patrol bombers, including several types of reliable, rugged reconnaissance floatplanes launched from surface warships or based alongside tenders. Several of the one- and two-place floatplanes—including the nimble Nakajima A6M2-N Zero variant—were capable of holding forth against Wildcats.

The premier Japanese long-range patrol bombers of the day were the Kawanishi H6K Mavis and the brand-new H8K Emily four-engine flying boats. The Mavis featured single-mount 7.7mm machine guns in the bow, two side blisters, an open dorsal position, and one 20mm cannon in a tail turret. The thoroughly modern Emily, which was just coming on the scene in mid-1942, could defend itself with five single-mount 20mm cannon—one each in bow, dorsal, tail, and two beam positions—and three 7.7mm machine guns—in two side hatches and a ventral hatch. The older Mavis was at least as good as any U.S. Navy airplane in a forward area in mid-1942, but it was of startlingly flimsy, flammable construction. The Emily provided some armor protection, partially self-sealing fuel tanks, and a carbon dioxide fire-fighting system, but it would prove to have little more staying power against fighter attack than the more vulnerable Mavis.

Unlike the U.S. Navy, the Imperial Navy had long fielded land-based bombers. The best by far was the new Mitsubishi G4M1 Type 1 Betty "land attack" bomber, which became available in very small numbers over China in August 1941 and which was only just coming into widespread use in mid-1942. The Betty—rated a medium bomber by Americans—was capable of carrying up to 1,000 kilograms of bombs (typically four 250-kilogram or two 500-kilogram bombs) or a single 800-kilogram Type 21 aerial torpedo. The Betty had a combat radius of more than 1,200 miles, a cruising speed of 195 miles per hour, and a service ceiling of more than 30,000 feet, and it was extremely maneuverable. Like most of the lightly constructed Japanese warplanes, however, the Betty was highly flammable and simply could not take much abuse in the form of a Wildcat's six .50-caliber machine guns. Its defensive armament consisted of two 7.7mm machine guns in the nose, one 7.7mm machine gun in each of two beam mounts, a single 20mm cannon in a dorsal turret, and another 20mm cannon in a tail turret.

Thus, aside from scout types and the singular niche filled by the Japanese Betty, both navies deployed roughly equivalent aircraft in mid-1942. Japan had, by far, the better and more reliable aerial torpedo, and all of its carrier aircraft were faster and longer ranged than their American counterparts. On the other side, however, all of the American carrier models were far and away more rugged and better armed than their Japanese counterparts, and every U.S. Navy airplane of the day was equipped with a radio—a tremendous, often decisive, advantage in combat.

◆

The organization of carrier air groups, squadrons, and smaller formations employed by the two sides was quite different.

American fighter squadrons, employing up to thirty-six airplanes each by mid-1942, were organized into more-or-less standing four-plane divisions of two two-plane sections each. Because of their limited range, Wildcat fighters were not *ipso facto* expected to undertake escort duties for air strikes; if enemy targets were well within the Wildcat's 250-mile combat radius, four or eight fighters might be sent along all or part of the way. Or none might be sent with the bombers. The Wildcat was primarily an interceptor: At all times during the day, four to eight Wildcats were aloft over the friendly carrier, and four or eight were ready to take off at short notice. Other Wildcats might supplement the bombers on antisubmarine patrols around the friendly carrier, but that practice was in decline by mid-1942.

Doctrinally, American carriers depended mainly upon their own fighters to stave off enemy bombers. This meant that few fighters would be used to escort air strikes even against targets within the Wildcat's operational range. U.S. Navy surface ships accompanying the carriers could certainly put up formidable antiaircraft defenses, as could the carriers themselves, but the burden of defense fell upon a distant barrier of radar-vectored interceptors whose primary mission was to fend off incoming enemy air attacks.

In the rapidly emerging, ever-changing doctrine of the period, the fighter division was the basic maneuver element, its two two-plane sections operating as an integrated team, attacking enemy airplanes and defending themselves in tandem. The reality of swiftly moving aerial combat often resulted in the sections—and even the teams of section leader and wingman—becoming unglued. Training included all possible permutations, and every pilot could perform in every slot used in all formations up to a full squadron formation. No pilot was so senior that he could not take over the wing slot on a junior pilot, if that is what the situation demanded.

SBD and TBF squadrons used as offensive strike forces were organized into three-plane sections built up into six-, nine-, twelve-, fifteen-, or eighteen-plane units, depending on availability, the mission, and the array of targets. SBD airplanes and crews nominally organized into separate scouting and bombing squadrons were completely interchangeable in the strike role, but scouting units did spend more time training for that important task. Since the doctrine of the day called upon Dauntlesses to undertake arduous long-range searches and close-in patrol missions, there was always a number of Dauntlesses that could not be launched for attacks, either because they were busy elsewhere, had to be held back for other missions, or were down for maintenance. The same was essentially true for the less numerous Avengers.

The American scout and torpedo bombers of the day were solid, maneuverable airplanes with enough firepower to hold off Japanese fighters, though rarely to defeat them. The standard stepped-down vee-of-vees formation employed on the way to and from strike targets was defensive in nature. Awesome firepower in the form of massed forward- and rear-firing machine guns presented attackers with a formidable deterrent. In a few extreme cases, lone Dauntlesses had shot down Japanese fighters and bombers in one-on-one combat.

One overriding shortcoming of the U.S. Navy's carrier doctrine was that there had not yet evolved a means for smoothly combining and integrating the offensive or defensive capabilities of two or more carrier air groups operating together. Only the crudest control could be exerted by a carrier's fighter direction officer (FDO) over his own defending fighter divisions. Handling more than one squadron at a time was simply beyond the capabilities of the crude radars and experimental fighter-direction systems then available. The same was true for coordinated air strikes. There was simply no means for having a designated strike commander oversee air strikes by more than a single carrier air group.

The Japanese carrier air group *(hikokitai)* looked similar to its American counterpart, but it was doctrinally dissimilar in a number of ways, both in capabilities and in outlook.

Japanese carrier-based fighters were organized into sections—*shotai*—of three airplanes and then into flights—*chutai*—of six to nine airplanes. The three-plane fighter *shotai* operated as a nearly inviolate unit, with a senior pilot and two wingmen. In most cases, one wingman was stationed off either of the senior pilot's wings, and just to the rear. Also, the *shotai* often operated in left- or right-echelon formations. In a left echelon, for example, the first wingman was stationed off and behind the leader's left wing, and the second wingman was stationed off and behind the first wingman's left wing. In most cases, also, the three launched coordinated attacks against targets selected by the senior pilot, and they operated as a team when on the defensive. But defense was not one of the things for which the Zero fighter was built, nor were Japanese pilots as defense minded as they were finely honed predatory beasts.

In defense of their carriers, Japanese fighters did not have access to even the rudimentary carrier-based fighter direction enjoyed by the Americans—because of a paucity of radar. In general, Japanese combat air patrols were smaller than the American combat air patrols, but their ready fighters could get to altitude a good deal faster than American ready fighters. Japanese carriers depended upon fighters to keep American bombers at a distance; but if the carrier group was away on a strike of its own, most of the fighters would be with the strike. Thus the burden of Japanese antiaircraft defense lay with the escort vessels. Strangely, the Japanese carriers themselves were grossly undergunned for a meaningful self-defense role, and few surface warships were ever designated to undertake close-in defense of the carriers.

There were twenty-one to twenty-seven Zero fighters available to each Japanese carrier air group, largely because there was no folding-wing variant available for denser storage. (The A6M2 Model 21 had folding wingtips, which saved a little space.) Offsetting this particular disadvantage was the habitual pairing of Japanese fleet carriers in offensive operations. Unlike their American counterparts, the Japanese fighter pilots were used to operating under the senior fighter command pilot—from any ship—in the air at the time of offensive or defensive operations. Only the basic maneuver element, the three-plane *shotai*, was more or less structurally inviolate.

The Val and Kate squadrons also were organized into three-plane *shotai* and thence into *chutai* of six to nine airplanes, which usually flew in inverted vee-of-vees formations. As with the fighters—and unlike their American counterparts—Japanese offensive strike groups were highly flexible. Mixed groups from two or more carriers were often placed under the senior strike commander on the scene.

An unusual feature of the Imperial Navy's air-command setup was that a senior bomber commander—from air group commander to strike leader to *chutai* leader—was not necessarily a pilot. Very often, the commander rode as an observer in a Val, Kate, or Betty. This was never the case in any U.S. Navy flight formation; every American commander in the air was a rated pilot who flew his own airplane.

In many ways, American fighter doctrine was superior in the defense, and Japanese fighter doctrine was superior in the offense. And the more flexible Japanese strike doctrine was generally superior to American strike doctrine. Ultimately, however, any decision in a battle between carrier air groups would be determined by the size of the competing forces and by the staying power of the airplanes and the men who flew them.

Chapter 3

Until 1935, almost all U.S. Navy officer pilots were Regular line officers, usually graduates of the U.S. Naval Academy, and all enlisted pilots (Naval Aviation Pilots, or NAPs—no more than 30 percent of all pilots) were specially selected from the Fleet. Because the U.S. Navy promoted only qualified pilots to command its carriers, many senior officers, up to the rank of captain, attended flight school throughout the 1920s and 1930s.

When the Navy and Marine Corps vastly expanded the strengths of their separate air arms in 1934, it was realized that the pool of qualified Regular line officers could not fill all the available billets, so the Aviation Cadet Act of 1935 provided for the selection and training of specially qualified Reserve pilots. Recruiting took place mainly among college graduates between the ages of twenty and twenty-eight. The initial AvCad course was extremely rigorous, including one year at flight school at Pensacola, Florida (465 classroom hours and 300 flight hours to qualify for wings). Once the AvCad earned his coveted Wings of Gold, he spent three years flying with the Fleet ranked somewhere between warrant officer and ensign. The AvCad finally received his commission as a Navy ensign or Marine second lieutenant four years after qualifying for flight school. At the same time as he was commissioned, however, the early AvCad was placed on *inactive* status with the U.S. Navy or Marine Corps Reserve.

The AvCad program was substantially upgraded by the Naval Aviation Reserve Act of 1939. This provided for six thousand trainees who would receive commissions upon completion of flight training at Pensacola and who would serve a total of seven years on active duty. AvCads who had earned their wings prior to the inception of the new act were immediately commissioned, and those who had gone on Reserve status were given the opportunity to return to active duty.

In 1940 the Congress expanded the act to train enough pilots to man fifteen thousand Navy and Marine aircraft. On December 7, 1941, the Navy and Marine Corps had a total of six thousand five hundred qualified active-duty pilots. About half of them were AvCads trained at Pensacola or newer flight schools at Corpus Christi, Texas, and Jacksonville, Florida. In addition, many hundreds of additional AvCads were in the pipeline, days or months away from graduation.

As the AvCad program expanded alongside flight training programs for Regular officers and enlisted cadets, the vastly expanded needs of the day resulted in relaxed entry standards. Early in the program, only perfect physical specimens were selected (no dental fillings, no broken bones). This was to help reduce the vast pool of otherwise qualified applicants clamoring for admission to a very small program. When more cadets were needed than the perfect-specimen pool could provide, some of the most extreme physical criteria were relaxed, and the educational requirement was rolled back to two years of college. As an added inducement, AvCads were to earn a bounty of $500 per year for four years, payable when they mustered out. Many a Depression-poor college sophomore signed up in the hope of earning enough in four years to pay his junior- and senior-year tuition bills.

At the same time that entry qualifications were being relaxed, cadets were required to weather fewer and fewer classroom and flight hours. Ultimately, the scaled-down twenty-six–week course called for just 207 flight hours prior to commissioning and assignment to advanced specialized training. Even the speeded-up syllabus barely provided enough qualified— which is not to say "seasoned"—pilots to man the carrier air groups following the attrition resulting from the war's early carrier battles at the Coral Sea and Midway. Older AvCads, Regular officer pilots, and NAPs held the line as the new wave of AvCads, along with a sprinkling of qualified Regulars, learned the art of survival in the air—literally on the fly. In the weeks after Midway, more than one rookie pilot undertook his first real carrier landing as he was reporting in to his first operational squadron.

The American genius for mass training barely won the battle of time in the case of carrier-based combat pilots. But that particular genius had held the line. The same was not true for the Japanese survivors of the vicious early carrier battles.

Nearly all Japanese officer carrier pilots were graduates of Eta Jima, Japan's naval academy. Because Japanese carrier captains and carrier-fleet commanders did not need to be qualified pilots, however, few older officers undertook the rigors of flight training. (A notable exception was Capt Isoroku Yamamoto, who was to command the Imperial Navy's Combined Fleet during the first eighteen months of the Pacific War.) Each young Eta Jima graduate was commissioned following a rigorous three-and-a-half–year course and before beginning flight training. Far from following the American model of compacting the flight-training syllabus, the Japanese in 1940 lengthened their officer's course from about eight months to a full year. Also, whereas American pilots in the prewar years might be called upon to fly all types of airplanes available to the United States Fleet, most Japanese pilots specialized exclusively in fighters, single- or multi-engine bombers, or reconnaissance types.

Japanese enlisted pilots came either from the Combined Fleet, following several years' line service, or they were recruited directly from the population. During the 1930s, the naval aviation community recruited many fifteen- and sixteen-year-old boys, which obliged the Imperial Navy to undertake secondary education as well as flight training. An emphasis in selection was placed upon physical strength, coordination, and agility. Pre-flight training discipline was particularly brutal as a conscious means to weed out *most* candidates.

The selection, schooling, and training process was comprehensive but very slow. Belatedly, the Imperial Navy streamlined the system in August 1941, when it set a goal of training fifteen thousand pilots.

By the time the war started, some early enlisted pilots had been commissioned as special-duty ensigns, and many were warrant officers. By the time an Eta Jima graduate reached an operational squadron following theoretical and flight training, he was usually a newly promoted lieutenant junior grade.

By the time the Japanese enlisted pilot reached an air group, he had spent seven to nine months undergoing flight training, including rudimentary instruction in his specialty. In that time, nearly two-thirds of his classmates washed out of flight school. (Pensacola graduated about two-thirds of its cadets.)

The differences between the services became more pronounced at the operational level. American pilots were largely interchangeable, though there was a trend toward placing an individual pilot in a job for which he had the most aptitude. The average Japanese pilot was specialized early in his training. American pilots were all selected for leadership traits, whereas only Japanese officers, warrant officers, and very senior enlisted pilots could lead other pilots into combat. The vast majority of Japanese enlisted pilots were merely taught to follow the leader.

The most important difference was the permanence of postings. Japanese rookie pilots were assigned to a particular air group, which served as his advanced-training command. If the group happened to be engaged in combat, the rookie very often learned the finer points of his profession under the gun—or he died trying. If the rookie's air group had been gutted by combat losses—as was the case for many once the Pacific War got under way, but also during the long years of the so-called China Incident—there was a chance that he would rise to a key level of intermediate responsibility before he was quite ready. This tendency was not aided by the creation of many new carrier- and land-based air groups in late 1941 and early 1942, a trend that tended to siphon off many of the skilled senior pilots, who also served as trainers, mentors, and examples to younger pilots.

The rookie American naval aviator usually underwent advanced training in his specialty before joining an operational air group. For example, all fighter pilots honed their skills and flew the latest fighters at the Miami Naval Air Station. Also, the fledgling U.S. Navy pilot bound for carrier duty would train for several weeks to a month or two with an advanced carrier training group (ACTG). There, he simply learned to take off from and land on a carrier deck (most often a simulated carrier deck superimposed on a land-based runway). If there was time, he stayed with the ACTG until he mastered carrier operations or, if he could not, until he was sent elsewhere, usually to fly multi-engine planes.

As the competition for new pilots decreased after the Midway losses had been made good, the U.S. Navy began forming numbered reserve carrier air groups. One of the first, Air Group 10, received a draft of battle-experienced veterans, some older pilots who had thus far missed combat (mostly due to training duties), and a large component of recent ACTG graduates. If everything went as planned, Air Group 10 would exchange places with a group serving in the Pacific aboard a fleet carrier. There would always be a need to directly replace individual pilots lost in combat and operational accidents, but the reserve carrier air groups would provide young American rookies with the time and the place to learn the ropes from veterans. It was a golden opportunity most Japanese rookies missed.

The clear implication of the vastly different "polishing" phases was that the U.S. Navy was turning out pilots to spare while the Japanese were under the gun from the start. The Americans had staying power the Japanese lacked.

Of equal importance was that the reserve carrier air groups would eventually provide veteran American carrier pilots with an opportunity to recuperate from the rigors of war cruises, whereas the veteran Japanese carrier pilots would have to keep flying and fighting as long as their home carriers were in the war zone. Veteran American pilots could train rookies far from the sound of the guns, but Japanese veterans often could not. The potential for simple fatigue to have a negative impact on group operations was greater on the Japanese side. And, because the Japanese squadrons were manned by increasing numbers of raw fledglings, an increasing share of the burden inevitably fell upon the decreasing number of veterans. It was virtually impossible for the decimated Japanese carrier groups to draw experienced replacements—particularly command pilots—from land-based groups because of early and ongoing specialization in mission training.

If the war was not decided quickly—in a matter of months—the Japanese carrier air groups stood the better chance of simply being ground down.

Chapter 4

The only reason for building, maintaining, and defending aircraft carriers was the mobility they afforded airplanes in moving across vast oceanic distances. The heart of the aircraft carrier and the carrier task force was air operations.

Prior to taking off on a typical search or combat mission, duty pilots gathered in their squadron ready rooms, which were steel cubes located on the deck just beneath the flight-deck level. They were like very small theaters with eight rows of four upholstered seats per row. On the forward bulkhead, to the left, was a teletype machine fitted with a red typewriter ribbon. A large chartboard dominated the center of the forward bulkhead. On a table set against the rear bulkhead was a perpetually filled coffee urn and white enamel mugs. The room was consistently hazy from cigarette smoke and was invariably dimly lighted. At night the lights were red to prevent night blindness.

When a pilot was to leave for a search or patrol mission away from the task force, the teletype clattered out a message to keep him abreast of the speed and planned course of the carrier, known magnetic variations, and other navigational data that would help him to a safe return.

If a long flight by all or most of the squadron was planned, the squadron engineering officer—a senior pilot with that additional squadron duty—might brief on how to get absolute maximum gas mileage by leaning out the fuel mixture to the point where engine temperature rose to the allowable limit.

In the event of a strike mission, the carrier's air officer—a senior pilot on nonflying duty as part of the ship's company—would usually come down from the bridge to cover special points and answer questions. As data continued to be updated via the teletype, individual pilots jotted down their own navigational notes on their plotting boards—16-by-18-inch navigational devices that fit under the airplane dashboard and could be referred to and updated during flight. Fighter pilots and the radiomen assigned to the bombers were given radio call signs and a schedule of frequencies and emergency bands for the mission and nearby bases.

When all had been said and done and it was time to leave, pilots and aircrewmen climbed from their separate ready rooms to the flight deck—usually to the accompaniment of tinny voices sounding orders over the ship's public address system: "Pilots, man your airplanes."

Once on the flight deck, a mission pilot might walk around his airplane to inspect it and the load of ordnance slung beneath it. Then he would climb aboard by way of the left wing. Once in the cockpit, the pilot shrugged into his seat and parachute harnesses, usually with a helping hand from his plane captain. Then he plugged in his helmet-mounted earphones and microphone. Following a briefing from the plane captain on quirks and potential problems—invariably followed by a thumbs-up for luck from the man who would stay behind—the pilot waited for clearance to run up the engine to check it and the magnetos. If there was a problem and the plane had to be scrubbed from the mission—the decision was the pilot's—the pilot had to signal the plane captain and then shut down the engine. If that happened, plane handlers would swarm around the airplane in a race to get it out of the way before the launch schedule was totally destroyed. If all seemed well with the power plant and the electrical system, the pilot waited his turn until signaled by the deck boss or the deck boss's assistant to taxi his airplane forward to the take-off spot. Within a few seconds, as the engine wound up to full power, he had to get his completely loaded fighter or bomber airborne—from a standing start to fully airborne within a too-few hundred feet. As soon as the airplane was steady on the take-off spot, the pilot pushed both feet into the brakes and nudged the throttle forward with his left hand until the engine achieved maximum take-off power.

At a signal from the deck boss, the pilot lifted both feet simultaneously from the brake pedals and gently set them on the rudder pedals. The plane was rolling. To keep it steady, the pilot alternately nudged first one rudder pedal and then the other as he held the control stick steady with his right hand and pushed the throttle forward with his left.

To increase the lifting power of aircraft wings, the carrier invariably raced at high speed directly into the wind during the launching operation. Depending on how full the flight deck was, any given airplane would be able to use more or less than one-half the total length of the flight deck for takeoff.

Predawn or evening launches were always a thrill because, in addition to normal perils, carriers in operational areas showed no lights whatsoever on the flight deck or superstructure. The total darkness did nothing to enhance depth perception ahead or to the sides. About all most pilots had to guide them in predawn or evening launches was the flickering blue flames emitted from the engine exhaust stacks of the airplane just ahead. From time to time, a pilot became disoriented during a launch in the dark and flew toward lights that were in fact reflections on the surface of the ocean. At other times, day or night, the airplane engine did not have enough power to keep the airplane airborne. And sometimes the air was too humid for the physics of a launch to quite work out. Airplanes were lost and men were killed in carrier launches; it was an occupational risk.

Seasoned pilots with a decade or more of experience in carrier flight operations were only just slightly less prone to operational accidents than the rawest novice. In addition to inexperience and exhausting schedules that often muddled judgment or slowed reflexes, work-weary airplanes and the relative inexperience among the burgeoning groundcrew population contributed to high operational losses.

A fully loaded SBD with a 1,000-pound bomb, four hundred .50-caliber rounds, and twelve hundred .30-caliber rounds, plus a full load of gas, had a tendency to waddle down the flight deck and more or less fall off the bow of the ship. If by that point the airplane had not powered up to 65 or 70 knots of air speed, it simply was not a flying machine and would fall into the water.

At a moment only the inner ear could gauge, the pilot smartly pulled the stick in his right hand toward the pit of his belly to get the nose up. He was committed to flight.

If the warplane did become airborne, the pilot immediately had to pull up the landing gear and flaps. These tasks—coupled with keeping the nose high and turning leftward away from the ship—were made more difficult by the need to accomplish both jobs more or less simultaneously through cross-hand actuation or by shifting the stick from one hand to the other and back again. Carelessly dropping the left wingtip into the water was a fairly simple mistake while undergoing these gymnastics, and the sudden drag that error generated would easily flip a fully throttled airplane into the water.

Wildcat pilots had to turn a hand crank twenty-seven times to pull up the landing gear while fighting the airplane's marked tendency to pull to the left because of high engine torque. Turning the hand crank usually caused the newly airborne Wildcat to wobble across short arcs until the landing gear was safely up and secured.

Avenger pilots had the best airplane by far for carrier takeoffs. The huge-winged TBF was often airborne long before it reached the bow, and it was usually uphill all the way.

A typical daily mission for carrier scout- and torpedo bomber crews was a dawn or afternoon search for enemy vessels. Each search sector usually consisted of a wedge of ocean 200 to 250 miles in length covering ten degrees of a 360-degree circle centered on the carrier. Depending on the needs of the moment, anywhere from eighteen to thirty-six 10-degree sectors would be searched. And depending upon the availability of SBDs and TBFs, each pie-shaped sector would be searched by one or two airplanes.

The searcher had to know his position at all times, both as a means for returning safely to his ship and in order to accurately report the position of whatever he might encounter. Each searcher was typically armed with a single 500-pound General Purpose bomb, though his mission was less to engage enemy ships than to find, track, and report on them. Only in extreme circumstances, or if the opportunity was too good to pass up, was a search pilot to launch an attack upon, primarily, an enemy carrier—and only after he was dead certain he had made an accurate position report that had been received by a friendly vessel.

Most of the hundreds of weekly search sorties were simply boring. Most of the search pilot's energy went into scanning the endless sea and checking his position relative to his carrier, which was usually on the move to a position far from the point at which the searcher had been launched.

Usually, the search pilot flew out from the task force right on the surface, because climbing to altitude used up a great deal of fuel. In any case, it was impossible for the pilot to read the play of the wind on the surface of the ocean at altitudes higher than 150 feet. By knowing the strength and direction of the wind, the pilot could determine which way and how far the airplane was being blown off course. This was the only way he could go out up to 250 miles and expect to find his way back home with reasonable assurance.

All carrier planes had small radio receivers that could pick up homing signals in every direction from the carriers. Depending upon the code the pilot and radioman could hear, the pilot could fine-tune his final approach to the left or the right to find the carrier. If an airplane flew past the carrier in bad weather or at night, the homing radio would tell him so—if he was in line-of-sight VHF range. The key to the system was letter signals; the pilot knew which way to fly based upon which Morse code letter he was receiving on the radio.

Once settled on the first search leg, the pilot could stop watching his compass and air-speed indicator to the exclusion of all else and look around. Indeed, the search pilot's main purpose was looking far and wide to see what was out there. If he saw anything of note on the search leg or cross leg—enemy ships or an inbound hostile strike force—he was to report all the details to his ship.

The third, or intercept, leg of the three-legged pattern was the most crucial. If all the navigational computations—mainly direction and wind speed—had been correct, the search pilot would find his way home to

Point Option—the place the carrier would be four to five hours after the searcher had been launched. In the words of Ens Fred Mears, a member of Torpedo Squadron 3 in mid-1942, "If he has done his navigation correctly and Point Option has not changed without his knowing it, the fleet will appear at the proper time. If not, there is still only water and more water."

Once the returning pilot found the carrier, he had to undergo the stress of landing upon what invariably looked like a short, narrow flight deck that was moving *away* from him at high speed.

As soon as the pilot visually acquired the carrier, he would wheel into the imaginary oblong landing traffic pattern down the port side toward the stern of the ship. If landing operations were under way, the planes in the landing traffic pattern would pace themselves to begin final approaches at 40-second intervals. Airplanes low on fuel or having mechanical problems would receive priority clearance if there was time.

Each pilot in the landing traffic pattern would tick off his prelanding checklist: canopy back and locked (for quick escape in the event he somehow hit the water), fuel on rich mixture (for immediate added power if he suddenly needed to fly away from the groove), fuel coming in from the fullest internal tank (so his engine would not suddenly die from fuel starvation while his mind was on other matters), cowl flaps partly open (to keep the engine cool), and prop in low pitch (so he could bite the maximum amount of air at the low landing speed).

If the checklist checked, he was ready to land.

In the case of landing a Wildcat, for example, the pilot next reached across his body with his left hand, found the required lever, and dropped the tail hook. He had by then slowed his fighter to an indicated air speed of 120 knots. Next he lowered his landing gear and landing flaps; the latter caused a slight downward pitching motion. As he slowly flew up the carrier's wake, right in the groove, his air-speed indicator should have registered the desired 90 knots, and the fighter should have been in a perfect nose-high attitude. The experienced carrier pilot was able to fly by feel alone, which totally freed his eyes to follow the motions of, to all carrier pilots, the most important man in the world, his landing signal officer (LSO).

In its essence, a carrier landing consisted of a sequence of these phases: While the carrier sailed at top speed into the wind, the pilot lowered his airplane's tail hook and approached the carrier flight deck from dead astern; guided by the LSO, the pilot lined up on the flight deck at just the right altitude, attitude, and speed; if the LSO was satisfied that the airplane was in the correct position relative to the deck, he signaled the pilot to land; if the airplane was not in the correct position and could not be guided into the groove in the time remaining, the LSO would wave it off for another try. If the pilot was allowed to land, he quickly dropped to the deck in what can only be described as a controlled stall with the intention of catching the extended tail hook on any of the dozen stout cables running the width of the deck; if the tail hook caught a cable, the cable gave a bit while the airplane was forced to a rapid stop; if the tail hook missed all the cables, and if the deck was clear, the pilot simply gunned the engine and took off for another try; if the tail hook missed the cable and the deck was obstructed, the nose of the plane was arrested by a flexible barrier, which usually ruined the propeller but prevented a flaming collision between the airplane and whatever obstructions lay ahead.

Only the LSO could determine when an approaching pilot was ready for the carrier. He would signal his opinions with his two outstretched luminous paddles.

By that time, the pilot was going over part of the litany again: A one-second delay in cutting the throttle makes the difference between a normal cable-arrested landing and a crash on the flight deck. Never touch the throttle until safely on the deck. If you miss the cables, immediately push the throttle forward to acquire liftoff speed. If the airplane is properly arrested, cut power to the absolute minimum and taxi off as soon as the hook and the cable have been separated by a deck crewman.

The pilot had to totally concentrate on altitude, attitude, propeller pitch, throttle setting, landing gear, flaps, tail hook, the rapidly approaching LSO, and the tossing, twisting postage-stamp–sized flight deck.

The LSO stood tall in front of his protective windscreen on the starboard aft corner of the flight deck. A pilot who had once naively asked the LSO what the screen was for had received a sarcastic answer that the ship would be doing 18 to 20 knots, which, combined with a wind-speed factor of anywhere from 0 miles per hour to infinity, usually created enough of a breeze to pitch a sturdy LSO into the drink. The dark-colored screen also aided the pilot in finding and following the motions of the LSO, who was invariably clad in light-colored clothing.

On the far side of the screen was the LSO's assistant. It was his job to see if the tail hook, landing gear, and flaps of the approaching plane were down. If so, he would yell above the wind, right into the LSO's ear, "All clear." Then he would turn to watch the deck as the landing plane hurtled past the LSO platform into the cable.

Many LSOs waved their paddles with a great deal of energetic flair, but most passed the standard thirteen landing signals in a straightforward manner. Ten of the signals told the pilot of some specific error in technique or procedure—wrong height, wings not level, approach speed too fast or too slow, even that the tail hook was not deployed or the main landing gear was not down. The remaining three signals were "roger," "cut," and "wave-off."

Pilots wanted a "roger" on the first pass. If the plane was correctly lined up, the LSO would hold his paddles straight out from the shoulders to signify that the airplane was "in the groove"—that the approach was satisfactory.

Just as the pilot sensed that his airplane's nose was hovering several feet over the fantail, the LSO dropped his left arm to his side. Then his right arm lifted and the right paddle abruptly slashed across his throat. That was "cut."

The pilot immediately chopped back his throttle and held the control stick rock steady. The airplane was now in a perfect three-point landing attitude, which meant that all three wheels would strike the deck at the same instant. Things happened fast from that point. There was literally nothing for the pilot to do; the laws of physics were running the show.

The pilot next felt the shock of the landing gear as they hit the solid flight deck. Then he felt the tail hook grab hold of the wire. If it was the first wire, the landing was perfect. The mass of the fighter rapidly decelerated and came to an abrupt no-brakes near stop. Immediately, the tension on the arresting cable eased, and the fighter's remaining momentum pulled it forward about 40 feet with the hook still attached. This brought the fighter to a slow, controlled stop. At that point, the pilot came under the direction of the deck crew and plane handlers. No more than five seconds had passed from "cut" to the rolling stop.

Once the pressure was off the tail hook, the pilot and his airplane became the center of furious activity. A quick glance into the rearview mirror would reveal a deck crewman ducking beneath the tail to release the hook from the cable. At almost the same instant, another deck crewman took charge of the taxi routine by using his unique set of signals. First, on signal, the pilot retracted the tail hook. Then he had to get lined up with the centerline of the deck to get into taxi position. The vertical barrier, which looked like a large tennis net and was raised for all landings, was dropped as soon as the tail hook caught the cable. The instant the tail wheel was clear of the barrier, the obstruction was raised again in preparation for the next landing.

As soon as the airplane cleared the barrier, the LSO's assistant, who was standing with his back to the LSO, turned aft and yelled "All clear" into the LSO's ear.

If the recovery operation was perfect, the succeeding airplane was in position to take the "cut" just as the previous airplane cleared the deck barrier.

Often, in a large landing operation, the LSO had to pass the "wave-off" signal to two or three pilots as they felt their way into the groove one after another. To pass this signal, the LSO simply waved both paddles over his head. The wave-off had the force of absolute law. Even if the pilot was in fact right in the groove and lined up for a perfect landing, he had to obey the wave-off signal, as there might be an emergency beyond his knowledge or range of senses—such as an imminent enemy attack. Pilots were not given the option of overruling an LSO's orders, especially in the case of a wave-off.

In early August 1942, Ens Fred Mears had to make an emergency landing aboard the *Enterprise*. He was just completing an exercise torpedo run on the ship when his motor began to cut out for a second or two and then catch again. Mears thought there was a clog in the fuel line. After circling the ship twice, trying to make the plane run true by adjusting the controls and having no success, Mears made an emergency pass down the starboard side of the ship with his tail hook down—the signal for a "delayed forced landing." The ship did not clear the flight deck, so Mears circled again and passed down the port side, which is the signal for an "immediate forced landing." Only then did the *Enterprise* swing into the wind. Ensign Mears got into the landing circle and began his approach. As Mears came up the groove, he was given a "low" signal by the LSO. He added throttle, but the engine conked out again astern of the ramp. Then it revived just in time. The LSO gave Mears the "cut," and the motor died as soon as the pilot chopped the throttle. The mechanics later told Mears that there was a stoppage in the carburetor. It was fortunate for Mears and his two aircrewmen that they were not hundreds of miles away over open sea when the engine began acting up. Too many of Mears's contemporaries had disappeared without a trace, no doubt because of "routine" malfunctions like the stopped carburetor.

Maintaining and servicing the warplanes of a carrier air group required endless hours of work by dedicated groundcrewmen.

AMM2 Bernard Peterson, who was awaiting word on his application for flight training, was in charge of the aircraft hydraulic and rigging crew for all of Torpedo Squadron 3's Grumman TBF Avengers. He had four seamen strikers working for him; they were younger seamen working their way up the rungs of the promotion ladder, trying to get their aviation machinist's mate ratings.

The permanence of the flight crews was fairly well established during a combat situation. During routine operations, however, many of the senior groundcrewmen flew on training missions to qualify for standby crew duty and to enable them to receive flight pay, a sort of reward for extra services. AMM2 Peterson had been trained as an alternate aircrewman, but his maintenance specialty required that he spend far more time taking care of the TBFs than flying them.

Typically, the commanding officer (CO), executive officer (exec), and flight officer of a carrier squadron had their own personal airplanes and crews. The junior officers often flew any airplane assigned to them, often with a strange crew.

Each plane had its own plane captain permanently assigned. That was *his* plane, and his plane only. He and the pilots who flew it would call upon the ordnance, engineering, and radio sections of the squadron for corrective action or maintenance, as required. The ship's company did the plane handling on the hangar and flight decks, plus refueling and respotting airplanes.

Most of the aircrewmen in the torpedo, scouting, and bombing squadrons held radioman ratings, but a small percentage were aviation machinist's mates or even aviation ordnancemen.

Torpedo Squadron 3 consisted of approximately twenty-four pilots, fifty aircrewmen, four ground officers, and twelve nucleus groundcrewmen. The scouting and bombing squadrons were slightly smaller because they rated fewer aircrewmen. In addition to flying duties, everyone, including the pilots, had certain ground or shipboard duties.

Nearly all the torpedo, scouting, and bombing squadrons had between twelve and eighteen operational airplanes at any particular time. Attrition was usually through accidents and maintenance problems.

Part II

★

Invasion
August 7–9, 1942

Chapter 5

The Japanese Pacific juggernaut that began at Pearl Harbor and the Philippines on December 7, 1941, rolled over the Australian- and British-mandated Bismarck Archipelago and Solomon Islands between late January and early May 1942. The occupation of the principal islands of both groups was undertaken by small naval surface forces and naval landing parties virtually without opposition.

The occupation of the Solomon Islands was both beyond the scope of the early Japanese war aims and far ahead of schedule. Although the Japanese plans called for the eventual seizure of the French New Hebrides, New Caledonia, Fiji, and Samoa, the need to rest and regroup resulted in a halt in the vicinity of Tulagi, an anchorage in the eastern Solomon Islands capable of protecting a very large component of the Combined Fleet, the fighting arm of the Imperial Navy. There, at Tulagi, the Japanese decided to build fleet and air bases from which future operations to the south and east might be supported.

American senior naval strategists meeting in San Francisco in late June 1942 selected the Tulagi anchorage as the lead-off objective for their projected Pacific counteroffensive, which was to begin in midsummer. All the planners would have preferred a straightforward drive across the Central

Pacific, an offensive carrier-supported surface-fleet operation that had been
the basis of all U.S. contingency planning since the 1920s. But the danger
lay to the south, across the vital shipping lanes linking Australia and New
Zealand with the United States. Tulagi was simply the Japanese base closest to the shipping lanes and to the tiny island-bound Allied bastions guarding them.

After the objective had been selected, as the San Francisco meeting
was breaking up, news arrived from an Allied "coastwatcher"—a volun-
teer who had stayed behind when Crown forces retreated from the eastern
Solomons—that the Japanese had crossed the 20-mile-wide channel between Tulagi and Guadalcanal Island to begin building a new airfield. The
airfield immediately became the main objective of the first Allied Pacific
counteroffensive, and the schedule was precipitously moved up. An
amphibious landing force, guarded by numerous surface warships and all
available American fleet aircraft carriers, was to be set in motion. The
invasion was to take place in early August 1942.

A number of top-level strategists hoped, among other things, that Japanese fleet carriers would be drawn into the upcoming confrontation. Many
of the airmen manning the American carriers wanted to follow up on their
clear, tide-turning June victory at Midway.

But the main objective of the invasion was to forestall a renewed Japanese drive toward the New Hebrides. The Americans were invading the
eastern Solomons because they had to.

The Allied invasion fleet arrived in the eastern Solomons from its stag-
ing area in Fiji in two parts. Task Force 62 incorporated the troop transports carrying the reinforced 1st Marine Division and a mighty surface
escort force composed entirely of cruisers and destroyers. The support force,
Task Group 61, comprised three of the U.S. Navy's four remaining fleet
aircraft carriers—the *Enterprise,* the *Wasp,* and the *Saratoga*—and a screening force of cruisers, destroyers, and a battleship.

Despite realistic fears to the contrary, the approach of the invasion
armada went completely undetected by the burgeoning Imperial Navy headquarters and air base complex in Rabaul, 600 air miles to the northwest.
The Japanese defenders—little more than a battalion of bluejackets and

the airfield-construction and base forces it guarded—were to be taken completely by surprise.

The landing of Marines on Guadalcanal, Tulagi, and several nearby islands was to begin at 0800—eight o'clock in the morning—on Tuesday, August 7, 1942.

While surface warships attached directly to the invasion fleet were still closing on darkened beaches on both sides of Sealark and Lengo Channels, the airmen of the three carrier air groups were preparing for their day's work. The *Saratoga* Air Group—consisting of Scouting Squadron 3 (Scouting-3), Bombing Squadron 3 (Bombing-3), Torpedo Squadron 8 (Torpedo-8), and Fighting Squadron 5 (Fighting-5)—was to provide direct support for the Marines landing on Guadalcanal's northern shore. The warplanes of the *Wasp* Air Group—Scouting-71, Scouting-72, Torpedo-7, and Fighting-71—were to provide support for Marines landing at Tulagi and other islands on the north side of the channel. Most of the *Enterprise* Air Group—Scouting-5, Bombing-6, Torpedo-3, and Fighting-6—was to guard the carrier and surface invasion forces, as well as provide a ready reserve of nine dive-bombers and eight fighters for its sister air groups.

In sum, the three fleet carriers and their air groups comprised 75 percent of the aerial offensive striking arm of the United States Fleet. The need to adequately support the first Allied counterstroke in the Pacific had been carefully weighed against ominous potential consequences. The Japanese strategy for the early phase of the war had been to draw out the American carriers and destroy them. Thus far, two of only six U.S. fleet carriers that had been available at the start of the war had been destroyed. The *Lexington, Saratoga's* sister ship, had been lost in the Coral Sea turning back a Japanese invasion fleet bound for Port Moresby, New Guinea. And the *Yorktown,* sister to the *Enterprise* and *Hornet,* had been lost at Midway. In return, the Americans had sunk one Japanese light carrier in the Coral Sea and four Japanese fleet carriers at Midway. The odds had been made nearly even at Midway, but the carrier force available to the Combined Fleet commander, Adm Isoroku Yamamoto, was by far more formidable than anything the Allies could maneuver in Pacific waters.

Still, because they enjoyed the fruits of two victories, a number of the

American strategic planners who had conceived of the Guadalcanal invasion in San Francisco in June were not wholly averse to the notion of fighting the grand carrier battle Admiral Yamamoto so clearly desired. So far as some of them were concerned, August 1942 was as good a time as any to decide the future course and possible outcome of the war.

But there were cautious dissenters who believed that the United States needed to win time to fully engage her awesome industrial might in the building of an unstoppable war machine. These leaders often cited simple statistics: It would take until early 1943 to complete the first new carrier construction of the war. After that, carriers of several sizes and types would be joining the United States Fleet in accelerating numbers. Those in the know cited similar statistics to bolster the argument: Japanese industry had no hope of keeping pace with America's awakening industrial might and, indeed, would be hard pressed simply to replace the losses sustained by the Combined Fleet at the Coral Sea and Midway. These strategists advised against initiating an early final confrontation. So long as some forward momentum could be maintained, they were all for awaiting the first fruits of the all-out wartime carrier-construction program.

In the end, it came down to one man—the overall commander of the Allied Solomons invasion fleet, VAdm Frank Jack Fletcher. Though under the command of a shore-based area commander, Fletcher was the man on the scene in the eastern Solomons. If the Japanese carriers sallied from home waters to rescue Guadalcanal's airfield, he would fight or withdraw, as *he* saw fit.

Chapter 6

Guadalcanal. *August 7, 1942.* Lt(jg) Smokey Stover, a Wildcat section leader with the *Saratoga* Air Group's Fighting-5, was to be among the first U.S. Navy airmen launched against Japanese shore installations near Guadalcanal's Lunga Point. Though Stover had spent a sobering, pensive evening in his stateroom—writing his will and accompanying letters to his family—he did not really believe he was going to die in the morning.

The Fighting-5 pilots had attended lectures every evening for the two weeks leading up to D day. Smokey Stover felt he was well acquainted with the squadron's targets and with the general situation at Guadalcanal and Tulagi. He was not certain about reports of possible opposition; some reports had placed Imperial Japanese Navy land-based Zero fighters on Guadalcanal's new airfield, but others claimed the runway was not yet operational. The latest report indicated that there were no Japanese land-based fighters in the eastern Solomons, but that a contingent of float fighters was definitely based at a seaplane base 20 miles north of Fighting-5's strike objective. This potential opposition seemed inconsequential to Stover, because the float fighters were not nearly as maneuverable as the Grumman F4F Wildcat fighters he and his comrades would be flying.

Three four-plane divisions of the *Saratoga* Air Group's Fighting-5 and two four-plane divisions of the *Enterprise* Air Group's Fighting-6 were to launch well before dawn and fly to Lunga Point in time to begin strafing airfield facilities by 0630, fifteen minutes before sunrise. If reports of submarines and patrol boats based around Lunga were accurate, these fighters were to help the main bodies of two *Saratoga*-based dive-bomber squadrons, Bombing-3 and Scouting-3, work them over. After that, the fighters would be free to use their remaining ammunition against targets of opportunity and then independently return to the *Saratoga*.

The *Wasp* Air Group's Fighting-71 and Scouting-71, plus nine Scouting-5 dive-bombers from the *Enterprise* Air Group, were to conduct similar initial strikes against targets 20 miles to the north of Lunga—against Tulagi, Florida, Makambo, Gavutu, and Tanambogo islands. And many of the remaining *Enterprise* Air Group dive-bombers were on call to lend a hand in general support, wherever needed, while most of Fighting-6 and elements of Fighting-5 and Fighting-71 maintained combat air patrols over the carriers. Torpedo bombers from the three carriers had no initial strike duties, but they were on call to undertake horizontal bombing missions or help the remaining dive-bombers conduct a wide range of patrol missions over the carriers or elsewhere in the eastern Solomons.

Lieutenant (jg) Stover had begun his military flying career on December 30, 1940, when he arrived at Pensacola, Florida, to attend flight school. He was designated a naval aviator and awarded his coveted Wings of Gold and a commission on July 2, 1941. He was subsequently assigned to the USS *Hornet's* Fighting-8, and he went to sea for the first time aboard his brand-new carrier on December 27, 1941. He had been a bystander during U.S. Army Air Forces LtCol Jimmy Doolittle's Tokyo Raid, which was launched from the *Hornet's* flight deck on April 18, 1942. He had come close to seeing first combat at Midway, but never saw an enemy airplane nor any of the enemy carriers. The first time Smokey Stover fired in anger was on a strafing mission in which he undoubtedly killed survivors of a sunken Japanese cruiser.

The battle-depleted air groups of America's surviving carriers were extensively reorganized after Midway, and Lieutenant (jg) Stover was reassigned to Fighting-5. He reported to his new unit in Hawaii on July 3, 1942, just in time to prepare to ship out for the Solomons aboard the *Saratoga*.

Smokey Stover was awakened with all the other *Saratoga* Air Group pilots and aircrewmen at 0400, August 7. He had time to wolf down an unenjoyable breakfast, attend final briefings, and check out his Wildcat fighter before launching in the dark at 0530.

By manning their airplanes early, beginning at 0500, all of the strike pilots were able to become pretty well acclimated to the dark. The half-moon out in the predawn hours gave off a fair amount of light, but it was hidden by clouds part of the time. Lieutenant (jg) Stover's main concern was that there would be enough moonlight to brighten the horizon. If not, he would have to resort to flying less certainly with the aid of instruments than by using direct sight.

The day's launch began promptly at 0535, when a Fighting-6 Wildcat fighter left the *Enterprise's* deck to begin screening the carriers and their surface escorts. Once the eight Wildcats assigned to the combat air patrol were clear of the *Enterprise,* all three carriers began launching strike aircraft and others meant for various patrol assignments over the carriers or the distant invasion fleet.

When it was Stover's turn to launch from the *Saratoga*—he was fairly far back in the fighter pack but ahead of any of the dive-bombers—he gave his engine full throttle and roared off into the darkness. As with all carrier launches, the heavy Grumman fighter dropped a bit as it cleared the end of the flight deck. Stover smoothly pulled back on his control stick and followed the preceding fighter, which was marked only by a few faint lights receding into the dark sky.

There was a mix-up right behind Stover, whose wingman went astray. A division of Fighting-6 Wildcats freshly launched from the *Enterprise*—which was only 5 miles away from the *Saratoga*—joined on the wingman, who then led them away from their assigned objective. Another Wildcat joined on Stover's wing, but it later disappeared. In fact, many fighters from all three squadrons went astray in the crowded sky over the carriers, but all ended up over Guadalcanal or Tulagi, one way or another.

♦

Lt(jg) Slim Russell, a dive-bomber pilot with Scouting-3, was near the end of the string taking off from the *Saratoga*. He noticed just before he taxied forward into his take-off spot that a searchlight was playing from the carrier's starboard side. Russell fleetingly assumed that the light was probing the darkness for a submarine, then forgot about it; submarines were not his immediate concern—a safe launch was.

Lieutenant (jg) Russell was flying the number-two spot on Lt Ralph Weymouth, the leader of Scouting-3's six-plane 3d Division. The division rendezvoused ahead of the carrier at 500 feet and made two sweeping left-hand circles while it joined with the squadron's other divisions. Then Scouting-3 headed directly for its target at Kukum, 68 miles to the east-northeast on Guadalcanal's northern shore. All the Dauntless pilots shut off their lights as soon as the squadron rendezvous had been completed—except for Slim Russell's wingman, the number-three man, on Lieutenant Weymouth's other wing. The dive-bombers—brightly marked by the single set of navigation lights—were over Guadalcanal's southern mountain range before the green ensign was finally snapped from his reveries by the wild maneuvering of several other pilots, who eventually made him understand how he was endangering the entire formation.

Fighting-5 flew in full darkness northwest toward Guadalcanal's western cape and did not turn off running lights until the fighters were 40 miles away from the carrier. The moon broke through the clouds as the Wildcats rounded the cape—Cape Esperance. In eerie moonlight, the fighters turned east and felt their way along Guadalcanal's northern coast. They were scheduled to arrive over Lunga Point at about the time the slower Scouting-3 Dauntlesses completed their direct hop over the island's interior.

Lt(jg) Smokey Stover saw what he feared were antiaircraft guns far ahead. He had expected to be tracked by shore-based guns, but these flashes appeared to be rising from the middle of the channel north of Lunga. After tense minutes, Stover realized that the flashes were from friendly warships, which had just opened their bombardment of the shoreline from Kukum eastward to the Marines' landing beach. Stover maintained formation while watching the colorful display. At regular intervals, bright yellow flashes flared from one of the now-visible dark splotches on the water. Each new bright flash soon resolved itself into three tiny white spots that soared aloft in long, glowing arcs before impacting brightly among the coconut palms around Kukum or Lunga.

At twenty minutes before sunrise, it was still so dark that Smokey Stover could see little more than the darker silhouette of the island. Far to the left, he could see warships bombarding Tulagi, where five or six fires were evenly spaced along that island's dark shore.

Scouting-3's Lt(jg) Slim Russell, who was just then arriving from the south, could also see huge flashes of flame as the cruisers and destroyers pounded the beaches. A large fire was raging beyond Kukum, but Russell could not see northward as far as Tulagi.

The first U.S. Navy carrier planes over the target area were eleven Fighting-71 Wildcats led by the squadron commander, LCdr Courtney Shands. Their job was to engage Japanese float fighters if any were in the air, or to destroy them and a number of large amphibian patrol bombers at their moorings off Tanambogo and Florida islands. As it turned out, none of the Japanese aircraft was airborne.

Two of the Wildcats held at 5,000 feet to cover the others, three fighters strafed a coastal village on Florida at which Marines were shortly due to land, two fighters peeled off to attack the seaplane anchorage and other targets at causeway-linked Gavutu and Tanambogo islands, and Lieutenant Commander Shands led three other fighters against possible targets along a fair stretch of Florida's coast and nearby Makambo Island. As it turned out, Shands fired at some likely looking dark objects off Makambo and wound up setting a moored Imperial Navy H6K Mavis flying boat afire. The other members of Shands's division joined in, and three moored Mavises and several small craft were left in flames. The two Fighting-71 Wildcats sent against Tanambogo also found four Mavises moored off the north coast, and these were also flamed. At 0620, Lieutenant Commander Shands and his wingman located a nest of six A6M2-N Zero float fighters moored off Halavo, a village on Florida's coast to the east of Tanambogo. Before any of the Japanese pilots could man their waiting fighters, the two Wildcat pilots strafed them from low level and flamed them all.

By the time Shands's Fighting-71 Wildcats had finished off the Japanese air contingent and gone on to strafe shore targets, eleven Scouting-71 and nine Scouting-5 Douglas SBD Dauntless dive-bombers were at work with 1,000-pound bombs and machine guns against various shore targets on Tulagi, which was the target of an imminent landing by two Marine infantry battalions.

Upon arriving over the Guadalcanal target area, twenty-three *Saratoga* Air Group SBDs split up and circled in the dark. Following his division leader, Lt(jg) Slim Russell flew in and out of the sparse cloud cover, which was at about 6,000 feet. He could easily see the long runway behind Lunga Point. The dive-bombers had arrived a bit early, before the cruisers offshore had completed their scheduled bombardment. There was no sign of antiaircraft fire nor, for that matter, any other form of opposition.

Then Russell saw that the Fighting-5 Wildcats were going in.

The three Fighting-5 divisions had been at about 5,000 feet when they rounded Cape Esperance and started a shallow descent toward Lunga. They had gained considerable speed between the cape and Lunga Point. Fighting-5's 1st Division, which was led by the squadron commander, LCdr Roy Simpler, pulled ahead of the pack, forcing the pilots in the rear divisions to add a lot of throttle to keep up. Lt(jg) Smokey Stover had to race simply to keep sight of his own division leader, Lt Walter Clarke, who was only two planes ahead. Clarke momentarily disappeared from Stover's view whenever he got lower than Stover, and he was barely visible against the forest below when he was level with Stover.

The fighters swung a little south of where the cruisers were shelling Kukum and swept over the airfield from the west. A mile ahead of Clarke's 3d Division, Simpler's 1st Division began firing at targets on the ground. Moments later, the four Wildcats of Lt Dick Gray's 5th Division opened fire, too. Stover could easily see tracer ammunition ricocheting off the runway surface. At first, he thought the ricochets were the feared antiaircraft fire, but he observed the same effect as soon as Lieutenant Clarke opened fire, and realized that he was in no immediate danger from guns on the ground. Each burst from the fighters' six .50-caliber wing-mounted machine guns—a mix of one tracer in every four rounds—slowly sank toward the buildings and partially completed revetments, then ricocheted up in red splashes as if from a Roman candle. It was still so dark that Stover could not use his Wildcat's electric gunsight, which reflected a bright calibrated ring on the fighter's Plexiglas windscreen. Even turned down to its lowest setting, the sight would have blotted out everything beyond it.

To conserve ammunition, Stover initially fired only his four outboard machine guns, a standard practice. He aimed by firing short bursts, then corrected as he saw the fall of the bullets, which seemed to spray over half the field. Stover still expected return fire from the ground, so he pulled up in a climbing, twisting turn. But there was no answering fire.

The fighters returned again and again to shoot up everything that possibly could have sheltered airplanes or men. Lieutenant (jg) Stover observed no human beings and no return fire. On one pass, he streaked at full throttle across the runway at only 50 feet to lay his gunfire beneath the roofs of several low metal-walled buildings. The buildings appeared to have been abandoned by their Japanese landlords. In a way, it all seemed too easy.

While pulling out from one low pass to seaward, Stover saw in the gray dawn a moving mass in an open field. He flexed his thumb on his control stick's gun-button knob, ready to fire. Then he realized he was aiming at cows. Stover did not shoot, but at least one other fighter pilot did. The carnage disturbed Stover, though he was certain his comrade had fired in haste, too keyed up to stop himself.

The Wildcats—numbering twelve from Fighting-5, five from Fighting-6 that had been assigned to attack possible beach-defense positions around Lunga Point, and four Fighting-71 stragglers—caused a great deal of damage against negligible opposition. In addition to shooting up a large headquarters building and six hangars, they destroyed several vehicles and some earth-moving equipment. And two of the Fighting-5 pilots set fire to a 200-foot schooner that was apparently laden with a cargo of aviation fuel.

As soon as the fighters had completed their strafing runs—they were actually ordered to stand clear by the *Saratoga* Air Group commander, Cdr Don Felt—twenty-three Scouting-3 and Bombing-3 Douglas SBD Dauntless dive-bombers, with four Scouting-71 stragglers thrown in, started dropping their 1,000-pound bombs along the coast and on the airfield. Many of the dive-bombers' rear gunners strafed buildings as the pilots pulled out of the bombing runs.

Lt(jg) Slim Russell watched the fighters leave and then pushed over against a dimly perceived gun emplacement 5,500 feet below. As Russell dived, he fired his two cowl-mounted .50-caliber machine guns at the emplacement to suppress possible return fire. As he neared the objective, however, he could see that there was no gun in the emplacement. The wind was blowing him away from his point of aim by then, but he decided to drop his 1,000-pound bomb anyway. Russell pulled the bomb-release toggle at 1,800 feet and pulled out. The bomb hit about 100 feet off the beach, in the water. It caused no visible damage.

As Russell castigated himself for the bad drop, he circled and came back at about 60 feet over Kukum to strafe buildings and presumed supply dumps with his forward machine guns. He was so intent upon strafing that he almost flew into the water.

Next, Russell joined several other SBDs over Lunga Point and strafed targets there. After the first pass at Lunga, as Russell flew back over the coconut trees, he saw streaks of red tracer coming at him from out of the trees. He pulled up and the tracer all fell behind and below his dive-bomber. He cautiously climbed and then dived again to strafe the spot from which the fire had come. No fire rose to meet Russell on the way down, but red tracer chased his tail as he pulled up. He expended a great deal of his ammunition strafing the coconut groves but was unable to observe tangible results.

Most of the early-morning aerial effort against Guadalcanal turned out to be of limited value. Nearly 2,500 Japanese and Korean laborers and approximately 250 Imperial Navy combat troops bolted from their bivouacs and the airfield area as soon as the shelling and strafing began. There were no land-based Japanese aircraft in the eastern Solomons; though the 2,624-by-197-foot Lunga runway was to have been declared operational that very day, the first contingent of land-based warplanes was not due to arrive for another week.

Lt(jg) Slim Russell finally had to quit at 0720 and return to the *Saratoga*. When he glanced around, he saw that he was alone except for a cruiser-launched SOC observation plane and several carrier fighters. He turned back over Guadalcanal and flew south to the ship. On the way, he noted how very rough the interior of the island appeared. Great rolling hills and mountains covered with dense green foliage were interspersed with occasional meadows beside which islanders had built tiny villages.

When Russell landed, everyone looked at him with wonder. They all thought he had spun into the water on takeoff. The searchlight Russell had thought was trying to pinpoint a submarine was actually trying to pinpoint a Dauntless that had indeed spun in. It turned out that a Scouting-3 SBD two places ahead of Russell had lost power just after clearing the *Saratoga's* deck. Its pilot and radioman-gunner were never found.

Slim Russell grabbed a sandwich and a cup of cocoa while Scouting-3's twelve operational dive-bombers were being rearmed and refueled. After taking off at 0930 and circling over Kukum and Lunga for two hours, four Scouting-3 SBD dive-bombers struck an ammunition dump with 1,000-pound bombs and blew it up. Russell's second 1,000-pound bomb of the day was dropped into a wooded area, where it burned up two large tents and knocked down a frame building. Russell returned alone to the *Saratoga* at about noon, and turned in for a nap after he ate lunch. By then, the ground troops ashore didn't appear to need any further support from the carrier bombers, though flights of SBDs and even some bomb-armed Grumman TBF Avenger torpedo bombers were kept on station in the event they were needed.

Lt(jg) Smokey Stover returned to the *Saratoga* from his early-morning strafing mission without incident at 0730. After his fighter was refueled and rearmed, he took off at 0930 to fly a routine combat air patrol over the carriers. He thus missed the opening air battles over the eastern Solomons.

Chapter 7

Rabaul had little on which to go. Moments before Allied cruisers opened fire on August 7, 1942, Tulagi Island's radio station transmitted a brief, perplexing message: "Large force of ships, unknown number or types, entering the sound. What can they be?"

RAdm Sadayoshi Yamada, the veteran pilot (one of the Imperial Navy's first) commanding the land-based 5th Air Attack Force, supposed that Tulagi was being raided in force, so he sent out a Mavis long-range reconnaissance bomber to investigate. But long before the reconnaissance could be completed, the commander of Tulagi's defunct seaplane detachment transmitted a second—final—message: "Enemy forces overwhelming. We will defend our posts to the death, praying for eternal victory."

Bomber and fighter squadron leaders and air staff officers were summoned to Yamada's headquarters. Twenty-seven twin-engine, land-based Mitsubishi G4M1 Type 1 Betty medium bombers from the 5th Air Attack Force's 4th Air Group had already been briefed and armed to undertake a morning mission against a newly discovered Allied airfield at Rabi, in eastern New Guinea. Rabi was considered an important target, for its presence was a serious threat to Japanese bases in northeastern New Guinea, but Admiral Yamada decided within a matter of moments that the greater threat—perhaps including an imminent attack on Rabaul itself—lay to the south, at Tulagi. The mission to New Guinea was postponed, but the fear of an early attack by U.S. Navy carrier aircraft was so great that Yamada and his flight leaders and staff officers decided to get the bombers off with the bombs they already had aboard, rather than switch to torpedoes, a lengthy process that would leave the bombers vulnerable on the ground for several hours. Serious disadvantages would arise from the decision to attack ships with bombs meant to hole a runway, but time was of the essence and it overrode all other considerations.

LCdr Tadashi Nakajima, the veteran flight commander *(hikotaicho)* of the crack Tainan Air Group, perhaps the finest fighter unit Japan ever put into the air, vigorously protested that the 1,200-mile round trip to Tulagi and back was at the extreme range of his unit's Mitsubishi A6M2 Type 21 Zero fighters and could lead to the loss of half his command. With a maximum range of 1,675 miles and a combat radius rated (but never previously confirmed) at 600 miles, the Tainan Air Group Zeros would be cutting it close on a mission from Rabaul to Tulagi. The distance from base to target was almost exactly 600 miles, and no one had ever flown a fully fueled and combat-loaded Zero that far for a fight. Except for an abandoned former Royal Australian Air Force runway at Buka, 160 miles southeast of Rabaul, there were no intermediate bases at which Zeros suffering from mechanical difficulties, lack of fuel, or battle damage could land. Lieutenant Commander Nakajima had an undisputed reputation for bravery, but he considered the proposed escort mission to Tulagi to be suicidal. A fierce argument ensued. Admiral Yamada would not back down, but he did finally agree to reduce the number of escorts from all of the Tainan Air Group's twenty-four operational Zeros to just eighteen. The remainder, along with sixteen short-range Zero Model 32 interceptors that had arrived on August 6, were to guard Rabaul's two airfields against the feared carrier-based air attack—and perhaps take part in an attack against the carriers themselves.

The Tainan Air Group had been created in October 1941, but many of the pilots on its rolls had served long tours in combat over China. At the start of the Pacific War, the group had been based on Formosa, from which it had taken a leading role in the earliest strikes against American bases on

Luzon, in the Philippines. It next served through the conquest of the Netherlands East Indies, and since April 1942 it had flown mainly from Lae, in northern New Guinea. Beginning with their initial action over the Philippines, and heating up during combat over the East Indies and New Guinea, many of these land-based naval aviators had honed their predatory skills against obsolete U.S. Army Air Forces and Royal Australian Air Force fighters and bombers and their pilots. By August 7, 1942, the group boasted a number of Japan's leading fighter aces. The very best of these were the men Lieutenant Commander Nakajima led down the dust-shrouded Lakunai strip—an active volcano brooded nearby—on what was to be the longest round-trip fighter mission to that time. The Zeros began taking off at 0950.

The 4th Air Group was a newer unit than even the Tainan Air Group. It had been formed at Truk, Japan's principal naval fortress in the Caroline Islands, in February 1942. Its only combat experience had been in attacks on targets in New Guinea as a component of the 5th Air Attack Force (formed in April 1942) while based at Lae and Rabaul. Commanded by Lt Renpei Egawa, a nonpilot command officer, the twenty-seven 4th Air Group Bettys, each laden with two 250-kilogram bombs and four 60-kilogram bombs, began taking off from Vunakanau Airdrome at 1006.

The Allied fleet in the eastern Solomons was amply alert to the oncoming bomber force. At about 1130, a coded message from Pacific Fleet headquarters in Hawaii warned VAdm Frank Jack Fletcher's Task Force 61 that, according to intercepted and decoded Japanese radio messages, eighteen bombers and seventeen fighters were on the way to the Tulagi area from Rabaul. Targets might be the invasion fleet (Task Force 62) off Lunga or the carriers off southern Guadalcanal. A short time later, Royal Australian Navy Petty Officer Paul Mason, a forty-one-year-old Australian planter turned covert observer, spotted the Japanese formation from his vantage point atop a hill in southern Bougainville and immediately radioed the news in the clear on a priority frequency: "24 bombers headed yours." Mason's message was picked up at Port Moresby, New Guinea, and relayed to Townville, Australia, which boasted the strongest transmitter in the region. From Townville, the news was flashed to Pearl Harbor and, finally, retransmitted to the fleet off Guadalcanal, which sprang to action. Paul Mason's position in southern Bougainville was approximately 300 miles northwest of Guadalcanal's Lunga Point—a distance the Bettys would be able to cover by a little after 1300.

Seventeen Japanese fighters (one had aborted with a landing-gear problem) and the twenty-seven Bettys came within range of American shipborne radars shortly after 1300, dead on time. While one "challenge" section of five Zeros led by Lt Shiro Kawai, the Tainan Fighter Group's senior division leader *(buntaicho)*, went in early to draw off the American fighter combat air patrol, the two remaining six-plane sections, under Lieutenant Commander Nakajima and Lt(jg) Junichi Sasai (a junior *buntaicho*), were to remain tethered to the Bettys, which were to execute precision high-level attacks on shipping with their antipersonnel and runway-busting bombs.

Two four-plane divisions of Fighting-5 F4F Wildcats under the command of Lt Pug Southerland and Lt Pete Brown were launched from the *Saratoga* beginning at 1203. They were to relieve other carrier fighters patrolling over the Task Force 62 anchorages between Guadalcanal and Tulagi. Also, eight other Fighting-5 Wildcats were launched at this time to relieve the combat air patrol over the carriers, Task Force 61. It was the third mission of the day for many of these sixteen fighter pilots.

At about the same time as Lieutenant Brown's and Lieutenant Southerland's Wildcat divisions were being launched from the *Saratoga*, four Wildcats under Lt Lou Bauer, the Fighting-6 commanding officer, were launched from the *Enterprise*, also to relieve fighters patrolling over the invasion fleet. Two other Fighting-6 Wildcats accompanied Lieutenant Bauer to Lunga, where they were to relieve the escort for the ground-support strike coordinator, who at that hour happened to be the commanding officer of the *Enterprise* Air Group, LCdr Max Leslie, at the controls of a specially equipped TBF command plane.

Shortly after it arrived on station over Task Force 62 and detached the command-plane escorts—about 1230—Lieutenant Bauer's four-plane division was ordered by one of the invasion fleet's two shipborne fighter direction officers (FDOs) to fly to the northwest at an altitude of 8,000 feet;

there were "bogeys" out there, and Bauer was to intercept them as far from the anchorage as possible. Bauer was unaware that four Fighting-71 F4Fs and four Fighting-5 Wildcats he left on station pending relief by Brown and Southerland were critically low on fuel and had to immediately depart for their ships. Other fighters were then being launched, but they were a half hour or more away.

Lieutenant Bauer's four F4Fs were nearing Savo Island—and heading toward the incoming Japanese warplanes—when they were ordered south, back toward the carriers. Bauer requested a confirmation, which he received, and an explanation, which he did not receive. Though puzzled, he had no choice but to comply. As he was turning south toward the carriers at about 1300, he heard that a Fighting-6 division under Lt(jg) Dick Gay was being launched and vectored toward the invasion fleet. This really puzzled Bauer, who was unknowingly being positioned to stand between the carriers and the incoming Japanese bomber force.

At 1311, the *Enterprise* launched four Wildcats under Lt(jg) Gordon Firebaugh to reinforce the combat air patrol over the invasion fleet. Accompanying Firebaugh's division were two Wildcats that were to relieve the two escorting LCdr Max Leslie's command TBF. At 1319, the *Wasp* launched the first of sixteen Fighting-71 Wildcats that also were to be sent to cover Task Force 62.

The eight Fighting-5 Wildcats under Lt Pug Southerland and Lt Pete Brown arrived over the anchorage at about 1300 and at 12,000 feet. The sky above was overcast, all but precluding the visual sighting of the approaching Japanese bombers.

Minutes after reporting in on the FDO channel at 1300, Lieutenant Southerland's own four-plane division was ordered to the northwest. And minutes after that, Lieutenant Brown's division was ordered to follow.

Shortly after 1300, the Japanese bomber leader, Lt Renpei Egawa, ordered the pilot of his lead Betty to begin a gentle descent through the clouds from 16,400 feet. Egawa intended to level off just beneath the clouds and attack the enemy shipping from there. By the time the 4th Air Group Bettys began their shallow descent, the Tainan Air Group Zeros had gone higher: Two six-plane *chutai* under Lieutenant Commander Nakajima and Lieutenant(jg) Sasai flew up to nearly 20,000 feet, and the five-plane challenge *chutai* under Lieutenant Kawai went to nearly 28,000 feet. As the attack force passed the Russell Islands, 65 miles from Savo, Lieutenant Kawai's *chutai* surged ahead to take on any fighters it could find between the main attack force and the enemy ships.

While approaching Savo Island, at the western end of the Allied fleet anchorage off Guadalcanal, Lieutenant Egawa was unable to see any enemy transports, so he decided to attack a number of the many warships that he and his bombardier could see. All twenty-seven bombers—arrayed in a broad, shallow vee-of-vees formation with its three nine-plane *chutai* nearly abreast—bellied through the clouds into clear daylight at about 1315. They were at 12,000 feet and only 500 yards from an astonished Lt Pug Southerland, also at 12,000 feet and on a reciprocal heading.

"Horizontal bombers, three divisions, nine planes each, over Savo, headed for transports, Angels twelve [12,000 feet]," Southerland rattled off through his throat mike. "This division from Pug: Drop belly tanks, put gun switches and sight lamps on. Let's go get 'em, boys!"

Chapter 8

By the time the 4th Air Group Bettys were first seen by Lt Pug Southerland, they had opened their bomb bays, ready to bomb the shipping below. Though there was precious little room to maneuver, and a perfect attack was out of the question, Lieutenant Southerland instantly dropped his fighter into a tight low-side run from the bombers' left and fired several bursts from his six .50-caliber wing guns at the leading bomber *chutai*. As he hurtled by, he aimed at the right nine-plane *chutai* and fleetingly fired into it from long range. Shortly, he was able to fix his aim upon a bomber near the center of the left *chutai*. He saw his bullets start a fire in the fuselage just forward of the open bomb bay. Southerland did not see the result, but this Betty was a goner. It nosed down in flames and fell all the way to the surface. Meantime, as Southerland banked left and down, Japanese 7.7mm bullets cracked the bulletproof Plexiglas windscreen in front of his face, and an incendiary bullet started a fire behind his cockpit. Undeterred, Southerland banked around to execute a low-side attack against the right *chutai*. He poured all his remaining ammunition into another Betty's right engine and wing. This Betty, piloted by PO1 Yoshiyuki Sakimoto, fell back in the formation, but Southerland could not finish it off. Nor could he hang around in his smoking F4F to see what happened to it. He dived out of the fight, having unknowingly scored the first American aerial victory of the Guadalcanal Campaign.

The other three Wildcats in Southerland's division were jumped by Lt Shiro Kawai's five challenge fighters before they could attack the bombers. Lieutenant Kawai had missed seeing the Wildcats as he passed over Savo at 28,000 feet ahead of the bombers, but he suspected something was amiss, retraced his route, and led his fighter *chutai* lower just in time to catch the three Wildcats as they followed Lt Pug Southerland against the Bettys.

Ens Don Innis, the division's tail-end charlie, saw Kawai's Zeros coming a split second before the attack was sprung, and he took defensive action. However, the two Wildcats between Southerland and Innis were simply shredded as the five Zeros cut through the center of Southerland's division. Southerland's wingman, Ens Robert Price, and Innis's section leader, Lt(jg) Charles Tabberer, were shot down and killed, probably before either of them fired a shot or even knew what hit them.

Ensign Innis managed to evade certain death by climbing head-on into the diving Zeros and firing all his guns at every one of them. One of the Zeros managed to turn onto Innis's tail, and the Wildcat endured a shredded elevator and forty-nine bullet holes before Innis flew into a cloud.

Lt Pete Brown's Fighting-5 division was moving to aid Southerland's division when Brown first spotted the bombers, which were his primary targets. He briefly thought about attacking Kawai's Zero *chutai* as it dived through Southerland's division, but he opted for the bombers, for the warships they were about to attack were more important than a few fighters, more important even than the fellow Fighting-5 pilots at the controls of those fighters.

Brown was turning into a favorable attack position when his division was beset by five Zeros from LCdr Tadashi Nakajima's *chutai*—an enraged Nakajima stayed with the bombers—and possibly two from Lt(jg) Junichi Sasai's. Brown wanted the bombers, but he had to deal with the Zeros. He sent his second section—Lt(jg) Bill Holt and Ens Joe Daly—after the Bettys and turned to take on the Zeros with the help of his wingman, Ens Foster Blair.

Brown turned into the highly maneuverable Zeros and climbed to attack them head-on. This worked fine for a moment—he bluffed two Zeros out of his way—but another Zero parked on his tail and opened fire. Miraculously, this Zero was too close to Brown, so two streams of 7.7mm machine-gun bullets passed along both sides of Brown's cockpit and converged ahead of the Wildcat. Brown rolled down and shook the Zero from his tail.

Ensign Blair was right behind Brown through the head-on maneuver, and he squeezed off a few rounds at the Zero parked on Brown's tail before he was forced to evade another Zero that got on his tail. That separated him from Brown, but it also forced the Zero on Brown to evade Blair's bullets and leave the division leader alone. Blair reversed course and lost altitude in a split-**S** maneuver and hid out in a cloud.

Even before Blair forced the Zero from his tail, Brown was beset by a Zero that attacked from ahead and above. The Japanese pilot executed a neat overhead pass and opened fire on the way down. Lieutenant Brown was struck in the right hip with an incendiary smoke round. Other bullets shattered instruments and fixtures in Brown's cockpit and filled the compartment with smoke. Brown pulled up to evade the Zero and cracked the cockpit canopy, ready to bail out if the smoke and fumes did not give way to fresh air. At this point, the Japanese pilot who had nailed the Wildcat pulled up alongside. The opposing pilots stared at one another until the Japanese pilot grinned, waved, and surged ahead. Brown felt a momentary impulse to let the Zero get away, but he opened fire. However, the recoil of the guns caused the Wildcat to stall and spin away. Brown regained control and continued down. He fired at a Zero that flashed past his gunsight and then flew into a cloud. Brown's Wildcat was becoming unstable and the pain and blood from his hip wound were worrying, so he called it a day and set course for the *Saratoga*. He wasn't at all sure he would live to get there, or that the Wildcat would fly that far.

The Bettys were getting ready to release their bombs when Lt(jg) Bill Holt and Ens Joe Daly—Pete Brown's second section—roared through Lt(jg) Junichi Sasai's Zero *chutai* and delivered a diving high-side attack upon the lead aircraft in the left bomber *chutai*. Both U.S. Navy pilots scored hits on bombers in the far-left trio, but there was no visible damage and all the bombers kept formation. The two Wildcats flew all the way through the Betty formation and used their high diving speed to swoop up to do it all over again. At about this time, as reported earlier, a Betty in the right *chutai* fell away under Lt Pug Southerland's guns. Also, antiaircraft fire from the warships below began bursting in and around the 4th Air Group formation.

Shrapnel sprayed the formation and caused damage to several of the bombers. Then one antiaircraft round struck the right wing of the Betty to Lt Renpei Egawa's immediate left. It looked like the engine was going to twist from its mount, but the bombers were over their targets, and the pilot of the damaged bomber, PO1 Asayoshi Nakamura, fought for control long enough to get the bombs dropped.

At 1320, the bombardier in Lieutenant Egawa's Betty salvoed his bombs from just above 12,000 feet, and then all the Bettys let go with a total of 156 bombs. Their target was a string of speeding warships and a squadron of transports. The combination of the fighter attacks, the altitude, and the number of moving targets below threw the Japanese bombardiers off their mark. Most of the bombs fell wide of the many targets, but it seemed to several Japanese airmen that a transport and a destroyer were hit. In fact, no real harm was done.

Bill Holt and Joe Daly struck the bombers from above again only seconds after the bombs were toggled. As they did, Petty Officer Nakamura's damaged Betty fell out of the formation. Ensign Daly put many rounds into two other bombers in the center *chutai*, and fires started in both of them. In return, tail gunners manning 20mm stingers holed Daly's wings and tail. In the next pass, one of the Wildcats set fire to an engine of a Betty in the left *chutai*, but the Betty was able to stay in formation. Another Betty in the right *chutai* took hits in a fuel tank, but it did not burn. And yet another Betty in the left *chutai* was hit many times through the fuselage. This last Betty eventually fell out of formation and was never seen again; it is the only Betty that Holt or Daly hit that went down.

Ens Foster Blair rejoined the fight at this point, and he severely damaged the Betty in the right *chutai* piloted by PO1 Yoshiyuki Sakimoto—the same one that had been staggered but not downed during Pug Southerland's last pass at the bombers. Ensign Blair's bullets started a fire in the bomb bay, but despite that and the damage caused by Southerland to the right wing and engine, Sakimoto's airplane was able to keep up with the 4th Air Group formation.

Several Zeros, just barely under Lieutenant Commander Nakajima's control, finally regrouped and went after Holt and Daly. Holt forced a Zero off Daly's tail, but the Japanese fighter pilots were not deterred by the skill or aggressiveness of their adversaries. They set up three attacks on the scissoring Wildcat pair, but to little or no avail. While they regrouped, Holt and Daly tried for the bombers again, even though only two of Daly's wing guns remained operable.

The final Zero attack caught the Wildcats from astern. Holt and Daly tried to scissor their way out, but a 20mm round caught Daly's airplane beneath the cockpit, ripped open a fuel tank, wounded Daly, and set everything including the pilot on fire. Daly was sure he was about to die, but he opened the canopy, clawed out of his seat belt, and jumped from the burning airplane at 13,000 feet. He intentionally fell about 6,000 feet before deploying his parachute and drifted to the surface. He landed in the water off Guadalcanal, about 15 miles from the Marines' landing beaches. Daly had nine bullet holes in his leg, second-degree facial burns, and assorted other burns and bruises, but he was able to swim slowly toward shore. Eventually, he was rescued by an SOC observation plane and taken aboard the heavy cruiser *Chicago*.

Bill Holt was shot down moments after Daly, but it is not known how, or what became of him. After Daly was culled, no one ever saw Holt again.

Moments after delivering a fatal attack against a Betty in the right *chutai*, Ens Foster Blair was chased from the scene by two Zeros that holed his Wildcat's right wing. For the second time in a matter of minutes, he hid out in a cloud.

Lt Pug Southerland was diving through 11,500 feet on his way out of the fight when he was attacked by a lone Zero. As the Japanese pilot executed repeated firing passes, Southerland cranked his seat down and hunched behind the armor plate at his back. Then he went to work trying to recharge his guns. He thought his ammunition cans were empty, but he hoped the guns had merely jammed during his last firing pass on the Bettys.

By this time, the Zero was attacking from the starboard quarter, so Southerland pushed over as though diving to escape him. Then he immediately pulled out, cracked his landing flaps, and pulled his throttle to low power. When the Zero overran the suddenly slowing Wildcat, as Southerland had hoped he would, the Japanese pilot made a climbing turn to the left. Southerland easily turned inside the Zero and saw that an aviator's dream had come true; he had a Zero at close range and perfectly lined up in his gunsight for an easy quarter-deflection shot. But when Southerland pressed the gun-button knob, nothing happened. Now certain that all his ammunition had been expended on the Bettys, he knew he would have to fight the rest of the battle unarmed.

Two fresh Zeros joined the attack on Southerland. The three Japanese repeatedly dived at Southerland in changing pairs, firing first from one side and then from the other. Pug Southerland's job now merely consisted of determining which of the Zero pilots attacking almost simultaneously on either quarter was about to open fire first and then sharply turning toward him as he opened up. This gave the firing Zero a full-deflection (90-degree) shot so that he invariably underled the Wildcat. Countless bullets struck the Wildcat's fuselage from cockpit to tail but did little serious damage. The Wildcat's quick evasive turns also placed the second Zero directly astern so that Southerland was adequately protected by the armored back of his seat. When the Zeros' runs were not quite simultaneous, Southerland relied on his armor, placing the attackers directly aft in succession as they made their firing passes.

PO1 Saburo Sakai was one of Japan's three top-scoring aces. This day, he was leading Lt(jg) Junichi Sasai's second three-plane Zero *shotai* above the Bettys.

As Sakai joined on Sasai at 12,000 feet, he noted that his two brash young wingmen were gone, no doubt drawn to the action against Bill Holt, Joe Daly, and Foster Blair. As Sakai scanned the sky in the hope of spotting the errant pilots, he saw that three Zeros were trying to down a lone American Wildcat. Sakai spotted the melee just as two of the swift Zeros overtook and passed the slower Wildcat. It seemed to the ace that the Wildcat was winning the fight, so he flew up alongside Sasai's Zero and motioned for permission to join the action. Sasai nodded.

Saburo Sakai fired his Zero's two 7.7mm cowl-mounted machine guns and two 20mm wing-mounted automatic cannon from more than 600 yards, more to distract Pug Southerland than in the hope of destroying him. Southerland countered with a mock attack, snapping into a tight left turn to disrupt Sakai's firing run.

Where the other three Japanese had hunted Pug Southerland with superior firepower, Saburo Sakai hunted with his Zero's superior maneuverability. Two superb airmen were pitted against each other, but the battle was unequal, for Sakai was armed and Southerland was not.

This was Sakai's first encounter with the F4F Wildcat. He had routinely been shooting down Chinese, Dutch, and U.S. Army Air Forces pilots for five years—fifty-six kills claimed thus far—but he had yet to meet anything like the rugged Grumman carrier fighter he was taking on this day. He repeatedly maneuvered into superior attack positions only to find himself outmaneuvered by the slower but deftly handled Wildcat. Sakai pushed five separate attacks against Southerland but did not fire a round because he knew his bullets would not down the Grumman fighter. Since Sakai did not know that Southerland had no bullets left, he remained cautious lest he fall under the Grumman's mangling .50-caliber machine guns. When Southerland tried to pull out of the fight after Sakai's fifth abortive attack, however, the Japanese pilot realized that the Grumman was not in fighting condition.

All Southerland wanted to do was get over friendly territory and bail out of his stricken airplane.

Sakai withheld his killing pass long enough to snap a photo of the Grumman with his handheld Leica camera. Then he took careful aim and fired two hundred 7.7mm rounds from only 50 yards. Amazingly, though few of the bullets could have missed, and the Grumman seemed tattered and ripped to shreds, it doggedly continued to fly toward Guadalcanal. Even more amazing, Sakai found himself hurtling over the suddenly slowing Grumman; Southerland was dead on Sakai's tail and could have destroyed the flimsier Zero if he had had bullets.

The riddled Wildcat was in bad shape, but it was still performing to Southerland's satisfaction. The F4F's landing flaps and radio had been put out of commission, a large part of its fuselage was like a sieve, and it was smoking from incendiary hits, though it was not on fire. All of the ammunition-box covers on the left wing had been blown off, and 20mm explosive rounds had torn several gaping holes in the upper surface of the left wing. The instrument panel was badly shot up, the goggles on Southerland's forehead were shattered, the rearview mirror was broken, the windscreen was riddled, tiny drops of fuel were leaking onto the cockpit floor, and the contents of the punctured oil tank was pouring down Southerland's right leg and foot.

At length, curiosity, along with his esteem for his dogged enemy, got the better of Sakai. He pulled up beside the American, whose rudder and tail were so much scrap. The two stared at each other as they flew straight and level, then Sakai surged ahead and signaled the American to come and fight if he dared. Pug Southerland shifted his stick from his right hand to his left and made what looked to Sakai like a plea for mercy. It was not. Southerland was preparing to bail out, and he needed his right hand to free his legs and body from his seat harness. Sakai chopped his throttle, dropped behind the American, and switched on the pair of deadly 20mm cannon in his wings. His finger lightly rested on the gun button, then pressed down.

The 20mm burst from Southerland's port quarter struck just under the Wildcat's left wing root. The fighter finally exploded, no doubt because of the ignition of gasoline vapors that had been collecting in the cockpit and fuselage. When Southerland felt and saw the flash below and forward of his left foot, he was ready for it. He dived headfirst over the right side of the cockpit, just aft of the starboard wing root. The holster of his automatic pistol caught on the hood track, but he immediately got rid of it without quite knowing how.

Saburo Sakai saw Pug Southerland fall away, trailing a huge silken canopy as he drifted toward the water. Seconds later, Southerland thudded to earth on Guadalcanal, several miles from the coast and many miles west of friendly lines.

Lt(jg) Slim Russell, of Scouting-3, awoke at 1330 from his nap following two morning bombing missions and went up to the *Saratoga's* flight deck to see what was going on. Surprisingly, no one was working on the broad deck, and it took about a minute for Russell to find dozens of officers and sailors clustered around the carrier's antiaircraft gun galleries. Some-one said that Zero fighters were overhead. The *Saratoga* was nearing a storm front and the clouds were already very low, so Russell did not worry about Zero fighters. He walked past the Fighting-5 ready room and saw a naked form covered with blood. This was Fighting-5's Lt Pete Brown, who had just completed a hairy landing in a badly damaged Wildcat. Russell noted that Brown's Wildcat was badly shot up and that Brown had been hit in the fleshy part of the thigh and rump by an incendiary bullet. A medical corpsman told Russell that Brown's flesh was badly burned by white phos-phorous. The corpsman opened up the inside of the pilot's leg, cut to the path of the bullet, and scraped out the fragments of white phosphorous. It was a very messy job.

Of the eight Fighting-5 Wildcats in the two divisions Lt Pug Southerland had led off the *Saratoga* a few minutes after noon, only three returned to the carrier: the severely wounded Lt Pete Brown, Ens Foster Blair, and Ens Don Innis. Three of the eight pilots were lost without a trace, Lt Pug Southerland was missing, and Ens Joe Daly was soon to be rescued by a friendly warship. Lt(jg) Bill Holt, Ens Robert Price, and Lt(jg) Charles Tabberer were dead.

Pug Southerland fell to earth on Guadalcanal, miles and miles from friendly forces. He reached Marine lines with the help of islanders on August 10 and was air-evacuated to a rear-area hospital on August 12.

Chapter 9

The next American aircraft to tangle with the Japanese attack group were six Scouting-71 Dauntless dive-bombers that happened to be orbiting beneath the clouds overhanging Tulagi Harbor. These airplanes were under the control of LCdr Wallace Beakley, the commanding officer of the *Wasp* Air Group, who was working a shift as ground-support coordinator over Tulagi and Florida. At 1320, Lieutenant Commander Beakley had ordered three of eight orbiting *Wasp* SBDs to attack a small islet with their 500-pound bombs. Responding had been LCdr John Eldridge, the Scouting-71 commanding officer, and his wingmen, Lt Dudley Adams and Ens Jacob Paretsky.

Just as Eldridge and Adams toggled their bombs, Beakley blurted "Bombers above!" into the open bomber channel, and urged the SBDs to intercept them. Eldridge responded by leading Adams and Paretsky aloft. Lt(jg) William Kephart, a Scouting-71 section leader, ordered his two wingmen to jettison their bombs and follow the squadron commander. However, since Kephart's section started out higher than Eldridge's, Kephart had the lead. In all, six SBDs ended up in a loose formation, arrowing toward the Bettys.

As the SBDs topped the clouds, the Bettys were at 15,000 feet and climbing, but Lt(jg) Junichi Sasai and his two Tainan Air Group wingmen were at 7,500 and diving toward the U.S. Navy dive-bombers. They all met at 7,500 feet.

Kephart responded to the sudden appearance of three Zeros firing their 7.7mm cowl guns by twisting away and leading his two wingmen toward the water. There was no way the Zeros could catch the heavier SBDs in a dive. These three Dauntlesses ended up in a cloud, but they soon popped out and gave chase to the Bettys, which were by then making a wide turn toward home over Florida.

Kephart's section drew off Sasai and his wingmen, but two members of Lt Shiro Kawai's Zero *chutai* assailed Lieutenant Commander Eldridge's section from behind. They both attacked Lieutenant Adams's SBD, which was trailing Eldridge's and Paretsky's. Though the Zero pilots claimed three kills, they were in fact held off for a crucial moment by Adams's radioman-gunner, ARM3 Harry Elliott. And in that moment, the three SBDs broke formation and dived for the safety of the clouds.

Not content with escaping a duel with Zeros with his life, Lieutenant Adams, a 1939 Annapolis graduate, went after four different Zeros he spotted as they cut across the channel from Guadalcanal to rejoin the Bettys over Florida. These airplanes were flown by PO1 Saburo Sakai and the three other members of Lieutenant(jg) Sasai's *chutai* who had hammered Pug Southerland out of the sky.

The first Petty Officer Sakai knew of Lieutenant Adams's proximity was a .50-caliber bullet the Annapolis grad fired through the ace's canopy. Sakai looked around and saw that a blue-painted airplane was assailing him from off his port quarter. Sakai led his three wingmen up from 7,000 feet and turned back to deliver a high-side attack against the audacious man in the slower airplane. A burst of 7.7mm fire from Sakai's cowl guns killed ARM3 Elliott, in the rear seat of Adams's Dauntless, and severely wounded Adams. Certain of a kill, Sakai led his Zeros away while Adams managed to ditch beside a destroyer at 1337. He was rescued in a matter of minutes.

Lieutenant(jg) Kephart and his two wingmen never caught up with the swifter Bettys, and Lieutenant Commander Eldridge and Ensign Paretsky remained in the clouds until all the Zeros had cleared the area.

◆

Shortly after downing Lieutenant Adams, Saburo Sakai spotted eight *Enterprise* Air Group Dauntlesses under the command of Lt Carl Horenburger. Like Eldridge's, these Dauntlesses were orbiting at 7,800 feet to provide on-call air support for Marines fighting on Tulagi and Gavutu. Sakai mistook the distant dive-bombers for fighters, and he and his three wingmen launched a beam attack, never dreaming that their quarry was armed with rear-firing twin .30-caliber machine guns.

Lieutenant Horenburger's radioman-gunner, AMM2 Herman Caruthers, was the first to see Sakai's approach. At that moment, he was passing the time communicating with AOM2 Harold Jones, another radioman-gunner, by means of Morse code hand signals—open hand, closed fist. When Caruthers signaled the approach of enemy aircraft, Jones spotted the Zeros 800 feet below and nearly a mile astern his Dauntless. Suddenly, one of the Japanese fighters broke off, turned left, dived, and approached the Dauntless formation from underneath. Jones also saw a second Zero as it hurtled toward him from dead astern.

The Zero that Jones saw approach the Dauntless formation from underneath was one of Sakai's wingman, PO2 Kenji Kakimoto. The Japanese pilot approaching from astern—to within 300 yards—was Sakai himself. By the time Sakai had closed on Jones's dive-bomber, which was piloted by Ens Robert Shaw, he knew he had made an egregious identification error, but he was committed to the attack.

Ens Eldor Rodenburg was leading the lead three-plane SBD section. As soon as he was made aware of the enemy fighters in the area, he closed up his formation as tightly as possible with a wingman on each wing, and dropped back to a position slightly astern and below the division leader. Lieutenant Horenburger was leading four wingmen—one on his starboard wing and three on his port wing. Both sections were in tight stepped-down formations. As soon as Rodenburg's move had concentrated the firepower potential of most of the Dauntless rearseat gunners, Horenburger led the formation in a gradual turn to starboard.

Petty Officer Sakai was coming in directly from astern, and he started firing when he was about 500 feet away from the rear SBD. A 20mm shell hit the vane of Ens Robert Gibson's 500-pound bomb, then ricocheted upward and exploded beneath Gibson's armored seat. To Gibson, the detonation felt like a swift kick in the pants, but he was unharmed. By then several of the American gunners had responded with bursts from their twin .30-caliber machine guns. Several others, however, including AOM2 Jones, could not initially bring their guns to bear on Sakai without shooting up the tails of their own bombers. When Sakai turned to the right and pulled up in order to avoid colliding with the SBDs, every rearseatman could safely fire. And all of them did.

At a distance of little more than 100 feet, AOM2 Jones saw Sakai's cockpit explode in a bright orange flame. The Zero's canopy appeared to be torn from its tracks, and Jones saw something fly out of the cockpit. He also got a clear look at Sakai's face, and saw that the ace's head had been forced back against the headrest. He had the distinct impression that the Japanese pilot had been wounded. The Zero pulled almost straight up and then fell away, trailing smoke, but Jones immediately lost sight of it as he swung his guns to bear on Petty Officer Kakimoto's Zero, which was coming in from below.

Sakai's Zero began a vertical plunge toward the water. By incredible good fortune, Japan's leading ace overcame his severe head wounds and gravity to pull out at wave-top height and lurch for home. He later determined that the turbulence of the 7,000-foot dive must have extinguished the flames that threatened to consume his battered Zero fighter. Though severely wounded—a .30-caliber bullet had plowed a groove in his skull—and nearly blinded from severe facial and eye injuries, Sakai struggled on to complete an epic 560-mile flight back to Lakunai Airdrome in under five hours.

As AOM2 Jones fired at Petty Officer Kakimoto's Zero, his attention was again refocused when his pilot, Ens Robert Shaw, announced over the intercom, "Stand by to bail out." Shaw told Jones that their Dauntless's controls were very sloppy and that he did not feel he could fly the airplane. Shaw fell out of formation and slowed the bomber while Jones surveyed the damage. He told Shaw with considerable relief that only the right half of the elevator was hit. Shaw decided to fly back to the *Enterprise,* which was about 60 miles away. They made the slow return alone, and Shaw landed without incident.

◆

The fight over the fleet raged on as fresh *Enterprise* fighters came on station at 1330.

Lt(jg) Dick Gay, a former enlisted pilot with many years of military flying behind him, was leading his Fighting-6 division directly across Guadalcanal from the south when he was ordered by one of the FDOs with Task Force 62 to investigate antiaircraft bursts over the Tulagi anchorage. Gay's division was at 16,000 feet and passing across Guadalcanal's northern shore when all four pilots saw the telltale black puffs about 10 miles ahead and at about 13,000 feet.

Gay's wingman, Lt Vince de Poix, a sharp-eyed 1939 Annapolis graduate only a few months out of flight school, was the first to spot the riddled Japanese bomber formation over Florida Island as it was racing northwest for Rabaul at 180 knots. No Zeros were visible at that time, but eight of them were lurking 1,000 feet beneath the bomber formation—Lieutenant Commander Nakajima's entire *chutai* and Lieutenant Kawai and one wingman.

Lieutenant de Poix was the first to break formation. At 1345, he commenced a high-side attack from in front of the bombers. Dick Gay crossed to the left and commenced a steep high-side attack against the right *chutai*. The second Wildcat section—Mach Howell Sumrall leading Mach Joe Achten—commenced a run from starboard to port over the top of the bomber formation. While just going into his run, Gay spotted two Zeros, but he ignored them; they were below and behind the bombers, no threat at all for the moment.

Vince de Poix got a Betty in the center *chutai* in his sights and hammered it. Machinist Sumrall saw a fire erupt in this bomber, but it held formation.

Sumrall was just going to open fire when the light filament in his reflector gunsight burned out. He nevertheless opened fire on one of Lt Renpei Egawa's wingmen and pulled the tracer from his guns to the port engine, which he hit. As Sumrall's momentum carried him past this first target, he put his tracer through the wing of the third Betty in the right *chutai*. In fact, Sumrall thought he might have severed the Betty's fuselage at the trailing edge of the port wing, but he had not. Machinist Achten, who remained on

Sumrall's wing, hit another Betty in the right *chutai*, but none of the bombers hit by the two warrant machinists fell out of the formation.

Dick Gay pulled in for a second pass, and his gunsight fell on the twice-wounded Betty flown by PO1 Yoshiyuki Sakimoto—the same Betty that had been struck by bullets fired by Lt Pug Southerland and Ens Foster Blair. Already struggling to keep up with only one engine, Sakimoto was unable to overcome the added damage inflicted by Gay's guns. The Betty fell away and trailed smoke as it lost altitude. Lt Vince de Poix arrived on the scene at this point, and he fired into Sakimoto's Betty until it was burning from end to end and rolled away in a final plunge to the sea. De Poix got credit for the kill.

It was only as Sakimoto's Betty was falling away in flames that gunners aboard other Bettys attracted the attention of the two Zero pilots who had been obliviously trailing the bomber formation throughout the minutes-long attack by Gay's division. None of the Zeros carried radios; it took shots across the bows of these two to alert the wool-gathering pilots to the presence of the Wildcats.

The Zeros each latched themselves to the tail of a Wildcat—Gay and de Poix—and chased them away from the bombers. Gay's F4F was shot up as he fled into the clouds. Lieutenant de Poix was slightly wounded in the shoulder by a 7.7mm slug, and his instrument panel was shattered as he, too, was driven into the clouds by the Zero on his tail.

Following his first firing pass across the top of the bomber formation, Machinist Sumrall pulled out directly beneath the bombers in the hope of spoiling the aim of any belly gunners who might have been tracking him. (There were no belly gunners.) As Sumrall recovered to get into position for another sweep through the bombers, he saw a Zero below, slightly to the left and behind his Wildcat. It was clear to Sumrall that he would be under the Zero's guns before he could make the next run on the bombers. As the realization struck, the Japanese pilot opened fire. Sumrall kicked his F4F into a split-**S** maneuver to force the Zero into a head-on run. However, two of the Japanese pilot's 20mm cannon rounds exploded in the Wildcat's fuselage just aft of the left wing, and many 7.7mm bullets riddled other parts of Sumrall's airplane. Sumrall immediately attempted to alert the other Wildcat pilots, but his radio, which was located in the fuselage behind the wing, had been knocked out. By then, Sumrall's cockpit was filled with smoke and he was unable to see a thing. Certain his fighter was on fire, he opened the cockpit canopy. The smoke immediately cleared to reveal that Sumrall was in the midst of four Zeros.

The four Japanese fighters worked the lone Wildcat over for some moments, until Sumrall remembered hearing that a Zero's ailerons froze at speeds over 250 knots. To test the rumor, Sumrall went into a steep spiral to the left, which he reversed when his air-speed indicator nudged 250 knots. As Sumrall twisted to the right, he saw a huge cloud formation. Reasoning that the Japanese would assume he would make for the clouds, he pulled up into a climbing turn to the right, from which he hoped to catch the Zeros as they passed his projected former diving turn. But the Zeros were gone; they had flown back to protect the bombers. By then, Machinist Sumrall was flying on his 27-gallon reserve fuel supply, so he headed toward the *Enterprise* by the most direct route. He was concerned that solid 20mm hits in his wings—he could see great patches of ocean through the gaping holes—would affect the Wildcat's landing characteristics, but a quick test at altitude revealed that the abused fighter would behave.

Mach Joe Achten, Sumrall's wingman, was attacked by two Zeros before he quite completed his firing pass at the right Betty *chutai*. Fortunately, the lead Zero overran Achten's Wildcat, and Achten got a good burst into it from behind. Simultaneously, however, the wings and fuselage of Achten's F4F took solid hits from the second Zero's 20mm cannon. Achten shook this assailant by diving for the thick cumulus clouds over Florida Island, but he eventually had to land his Wildcat after the engine froze, the result of hits on an oil cooler that spilled all the airplane's oil. Achten landed safely on the water at 1350 and was rescued a short time later by a Navy transport.

Gay and Sumrall safely landed aboard the *Enterprise,* and de Poix put down aboard the *Wasp*.

Six Fighting-6 fighters led by Lt(jg) Gordon Firebaugh, a former enlisted pilot with ten years' experience and more than thirteen hundred hours in fighters, had been launched from the *Enterprise* at 1311, four minutes before Lt Pug Southerland met the 4th Air Group crossing over Savo toward the Allied fleet anchorage between Guadalcanal and Tulagi. The pilots of Firebaugh's own four-plane division, plus two manning Wildcats that were supposed to have relieved the escort for the *Enterprise* Air Group command TBF, spotted the retiring brown-green bombers as they passed over Florida on their way home, but it would require a long chase to catch up. Normally, the Wildcats would have been held on a 35-mile leash, but the FDO controlling them allowed them to continue on because they had plenty of fuel aboard, including 42-gallon drop tanks.

It was after 1400 and over the southern tip of Santa Isabel Island—about 150 miles from the invasion fleet—before the six Fighting-6 F4Fs finally caught up with the speeding bombers and their escorts. The Bettys were at 12,000 feet and the Wildcats were 2 miles to port at 14,000 feet when Firebaugh's belly tank ran dry. Sweeping the sky for Zeros before he would commit to an attack on the Bettys, Firebaugh saw three of them on his side of the bomber formation at about 10,000 feet. These were piloted by Lieutenant Commander Nakajima and two petty officers. Lieutenant Firebaugh did not see the five Zeros commanded by Lieutenant Kawai, which were well above the bombers, nor Lieutenant (jg) Sasai's *chutai* (minus Sakai), which was ahead of the Bettys.

Feeling that the three Zeros he could see were no immediate threat, Firebaugh ordered everyone to drop their belly tanks and split into two uneven sections. While he led his wingman, AP1 Bill Stephenson, against Lieutenant Commander Nakajima's three Zeros, Mach Bill Warden and RE Tommy Rhodes were to lead their wingmen—Ens Bob Disque and AP1 Paul Mankin, respectively—against the bombers.

Lieutenant (jg) Firebaugh led AP1 Stephenson straight down toward the three trailing Zeros and lined up on the leader—LCdr Tadashi Nakajima, the Tainan Air Group *hikotaicho*. But Nakajima had already seen the pair of Wildcats, and he was already leading his two wingmen in a climb so swift that he rattled Firebaugh a bit. Firebaugh opened fire at 500 yards and saw hits on the leader's cowling. Then he eased down to go below the

Zeros. As he did, a stream of 7.7mm bullets passed straight up by his right knee to tear up his Wildcat's instrument array. Firebaugh scissored to the right and watched *eight* Zeros pass underneath his airplane. He looked to see if Stephenson was okay, but his wingman's Wildcat was heading toward the sea in a 45-degree dive from which it never recovered.

In the meantime, Mach Bill Warden, RE Tommy Rhodes, Ens Bob Disque, and AP1 Paul Mankin deployed to attack the 4th Air Group Bettys from port to starboard, out of the sun. However, when Warden told Gordon Firebaugh that he could not release his belly tank, Firebaugh told him to stand off while Rhodes led the attack. Moments later, Mankin discovered that his vulnerable belly tank was also still firmly affixed to his fighter, so he stayed high to cover the others.

Rhodes and Disque made a single firing pass across the top of the left bomber *chutai*. As they pulled away, one of the rear Bettys lost its place in the formation and began to fall behind. At this point, Rhodes pulled away to look for Firebaugh and Stephenson, because Firebaugh had reported problems with the Zeros.

Ensign Disque elected to undertake a second run at the bomber formation. Under the impact of his bullets, yet another Betty dropped out of the right *chutai,* though it was unclear what damage Disque had caused. And on a third run, Disque closed in on one of the slowing Bettys and got solid hits on an engine or fuel tank. The bomber immediately trailed a long, bright orange flame with black smoke streaming behind it, but it continued on straight ahead in level flight.

Disque was so excited and entranced at the sight of *his* burning Betty that he pulled up beside it to look it over. He never thought about the nose, fuselage, dorsal, and tail gunners, who were probably banging away at him. All he could think was: If my dad could only see this!

After a few moments, as Disque started to climb after the rest of the formation, he heard Mankin call out that there was another cripple below. Disque warned Mankin that this might be a decoy, but Mankin had the bit in his teeth. Though he was still lugging his dangerously flammable belly tank, he executed a neat high-side run on the trailing Betty and flamed its port engine. It was a goner.

With that, Disque and Mankin, who were feeling invincible, climbed back to wreak some more havoc upon what remained of the 4th Air Group formation—still twenty-three of the original twenty-seven Bettys. They were not molested for several minutes, but then Mankin warned Disque, "There's a Zero on your tail." It was, in fact, Lieutenant Commander Nakajima, attacking alone and absolutely apoplectic because none of the other Zeros had bothered to re-form after breaking formation to chase Firebaugh and Stephenson.

Disque evaded Nakajima's first pass and adroitly maneuvered him into a head-on run in which both pilots failed to score any hits. Then Mankin arrived on the scene and fired tracers to scare Nakajima away. The *hikotaicho* took the hint; he turned in too tightly for Mankin to follow and dived away from the fight. With that, Mankin and Disque headed back to the carriers on their reserve fuel.

After Mach Bill Warden pulled out of the lead position from the four Wildcats sent to attack the Bettys, he rode off to the side to try to jettison his belly tank. He soon lost track of the fight, but the fight came to him anyway in the form of Lieutenant (jg) Sasai leading three other Zeros. Machinist Warden gamely took on all comers as they attacked, but he had to break out of the stacked fight when 7.7mm bullets shattered one of his oil coolers. Two of the Zeros let him go, but two others stuck with Warden until the gutsy Wildcat pilot turned back to confront them. In fact, Warden chased the two until they caught up with the rest of Sasai's *chutai,* and he barely survived the counter-counterattack that ensued. But survive he did, and he turned for home on an engine he was sure would die on the way.

RE Tommy Rhodes had made one pass at the bombers, then continued through the formation to help Lieutenant (jg) Firebaugh and AP1 Stephenson. The problem was that there was no sign of Firebaugh's section, though Rhodes did see a splash on the water that could have been Stephenson's Wildcat. An instant later, Rhodes was assailed by four Zeros. The Wildcat pilot evaded injury and serious damage for several moments, and then the Zero leader overran the Wildcat, ending up right in front of Rhodes's guns. The U.S. Navy pilot cut loose and set the Zero ablaze. Rhodes was convinced he had scored a sure kill, but the Zero pilot dived away and managed to extinguish the flames.

Radio Electrician Rhodes was in serious straits. His frantic calls for help were going unheeded and unacknowledged, and he had no idea how he was going to shake the three remaining Zeros. Fortunately, Machinist Warden happened along in his crippled Wildcat. Only three of Warden's guns would fire, but the brave man squirted bullets ahead of the lead Zero on Rhodes's tail and scared all three into taking evasive action. Rhodes was sprung. He pulled his thoroughly riddled Wildcat into a friendly cloud until the heat died down. Eventually, he turned for home.

After assisting Rhodes, Machinist Warden dived to wave-top height and ran, but at least one Zero gave chase. Warden emptied his three remaining guns at this Zero, but his oil-starved engine finally seized and he was obliged to land without power in the sea slightly to the north of the Russell Islands. Warden nearly drowned when his head was thrown against the instrument panel, but he revived in time to get out on a wing and free his life raft from its storage compartment behind the cockpit. He waved at Tommy Rhodes, who had no idea who it was as he passed overhead on his way home.

That left Lt(jg) Gordon Firebaugh, who evaded a surprise attack by eight Zeros that claimed his wingman, AP1 Stephenson. The division leader was given a moment's respite after he saw Stephenson going down, but Lt Shiro Kawai's entire five-plane *chutai* turned back to take him on.

Lieutenant Kawai led the attack from above and to the right. Firebaugh waited until the *buntaicho* was fully committed to the attack and within range of his guns. At precisely the right instant, he turned sharply inside Kawai's track, forcing the Zero leader to fire at full deflection—broadside—a very tough shot against a speeding fighter. Kawai's bullets missed the lone Wildcat and Kawai hurtled by. Firebaugh attempted to reverse his heading in order to get a clear shot at Kawai, but Kawai climbed out of danger before Firebaugh could fire. By then, the second Zero had found the Wildcat with its bullets. Firebaugh reversed, the Zero overshot, and Firebaugh fired all his guns. This Zero, piloted by PO1 Mototsuna Yoshida, a twelve-victory ace, twisted to the right and flew all the way into the water.

The third Zero scored multiple 20mm and 7.7mm hits on Firebaugh's Wildcat, from just behind the cockpit to the tail. The life raft was blown out of its compartment, and it dragged along behind, ruining the airplane's flight characteristics. For all that, Firebaugh battled on against repeated firing passes. At one point, another Zero overshot the Wildcat and it suffered what turned out to be a mortal riddling. But then the very next Zero fired at least one 20mm round into the main fuel tank and set gasoline ablaze around Firebaugh's cockpit.

Firebaugh knew his Wildcat was a goner and that he was in mortal danger. Severely burned, he dived headfirst out of the airplane at 3,000 feet, but he did not deploy his parachute until he was much lower, so afraid was he that a Zero would shoot him dead. His spine was injured when he jolted into the water before his parachute could slow him down enough. As a reward, however, the last Zero he had riddled earlier slammed into the sea nearby. Its pilot, PO1 Kunimatsu Nishiura, perished in the crash. Two Zeros came down to 300 feet to look Firebaugh over, and then they left for home. A few minutes later, Firebaugh saw two Wildcats flying south, right overhead, but their pilots—Disque and Mankin—did not see him.

After becoming lost for a time on the way home, Ens Bob Disque landed aboard the *Wasp,* which was the first carrier he came to and which, fortunately, was ready to recover airplanes. He ran out of fuel in the arresting gear. AP1 Paul Mankin barely made it aboard the *Enterprise* on the last of his fuel. RE Tommy Rhodes also landed safely aboard the *Enterprise*. Lt(jg) Gordon Firebaugh and Mach Bill Warden eventually reached safety, but nothing was ever again heard from AP1 Bill Stephenson.

In the first aerial clash attending the first Allied offensive operation of the Pacific War, nine of eighteen Wildcat fighters engaged and one Dauntless dive-bomber of sixteen on the scene were downed by Tainan Air Group Zero fighters. Four Wildcat pilots and one SBD radioman-gunner were killed. Tainan Air Group pilots were awarded twenty-nine confirmed victories for Wildcats, seven confirmed victories for carrier bombers, and seven unconfirmed victories for Wildcats. Two of eight Fighting-71 Wildcats that were launched against the 4th Air Group but did not catch up with it were lost in operational accidents, and one of their pilots was severely injured.

The U.S. Navy fighter pilots downed four 4th Air Group Betty bombers outright. Another Betty had to be crash-landed in the northern part of Buka, and a sixth wiped out on landing at Vunakanau Airdrome. Nineteen of the remaining twenty-one Bettys sustained varying amounts of battle damage, but none of these had to be scrapped. Twenty-eight 4th Air Group pilots and crewmen were killed.

Two Tainan Fighter Group Zeros were downed outright in the air battle—both by Gordon Firebaugh—and the two Japanese pilots were killed in action. PO1 Saburo Sakai made it home to Lakunai Airdrome, but his airplane had to be written off and he would be out of action for several years due to loss of sight in one eye. Ten of the fifteen remaining Zeros made it home to Lakunai at 1730, some with many holes but none in need of being written off. Five Zeros were unable to make it all the way to Rabaul, and they set down at the abandoned Buka strip, where one cracked up.

The significance of this air battle cannot be overstated: Though the Japanese Zero pilots downed 50 percent of the U.S. Navy fighter pilots they engaged, and the Japanese strike group escaped largely intact, the lessons for the U.S. Navy pilots and their handlers were immediate and profound. It was noted at the outset that the Wildcats had arrived on the scene and been committed piecemeal, and that their positioning by FDOs left much to be desired. The piecemeal commitment meant that they never outnumbered the vastly more experienced Imperial Navy fighter pilots, who had ample time between attacks to regroup and reposition, and that no U.S. Navy fighter or section or division achieved numerical superiority over any combination of Imperial Navy fighters. The bad positioning by FDOs at the outset of the action took several Wildcat divisions completely out of the fight—or never brought them in—and it forfeited the altitude advantage in every case. In addition, few U.S. Navy pilots had ever before engaged a Betty attack bomber; little was known of its vulnerabilities or of how it was armed and armored. Significant information was gleaned from the survivors of attacks upon the bombers, and that information was passed around the fighter-squadron ready rooms beginning immediately after the battle. Ditto information on the Zeros, for even as late as August 1942 the U.S. Navy had precious little useful data regarding that phenomenon. To be blunt, U.S. Navy fighter pilots were wary of the mighty and legendary Zero—

not because they knew so much about it, but precisely because they did not. On the other hand, despite the high percentage of losses, the survivors of the battle who made it home that afternoon could state with a fair amount of confidence that the Wildcat had a tendency to absorb punishment. It had its weak spots, to be sure, but it could take a beating, even in an unequal engagement. The new store of knowledge—positive and negative— would help considerably in future engagements.

More significant than combat information gleaned was the influence this air battle had upon the thinking of VAdm Frank Jack Fletcher. Added to other information and considerations—some of which were not yet apparent, or had not yet even occurred—the one-sided outcome of the action in which eleven of Fletcher's ninety-nine fighters were downed or wrecked and at least four others were severely damaged in a half day of combat and intense carrier-deck operations had a profound impact on Fletcher's thinking. It poisoned it.

Not one hit was scored and not one lick of damage was done by any Japanese airplane to any of the scores of Allied warships and other vessels in the vicinity of Guadalcanal. But the 5th Air Attack Force was not yet done for the day.

Chapter 10

It is unclear what RAdm Sadayoshi Yamada and his staff and command officers had in mind when they approved the second 5th Air Attack Force mission of August 7. Nearly all the operational Tainan Air Group long-range Zeros had accompanied nearly all the operational 4th Air Group Bettys to the Tulagi area, and the Rabaul air command felt an attack by U.S. Navy carrier aircraft was imminent. But someone must have convinced Admiral Yamada—or perhaps he convinced himself—that he had not committed enough to the attack against the Allied invasion fleet around Tulagi.

Very shortly after the 4th Air Group Bettys finished taking off, nine of the newly arrived 2d Air Group's sixteen Aichi D3A Val dive-bombers were also launched from their base at Rabaul. But unlike the Bettys and long-range Zeros, this attack force had no hope whatsoever of returning from the mission. If it flew all the way to Tulagi, it would not even be able to return as far as the Buka strip. All of the Vals were to be sacrificed. A seaplane tender and a Mavis flying boat were dispatched to pick up ditched pilots and crewmen in the Shortland Islands, off southern Bougainville, but no one could have had much faith in that plan.

The Val was a carrier bomber with an operational range of approximately 275 miles—enough for a carrier bomber under most circumstances, but not even close for filling in as a land-based bomber under conditions that held sway on August 7, 1942, in the region under attack by the Allies. There was no provision in the airplane's design for an auxiliary fuel tank— no way to eke out significant extra miles. Moreover, the land-based Vals in the 2d Air Group's inventory carried only two wing-mounted 60-kilogram bombs, and not a 250-kilogram centerline bomb. If they attacked Allied ships off Tulagi, there was very little hope that their bombs would sink any, or even cause very much significant damage.

There was to be no fighter escort. The 2d Air Group's own Zero squadron was equipped with short-range Zero interceptors that could not fly even as far as the short-range Vals, and there seemed to be no point in dispatching an escort of only six Tainan Air Group long-range Zeros, which is all the veteran land-based fighter group had left on operational status at Lakunai Airdrome.

Nine 2d Air Group Vals under the command of the *hikotaicho*, Lt Fumito Inoue, began launching at 1030.

About the only outside Allied combat organization that could provide assistance to the Guadalcanal invasion force was MajGen George Kenney's Allied Air Forces, which had several groups of bombers and fighters based in New Guinea, mostly around Port Moresby. It was no mean feat for the embattled U.S. Army Air Forces in the Southwest Pacific Area to provide the needed assistance, but provide it did. B-26 medium bombers flown by the V Bomber Command's 22d Medium Bombardment Group attacked Lae during the day to keep Imperial Navy bombers and fighters from being shifted to Rabaul to take part in strikes against the invasion fleet at Guadalcanal. And at 1220, thirteen 19th Heavy Bombardment Group B-17 heavy bombers based in Australia and refueling at Port Moresby attacked Rabaul's Vunakanau Airdrome. Leading the strike was LtCol Richard Carmichael, the veteran commander of the 19th Bomb Group.

The attack on Vunakanau was not the least bit altruistic. Allied intelligence had surmised that 150 Imperial Navy fighters and bombers were based there, and that fifty additional aircraft were at Lakunai. It was as important to Allied commands in New Guinea as it was to Allied commands in the South Pacific that these forces be reduced.

One B-17 taking off from Port Moresby crashed before it could become airborne, and two B-17s returned to base with mechanical problems only minutes after taking off. One of the returning B-17s was piloted by Capt Harl Pease, who immediately transferred his crew to another heavy bomber, which was known to be in something less than top flight condition. Pease rejoined the rest of the strike force over Vunakanau, where the heavies were intercepted by fifteen 2d Air Group short-range Zeros and three Tainan Air Group long-range Zeros. Captain Pease's bombardier was able to release the bombs aboard his airplane, but the B-17 was set upon by several Zeros and eventually cut out of the pack. It lagged farther and farther behind the rest of the group, and finally it fell from the sky, apparently killing all aboard. Captain Pease was awarded a posthumous Medal of Honor.

No Japanese aircraft were destroyed or even damaged on the ground, and no Zeros were downed despite claims for seven by the B-17 gunners. The Vunakanau runway, which did receive minor damage, was repaired long before Lt Renpei Egawa and LCdr Tadashi Nakajima returned with their 4th Air Group Bettys and Tainan Air Group Zeros. Shortly, the Allied Air Forces' General Kenney, who would become an excellent combat commander, heard via a decoded radio intercept that the 5th Air Attack Force had thirty Bettys operational at Vunakanau that evening. Deducting this number from the erroneous very high intelligence estimates that had precipitated the noon-hour Vunakanau strike led Kenney to announce that the 19th Heavy Bombardment Group B-17s had destroyed seventy-five Japanese bombers on the ground.

In point of fact, the number of Bettys available at Rabaul climbed by nine during the afternoon, when a *chutai* of the Misawa Air Group arrived from Tinian, in the Mariana Islands. It was the arrival of these Bettys that led to Admiral Yamada's report that led to General Kenney's erroneous deduction.

The level of energy and effort aboard the U.S. Navy carriers off Guadalcanal was frenetic following the end of the battle with the 4th Air Group Bettys and Tainan Air Group Zeros. Many fighters were launched from the three carriers, and search missions were dispatched to look for downed fighter pilots on Guadalcanal and in the sea near Santa Isabel. By

1400, forty-four Wildcats were over the carriers and eighteen were over the invasion fleet.

Also at 1400, a strange false alarm was rendered by the invasion fleet commander, RAdm Richmond Kelly Turner. Fighting-6's battle with the Bettys had not yet ended off Santa Isabel when Turner warned that an attack by Japanese dive-bombers was imminent. And then Task Force 61 transmitted a warning that twenty-five enemy bombers were attacking from 8,000 feet. There were no Japanese aircraft anywhere near Guadalcanal or the carriers at this time, but these warnings set everyone on edge, for the implication was that Japanese carriers were in the area—even though U.S. Fleet intelligence had correctly reported that all of Japan's carriers were in home waters.

The false alarm was not sprung by any of the Allied coastwatchers hiding out in the central or northern Solomons, for Lieutenant Inoue's 2d Air Group Val *chutai* was skirting the northern chain of islands at nearly 10,000 feet, far from the sight of any of the coastwatcher stations. This track brought the Vals to the northern side of Florida Island at 1430. They were beyond the range of U.S. Navy radars and U.S. Navy fighter patrols. When Inoue judged that his dive-bombers were opposite the invasion fleet, he signaled a turn to the south.

There were clouds over the northern flotilla of Task Force 62, but Inoue had a clear view of many ships to the south, off Guadalcanal. As the Val *chutai* neared these ships, Inoue motioned for the three-plane *shotai* under WO Gengo Ota to attack a force of cruisers and destroyers to the west while the remaining six Vals went after transports anchored off the invasion beach.

The first American to realize an attack was under way was Lt Scoop Vorse, who was leading a pair of other Fighting-6 Wildcats over the western anchorage off Guadalcanal. Vorse happened to look down from 11,000 feet in time to see Warrant Officer Ota's *shotai* rolling into its dive against the warships below. Vorse was amazed, a feeling he overcame in a split second and rolled straight into a dive of his own. His two wingmen saw him go, but they were unable to follow, and they did not see any targets in time to figure out what was going on. A little late off the mark—he was lucky to have been on the mark at all—Vorse was barely able to keep contact with the diving Vals. The best he could do for the moment was park well behind the tail of the rear Val and open fire from long range.

With all the fine, big targets ahead of him—cruisers galore—Warrant Officer Ota for some reason set his sights on the *Mugford*, an oldish destroyer holding station in the western antisubmarine screen. At 1447, according to the *Mugford's* log, a lookout spotted two fixed-gear airplanes diving out of a cloud astern of the ship and head right at him. The sailor shouted a warning, and then he saw two more airplanes dive out of the cloud. Though the *Mugford's* captain was uncertain as to what was going on, he instinctively ordered a sharp turn to starboard.

Ota and his wingman followed the destroyer into the turn and dropped their four 60-kilogram bombs. Ota's missed the ship to starboard, but one of PO2 Koji Takahashi's bombs struck the *Mugford's* aft superstructure and killed twenty-one crewmen. The third Val, commanded by PO2 Minoru Iwaoka and piloted by S1 Seiki Nakamoto, never made a move on the injured destroyer, or any other ship. Perhaps Scoop Vorse had killed Iwaoka or Nakamoto with his guns, which he had been firing all the way down; certainly his bullets struck the Val, for the airplane's descent was marked by a trail of smoke. Whatever occurred, the Val dived straight into the water without ever lining up on a ship or opening its dive brakes. Score one for Lt Scoop Vorse, who pulled out to chase Ota and Takahashi but could not find them.

The six 2d Air Group Vals led by Lt Fumito Inoue never did reach the Allied transports. As they crossed the channel between Florida and Guadalcanal at 10,000 feet, they were spotted by Lt Hayden Jensen, whose Fighting-5 section was part of a six-plane division led by Lt Dick Gray. Though the Vals were 3,000 feet above the Wildcats, and well to the west, Jensen happened to be looking right at them when they came into view. In fact, he caught sight of the Vals just as three of them—Warrant Officer Ota's *shotai*—split off to attack the warships farther to the west.

Rather than clutter the fighter channel, Jensen raced to the head of the fighter division and waggled his wings to signal an alarm. Then he put on full power and led the way toward the larger group of Vals. During the climb, one Wildcat dropped out when its pilot found that its guns were not working.

At about the time Gray's division, with Jensen in the lead, began climbing toward the six 2d Air Group Vals, Fighting-5's Lt Dave Richardson and Ens Charles Davy spotted the same enemy dive-bombers from their position at 13,000 feet and to the north. As Richardson arrowed down, he hoped he would arrive in time to meet the Vals before they commenced combat dives on any of the juicy targets in the channel. If the Vals did dive before Richardson and Davy reached them, there would be no way for these Wildcats to spoil the bombing attack.

Lieutenant Inoue probably spotted Dick Gray's five Wildcats as they climbed toward his Vals, and that apparently prompted him to switch targets. There was no way he could reach the transports before his slow dive-bombers were overtaken by the carrier fighters, so he opted to go after what he believed was a light cruiser that was much closer. In fact, it was another oldish destroyer, the *Dewey*, which was west of the transports, guarding against submarine attack.

The Vals had just reversed their heading to set up on the *Dewey* when Lieutenant Jensen arrived in range at the head of Gray's division. Attacking from the side on a slight climb, Jensen fired at the nearest Val, which staggered in flight as bullets clearly struck home. The wounded Val split off from the rest of the group and angled toward the water. Jensen stayed with it, firing all the way.

The *Dewey* and other ships opened fire at everything in the air. Huge puffs from time-fused 5-inch antiaircraft rounds and ribbons of tracer blossomed and snaked at all levels from quite a bit higher than the Japanese dive-bombers and U.S. Navy fighters to quite a bit lower. But the remainder of Gray's division pressed in. Lt(jg) Carlton Starkes and Lt Marion Dulfiho followed the Vals into their dive, firing all the way at whatever targets presented themselves. Ens Mark Bright had so much speed on that he overran the rear Val. Ignoring the danger from that dive-bomber's two 7.7mm cowl machine guns, he pressed his attack on the next-to-rear Val and was answered in kind by a stream of 7.7mm bullets from its observer-gunner. Undeterred, Bright stayed the course until flames blossomed from between the fixed landing gear and spread forward and back. Lieutenant Gray, who was trailing Bright, fired a burst into the rear Val, but he thought someone better look out for more attackers, so he pulled up short and went high. Lieutenant Richardson and Ensign Davy did not get there in time to beat the Vals into their dive, so they pulled out and, like Dick Gray, looked around for more attackers.

Lieutenant Inoue and PO3 Seiji Sato reached the drop point over the *Dewey* without being hit by antiaircraft fire or drawing any direct fire from the Wildcats. All four of their bombs missed. Seconds later, two Vals from the rear *shotai* reached the drop point, but their bombs also missed the twisting destroyer.

At this point, Mach Don Runyon arrived on the scene with the three other members of his Fighting-6 Wildcat division. Alerted by chatter on the fighter channel, Runyon knew where to go and what to do when he got there. He skirted the friendly fire from below and attacked the first Val that he could get into his gunsight. He must have scored hits, but the dive-bomber was really hammered by the leader of Runyon's second section, AP1 Howard Packard. The Val definitely crashed off Lunga, and Packard was given full credit, but it is certain that this airplane had suffered battle damage under the guns of Dulfiho, Starkes, and Runyon—and perhaps Jensen and Bright too.

Lieutenant Dulfiho spotted one of the rear *shotai* survivors as it completed its recovery off the *Dewey*. This Val broke to the south and attempted to evade by flying across Guadalcanal's mountainous interior. The veteran Wildcat pilot—his first combat had been a carrier raid in February—closed to only 50 yards off the Val's tail and opened fire. Unfortunately, at the crucial moment, Dulfiho's windshield was covered by oil thrown up by his own engine. He cracked the canopy and leaned out, resuming fire and attempting to adjust his aim on the fall of his tracer. But it was hopeless, and Dulfiho broke contact. By then, AP1 Packard was on the scent, and he went all out to catch up with the fleeing Val. But Don Runyon got there first, from ahead and below, and Packard's wingman, Ens Dutch Shoemaker, boxed it in from the side. All three Wildcats were firing when the Val flew into a ravine and blew up. Runyon was the division leader; he got the credit.

Lieutenant Inoue and one of his wingmen got clean away. However, the leader of the rear *shotai*, WO Seisuke Nakagaki, was fired on—and individually claimed—by both Ens Mark Bright and Mach Don Runyon as he flew clear of the Allied shipping. Then Nakagaki was caught by Ens Dutch Shoemaker and Runyon's wingman, Ens Harry March, as he neared Savo on a course toward the Shortland Islands. As Shoemaker set up for a high-side run, March roared up the Val's tail and fired despite a stream of bullets put out by Nakagaki's observer-gunner. March thought his bullets started a fire, but Lt Hayden Jensen, who was coming on fast, thought the stream of white smoke was from a nonfatal oil-line break. In any event, Jensen closed on the wounded Val and fired bursts into it from 350 yards and on down. His bullets definitely set Nakagaki's oft-wounded Val aflame, and the dive-bomber knifed into the water, for sure. Just about everyone involved was awarded a full official credit for this lone victory.

In all, the nine Fighting-5 and Fighting-6 Wildcat pilots who attacked Lieutenant Inoue's six Vals claimed thirteen full victories, and Lt Scoop Vorse claimed one of the three Vals that attacked the *Mugford*. Naval vessels firing at the Vals claimed two.

All four of the 2d Air Group survivors, who claimed a light cruiser damaged, reached the Shortland Islands at about 1700. Warrant Officer Ota and Petty Officer Takahashi set their Vals down in the water, as planned, and all four airmen in them swam to the waiting Mavis. Shortly, Lieutenant Inoue and his wingman ditched near the rendezvous with the seaplane tender. Inoue and his observer were rescued by the ship when it arrived on the scene, but the second pilot and his wingman simply disappeared.

In return for superficially damaging a U.S. Navy destroyer and killing twenty-one members of its crew—with one of eighteen 60-kilogram bombs carried 600 miles from Rabaul—the 2d Air Group lost all nine Vals and twelve of eighteen pilots and observers.

All of the Fighting-5 pilots involved in the engagement with Inoue's Vals landed in due course aboard the *Saratoga*. Vorse, Runyon, Packard, and March barely made it back to the *Enterprise* on the last of their fuel, and Dutch Shoemaker landed aboard the *Saratoga*.

Coming off an afternoon patrol over the transports, a Fighting-71 Wildcat became separated from its division and got lost. It ran out of fuel over Guadalcanal and crashed in a stand of trees far from friendly lines. The injured pilot ended up in Marine hands nearly a week later, but this was yet another Wildcat gone from Frank Jack Fletcher's original ninety-nine.

Later, at about 1730, Ens Dutch Shoemaker, Ens Earl Cook, and Mach Pat Nagle, all from Fighting-6, were launched from the *Saratoga* to fly an ad hoc combat air patrol over the transports. Nobody had any business launching fighters to a distant station so soon before dark, but someone in authority was clearly rattled by the day's two bombing attacks. Shoemaker's Wildcat developed engine trouble on the way out, and he was nearly shot down on the way home by fellow Fighting-6 pilots who recognized his Wildcat at the last moment and led him to their ship. Cook and Nagle were ordered back to the *Enterprise* as soon as they reported on station. Nagle developed an undisclosed problem on the return. Though he was reported by Cook as having completed a successful water landing, he was never seen again. Ensign Cook asked for help back to the ship with the aid of radar, and the carriers even showed their deck lights to help guide him in, but he kept missing the mark and finally reported himself out of fuel at 1915. He was never seen again, either. There is speculation that the two *Enterprise* Wildcats were never refueled during their hour-long stay aboard the *Saratoga*, an understandable omission on such a busy day, but no less tragic in its consequences.

Chapter 11

T he appearance of Lt Fumito Inoue's nine Vals had everyone in authority on edge. There was ample reason to believe that the Vals were
land-based—because the trusted Pacific Fleet intelligence section
said there were no carriers within thousands of miles of the eastern Solomons.
But the Vals themselves suggested there *might* be carriers loose to the
north, and that suggestion could not be overlooked or discounted. So, shortly
after the surviving Vals departed the scene, RAdm Leigh Noyes, who was
aboard the *Wasp* overseeing the entire air effort, directed that carrier bombers
from the *Wasp* Air Group search the next morning in all directions from
which Japanese carriers might be approaching. Further, the entire *Saratoga*
Air Group was to be held in readiness to attack any Japanese carriers the
Wasp searchers might find. This left the somewhat depleted *Enterprise* Air
Group to answer all calls for ground-support strikes as well as to guard the
carriers and the invasion fleet. It was clearly too much for one overworked
air group to handle.

Capt Dewitt Ramsey, the *Saratoga's* skipper, found Admiral Noyes's
plan lacking and decided to go up against it, especially after the invasion
fleet commander, RAdm Richmond Kelly Turner, asked that extra strike
aircraft be laid on to break heavy resistance on Tulagi, Gavutu, and

Tanambogo. Ramsey could not contact Noyes because of a radio blackout designed to confound the Japanese, so he decided to act on his own. He ordered about half the *Saratoga* Air Group bombers to fly out to the northern invasion area at dawn and there join *Enterprise* support bombers following the directions of Cdr Don Felt, the *Saratoga* Air Group commander, who would be taking his turn as air-support coordinator.

As the *Saratoga* bombers were taking off before dawn, so too did the *Wasp* searchers. They were organized into six pairs of SBDs and dispatched on search tracks between 280 degrees and 040 degrees to distances of 220 miles. They found neither carriers nor signs of any. Near Santa Isabel, LCdr Ernie Snowden, the Scouting-72 commanding officer, downed an Aichi E13A Jake reconnaissance floatplane that had been launched before dawn by a Japanese cruiser, but that was it.

Back at the American carriers, the ready reserves continued to dwindle as essential missions cropped up. Six *Enterprise* SBDs were sent out to look for Ens Earl Cook and Mach Pat Nagle, who had gone down in the dark, and Captain Ramsey allowed a division of Fighting-5 Wildcats to look for that unit's many downed aviators. Moreover, Ramsey added four Fighting-5 Wildcats to each normal rotation of sixteen Fighting-6 fighters over the carriers and invasion fleet.

When Admiral Noyes discovered what Captain Ramsey had been doing, he blew the roof off. In a terse message to Ramsey, the flag officer in charge of air operations asked, rhetorically and sarcastically, what the *Saratoga* Air Group was going to send against Japanese carriers, if any were located by the *Wasp* searchers. Ramsey immediately recalled all his airplanes and set in motion a flurry of arming, fueling, and deck-spotting activity that would keep the *Saratoga* Air Group deckbound for quite a while. Captain Ramsey's views, if not his actions, were vindicated at 1041, when the *Wasp* searchers reported that there were no Japanese carriers to be found in any of their search sectors.

But there were Japanese on the way to attack the Allied fleet off Guadalcanal. The reconnaissance floatplane that LCdr Ernie Snowden downed off Santa Isabel had been launched by an Imperial Navy heavy cruiser that was part of a surface battle force on its way to attack the transports, and the 5th Air Attack Force had launched a strike force at 0630.

♦

RAdm Sadayoshi Yamada concluded from all the eyewitness reports he heard or heard about on August 7 that at least two and as many as three U.S. Navy aircraft carriers had to be in the Guadalcanal area, supporting the Allied amphibious invasion. That conclusion was correct as far as it went, but Yamada also concluded that the carriers were on station to the northeast or east of Tulagi, and this was completely wrong.

During the night, the Japanese ground crews at Vunakanau Airdrome prepared every available Betty bomber for an attack upon the American carriers or, failing that, a conclusive attack upon the transports anchored off Tulagi and Guadalcanal. Given more than enough time to prepare, twenty-six Bettys were armed with aerial torpedoes, a tedious process that entailed the removal of bomb-bay doors to accommodate the large, bulky weapons. Three more Bettys and two Mavis flying boats were also prepared to search ahead of the attack force. And the Tainan Air Group mechanics at Lakunai Airdrome worked all night to put fifteen long-range Zeros on line to escort the torpedo bombers.

The three reconnaissance Bettys and two reconnaissance Mavises took off at 0630, in search of the American carriers. Then, at 0730, Lt Shigeru Kotani, the 4th Air Group's senior *buntaicho*, led seventeen of his unit's Bettys aloft, followed by the nine Misawa Air Group Bettys that had arrived the previous afternoon from Tinian. After forming up over Rabaul, they headed southeast on a course that would carry them to the supposed carrier patrol station. The fighters took off from Lakunai at 0845; they would easily catch up with the bombers along the way. Three of the 4th Air Group Bettys soon aborted, leaving fourteen from that unit and all nine from the Misawa Air Group, still a formidable attack force.

Many of the Betty pilots and crews had taken part in the first August 7 attack, but only two enlisted fighter pilots had done so. Based on the previous day's performance, and given that the Bettys were correctly armed for the task, everyone was extremely optimistic.

Had the Japanese known the state of chaos prevailing aboard and above the carriers and invasion fleet, their sense of optimism would have been off the charts. Though well meaning, Capt Dewitt Ramsey's early-morning efforts to bolster various search, patrol, and strike requirements with aircraft from the *Saratoga* Air Group was, in the end, denying the fleet ample coverage. Refueling, rearming, and respotting the entire air group was tedious and time-consuming, and it ultimately placed inordinate strains upon the *Enterprise* and *Wasp* fighter squadrons, which were spread too thin for the many tasks assigned to them.

The flurry of activity throughout the carrier force was pushed up several notches when news of an impending attack made its way to the hands of Admiral Fletcher by the now-common roundabout channels. The large formation of 5th Air Attack Force Bettys and Zeros was spotted at 0942 by Sub-Lt Jack Read, a thirty-five-year-old former Australian district officer, now a member of the Royal Australian Navy manning a coastwatcher post in extreme northern Bougainville. Read, who was 400 miles from Guadalcanal, reported by radio at 0957 that forty bombers were proceeding from northwest to southeast. This message did not reach the invasion fleet directly; it was relayed by a second coastwatcher, and then it was sent to the Royal Navy admiral commanding the Task Force 62 screen from aboard a Royal Australian Navy heavy cruiser. The message was read, then passed along to RAdm Kelly Turner, who ordered Task Force 62 to up anchor and take evasive action. News of the oncoming bomber force slowly made its way from surface ship to surface ship, but not directly to the carrier force, and so not to the people responsible for getting fighters aloft. It was not until 1059—an hour after Sub-Lieutenant Read's transmission—that Admiral Fletcher received notice of the impending attack.

The experts agreed that the Japanese bombers would be over the invasion fleet at 1130 or so. While the carriers went into overdrive getting fresh fighters launched, the FDOs with the transports began positioning the fighters already on station to intercept the bombers over Savo and then in succeeding bands all the way to the transports and their surface escorts. At 1100, there were fifteen Fighting-71 and three Fighting-6 Wildcats over the Guadalcanal-Tulagi area and eight Fighting-6 Wildcats over the carriers. In all, the three carriers had fifty-one additional fighters more or less ready to launch.

The first ready fighters to be launched were fourteen Fighting-6 F4Fs, which assumed responsibility for covering the carriers. These joined eight other Fighting-6 Wildcats already aloft over Task Force 61. Also, all carrier bombers on the three flight decks were launched, mostly to get them out of the way, but also, in the case of many SBDs, to create a low-level line of defense against torpedo bombers.

At 1105, Admiral Noyes finally gave up the ghost on finding Imperial Navy carriers in the area. He asked that a message be transmitted from the *Wasp* to the *Saratoga,* releasing Fighting-5's twenty-seven ready Wildcats to bolster the defenses over the invasion fleet. But the message did not traverse the few miles between the ships until 1135, and then there were several delays aboard the *Saratoga*—getting the fighters from the hangar deck to the flight deck, then lowering a number of them again to be fitted with auxiliary fuel tanks. It was 1141 before LCdr Roy Simpler, the squadron commander, finally led the first eight Fighting-5 Wildcats off the carrier and raced to get to his assigned altitude—16,000 feet—over the transports. By then, it was too late.

The *Wasp* had to recall her fifteen Wildcats from the invasion fleet at 1130. They had all been low on fuel when the attack warning reached the FDOs at 1059, but they had held station because, along with three Fighting-6 Wildcats, they were the proverbial "it" until ready fighters could get on station. When there was no sign of the Japanese attack bombers by 1130, there was no choice but to recall them. And it was not until 1140 that LCdr Courtney Shands, the Fighting-71 skipper, was launched in the lead of the nine remaining *Wasp* fighters.

So, for at least a half hour, the only U.S. Navy fighters over the invasion fleet would be Fighting-6's Mach Don Runyon leading Ens Will Rouse and Ens Dutch Shoemaker.

Meantime, the transports and their surface escorts sailed to the middle of the channel between Guadalcanal and Tulagi, matched speed at 13.5 knots, and deployed in columns and rows meant to maximize antiaircraft protection and enhance maneuverability.

The Japanese were coming on slow. They had given the searchers plenty of time to get ahead and locate the U.S. Navy carriers, but the search had been in the wrong quadrant—north and east of Tulagi rather than southeast of Guadalcanal. The one searcher in more or less the correct area did not see the carriers. When it was clear that the attack would have to be against the invasion fleet—still an honorable target—Lieutenant Kotani eased toward Tulagi. Unwittingly, his line of flight made it impossible for U.S. Navy radars to spot the bombers, because he flew on the eastern side of the mountains on Santa Isabel and Florida.

The first anyone knew of the 5th Air Attack Force's whereabouts was at 1155, when many lookouts aboard the transports and screen warships saw a large gaggle of airplanes descending over Florida's eastern tip. Immediately, scores of antiaircraft guns were trained out to greet them.

Moments after Lieutenant Kotani sent one 4th Air Group Betty ahead as a control plane, the remaining thirteen 4th Air Group and nine Misawa Air Group Bettys broke into three separate, uneven *chutai* formations. Then the various *shotai* fanned out to deliver torpedo attacks from 150 feet and on down to only 10 feet above the surface. In some cases, propwash blew long streamers of water over the bombers' wings—they were that low.

While the northern transports and surface escorts, which had little time to maneuver, opened fire, the southern force began taking evasive action while the Bettys were still out of range. The powerful fire from the northern vessels caused Lieutenant Kotani to sideslip the entire formation to the south and settle on course toward the maneuvering southern ships, with their scores of traversing antiaircraft guns.

The first U.S. Navy warplane to get into position to attack the oncoming torpedo bombers was a lone Scouting-71 SBD piloted by Lt(jg) Robert Howard. Howard had received no news of the attack in progress via the bomber channel, but he happened to glance toward the northern transport force in time to see the Misawa Air Group *chutai* evade the antiaircraft curtain. Howard was in a good position to make a firing pass, so he did—despite the dense antiaircraft fire from friendly ships. He got his gunsight on a Betty, but his two .50-caliber nose guns would not fire when he pressed the gun-button knob on his control stick. Howard had to pull out to find out what the problem with the guns was. He had forgotten to arm them.

For GM2 Jim O'Neill, aboard the light antiaircraft cruiser *San Juan*, the noise of the firing was almost overpowering. From O'Neill's vantage point, the Japanese medium bombers were being shot down like ducks in a shooting gallery. The *San Juan*, a modern light antiaircraft cruiser, claimed credit for five of the Japanese warplanes. O'Neill clearly saw rounds from his own quadruple-1.1-inch pom-pom mount stitch a pattern across one Betty's fuselage, and then he saw the Betty explode.

Unbelievably, many of the bombers in Lieutenant Kotani's lead *chutai* passed directly over the southern ships, right through the dense antiaircraft curtain. The second 4th Air Group *chutai* passed to the north, and the Misawa Air Group *chutai* passed to the south. Thirteen of the bombers fell broken into the water, and only a few launched their torpedoes.

One of the flaming Bettys from Kotani's *chutai* struck the transport *George F. Elliott*, another snagged the rigging of the transport *Barnett*, and another narrowly missed flying into the heavy cruiser *Vincennes*. It is not known how many torpedoes were actually launched, but only one found a target. At 1202, it seriously damaged the destroyer *Jarvis* when it detonated against the ship's starboard side.

While the Bettys were still approaching the southern surface force, two of the five Tainan Air Group Zero pilots that were escorting the control Betty spotted a six-plane Scouting-71 SBD division. The U.S. Navy dive-bombers were no threat to the Zeros or the Bettys; they had just completed a bombing run on a tiny islet in Tulagi Harbor and were withdrawing at low altitude toward the carriers. But the two Zero pilots impetuously broke formation and dived on the leader of the second SBD section. All three SBD radioman-gunners saw the Zeros coming, and they parried with their twin .30-caliber machine guns. The Zeros made one firing pass and flew on. Their bullets caused some minor damage.

Next the two Zero pilots spotted a lone SBD, also at low altitude. This was Lt(jg) Robert Howard, who had attacked the Misawa Air Group Bettys with uncharged machine guns. Howard had just figured out the problem when his radioman, S2 Lawrence Lupo, opened fire on the two Zeros approaching and firing from behind. The Zeros made four firing passes from astern without inflicting much damage on Howard's airplane, and then they set up for a fifth attack, this time from dead ahead. Lieutenant (jg) Howard had turned on his .50-caliber cowl guns, and his return fire was dead on; his bullets hit PO3 Yutaka Kimura's Zero square and started a fire. The Zero knifed into the water off Florida, an undisputable kill. But the wingman wasn't fazed. He attacked the SBD from behind and opened fire at close range. Seaman Lupo fired back, certain he was scoring hits. Perhaps Lupo did hit the Zero; he certainly hit his own airplane—ten times, including twice in the right main fuel tank. But he also drove the Zero off.

The three *Enterprise* Wildcats led by Mach Don Runyon—the only U.S. Navy fighters over the anchorage during the entire attack—did not see the Bettys arrive until people on the open radio frequency started talking about them. No one actually vectored Runyon and his two wingmen against the torpedo bombers.

Alerted by the radio chatter, the Wildcat pilots looked down from 17,000 feet and spotted Lieutenant Kotani's lead Betty *chutai* as it crossed the eastern tip of Florida so low that the propwash foamed the flat sea. Runyon immediately dived at high speed, but the surviving Bettys were clearing the southern surface force and heading west by the time he could close on them.

At 1205, Runyon opened fire on the five survivors of the seven-plane 4th Air Group *chutai* commanded by Lt Bakuro Fujita, who had led the heavily punished left *chutai* the day before and who apparently had succumbed minutes earlier to antiaircraft fire. When Runyon's first firing pass failed to dislodge a Betty that was flying at only 20 feet, the veteran fighter leader pulled up to go around again.

Ens Will Rouse succeeded in getting on the same Betty's tail and holding position there. Ignoring a stream of large tracer rounds from the bomber's 20mm stinger, Rouse fired until the Betty flamed and crashed. Meantime, Runyon set up a head-on run at another Betty and poured streams of bullets into the flight deck and engines. It crashed, too.

Emboldened by his success, Rouse shifted his sights to another fleeing Betty and fired until a stream of smoke issued from the bomber's fuselage or wing root. Like Rouse's first victim, this bomber caromed off the wave tops in a huge plume of fire and spray, then exploded in a fiery ball visible to many hundreds of onlookers.

The bomber *chutai's* Zero escorts were asleep at the switch. Two of the six Zeros were away chasing cruiser-launched observation planes— satisfying, but a waste of time—and only the Zero *chutai* leader, Lt(jg)

Tadashi Hayashitani, was able to attack Ensign Rouse following Rouse's destruction of the second Betty. Nearly as soon as Hayashitani set up on Rouse, Ens Dutch Shoemaker attacked the Zero leader and drove him away. As the Zero rolled away from Shoemaker, it flew right into the gunsight of Machinist Runyon, who had come around by then to commence a third firing pass on the bombers. The Imperial Navy officer had joined the Tainan Air Group in June, fresh out of flight school. Now his flying career ended, and so did his life. Don Runyon hammered him into the waves.

Hayashitani's second *shotai* of three Zeros arrived on the scene at this time and mixed it up with one of the Wildcats, probably Rouse. While the Zeros were preoccupied, Shoemaker mounted a beam attack on a Betty and shot it down.

And suddenly the battle was over. Only one of the seven Bettys Lieutenant Fujita had led to Guadalcanal this noon hour survived the trip home. Indeed, only three 4th Air Group Bettys and three Misawa Air Group Bettys survived the ordeal by gunfire and fighters, and one of these crashed during the flight back to Vunakanau, no doubt the victim of severe battle damage. In all, eighteen Bettys were destroyed in the air and 125 bomber pilots and crewmen perished. Every one of the officers aboard the Bettys was lost. Two Zeros and their pilots were also lost. Nine stunned or disabled Japanese aircrewmen were pulled by U.S. Navy warships from the channel between Tulagi and Guadalcanal, but the crewmen from one bilged Betty fired on a destroyer with pistols before killing themselves.

After taking part in the worst catastrophe of its kind to that point in the war or for nearly a year to come, the surviving Japanese airmen brought home news of a telling victory. They said that torpedoes had sunk five cruisers, two destroyers, and three transports, and that a cruiser, a destroyer, and six transports had been damaged. Admiral Yamada downgraded the claims to a cruiser, a destroyer, and nine transports sunk, and three cruisers and three unidentified ships damaged. The airmen also claimed three or four SBDs and four of ten Wildcats engaged.

In fact, the destroyer *Jarvis* was severely damaged by a torpedo, and the transport *George F. Elliot* was set on fire when a Betty crashed into her. The *Jarvis* was ordered to sail to safety alone under her own power, which she did during the night. Lt Ralph Weymouth and Lt(jg) Slim Russell, of Scouting-3, flew over her just south of Guadalcanal's Cape Esperance on the morning of August 9, but she was never seen or heard from again. The *Elliott's* crew was evacuated to a nearby transport, and the fires were left to burn themselves out after the ship grounded herself.

The bomber strength of the 5th Air Attack Force—the only Japanese combat air command in range of Guadalcanal and Tulagi—had been gutted in only two days of fighting. Though many senior U.S. Navy aviation officers were proud of the showing, the aggressive fighter pilots were generally let down about allowing so many Zeros to escape. This poor showing had benefits, though, for the fighter pilots got right to work improving their tactics and setting in motion events to straighten out the faulty chains of guidance and communication that had worked so much to the advantage of the Japanese in all three air battles on August 7 and 8.

On the night of August 8, a Japanese surface battle force composed of seven cruisers and a destroyer attacked and thoroughly surprised two Allied cruiser-destroyer forces screening the western approaches to the Task Force 62 anchorages. In the resulting melee, known as the Battle of Savo Island, four Allied heavy cruisers—the *Canberra, Vincennes, Astoria,* and *Quincy*—were sunk or left in sinking condition, and a fifth heavy cruiser—the *Chicago*—and several destroyers were damaged. This disaster hastened the withdrawal of the Allied invasion force from the Guadalcanal area, but the decision to depart had been made before the audacious Japanese night surface attack.

The loss of sixteen of Task Force 61's original ninety-nine fighters in two days of combat and flight operations appears to have been at the root of VAdm Frank Jack Fletcher's decision to withdraw his carriers during the night of August 8. In fact, five other Wildcats were down that evening with mechanical problems, which reduced the original fighter complement by nearly 22 percent. Some observers characterized Fletcher's mood in the wake of the August 8 torpedo attack as demoralized. Fletcher also cited a fuel shortage. That was real enough, but it could have been alleviated by the dispatch of one carrier at a time to refuel in safe waters. It was the appearance of a reported "forty" Betty torpedo bombers on August 8 that must have thrown Fletcher for a loop, whether or not he was in good spirits before then.

The 19th Heavy Bombardment Group B-17s that had attacked Vunakanau Airdrome at midday on August 7 were supposed to have destroyed as many as seventy-five Japanese bombers on the ground. If as many as forty land-based bombers had been launched from Vunakanau on August 8, there was no telling how many more bombers the Japanese commander might have at his disposal. And Fletcher had a limited and declining complement of fighters with which to protect both the transports and the carriers.

Whatever the cause and motivation, Fletcher announced that evening that he was withdrawing with the carriers during the night. He requested permission from his superiors, but he felt he would be backed up because he was the man on the scene.

Fletcher's decision—taken before the night surface battle—obliged the amphibious flotilla and its escorts to withdraw to safer waters before as much as half of the supplies needed by Marines ashore could be landed. The amphibious force had been ready to pull out on August 9 all along, but Rear Admiral Turner, the Task Force 62 commander, had been pondering an extra day's unloading work before Fletcher decided the issue for him and the Japanese cruiser attack sealed the deal. Fortunately, by the evening of August 8, all the land objectives—including the all-important airfield on Guadalcanal—had been seized, though some were only tenuously held.

Late on the morning of August 9, seventeen 4th Air Group and Misawa Air Group Bettys escorted by fifteen Tainan Air Group Zeros were sent south to attack the American carriers with torpedoes. They went to the right place this time, but the carriers were long gone. All they found was the wounded destroyer *Jarvis*, which they mistook for a light cruiser. The small warship's gunners shot down two of the Bettys and severely damaged another before they and all their mates were sent to the bottom with their ship. No trace of any of them has ever been found.

Part III

★

Preliminaries
August 10–23, 1942

Chapter 12

Once the Allied invasion fleet had retired from the Guadalcanal-Tulagi area on August 9, the primary objectives left to the abandoned 1st Marine Division were building up its defenses and getting the captured Lunga airfield operational as quickly as possible. Without air support, the Marines were altogether at the mercy of Japanese aerial and naval attacks, and extremely vulnerable to ground assault. It was fortunate that the Japanese were initially nearly as hamstrung as the Marine Lunga and Tulagi garrisons.

Almost as soon as the Lunga runway had fallen into the hands of Marine infantry units on August 8, the 1st Marine Division's air and engineering officers were on the field sizing things up. They reported that their construction troops could ready 2,600 feet of usable runway surface by August 10, and that another 1,200-by-160-foot section could be completed in the week after that. On the day before his invasion flotilla's abrupt departure from the eastern Solomons, RAdm Richmond Kelly Turner promised the Marines that aircraft would arrive by August 11, though it is unclear where he thought they were coming from; Marine combat aviation units were on the way, but they could not arrive at Lunga before around August 18. But that was the news on August 8. Extensive revisions had to be made on August 9, in the wake of Turner's retirement with nearly all the heavy equipment and engineering stores owned by the Marines' 1st Engineer Battalion.

Airfield construction commenced on August 9, when the 1st Engineer and 1st Pioneer battalions and assorted helpers gathered sufficient materials to get started. A miserable 15 percent of all engineering equipment and supplies had been landed, with the result that construction troops had to manhandle 100,000 cubic feet of earth fill to cover a depression in the center of the field because the Japanese had begun the runway at either extremity and built toward the center. A huge steel girder served as a drag, and a Japanese road roller packed the fill. In fact, the Imperial Navy contributed most heavily to the 1st Engineer Battalion's small store of engineering equipment. In general, the captured equipment was in poor condition, but ingenious Marine mechanics kept it working hour after brutal hour in their lively race against time. The only earth-moving equipment designed for the purpose was one angle dozer the Marine pioneers had managed to land. There was not one dump truck. The engineers performed incredible feats of improvisation to overcome monumental difficulties.

On August 9, VAdm Nishizo Tsukahara transferred his Eleventh Air Fleet headquarters from Lae, New Guinea, to Rabaul and personally assumed operational control of all air operations in the region from RAdm Sadiyoshi Yamada. The new operational command was to be known as the Base Air Force. Tsukahara immediately advocated a policy of strong reprisals against the Allies in the eastern Solomons, but due to the severe losses sustained by his bomber force during the first two days of aerial combat, the senior air commander was limited to mounting harassment and reconnaissance missions. Fresh aviation combat units were on the move toward Rabaul, but days or weeks would pass before the 5th Air Attack Force made good the losses of August 7 and 8.

From August 9 onward for several weeks, the two things the Americans had going for them in terms of aerial defense were the weakness of the 5th Air Attack Force bomber contingent and the distance between Guadalcanal and Rabaul. Though the Zero was at the time the longest-legged operational fighter in the world, the 1,200-mile round trip between Rabaul and Lunga nevertheless pushed its capabilities to the limit. Indeed, the extended range requirements forced on the world's premier escort fighter obliged 5th Air Attack Force components to fly by the most direct route from Rabaul to Lunga. Doing so meant adherence to a predictable time-table, with no margin for feints, nor for speeding up the throttled-back engines of the fuel-conserving fighters. Harnessed to the range-stretching tactics of the Zeros, Japanese bombers bound for Lunga had to fly over Buka, off northwestern Bougainville, then Buin, overlooking the Shortland Islands, then straight down the New Georgia Sound. A coastwatcher station overlooking Buka was manned by Royal Australian Navy Sub-Lt Jack Read, who usually sent the first word of an impending reconnaissance or air strike. Royal Australian Navy PO Paul Mason, whose station was near Buin, got the next word in. It was invariably two hours between Mason's warning and the arrival of the bombers over Lunga, so the Marines around Lunga could count upon several quiet hours during the early morning and late afternoon in which to get some work done on the Lunga airfield, as well as upon having at least two hours in which to find cover and take aim. (The period of vulnerability was known as Tojo Time.)

The American antiaircraft defense was built around the 90mm antiair-craft guns of the 3d Marine Defense Battalion, which were bolstered by the independent battalion's own light automatic weapons batteries and numer-ous infantry machine guns set up on antiaircraft mounts. All levels up to 25,000 feet could be covered after a fashion, so raiders and reconnais-sance bombers from Rabaul usually stayed above that level, which ham-pered the accuracy of bombing and reconnaissance.

Lt(jg) SLIM RUSSELL
Scouting-3

Diary Entry of August 11, 1942

Yesterday we heard the Japs really pulled a fast one at 0300, August 9. The cruisers and destroyers of our outfit were convoying the trans-ports out of the harbor. Suddenly, seaplanes were heard. They dropped flares around our fleet, and enemy cruisers and destroyers pounded torpedoes into our outfit.

We had word that on August 8, at noon, an enemy fleet was

approaching Guadalcanal from the northwest. At that time, it was only 240 miles away. Why our three carriers ran southeast—away from our fleet in the harbor—is something I can't understand.

The cruisers *Vincennes, Astoria, Quincy,* and *Canberra* were sunk. The Jap losses? We have not heard a word and probably never will.

I believe there are too many heads running this show. And too-old heads at that. Let's kick them out. A dark page in U.S. Navy history.

We have pulled back to a spot halfway to New Caledonia to re-fuel. The [heavy cruiser] *Chicago,* with fifteen troopships, etc., is somewhere to the west. Our next move? Probably back to Guadalcanal. I feel confident a Jap landing will be attempted soon on Guadalcanal.

Late on the morning of August 11, six Tainan Air Group Zeros based at Lakunai Airdrome strafed Marines working on the Lunga runway and reconnoitered the area. They got in and out too quickly to be endangered by the local antiaircraft defenses. This little hit-and-run affair starkly underscored the vulnerability of the Marines in the eastern Solomons to air and naval attack.

On the afternoon of August 11, as the American carriers were completing their first postinvasion refueling operation, VAdm Frank Jack Fletcher heard from his immediate superior, VAdm Robert Ghormley, the commander of the South Pacific Force, headquartered in Nouméa. First, Ghormley, who was Fletcher's Naval Academy classmate (1906), reiterated Task Force 61's primary goal: to destroy Imperial Navy carriers. However, until Imperial Navy carriers arrived in range—there was no news as yet to indicate any were on the way from Japan—Task Force 61 was to guard the line of communication between New Caledonia and Espiritu Santo, support the Marines at Guadalcanal and Tulagi against Japanese ship movements (especially the feared amphibious counterlanding), and cover the movement of Allied ships to Guadalcanal and Tulagi.

Ghormley's message to Fletcher made no provision for an aerial watch over Guadalcanal and Tulagi. Until the Lunga airfield could be put into operation, the Marines on the ground would have to endure whatever the 5th Air Attack Force dished out. Meanwhile, in order to fulfill his obligations under Ghormley's directive, at least until the Lunga airfield was operational, Fletcher had to tie his vulnerable carriers to a patrol area no more than a day's sailing time from airplane range to Guadalcanal.

On August 11, MajGen Millard Harmon, the administrative head of U.S. Army ground forces garrisoning bases in the South Pacific Area, wrote to the U.S. Army Chief of Staff, Gen George Marshall, concerning the situation in the lower Solomons: "The thing that impresses me more than anything else in connection with the Solomons action is that we are not prepared to follow up. . . . We have seized a strategic position from which future operations in the Bismarcks can be strongly supported. Can the Marines hold out? There is considerable room for doubt."

Far to the rear, in Hawaii, Adm Chester Nimitz, the Pacific Fleet commander, ordered Task Force 17, including the USS *Hornet,* to clear Pearl Harbor on August 17 and sail by the most direct route to the South Pacific. In order to bolster Fletcher with the *Hornet,* Nimitz had to go against standing orders from his boss, Adm Ernest King, the commander-in-chief of the United States Fleet. King wanted one carrier task force held in reserve at Pearl in case an emergency overtook another Allied base beyond Fletcher's range. Nimitz felt he had no other remedy, that circumstances demanded that all of his nation's fleet carriers be committed to supporting the Marines at Guadalcanal.

On August 12, Ens Robert Gibson and Ens Jerry Richey, of the *Enterprise* Air Group's Bombing-6, took off on antisubmarine patrol at dawn and almost immediately surprised a Japanese fleet submarine as it lay on the surface about 20 miles ahead of the *Enterprise.* Gibson went straight into a bombing run and dropped his SBD's 500-pound bomb within 50 feet of it. Richey followed Gibson and placed his 500-pound bomb within 20 feet of the hull. The target, which was down by the bow, lay on the surface for five or six minutes while both pilots made repeated strafing attacks; Gibson and Richey each fired their .50-caliber forward guns on the inbound runs, and their radioman-gunners fired their twin .30-caliber free guns while the scout bombers were outbound. Richey later claimed to have seen several Japanese sailors lying wounded or dead on the deck while other Japanese struggled in the water. At length, both pilots observed the submarine, which remained down by the bow and stationary throughout its ordeal, slip beneath the surface. Gibson and Richey received official credit for sinking the submarine, but Japanese records fail to confirm the loss.

Far to the north, several B-17s from the V Bomber Command's 19th Heavy Bombardment Group staged through Port Moresby and attacked shipping in Rabaul's Simpson Harbor. No damage seems to have been inflicted by either side.

Administratively, Task Force 63, the South Pacific Force aviation command overseen by RAdm John Sidney "Slew" McCain, was made responsible for providing aviation logistical support to Marine air units at Guadalcanal. (McCain was a Naval Academy classmate of Ghormley's and Fletcher's, as was RAdm Leigh Noyes, Task Force 61's senior aviator.)

At Guadalcanal on August 12, Navy Lt William Sampson, RAdm Slew McCain's aide and personal pilot, told ground controllers that the admiral's personal Consolidated PBY Catalina staff plane he was piloting had developed a serious mechanical malfunction that prevented him from putting down in the water off Kukum. Sampson was allowed to land amidst the dust and debris of the airfield construction effort. Mechanics who went to work on the PBY found no malfunctions. What they did find was a grinning admiral's aide who had conned his way into the history books. On the return to Espiritu Santo, Sampson evacuated two injured men, the first aerial casualty evacuation from a combat zone in the Pacific. One of the evacuees was Fighting-5's Lt Pug Southerland, survivor of one-sided fighter combat on August 7.

During the noon hour, three 5th Air Attack Force Bettys reconnoitered the Lunga runway—now dubbed Henderson Field after Maj Lofton Henderson, a Marine dive-bomber leader killed at Midway. The three attack bombers circled benignly overhead, out of range of ground fire, until they had completed the reconnaissance.

During the night, in the first ground action since August 8, a twenty-five–man Marine reconnaissance force was ambushed and virtually annihilated by Imperial Navy ground troops who had fled without a fight during the August 7 invasion.

On August 13, two Task Force 61 Wildcats were wiped out in landing accidents, but both pilots escaped without injury. And an Imperial Navy submarine surfaced off Tulagi and opened fire on shore targets with her deck gun. Shore batteries returned the fire, but neither side did any damage. Nothing could have underscored the Marines' vulnerability more than this submarine's galling display of impunity.

On the plus side of the ledger, the auxiliary carrier USS *Long Island,* a strange flat ship with no superstructure, arrived at Suva, Fiji, on her way from Hawaii to the eastern Solomons. Embarked on the little ship were eighteen Marine Corps F4F-4 Wildcats belonging to Marine Fighting Squadron (VMF) 223, twelve SBDs belonging to Marine Scout-Bomber Squadron (VMSB) 232, and one F4F-4 in the care of the executive officer of Marine Air Group 23. (Groundcrews, key personnel from Marine Air Group 23, and all the necessary ordnance, fuel, and supplies needed to begin air operations had departed Hawaii separately aboard a slower transport.)

The entire complement of Marine F4Fs and SBDs was to be launched to Henderson Field as soon as the base was ready and Task Force 61 could escort the *Long Island* to within launching range. The ship had left Hawaii on August 2 and had bent on all speed to get within range of Guadalcanal as soon as possible, but when the defenseless auxiliary carrier's captain had heard about the Savo debacle, he had headed straight for Suva to await clearance to advance and launch his cargo of precious combat aircraft. Another complication arose in Suva when the *Long Island's* captain, a veteran airman, expressed his frank doubts that many of the green Marine fighter pilots could survive a carrier launch, much less combat. Admiral Ghormley, who had hoped to complete the launch by August 18, bucked the matter to his aircraft commander, Slew McCain. In his turn, McCain suggested that the *Long Island* stop by Efate, in the New Hebrides, so the greenest of the VMF-223 pilots could be swapped for better-trained specimens from the resident Marine fighter unit, VMF-212—the only Marine combat aviation unit based in the region. Ghormley reluctantly assented to McCain's suggestion and ordered it done.

At Rabaul on August 13, an Imperial Army corps-level headquarters was established to oversee the recapture of Guadalcanal by Imperial Army units already in motion toward the area. This Imperial Army command was placed under the control of a new Southeast Area command established in

Rabaul on August 11 by VAdm Nishizo Tsukahara to oversee all Imperial Navy and Imperial Army commands operating in the Solomons and Bismarcks region.

Lt(jg) SLIM RUSSELL
Scouting-3

Diary Entry of August 14, 1942

Well, we're on our way back to Tulagi, back to hit at the Japs. Since the tenth, we've drifted southward, fueling, consolidating. The battered *Chicago* and fifteen transports passed quite near us on the eleventh.

Hear that the Japs are really laying for Tulagi. Hope we catch a big part of their fleet there. Would really be wonderful to let them have about forty 1,000-pound bombs down their stacks. Am anxious to get there, do a good job, and then hit for home.

Far from attacking a Japanese fleet, Task Force 61 was moving into position to escort a tiny flotilla of U.S. Navy destroyer-transports from the New Hebrides to Guadalcanal. These would be the first Allied surface vessels to enter the eastern Solomons area since Task Force 62, departed on August 9.

During the morning at Guadalcanal, three 5th Air Attack Force Bettys photographed Henderson Field while circling above the range of Marine 90mm antiaircraft guns.

Adding considerably to his and the Guadalcanal garrison's burden of woes, Slew McCain learned on August 12 that the transport embarking Marine Air Group 23's vital equipment and groundcrews had been delayed in its passage from Oahu and could not get to Lunga before August 19. The Marine headquarters on Guadalcanal reported that four hundred drums of aviation gasoline had been captured, but there was absolutely no equipment or other supplies on hand with which to service aircraft.

Fortunately, the South Pacific aircraft commander had the problem whipped overnight. Maj Charles Hayes, the executive officer of Marine Observation Squadron (VMO) 251, a photographic and reconnaissance unit based on New Caledonia and Espiritu Santo, was ordered by McCain to mount out for Guadalcanal with selected Marines from his squadron's ground staff, including air controllers and communicators who would be needed to facilitate flight operations from Henderson Field. Also, the five officers and 118 enlisted men for the U.S. Navy's Construction Unit, Base, 1 (CUB-1) happened to arrive at Espiritu Santo at noon on August 13. As the sailors were coming ashore, the ensign commanding was informed that his unit would be landed at Guadalcanal in two days. CUB-1 had to unload, repack, and reload as much of its gear as it could—and there was a hitch. It drew transportation aboard four U.S. Navy destroyer-transports, obsolete World War I-vintage four-stack destroyers converted to transport small Marine raiding forces. Each destroyer-transport could carry only 30 tons of cargo, so only essential materiel could be embarked. The most essential materials had been stowed at the bottoms of the holds of the ship that had brought CUB-1 to Espiritu Santo, so the navymen barely had time to trans-ship 400 drums of aviation gasoline, 32 drums of lubricants, 282 bombs of various sizes, belted machine-gun ammunition, and miscellaneous tools and spare parts. The men of CUB-1 boarded the destroyer-transports carrying light packs and small arms, but not one tent, nor even a can of food.

Royal Australian Navy Lt Hugh MacKenzie, who was to man a forward coastwatcher radio liaison station at Lunga, was embarked with CUB-1 and the VMO-251 people. It was hoped that news of aircraft sightings beamed directly from the north to MacKenzie at Guadalcanal would end the rash of garbled transmissions and lost and delayed sighting messages that had been plaguing the network since August 7.

The destroyer-transports streaked to Guadalcanal during the afternoon of August 15 and hurriedly unloaded men and supplies off Kukum after dark. As soon as the unloading was finished, the destroyer-transports streaked away again, before they could be discovered by Imperial Navy long-range reconnaissance bombers. Task Force 61 turned southeast again as soon as the destroyer-transports were beyond the range of land-based bombers.

♦

On the morning of August 16, CUB-1 moved to Henderson Field, where the newly arrived Navy and Marine groundcrewmen learned that the Marine division quartermaster could not make good all of the personal gear they had had to leave at Espiritu Santo. And Lt Hugh MacKenzie was severely let down when he sought a suitable site for his vital radio station; he had to settle for a narrow five-foot-high dugout on exposed ground north of the runway.

During the middle of the day, Tainan Air Group Zeros reconnoitered Henderson Field and dropped food parcels to Imperial Navy ground troops hiding out in the bush near the Lunga Perimeter.

Lt(jg) SMOKEY STOVER
Fighting-5

Diary Entry of August 16, 1942

Fortieth day on this cruise, and I'm ready to hit a port. My longest cruise so far. Haven't flown in a week and would like to get in the air again, even on a four-hour inner air patrol.

We have been circling around north of New Caledonia and about 300 miles from Tulagi, waiting for the Japs to make a counterinvasion, I suppose. They have been bombing there about every other day, with no opposition since we left.

AOM2 ALFRED CAMPBELL
USS Enterprise

Diary Entry of August 16, 1942

Yesterday, Tulagi was attacked by high horizontal Jap bombers. The damage was very small. The Marines had consolidated their beachhead positions and there is little resistance left in the rest of the islands. Bombers from Australia have been bombing Rabaul very regularly.

We are topping off fuel for the destroyers. And we are about 100 miles from Tulagi. At the present time we are protecting the supply line from Australia to the Solomons from attacks from the east and south. Cruisers are up north.

On August 16, Lt(jg) Bill Henry and Ens R. E. Pellesier, of the *Saratoga's* Scouting-3, were assigned a long-range patrol mission that would take them north toward Guadalcanal and Savo by way of Malaita Island. Normally, the two SBDs would have flown with 500-pound General Purpose bombs aboard, but while the pilots were checking out their airplanes, the ordnancemen removed the bombs without explanation.

As the Dauntlesses were flying north of Florida Island, Henry and Pellesier both sighted a Japanese two-stack destroyer steaming north-northeast at about 20 knots. At 1106, as Henry led Pellesier abeam the enemy ship, Japanese gunners opened fire on both American warplanes. The initial bursts were extremely close, but neither airplane was hit. Henry motioned to Pellesier to prepare to attack, then led the way up to 5,000 feet and ahead of the destroyer, wishing all the while he had contested the decision to remove the bombs.

Halfway through the initial strafing run, Henry's .50-caliber machine guns jammed after firing only twenty rounds each. Pellesier fired approximately four hundred .50-caliber rounds at the destroyer's stacks. Neither pilot observed damage to the ship, and neither plane was damaged.

After recovering at low altitude, Henry turned south for home. Pellesier was well off to his left, attracting close antiaircraft bursts until out of range of the Japanese guns.

Because strict radio silence had been imposed to mask the presence of the carriers so close to Guadalcanal, Henry could not transmit a fix on the enemy destroyer. He had to wait to fly all the way back to the fleet and drop a message to the *Saratoga's* flight deck. A follow-up attack was not launched.

AOM2 ALFRED CAMPBELL
USS Enterprise

Diary Entry of August 17, 1942

About 300 miles south of Tulagi.

Allied planes are patrolling around Tulagi and the other Solomon Islands, so we are in a position to intercept anything they pick up.

Cool weather.

The *Astoria, Vincennes,* and *Quincy* are three cruisers which, according to scuttlebutt [rumors], have been sunk by the Japs at Tulagi in the skirmish that took place a few days ago. No official information, though. Also, it is believed that the *Chicago* got her bows blown off.

The *Long Island* arrived off Efate, and VMF-223 swapped eight of its greenest Wildcat pilots for eight better-trained lieutenants from VMF-212.

During the night of August 17, five hundred Imperial Navy infantry bluejackets *(rikusentai)* and their equipment were landed by destroyer-transports at Kokumbona, a village just a few miles to the east of the Marines' Lunga Perimeter. This was the first fresh Japanese ground force to be sent to Guadalcanal since the invasion. No radio intercepts had given the Allies early news of the landing, and no one at Lunga knew for more than a day that the fresh troops were there.

On August 18, shortly after noon, eight 5th Air Attack Force Bettys bombed Henderson Field from 25,000 feet. Marine antiaircraft gunners did little harm despite their claims for five Bettys damaged, and almost no damage resulted from the bombing. But it was clear to all that the 5th Air Attack Force was resuming work. For the moment, nothing stood in its path.

The *Long Island* left Efate on August 18 and joined with Task Force 61. After refueling, the carrier force was to dash to a position off the southern tip of San Cristobal, 190 miles from Henderson Field, and the *Long Island* was to launch VMF-223 and VMSB-232 around midday on August 20.

To the north, six ships from the same flotilla of Imperial Navy destroyer-transports that had landed the five hundred *rikusentai* at Kokumbona during the previous night embarked 916 crack Imperial Army ground troops and were bearing down on Guadalcanal from Rabaul. The troops were part of a ground force the Imperial Army hoped would be able to overrun the Lunga Perimeter within the week. The Japanese lacked good intelligence; they had no idea how many Marines these Imperial Army troops would be facing. Nevertheless, the Imperial Navy knew how to sneak troops ashore under enemy guns. During the wee hours, the destroyer-transports stopped off Taivu Point, several miles to the east of the Lunga Perimeter, and landed all the soldiers without any Americans being the wiser. After the landing operation was completed, three destroyers departed immediately for Rabaul, but the other three stayed behind to bombard the Lunga Perimeter at dawn.

On the morning of August 19, three Marine infantry companies attacked what they and their commanders thought would be disorganized remnants of the original Japanese Lunga garrison holed up in the Kokumbona area. What they ran into was the main body of the five hundred fresh *rikusentai*. The Marines won a hard-fought battle, but they withdrew to the Lunga Perimeter during the afternoon. At the height of the amphibious portion of the operation, three Imperial Navy destroyers materialized on the scene without warning and threatened to destroy landing craft carrying one of the Marine companies ashore. Instead, an 11th Heavy Bombardment Group B-17 piloted by Maj James Edmundson arrived from Espiritu Santo at an altitude of 5,000 feet and laid a stick of four 500-pound bombs across the fantail of the destroyer *Hagikaze*. This startlingly accurate attack caused the three destroyers to retire. Hundreds of Marines who could see Major Edmundson's bombing runs and the resulting tall column of black smoke from the *Hagikaze* were delirious with relief and approval, for Edmundson's was the first Allied warplane any of them had seen since Task Force 61 sailed away on August 10.

While the three-company Marine force was overcoming resistance at Kokumbona, to the west of Lunga, a reinforced Marine platoon patrolling east of the perimeter ran headlong into an estimated fifty Imperial Army officers and men who were preparing to reconnoiter the Marine defenses. The Marines killed thirty-five of the Japanese—mostly officers—in a brief, sharp firefight, and they captured maps and documents indicating that a counteroffensive against the Lunga Perimeter was imminent.

CUB-1 and the 1st Engineer Battalion reported Henderson Field fit to support air operations on August 19. The facilities were crude, but the base was ready.

♦

AOM2 ALFRED CAMPBELL
USS Enterprise

Diary Entry of August 19, 1942

Launched SBDs and TBFs to scout over Tulagi. Returned about noon. Had General Quarters about 1400. Reported enemy aircraft, but turned out to be a PBY. Took bombs off TBFs and put on torpedoes.

Lt(jg) SMOKEY STOVER
Fighting-5

Diary Entry of August 19, 1942

Plan of the day for tomorrow says, "Clear Ships for Action." We're going north!

In their deepest penetration into the area to date, several B-17s from the V Bomber Command's 19th Heavy Bombardment Group attacked a Japanese ship or ships at Faisi in the Shortland Islands.

Only the top Allied commanders and their close advisers knew it, but the Japanese were on the march. Several Imperial Navy aircraft carriers were on the way to the Solomons from Japan, and a counterattack on land appeared to be imminent.

Chapter 13

The Battle of Midway was not the beginning of the end for the hegemonic Empire of Japan. She lost the battle, it is true, but she could yet have won the Pacific War, though not ever in a pure contest of her material strength against the United States of America's material strength. Japan could never defeat the United States in a protracted war based on economic power, but she reckoned she might do so in a short war in which her repeated early victories overwhelmed the will of the American people. No. Midway, stunning and humiliating as it was, was not the beginning of the end for Japan.

Midway was the beginning of the beginning for the United States. It tested her will, and found her admirals and airmen sound—of the sort of stamina and backbone it would take to win this vast, looming war at sea. This singular battle granted the United States the opportunity to defeat Japan, the will to defeat Japan, and the pride and self-confidence to defeat Japan. While the Japanese viewed Midway as a temporary setback, Americans saw in Midway that the long chain of defeat had been severed and that ultimate victory was at least possible.

The beginning of the end for Japan began on August 7, 1942, when the 20,000-strong U.S. 1st Marine Division assaulted Guadalcanal and neighboring islands at the periphery of the Empire of Japan. A war hitherto thoroughly defensive became a war haltingly offensive. An American mindset hitherto dominated by pessimism and caution became conditionally optimistic and breathtakingly bold. But American leaders knew from the outset that the first Pacific offensive had to succeed, for a clear defeat or even an equivocal victory in the eastern Solomons would wipe away any vestige of optimism upon which the long haul, however far it needed to go, would have to be based.

No one involved at the beginning could have divined what the Guadalcanal Campaign might become. But one side knew and accepted the immense stakes from the inception, from the very agreement to go there. And the other side did not; it had no idea what monumental national resolve it was finally facing. On such differences of vision are the fates of nations determined.

To put it mildly, the Japanese seriously misjudged both the objectives and the strength of the Allies' August 7 foray into the eastern Solomons. Their intelligence services completely failed them, and their preconceived notions seriously deceived them. At the moment the reinforced 1st Marine Division invaded Guadalcanal and Tulagi, the attention of most Japanese senior commands in the area—and of Imperial General Headquarters in Tokyo—was riveted on a burgeoning campaign to seize Port Moresby, New Guinea. An Allied incursion into the eastern Solomons was a complete surprise and a most unwelcome diversion.

Disbelieving that the Allies were even capable of mounting a major amphibious counterattack anywhere along the remote perimeter of the Greater East Asia Co-Prosperity Sphere, the Japanese assumed that the incursion was merely a raid in force, perhaps an effort to divert Japanese attention and resources from beleaguered Port Moresby. Perhaps, the Japanese hoped, the Allied ground and naval forces in the eastern Solomons would leave when they were properly challenged. Moreover, the Japanese disbelieved that the Allies had a large enough infantry force available in the entire New Guinea-Solomons region with which to hold the Lunga airfield and Tulagi. And so, from the outset, the measures the Japanese took were aimed at giving a much smaller force than was really there an excuse to withdraw.

◆

Locally, it took the Japanese no time to react. RAdm Sadiyoshi Yamada's Rabaul-based 5th Air Attack Force had gotten its first strike away within two hours of the first news that Allied ships were in the Tulagi-Guadalcanal area. And the cruisers and destroyer of VAdm Gunichi Mikawa's newly created Outer Seas Force had taken only a few hours to clear Rabaul's harbor on a sally that would culminate on the night of August 8–9 in the mauling of the Allied surface screen off Savo Island. Moreover, as far-flung Japanese commands and commanders reluctantly came to grips with the Allied incursion into the eastern Solomons, the inflated claims by 5th Air Attack Force aviators and the eventual very real claims of the Outer Seas Force led them to believe that Allied naval and air losses were unsustainable even if the enemy's intention all along was to stay and use the Lunga base as a springboard for an even broader counteroffensive with Rabaul as its ultimate goal.

In short, from the outset, the Japanese commanders saw in the unfortunate and ill-timed eastern Solomons incident what they most hoped to see— a diversion of little consequence that was costing the Allies more in ships, airplanes, and lives than the Allies could afford to sacrifice for so hopeless a cause as winning back the Solomon Islands and retaining control of the Port Moresby area. But the Japanese were obligated to react, and they did so in what they believed was overwhelming fashion.

On August 8, aboard his flagship, the new super battleship *Yamato*, Adm Isoroku Yamamoto, the commander-in-chief of the Imperial Navy's vaunted Combined Fleet, told his subordinates that he wanted "decisive battle forces" massed in order to eject the Allies completely and permanently from the eastern Solomons. Adequate naval surface forces were at hand, under the control of VAdm Nobutake Kondo's Second Fleet, then headquartered in Japan. And the Imperial Navy's two remaining operational fleet carriers had just completed a reorganization at Kure. Available for the counteroffensive were the two fleet carriers and one light carrier under the control of VAdm Chuichi Nagumo's new Third Fleet. In addition, Yamamoto ordered that a support force be created for the operation at hand, and that all these naval forces be placed under Admiral Kondo's operational command and control. From the standpoint of the Imperial Navy, the Combined Fleet's necessary support of the Port Moresby offensive would be postponed until, as Yamamoto put it, his forces had finished "cleaning out" the Guadalcanal-Tulagi area.

Imperial General Headquarters pretty much concurred with Admiral Yamamoto's assessment and ranking of objectives. But the early underrating of the Allied invasion force caused it to limit the ground force assigned to drive the Allied ground force out of the eastern Solomons. Initially, one 6,000-man independent infantry brigade, a 2,000-man special infantry assault regiment, and a 600-man special naval landing force—all of which simply happened to be available in proximity to the battle arena—were assigned to conduct the counteroffensive on land. Another 500-man ad hoc naval landing force was scraped together from naval infantry troops in the Rabaul area, and it was hoped that organized remnants of the original Guadalcanal and Tulagi garrison force could be located and pressed into service. But that is all any Japanese senior commander, from Tokyo to Truk to Rabaul, thought would be needed to achieve a knockout blow on land. Then, Tokyo hoped, many of these very same ground troops could be used to bolster the forces already on the offensive against the real goal—Port Moresby. For the moment, Imperial General Headquarters and even Admiral Yamamoto didn't give any thought to how the strategic situation would change if the Allied force managed to get the Lunga airfield in operation and man it with offensive bombers.

Chapter 14

The essence of the Japanese battle plan—dubbed Operation *KA* after the first syllable of *Guadalcanal* rendered in Japanese—was pretty much fixed by August 10. On the surface, the agenda was built around the delivery of fifteen hundred infantrymen to Guadalcanal, but at its real heart was an ambition to engage and defeat the American carrier fleet. At the time the *KA* plan was set forth, the Combined Fleet was not in position to sally into the eastern Solomons area, so the initial version called for the ground troops to be landed around August 21.

The main surface components of VAdm Nobutake Kondo's powerful Guadalcanal Support Force—a name to indicate its role in seeing the ground troops safely to their destination—sallied from Japanese ports on August 11 and made their way slowly toward the southeastern area. The warships under Kondo were designated to fulfill specific tasks within the overall plan: Kondo himself would command the Advance Force, whose main body comprised five heavy cruisers, a light cruiser/destroyer leader, and five fleet destroyers. Also under Kondo was a Support Group consisting of a battleship and three fleet destroyers. These surface forces were to provide support for a carrier component and might be employed to mount bombardments against Henderson Field or other Allied bases. Also under Kondo was a Seaplane Group consisting of the auxiliary seaplane carrier *Chitose* and one fleet destroyer. Another separate formation under Kondo's command was VAdm Hiroaki Abe's Vanguard Force. Composed of two battleships, three heavy cruisers, a light cruiser/destroyer leader, and six fleet destroyers, its mission and goal was to close on the American battle fleet— including the carriers—and defeat it in a surface battle. Providing at-sea air support and the best means for attacking the American carriers was VAdm Chuichi Nagumo's Mobile Force *(Kido Butai)*, which consisted of the veteran fleet carriers *Shokaku* and *Zuikaku*, the light carrier *Ryujo*, and an escort force composed of one heavy cruiser and seven destroyers.

In addition to the powerful fleet units on their way from Japan, VAdm Gunichi Mikawa's Rabaul-based Outer Seas Force was to play a significant role in the unfolding operation. For the operation at hand, Admiral Mikawa oversaw four heavy cruisers and eight fleet destroyers. These ships were to provide close-in cover for the troop-laden transports and to mount spoiling attacks against the American bases at Lunga and Tulagi.

Under the direct control of VAdm Nishizo Tsukahara, in his capacity as commander of the new Southeast Area, and set to sail from Truk at the right moment, was the all-important Reinforcement Group, commanded by RAdm Raizo Tanaka, a hero of destroyer action in the Netherlands East Indies early in the year. It consisted of an Imperial Navy transport carrying the 600-man Yokosuka 5th Special Naval Landing Force, two slow Imperial Army transports carrying the 1,000-man second echelon of Col Kiyano Ichiki's crack Imperial Army infantry ground force, and an escort comprised of a light cruiser/destroyer leader and three patrol boats (small obsolete destroyers rigged out as destroyer-transports). In addition, Tsukahara held sway over two fleet submarines and one coastal submarine, to be used as weapons of opportunity as soon as the enemy fleet could be fixed. On station to help Tsukahara's land- and tender-based patrol aircraft fix the enemy fleet was the Advance Expeditionary Force—nine fleet submarines controlled out of Truk and operating along an advance patrol line in the direction of the supposed location of Task Force 61. Finally, at sea, a heavily escorted group of fleet oilers would be stationed north of the Stewart Islands.

Imperial Navy land-based air units at the disposal of Admiral Kondo's formidable naval command were under the immediate control of Vice Admiral Tsukahara's Base Air Force. As the confrontation neared, there were nearly one hundred Imperial Navy warplanes based at Rabaul, chiefly Betty medium bombers and land-based Zero fighters, both long-range escorts and short-range interceptors. Numerous long-range patrol aircraft were operating from Rabaul and a seaplane tender anchored in the Shortland Islands, and lighter seaplane-scouts and seaplane-fighters were operating from another tender anchored in Rekata Bay, Santa Isabel.

What the Japanese intended to make of this formidable and potentially overwhelming array of naval and air power was based on history—the history of the Imperial Navy, the history of the first eight months of the Pacific War, and the history of the commander-in-chief of the Imperial Navy's Combined Fleet.

It is a common impulse for practitioners of the military sciences to draw upon the lessons of the past while planning the battles of the future.

When one gets to the core of military history and the exercises in manipulation that arise from it, one finds that all strategies and all tactics remain more or less ageless: One side attempts to mass its manpower and weapons in such a way as to defeat the other in the attack or on the defense. This is true for land armies, and it is true for navies.

Military science is largely the art of the known coupled with human audacity, intuition, and luck.

The beginning of World War II saw the addition of an element of warfare whose consequences upon the modern battlefield were not yet known. Theory, audacity, intuition, and luck would play their roles in the new war, but air power would forever change the nature of war on land and at sea. Even by mid-1942, thirty-nine years after the world's first successful powered, manned flight, no one had yet synthesized the true lessons of air power, no one yet knew quite how to best use it, what might happen as a result of its presence over the battlefield, its full impact upon strategies and tactics.

For men inculcated in the traditions and lessons of nineteenth-century warfare—and that included every man who had, by mid-1942, attained flag rank—air power was a chimera.

♦

One of the most overrated characters of modern military history is Isoroku Yamamoto, commander-in-chief of the Combined Fleet, the Imperial Navy's operational arm.

Not quite the visionary extolled by his countrymen, nor quite worthy of the almost unseemly posthumous praise heaped on by the men he defeated (a convenient impulse—raising the apparent architect of one's defeat to godlike stature), Yamamoto was a bright, forceful leader, but he was no innovator. The surprise-attack strategy he forced upon his service and nation were cribbed from his hero and mentor, VAdm Heihachiro Togo, who launched surprise war upon the Russians at Port Arthur in 1904. A late-blooming pilot, Yamamoto was no air-power strategist, and certainly no air-power innovator. The innovators were on his staff or, more correctly, on the staffs of his subordinates.

Yamamoto loved the *idea* of aerial warfare—particularly carrier-air warfare—but, when it came time to play his hand, this inveterate gambler always hedged.

Yamamoto drew the wrong lessons from his youthful experience at Port Arthur, and he drew the wrong lessons from Midway, a defeat he, as much as anyone, inflicted upon his nation.

In the final analysis, Yamamoto, whom history has labeled a carrier-warfare genius, was the overseeing technician of rather standard battleship strategies. There is ample evidence to support the view that he mistrusted the ability of his carrier squadrons to play a strategic role, or misunderstood their worth.

The strategy Isoroku Yamamoto and his staff cobbled together in the face of the Allied incursion into the eastern Solomons had one aim, never before successful: to place Japanese *surface* forces in contact with the American carriers and their escorts. This was the vaunted Midway strategy coupled with the tactics of the Coral Sea draw. It was used and used again, in draws and defeats, because it was the pet theory of Japan's most revered naval leader after Togo, the mythical Isoroku Yamamoto.

A convoy of vulnerable troop transports would move on Guadalcanal accompanied at a distance by a naval surface bombardment force whose task it was to close down Henderson Field. Air groups from the two Japanese fleet carriers were to launch surprise strikes against American carriers drawn into range by the need to defend Guadalcanal against reinforcement or bombardment, depending upon which surface force the Americans located and their carriers attacked. Until the American carrier air groups were committed to attacking the transports or any of the surface forces, the Japanese carrier air groups and the carriers themselves would lay low beyond the range of Allied carrier- and land-based search aircraft. After the Japanese carrier air groups crippled the American carrier fleet, a powerful battleship-cruiser-destroyer flotilla positioned ahead of the Japanese carriers was to dash in against the American carriers and their surface escorts—to destroy them by gunfire.

The role of the Japanese carrier air groups—as at Midway—was to attack the American carriers, support follow-up operations by Japanese surface forces against American carrier and surface forces, and support a landing operation aimed at defeating American troops ashore. There was an important departure from the Midway battle plan. Since there were adequate land-based bombers in range of Guadalcanal, Japanese carrier aircraft would not be put at risk in attacks against ground targets, which in the past had meant fewer of them being on hand to attack the American carriers.

The upcoming battle was to be a slightly smaller version of the cataclysmic surface engagement between the main components of two modern fleets that was to have taken place at Midway. It was to be the battle Japanese naval strategists had been planning for two decades. Indeed, it was to be Japan's third attempt in four months to bring to reality a set-piece battle strategy that had been drawn and redrawn for endless map-table battles throughout the 1920s and 1930s. Above all, it was to be Isoroku Yamamoto's vindication for the defeat he had suffered at the hands of Fate—and not at the hands of the United States—at Midway.

And what can be said of Yamamoto's adversaries? Fate, and little else, prevented the U.S. Navy from following Yamamoto's cherished ideals of carrier-surface strategy. In the greatest unperceived irony of modern warfare, carrier forces operating under Yamamoto's subordinates destroyed the prime ingredients of ironclad American surface strategy. The battle-ships severely damaged or permanently sunk by Japanese carrier strikes against Pearl Harbor compelled the weakened U.S. Navy to undertake four carrier-versus-carrier clashes in the Pacific from May to October 1942. And the aggregate outcome of those clashes—not foresight—suggested the carrier-based strategy that eventually contributed so heavily to Japan's ultimate defeat.

The American focus upon aircraft carriers at the Coral Sea and Midway did not, in the minds of the leaders of the time, constitute a new broad-based naval strategy. Rather, it signaled the paucity of American battle-ships in the combat arena. So-called "black-shoe" battleship-cruiser admirals dominated the U.S. Navy of 1942 and would continue to dominate it well into 1943. Indeed, a number of the leading "carrier" admirals of 1942—VAdm Frank Jack Fletcher being chief among them—were, in fact, cruiser and battleship admirals, not aviators at all. And many of them were serving in positions well beyond their professional grasps.

Yamamoto's imperfect carrier-surface amalgams—lightly screened multicarrier task forces operating in conjunction with and usually acting in support of battleship-cruiser-destroyer maneuver forces—were based upon the overwhelming superiority the Combined Fleet enjoyed in surface assets.

Far from being the products of a perfect vision of how war should be waged in the vast Pacific, American carrier task forces—groupments of single carriers, each surrounded by its own screen of defending surface vessels—operated the way they operated because of a keenly felt scarcity of both carriers and screening warships. The first three weeks in the Guadalcanal arena cost the Allies—chiefly the United States—four heavy cruisers sunk, one heavy cruiser damaged, and several destroyers sunk or damaged. All of these ships but one destroyer were sunk or damaged by Japanese surface forces operating virtually within sight of Marine positions on Guadalcanal. Such losses appreciably added to the pressure already heaped upon the carrier task forces to achieve some lasting results in a type of warfare by then demonstrably more prone to Fate than most.

♦

All but ignoring the avowed purpose of the late-August exercise—landing troops on Guadalcanal and supporting their assault against what its intelligence service labeled "about 2,000 Marines"—the Combined Fleet managed to amass a staggering array of nearly sixty warships, plus transports and submarines. The intention was little more than to destroy any aircraft carriers the Americans sent to support the Marines at Guadalcanal.

The senior Japanese admirals feared American carriers far more than they respected their own. Those few American carriers loomed larger in Japanese minds in August than they had even in May, before the crushing humiliation of Midway.

Americans certainly feared risking their few carriers in action against Japanese carriers. But they had won big at Midway, so they well appreciated the potential fruits of carrier-versus-carrier warfare. More important, however, they *had nothing else but their carriers* with which to counter the Japanese carriers—nothing at all but their carriers to parry Japanese moves and buy time for the hurried, harried home-front builders of yet more carriers and a new generation of . . . battleships!

Chapter 15

Lt(jg) SLIM RUSSELL
Scouting-3

Diary Entry of August 20, 1942

Tulagi bearing 303 [degrees], distance 228 [miles].

On August 18, we fueled from the tanker *Platte* and received mail. The mail was from June 21 to July 7.

Yesterday morning, three destroyers and one submarine were reported to have shelled Tulagi.

This past week we have done little except go around in circles. Yesterday, I flew nine hours. One 200-mile search with Ens Bob Balenti, and I flew on Lt M. P. MacNair for a 250-mile hop in the afternoon. Supposedly an enemy force out there, but no could find. Did sight two islands. Also two PBYs.

This morning we had battle stations and stripped the ship for action. One [Japanese] heavy cruiser, one light cruiser, and three destroyers were reported shelling Tulagi at 0600. The *Wasp* sent search planes out at 0800. Three destroyers and one light cruiser reported

30 miles, bearing 270 [degrees], from Savo Island on course 330 degrees at a speed of 25 knots. Leaving us in a hurry! We were then 258 miles from them. A heavy cruiser was reported in Tulagi Harbor, possibly damaged by a B-17. Since that time, I have not heard anything more. The ship has been at General Quarters all day.

The *Long Island,* a small converted carrier, joined us last evening and is with us now. She has nineteen fighters and twelve dive-bombers with her. Marine planes. She is to send them into Lunga field soon.

This afternoon, we had quite a few bogies [unidentified aircraft] reported. Believe at least one of them was a Jap floatplane.

A 14th Air Group Mavis operating from the advance patrol base in the Shortland Islands began tracking the *Long Island* force—a cruiser and two destroyers, but not the little auxiliary carrier herself—at about 1020, and it transmitted news of the sighting. At 1130, the Mavis reported sighting the aircraft-laden *Long Island.* Unnoticed by U.S. Navy radars or any of the patrol aircraft in the air at the time, the Mavis eased to within 40 miles of the carrier and continued tracking her course. At 1334, the Mavis was finally picked up by the *Enterprise's* CXAM air-search radar. Fighting-71 Wildcats nearest to the bogey were vectored out, but the first U.S. Navy warplane to reach the Mavis was a Scouting-71 SBD piloted by Ens Harlan Coit.

The Mavis pilot spotted the SBD moments after Ensign Coit spotted the Mavis, and the huge reconnaissance bomber veered toward home at full power. Coit made several firing runs in the face of heavy machine-gun and cannon fire, but he was unable to hit it in a vulnerable spot. The Mavis escaped as Ensign Coit rushed to the *Wasp* to make an emergency landing. His Dauntless was full of holes and its hydraulic system was out of commission, but neither Coit nor his gunner had been hit.

At about 1345, the *Long Island* turned into the southeast trade wind, black smoke pouring from her horizontal starboard funnels, and catapulted a dark blue Douglas Dauntless SBD-3 dive-bomber out over the waves. The flattop ship and her escorts were off southern San Cristobal, 190 miles from Henderson Field.

Maj Dick Mangrum, a former flight instructor and fighter pilot with twelve years in the Marine Corps and many hundreds of hours in the air, deftly recovered control of the projectile that was his ride and slowly raised flaps to begin his long climb. Next up was 2dLt Larry Baldinus, a Polish expatriate and former enlisted pilot. The most experienced airman in the squadron after Dick Mangrum, Baldinus had been commissioned shortly after Pearl Harbor.

The third Dauntless was piloted by a more typical specimen of the day, 2dLt Hank Hise, a very young Texan who had graduated from flight school in May 1942 with a shade over two hundred flight hours under his belt. Hise had amassed more flight time during carrier training in California and check flights in Hawaii, but he was no veteran.

The force of the catapult caused the young pilot to pull back on his control stick, so the nose of the airplane pulled up smartly. Hise reacted by jamming the stick in his right hand forward, then had to fight to keep the Dauntless out of the water. The novice regained control and pulled up to join Mangrum and Baldinus.

Three of the twelve SBD pilots were survivors of Midway. One had attacked a Japanese carrier and had then landed his crippled dive-bomber on one wheel at Midway between rows of parked aircraft. Another had been wounded in the same attack and had returned to Midway with a critically wounded gunner. Their stories, and the stories of the two or three veteran fighter pilots accompanying them aboard the *Long Island,* had raised the hairs on the necks of the novice dive-bomber pilots.

The dozen Dauntlesses of Mangrum's VMSB-232 formed up and orbited to await the escort of eighteen shorter-legged Grumman F4F-4 Wildcat fighters from Capt John Lucien Smith's VMF-223 and a command fighter piloted by LtCol Charlie Fike, the Marine Air Group 23 executive officer.

Major Mangrum turned his three-plane section to the northwest as the last of the fighters joined up. The Lunga plain was 190 miles ahead.

Second Lieutenant Hise was surprised by the height of the hills as he flew up Lengo Channel on Maj Dick Mangrum's right wing and banked around in a 180-degree turn to begin his approach from the east. The diamond-shaped formation of four sections of three Dauntlesses each broke up with practiced ease; first Mangrum broke to the left, followed three seconds later by Baldinus, and three seconds after that by Hise. Landing gear was lowered by the pilots at 1,000 feet as they made their downwind approaches, and then flaps were lowered. Mangrum spotted Maj Charles Hayes—one of the Marine Corps' few qualified carrier landing signal officers—standing on the hood of a truck at the end of the strip, his arms held straight out in the "roger" position, indicating that it was okay to land.

Mangrum glided slowly to a mere 20 feet, then went around again. He cut back on the throttle and his airplane dropped smoothly to the surface. Second Lieutenant Baldinus made his usual perfect landing. Intent upon his instruments, Hise nearly plowed into the high stand of trees too close to the end of the runway, pulled up reflexively, gave a last spurt of power, chopped back the throttle, and plunked onto the ground in a cloud of dust.

While the Wildcats flew top cover, the remainder of the Dauntlesses landed. Major Mangrum followed a ground-control jeep to the dispersal area and jumped to the ground as soon as his Dauntless's engine stopped. There he had his hand wrung profusely by MajGen Archer Vandegrift, the 1st Marine Division commanding general.

Thousands of thankful Marines shouted themselves hoarse and pounded one another on the back in a thundering release of emotion. In a sense more real than symbolic, Dick Mangrum and his fellow pilots and aircrewmen were bringing their nation into the war as active participants.

Lt(jg) SMOKEY STOVER
Fighting-5

Diary Entry of August 20, 1942

At General Quarters all day from 0900. Quite useless and tiring for everyone, in my opinion. Came up to about 190 miles from Tulagi.

This afternoon, a *Wasp* scout plane tried to down a four-engine Jap patrol plane, but he got a 20mm shell in his plane, so he quit. The SBD came by the *Saratoga* giving a deferred forced landing signal, but we couldn't take him aboard.

We had a couple of alarms and manned our planes, and *Wasp* fighters went out after a Jap seaplane. Fighter Direction broke radio silence, but he got away.

Turned at about 1600 to course 100 [degrees] at 14 knots. Running away again!

The *Long Island* launched Marine fighters and some SBDs going to Lunga field on Guadalcanal. They may be able to discourage Jap raids for a while. Wish we could catch a good raid coming in!

AOM2 ALFRED CAMPBELL
USS Enterprise

Diary Entry of August 20, 1942

Sent out scouts early in the morning. They spotted some Jap ships. They came back and were rearmed with 1,000-pound bombs. We stood by to launch an attack group. We speeded up to better than 20 knots, but decided to discontinue until tomorrow.

The Japanese commanders were elated over the Mavis's sighting reports on the *Long Island,* but they misread their significance. It seemed to the Japanese that the carrier was stalking RAdm Raizo Tanaka's slow Reinforcement Group, which had departed Truk in two echelons on August 16 and 17. The American carrier was beyond the range of any Japanese strike aircraft, but Tanaka was within range of the unidentified American carrier.

No Japanese naval force was remotely in range to exploit news of the carrier sighting. The Imperial Navy carriers under VAdm Chuichi Nagumo and a large surface force were still far to the north—several days' sail beyond range—and VAdm Nobutake Kondo's mighty Advance Force was anchored in Truk Lagoon. Thus, VAdm Nishizo Tsukahara ordered Tanaka to depart from his route and schedule toward Guadalcanal and turn directly toward Rabaul. If the Americans really knew where Tanaka was, they might chase him and thereby sail within range of his Rabaul-based 5th Air Attack Force Bettys.

The news got better—but cloudier—at 1340, when the Mavis in the next search sector over from the *Long Island's* position reported the presence of a second aircraft carrier and an array of surface escorts. At 1415, the same Mavis reported that the carrier and its escorts were retiring to the south. This seemed unreasonable, but only because neither Mavis had seen or reported the launch of Marine Air Group 23 Wildcats and Dauntlesses to Guadalcanal. Once the Marine aircraft were away, the vulnerable *Long Island* headed out of range at full speed, and so did Task Force 61.

Aboard the battleship *Yamato*, which was well to the north of Truk, Adm Isoroku Yamamoto initially felt that the data indicated that the Americans were attempting to locate and attack Tanaka's Reinforcement Group. He ordered the only battle force remotely within range—Kondo's Advance Force—to sortie from Truk as soon as possible. He also ordered the Support Group, still far to the north of Truk, to race south at full speed to bolster Kondo. And Yamamoto ordered VAdm Chuichi Nagumo to skip a scheduled stopover at Truk in order to rendezvous his carriers with Kondo's force 120 miles east of Truk on the morning of August 21.

Everything changed for Yamamoto when he received an evening broadcast from one of the infantry forces on Guadalcanal. The new report indicated that a force of Navy-type fighters and light bombers had arrived at the Lunga airfield. The penny finally dropped; a permanent complement of American aircraft at Lunga radically changed the strategic equation. The American carriers were still important, but the Lunga airfield was all-important. Moreover, the withdrawal of the American carrier, as reported by the second Mavis, finally made sense; the American carriers had been delivering the aircraft to Guadalcanal, not stalking Tanaka.

And so Admiral Yamamoto ordered another radical change in plans. At 2242 all combat commands in the region and approaching the region were told to set their sights on the Lunga airfield; it was to be pummeled into submission by air and naval bombardment and then overrun by the ground troops already ashore on Guadalcanal and soon to be delivered by Tanaka's Reinforcement Group. To help things fall into place, he gave Tanaka an extra twenty-four hours—until August 24—to deliver the ground troops to Guadalcanal's Taivu Point. (The veteran six thousand–man 35th Infantry Brigade had left the Palau Islands on August 15, but it could not reach Guadalcanal before August 28, and so might arrive too late to take part in winning back the Lunga airfield.)

For all that, never losing sight of his primary war strategy, Yamamoto also ordered VAdm Nishizo Tsukahara to relocate and continue to track the American carriers. He wanted them too.

Chapter 16

Once the Marines who killed them got to looking around, there were several strange things about the Japanese who had died in the unexpected August 19 meeting engagement east of the Lunga Perimeter. As his Marines collected souvenirs and documents, 2dLt John Jachym, a platoon leader with Company A, 1st Battalion, 1st Marine Regiment (1st Marines), noticed that there were too many map cases, swords, binoculars, and documents for so small a patrol. And there were far too many officers present. *And* the corpses were too well dressed. *And* their helmets bore the red enamel star insignae of the Imperial Army—not the anchor-and-chrysanthemum of the Imperial Navy *rikusentai* who had been garrisoning the Lunga area on August 7.

Intent upon his mission, the combative company commander, Capt Charlie Brush, wanted to collect the documents, proceed with the destruction of a Japanese machine-gun detachment east of Tetere, and *then* return to the Lunga Perimeter to file a report and turn in the documents. Lieutenant Jachym had three wounded Marines to think about, and he was loath to leave them behind when he was certain that at least a few Japanese had survived the fight; leaving a squad to defend them would further weaken the reinforced platoon Captain Brush had at his disposal. Brush relented.

Three Marines who had been killed in the firefight were left in shallow graves with their feet sticking out to aid recovery efforts, and stretchers for the wounded were rigged from ponchos and cut saplings.

Though all hands, including the officers, took turns carrying the wounded men up and down gullies, across streams, and through the loose sand of the beach, everyone was done in by the time the platoon met an ambulance that had been sent out in response to a radio report. It was well after 2100, August 19, before Captain Brush and Lieutenant Jachym reported their findings and turned in their haul of data and artifacts.

As 1st Marine Division intelligence linguists unraveled the history and mission of *Ichiki Butai,* many were surprised to learn that the Imperial Army troops had been ashore for only a day when they ran into the Brush patrol. What struck them the most was the graphic on a captured map; the eastern Lunga Perimeter defenses along Alligator Creek, which were quite weak at that moment, had been sketched in accurate detail.

Following deliberations with the 1st Marine Division operations staff in the morning, Col Clifton Cates, the commanding officer of the 1st Marines, ordered LtCol Al Pollock's 2d Battalion, 1st Marines, to dig in at the mouth and along the west bank of Alligator Creek. A pair of 37mm antitank guns from the 1st Special Weapons Battalion was sent to the sandspit, and twelve 75mm howitzers of the 3d Battalion, 11th Marines, were tightly registered on the area. It was adjudged that the new defensive line would be capable of withstanding an assault by the following night, August 20.

Nothing much happened through the daylight hours of August 20. The nine hundred-odd Marines of the 2d Battalion, 1st, put on a furious burst of entrenching activity along Alligator Creek and the beach west of the sandspit, and everyone else in the Lunga Perimeter went to full alert. All hands took time off to cheer the arrival of Marine fighters and dive-bombers in the late afternoon. Scuttlebutt—the gleanings of the rumor mill—was rife. The blooded *veterans* of Jachym's platoon gave advice based upon their half-hour combat experience.

SgtMaj Jacob Vouza, the chief scout commanded by a British coastwatcher, Capt Martin Clemens, led a patrol of fellow islanders on the evening of August 20 to reconnoiter along the coast east of Alligator Creek. The small party made its way rapidly along the coastal trail until the lead scout detected movement ahead. While the main body moved ahead from a fork in the trail, Vouza dropped back to discard a tiny souvenir American flag he had foolishly carried with him. Before the chief scout could act, however, a Japanese patrol blundered up to him and held him stock still at riflepoint.

A proud, volatile individualist, Vouza disdainfully glared at his captors and refused to answer any of their questions. He was bound to a tree and searched. The American flag was discovered, and several pointed questions were asked and ignored. Vouza was beaten, stabbed, and left to die. But the islander remained calm and immobile, awaiting the return of his strength. Then he gnawed through the straw ropes and made for the Lunga Perimeter, taking care to avoid the numerous Japanese soldiers who had by then infiltrated the area.

The Americans had no inkling as to Japanese movements, but they were fully alerted. Marines manning a listening post near the mouth of Alligator Creek detected an individual staggering toward the stream. Several men sent to investigate found a bleeding islander—Vouza—in a high state of agitation, incoherently babbling away. Capt Martin Clemens was called out from the 1st Marine Division command post as Vouza was carried to the west bank.

Clemens, who furiously drove from the division command post, was shocked at the scout's condition; Vouza had been wickedly gashed across the throat and was bleeding copiously from several body wounds. He asked Clemens to take down his last will, which he proceeded to dictate at great and boring length. At once sensing that the scout would recover, while fearing that he would not, Clemens held one of Vouza's hands and furiously transcribed.

As Martin Clemens wrote, the first files of nearly nine hundred *Ichiki Butai* soldiers who had arrived on Guadalcanal fewer than forty-eight hours earlier moved stealthily upon the listening posts guarding the sandspit at the mouth of Alligator Creek. Their colonel, Kiyano Ichiki, had panicked at news of the deaths of so many of his officers and the discovery of his assault force's first echelon so soon after landing on Guadalcanal. Fearful that the Marines would be given time to dig in or mount a spoiling attack, he decided on his own to launch an immediate assault upon their lines. Had Ichiki waited and looked and learned, he certainly would have discovered that the Allied presence on Guadalcanal was far more powerful than any Japanese commander realized. If he had waited and looked and listened, he might have warned higher headquarters that the ground assault they had planned was futile with so few troops. But Colonel Ichiki did not wait or look or listen. He did not even report to higher headquarters. He simply ordered an immediate attack by the nearly nine hundred soldiers he had with him—against a battle line held by at least an equal number of thoroughly alerted Marines.

Pvt George Turzai, an eighteen-year-old serving with Company E, 2d Battalion, 1st Marines, was sound asleep in his foxhole when the Japanese vanguard of scouts attacked or blundered into Marine listening posts near the mouth of Alligator Creek, about 200 feet to the north. Turzai and his foxhole buddy, a close-mouthed older private named Moser, were exhausted after digging their fighting hole, a three-by-six-by-three-foot-deep affair about 20 feet from the west bank of the sluggish creek. Neither Turzai, who was asleep, nor Moser, who was on watch, knew a thing about the Japanese advance until a piercing scream wrenched them to full awareness.

Everything went dark and quiet for a moment. Then the sky was lighted, clear as daylight, and rifle and machine-gun fire erupted from within and in front of the strongpoint Marines had built up at the sandspit at the creek's mouth. A flare landed on the bank directly in front of Turzai's fighting hole. Private Moser, who was older and smoother than George Turzai, urged his partner to crawl into the open and douse the light. Turzai affixed his bayonet to the end of his bolt-action, five-shot Springfield M1903 rifle and crawled forward to knock the flare into the water. As Turzai lay still, recovering his night vision, he saw a sword-wielding Japanese officer leading nearly two hundred soldiers from the stand of coconut palms on the east bank.

A machine gun momentarily stopped most of the Japanese, but at least six who were racing directly at Turzai kept coming. The young Marine snapped his rifle to his shoulder and put out the five rounds in its magazine as quickly as he could work the bolt and trigger. He had no idea if he was hitting anyone, and cared less, for two live ones were upon him. Turzai stood up in time to parry a bayonet thrust; the Japanese steel clanged against the American rifle barrel, nearly severing Turzai's left pinky. The second Japanese, confused or overexcited, felled his own countryman with a well-directed bayonet thrust, and then his face splintered under the impact of Turzai's heavy rifle butt. George Turzai beat a hasty retreat.

Pvt Johnny Rivers was manning the .30-caliber water-cooled medium machine gun in the log-and-earth emplacement only yards from George Turzai's foxhole when the Japanese burst from the trees on the opposite bank. A promising welterweight whose reactions had been honed to perfection during a year's training as both gunner and boxer, Rivers snapped his weapon onto the first target he saw and lifted the butterfly trigger tab. Japanese in the arc upon which the medium machine gun could bear scattered or dropped, but several who approached from the sides got to within arm's length of the burly boxer and had to be punched to submission. The very instant the machine gun cut loose again, a bullet from the far bank passed through the firing embrasure of Rivers's bunker and killed the young gunner. Dying fingers froze upon the trigger, and nearly two hundred rounds were pumped into Japanese bodies before Rivers slowly toppled over. Cpl LeRoy Diamond resumed firing until he was wounded.

The Japanese appeared to the third man in the dugout, Pvt Al Schmid, as hysterical cattle charging into the water in massed waves. The bucking machine gun mowed down the lead rank, but Japanese to the rear pressed into view—and fell under Schmid's well-directed bursts. Within minutes, however, a hand grenade exploded at the embrasure and blinded the gunner.

Pvt Whitney Jacobs heard shouts for help from within the dugout, dashed through heavy gunfire, entered the emplacement, and hurriedly staunched the wounds of the bleeding gunners. Then he excitedly returned to his own fighting hole.

Schmid and Diamond took stock. The corporal could see, but his wounds prevented him from firing the gun. Al Schmid was blind but otherwise able to direct the key weapon. Schmid resumed his position between the spread rear tripod legs, squeezed the release, and, with Corporal Diamond issuing directions in his ear, lifted the trigger and resumed his job of killing and maiming Japanese soldiers.

Nine hundred Japanese in all, the half of *Ichiki Butai* that had been landed only days earlier, attacked LtCol Al Pollock's reinforced 2d Battalion, 1st, at Alligator Creek. Most of them made for the sandspit, right into the teeth of a pair of 37mm antitank guns manned by members of Battery B, 1st Special Weapons Battalion. The gunners fired canister into the packed Japanese, momentarily halting them as riflemen and machine gunners fought to recover from the shock of first contact.

The ready reserve of the 2d Battalion, 1st's posted about 300 yards west of the sandspit, was 2dLt George Codrea's 1st Platoon of Company G, which was formed into a column of squads and in motion toward the sound of the firing within minutes of the opening exchanges. The last hundred yards had to be traversed on hands and knees under an umbrella of Japanese machine-gun fire which was overshooting the Marine defenses at the front.

As the reserve platoon approached the embattled sandspit, Lieutenant Codrea formed his men into a skirmish line and ordered them forward. When the 6-foot-4-inch officer was hit twice in the arm, he dropped back, prepared to sit the fight out. But when Cpl John Spillane's squad was stopped by a mortar round right beside him, Codrea sensed the need for some drastic action. He yelled, "Follow me!" and headed directly for the apex of the sandspit, a spot that would be known as Hell's Point.

Corporal Spillane was right at Lieutenant Codrea's heels when three rounds penetrated his helmet in quick succession. Stunned but unscathed, he loosed a violent oath, grabbed a helmet from a dead man, and thrust himself back into the attack.

Pvt Harry Horsman was baptized in blood when the platoon's first fatality fell with a head wound and deposited brain matter all over Horsman, who dropped to the sand and opened fire on anything that even seemed like a target.

As eerie shadows played death games in the light of colored flares, bright yellow and pink tracers arced hypnotically across the silvery water and among the pitch-dark stands of stately palms. Two Marine infantry companies, most of a Marine weapons company, and two Marine 37mm antitank guns withstood the repeated blows of nearly a battalion of superb, extremely brave Japanese infantry.

Jammed or balky weapons seriously affected the Marines' ability to defeat the attackers. Old ammunition and the excitement of the fight were at the root of the trouble. When Cpl John Shea's Thompson submachine gun jammed, he rolled over onto his back to fix the weapon. After a moment, he felt someone hacking at his left leg with a bayonet. Astounded, Shea pinned his assailant against the wall of his fighting hole with the injured leg and released the bolt of the weapon, thereby pumping five rounds into the attacker. Pvt Joe Wadsworth, manning a foxhole right on Hell's Point, fired into the Japanese until his Browning automatic rifle (BAR) jammed. He picked up a discarded Springfield rifle and fired it until several Japanese got within bayonet range. Wadsworth parried and jabbed for some moments, but was overwhelmed and left for dead. Pvt Ray Parker wriggled out across the sand, sheltered by a low dune, to a position from which he could place enfilade fire upon a Japanese machine gun emplaced on the east bank. His BAR jammed within minutes, and he had to continue with a slow-firing Springfield '03 rifle he happened to find. Cpl Dean Wilson's BAR jammed just as three Japanese loomed out of the darkness and charged his foxhole. He threw aside the useless automatic rifle and grabbed for the nearest weapon—a machete—with which he took a swipe at the nearest attacker. The man reached for his belly too late to hold back the torrent of intestines that cascaded over his feet. Wilson also hacked the other two Japanese to death.

Unable to fully assess the Japanese assault force, LtCol Al Pollock was loath to commit the remainder of his reserve company. He would hold with what he had for as long as he could, using whatever supporting arms Regiment and Division could direct to his aid.

As *Ichiki Butai's* first and major effort subsided in the face of unexpectedly strong and determined opposition, Colonel Ichiki ordered his officers to re-form the troops while his mortars and light 70mm battalion guns softened up the sandspit.

Maj Robert Luckey, the commanding officer of the 1st Special Weapons Battalion, rushed to the 1st Marines command post as soon as the attack developed, to coordinate the 2d Battalion, 1st's supporting arms. Messages from the line soon convinced Luckey that fire from the infantry battalion's four 81mm mortars and the 3d Battalion, 11th Marines' twelve 75mm howitzers was falling on friendly troops. Luckey was about to order corrections when an icy calm Col Clifton Cates told him, "That's an old trick, Bob. Keep right where you are." Cates was right; the Japanese were firing their mortars in such a way as to give the illusion that friendly fire was falling short.

The lull gave LtCol Al Pollock a few free moments to talk to observers on the line and dope out the best use for the uncommitted portions of Company G, which he had held back for forty-five of the longest minutes of his life. Following quick consultations with his company officers, sundry observers, and Regiment, Pollock ordered the bulk of Company G to counterattack the Japanese trying to force his line at the sandspit.

The Company G attack slowly forced the Japanese toward the east bank and seemed assured of success, when several hundred Japanese soldiers waded into the breakers preparatory to attacking Pollock's flank. Marines met the threat with everything they could bring to bear. All twelve of 3d Battalion, 11th's 75mm pack howitzers opened fire, as did a pair of 1st Special Weapons Battalion halftrack-mounted 75mm antitank guns that had been rushed forward. A ghastly toll was exacted before the surviving attackers tumbled over one another in headlong flight for the coconut grove.

The Japanese launched no other significant mass assaults, but hours of intense exchanges and local assaults ensued.

Pvt Andy Brodecki, of Company G, fired his BAR for so long that he had to stop to allow it to cool down. Still, Brodecki was in a good spot and felt he should do something to ward off the Japanese. He asked Marines to his rear to pass forward a weapon, and was amazed when someone handed him a Thompson submachine gun and ten magazines of ammunition. That started an avalanche of weapons and ammunition from the rear to the hands of the men in the best firing positions. Brodecki and his foxhole buddies received dozens of hand grenades, which they lobbed blindly whenever they wanted to stir things up across the way.

The Marines kept the sandspit bathed in flare light, but Japanese snipers in the coconut grove used the light to zero in on their most dangerous adversaries, the 37mm gun crews. One after another, the gunners were felled by the patient snipers.

The 37mm platoon commander, 2dLt Jim McClanahan, took rounds in the arm, leg, and buttocks before becoming convinced that he could no longer take part in the exchange of gunfire. He nevertheless refused evacuation and went to work fixing numerous jammed automatic weapons. His second-in-command, GySgt Nelson Braitmeyer, launched a one-man assault against several Japanese who were setting up a machine gun that would be able to sweep the antitank-gun emplacements. He was shot to death. Pvt Elmer Fairchild, manning one of McClanahan's .50-caliber air-cooled heavy machine guns, had the three middle fingers of his right hand shot away. Nevertheless, and despite shrapnel wounds in both legs, Fairchild wrapped his bleeding right hand in his shirt and carried on.

It was getting light when Pvt Harry Horsman, of Company G, noticed that the 37mm gun adjacent to his fighting hole had gone silent. He and another rifleman ventured over the low sandbag wall and found that no one was tending the weapon. The two riflemen decided to give it a try themselves. While the other Marine loaded, Horsman aimed and fired by trial and error. A corporal from their squad soon joined them, but none of the three really knew what they were doing. When Sgt James Hancock, their squad leader, came over the wall, the riflemen suddenly became a real guncrew, for Hancock had been an artilleryman before the war. The ad hoc guncrew fired the 37mm gun with adequate results until a tremendous explosion engulfed the gun pit and severely wounded Sergeant Hancock.

The first gray streaks of dawn were breaking over the palms on the east bank of Alligator Creek when Pvt George Turzai rose to meet a handful of Japanese who had crossed the sluggish stream. Turzai quickly emptied a fresh five-round magazine and watched five of the Japanese falter and drop, not knowing or caring if he or other Marines had hit them. One of the attackers met Turzai's bayonet lunge with a well-timed parry. Turzai tried to jab the man head-on, but the Japanese soldier pressed his rifle's muzzle against the Marine's neck and squeezed off a round. The stunned Marine left his assailant to others and crawled and ran over mounded dead and wounded men in the hope of finding help. Marines from his platoon passed him in the opposite direction, charging a platoon of Japanese that had forced a penetration. Then Turzai passed out and fell to the ground, where he would be found and cared for hours later.

The sparring continued past sunrise. Neither side was quite able to muster a decisive blow, but, while the Japanese had been spending their limited resources on futile efforts to unseat the Marine line, the Marines had been readying their reserves.

Col Clifton Cates had been planning a counterattack together with LtCol Gerald Thomas, 1st Marine Division operations officer, and LtCol L. B. Cresswell, the commanding officer of the 1st Battalion, 1st. Cresswell's companies had been shaken from their bivouacs in the dead of night and were ready to move at a moment's notice, as soon as the best direction for the attack had been ascertained from conflicting reports.

As the fighting around Hell's Point subsided, a company of the 1st Engineer Battalion arrived to help Pollock's troops dig antitank obstacles and install a minefield across the sandspit, which was gruesomely littered with Japanese corpses. The line had been well wired-in the previous day, and that probably saved Pollock from being overrun. But for desultory sniper fire, the creekfront was fairly quiet. *Ichiki Butai* had drawn back to lick its wounds.

While 2d Battalion, 1st, and its supports retrenched along Alligator Creek and Hell's Point, LtCol L. B. Cresswell's 1st Battalion, 1st, was ordered to envelop what remained of Colonel Ichiki's command. The battalion crossed Alligator Creek at 0700, well south of the coconut grove that sheltered *Ichiki Butai*. While posting most of Company D, the battalion weapons company, along the way to cut possible escape routes, Cresswell pushed his infantry companies toward the enemy. After crossing Alligator Creek well south of the coast, the battalion angled slightly to the west to arrive behind the Japanese and pin them between the beach, Alligator Creek, and itself.

Second Lieutenant John Jachym spent hours listening to his platoon sergeant bitch and moan about the needless firing that had forced the battalion into the attack; the sergeant was dead certain that no more than a half-dozen Japanese stragglers had set off the whole shooting match. Jachym was not so certain.

Pvt Andy Poliny, a Company A BAR-man, was in agony. His ammunition belt, loaded with 240 .30-caliber rounds, had chafed the skin from his hips. When Poliny dropped his pants during one rest break to check on the injury, he found that he was actually bleeding from the chafed spots.

Pvt Adam Sowa, a Company C 60mm mortar gunner, had been spooked by the sudden onset of his battalion's movement in the night, but things seemed to be going as he had been told they would, so he found himself relaxing despite the fact that first combat was drawing closer. Sowa was pleasantly surprised when he emerged from the rain forest and found the beach on his right; Company C had gone completely around the Japanese in secrecy. He was particularly impressed at the way Marine artillery simply shut itself off the moment his battalion opened its attack.

The onset of the battle was sudden, startling. As 1stLt Nick Stevenson's Company C broke out of the forest directly into the coconut grove, a Japanese infantry platoon holding tiny Block Four Village opened on the Marine point. LtCol L. B. Cresswell ordered Stevenson to backpedal a bit to encircle the huts and isolate the Japanese rear guard from the Japanese main body, which was farther to the west. The eager Company C riflemen drew first blood when the Japanese guarding Block Four Village charged head-on. Deployed in a loose skirmish line, they blasted the attackers and turned the survivors toward the beach, where the Japanese ran into the surf. Marines standing on the beach casually squeezed off rounds at the bobbing heads.

Pvt Andy Poliny, of Company A, forgot his bruised and bleeding hips as soon as he stepped out of the rain forest and saw enemy soldiers turn to fight. Marines around Poliny cheered as they closed on the enemy, but their spirits were rapidly subdued when several of them were shot. The action turned positively grim when a dozen Japanese broke from cover to escape along the beach. They were felled, one after another, as Capt Charlie Brush coolly directed the fire of his rear guard.

The Japanese in the coconut grove were contained by 1400.

As Pvt Andy Poliny's squad was about to drag two Japanese corpses from a shallow depression among the palms, an officer ordered the Marines to bayonet the bodies. Two Marines moved to undertake the grisly order, but one of the Japanese rolled over and shot one of them in the face. Poliny leveled his BAR and fired on full automatic. A short time later, two Japanese emerged from the trees carrying a wounded comrade. The company gunnery sergeant bellowed, "Cut 'em down!" The two uninjured Japanese pulled hand grenades from their tunics, but they died in a hail of gunfire before the grenades could be armed.

Though the Marines had clearly won the battle, the Japanese survivors were not about to concede defeat until they had had an opportunity to draw as much American blood as they could. That attitude meant a battle to the death.

The action was transformed into a hunt. Wily Japanese and Marines used every conceivable trick to stalk one another. Bullets whisked through the coconut grove from every direction, tearing up trees and American and Japanese flesh.

Pvt Andy Poliny was caught flatfooted when a machine gun opened fire as his squad crossed a small open space. Poliny flopped to his stomach in front of the nearest palm tree. While his heart pounded against his ribs, splinters rained down on his helmet as the Japanese gunner tried to chew the palm to pieces inches above his head. But the gunner never depressed the barrel of his weapon, and Poliny was released from his cruel prison when other Marines destroyed the machine-gun nest.

The heat of the day took its toll. As exhausted, dehydrated Marines fell under the impact of the stifling heat and humidity, their experienced non-commissioned officers stalked among them, admonishing them to conserve water by merely wetting their lips and mouths rather than gulping from their canteens. Some men obeyed, but most did not.

When a large group of Japanese broke through the Marine skirmish line and headed down the east bank of Alligator Creek, a Company B platoon stood fast and obliterated the opposition. Another group ran headlong into a blocking position built around a machine-gun section and it, too, was ground to dust.

When the encirclement had been completed and tightened, four VMF-223 Wildcats lifted off the muddy runway that was the object of the blood-letting and mounted the first close air support operation of the campaign.

They hit the main body of *Ichiki Butai* in the coconut grove and did a ghastly execution with their machine guns.

As the chaotic afternoon fight wore on, MajGen Archer Vandegrift despaired of completing the annihilation of *Ichiki Butai* by nightfall; he wanted the survivors killed or captured, every one of them. A platoon of six light tanks that had been unable to accompany Lieutenant Colonel Cresswell's battalion in the dark was ordered across the sandspit in the middle of the afternoon. One tank was wrecked by a Japanese who died placing magnetic mines on its steel hull, and two others were damaged in accidents brought on by limited visibility and the broken ground. The last three were ordered by Cresswell to simply reconnoiter the Japanese position in the coconut grove.

When the three surviving light tanks had formed up on the sandspit, the tank platoon leader, 1stLt Leo Case, ordered them to drive forward and direct point-blank fire at the Japanese. This was quite a bit more than Lieutenant Colonel Cresswell had envisioned, but the armored attack flushed numerous survivors into the sights of waiting riflemen.

The battle was pretty much over by 1700 hours, fully sixteen hours after it began. The survivors of the advance detachment of *Ichiki Butai* fought to the death.

Considerable food, equipment, weapons, ammunition, and data was scavenged from the 871 dead and 15 captured members of *Ichiki Butai*. The cost was thirty-four dead and seventy-five wounded Americans.

Late that evening, Col Kiyano Ichiki buried the colors of the 7th Infantry Division's 28th Infantry Regiment in the coconut grove, drew a ceremonial dagger, and disemboweled himself in the soft sand by Lengo Channel.

Chapter 17

U pon hearing of the attack on the Lunga Perimeter—and receiving pleas from MajGen Archer Vandegrift to send help—VAdm Frank Jack Fletcher turned Task Force 61 toward Guadalcanal at 0640, August 21, and raced to reduce the 400-mile separation he had opened between his carriers and Henderson Field since 1400, August 20. Just before 0900, Fletcher told his fellow task force commanders, RAdm Leigh Noyes and RAdm Thomas Kinkaid, that Task Force 61 would be launching strikes if word was received that Japanese warships were in position or moving into position to bombard the airfield. He also asked RAdm Slew McCain to launch PBYs to search as broad an area as possible.

Early on August 21, on a scouting hop that covered the Santa Cruz Islands, Scouting-71's Lt(jg) Charles Mester and Ens Robert Escher discovered a seaplane tender, two destroyers, and several patrol planes in Ndeni Island's Graciosa Bay. Upon receiving no recognition signals from the vessels, and after identifying them as Japanese, the two SBDs initiated a bombing and strafing attack.

When already well into his dive, Mester saw stars on the wings and fuselages of the patrol planes. They were friendly PBYs! He immediately pulled clear, but Ensign Escher did not recognize them as friendly and completed his attack. His 500-pound bomb landed just off the beam of the seaplane tender and he retired under heavy antiaircraft fire from the ships.

The U.S. Navy seaplane tender was the *Mackinac*. Ensign Escher soon learned that his well-placed bomb had wrecked two OS2U observation-scout planes, damaged the tender's gasoline system, and injured several islanders who happened to be nearby in canoes.

At 0807, the 5th Air Attack Force launched twenty-six torpedo-armed Misawa and 4th Air group Bettys and thirteen Tainan Air Group long-range Zeros to locate and attack Task Force 61. The Rabaul-based strike force searched a vast area toward the last known position of the American carriers, but at 1140 the bomber leader decided that the ships were beyond the range of Rabaul-based strikes. VAdm Nishizo Tsukahara agreed; he ordered RAdm Raizo Tanaka to turn the hovering Reinforcement Group toward Guadalcanal again and to land the fifteen hundred ground troops in his care on August 24, east of Henderson Field, where they would join with the *Ichiki Butai* advance echelon.

The Bettys were not armed for an attack against a land target, so they turned back to Rabaul, but Lt Shiro Kawai, the fighter *buntaicho*, made course for Henderson Field to shoot up the Marine base. The thirteen Zeros arrived over the Guadalcanal area at about 1205, and there they were challenged by four Marine Wildcats commanded by Capt John Lucien Smith, the VMF-223 commanding officer. In the brief clash, Smith claimed one Zero destroyed, but no Japanese were in fact downed. The Japanese claimed damaging strikes on two Wildcats, which was true enough. But the damage was actually cause for celebration, for the Wildcat proved itself to be a rugged airplane in the eyes of Marine pilots who either had never seen combat or had been mauled at Midway.

Lt(jg) SMOKEY STOVER
Fighting-5

Diary Entry for August 21, 1942

General Quarters all day as we are rather close in [to Guadalcanal].

Finally got a flight. Combat air patrol from 1015 to 1345. Started out as dull as preceding ones, but three of four vectors had something at their ends. First one was a blank, but on the second we got about 20 miles from the fleet to see a tall column of smoke on the water. Saw one SBD leaving in the direction of the fleet. Found nothing but an oil patch on the water and a little smoke cloud drifting away. Within two minutes later, a wing section and a lot of other debris came up and was very thick around the slick. The wing was very broad with a large red circle (solid) toward the rounded tip and a float close to the other end, where it had broken off. Saw neither bodies nor survivors. Found out later that a *Wasp* SBD had shot down a four-engine Jap patrol plane. He beat us to it by only five minutes, at the most.

On the third vector we found a B-17 streaming along at about 150 knots. After identifying it, we flew up alongside and waved in return to their greetings.

Found an SBD about 15 miles out on our last vector. Apparently he hadn't turned on his IFF [identification, friend or foe transmitter].

LCdr Roy Simpler [of Fighting-5] found a PBY, and Lt Dick Gray's division found a couple of B-17s.

I hear the Japs have made a landing on Guadalcanal to the east of our Marines, who are hollering for help. Don't know if we will go in.

The patrol bomber Smokey Stover's Fighting-5 division barely missed tangling with was a Yokohama Air Group Mavis out of the Shortland Islands advance patrol base. At 1045, just more than thirty minutes before its demise, the crew had spotted and reported the presence of five surface warships heading a bit south of west at 20 knots. While following a reciprocal heading, the Mavis ran into a Scouting-72 SBD piloted by Lt Robert Ware. The Mavis turned for home at full speed, and the SBD gave chase at barely higher speed. It took fifteen minutes for Lieutenant Ware to get within range, and he fired his .50-caliber cowl guns more or less continuously until he was only 50 feet away from the massive amphibian. By then, a fatal fire was burning in the left wing, which fell off at 1,000 feet. When the Mavis fell into the water, it was only 15 miles from Task Force 61.

Ens Foster Blair, who was flying in the same Fighting-5 division as

Lt(jg) Smokey Stover, vented his frustration in his diary: "Wish the damn scouts would tend to their own business." For sure. The Navy SBDs had downed two Mavises in two days, and the fighters had not scored a single victory since August 9.

Late in the morning, Task Force 61's escort was bolstered by the arrival of Task Force 44, which was composed of a Royal Australian Navy heavy cruiser, a Royal Australian Navy light cruiser, and three U.S. Navy destroyers.

At 1214 a Patrol Squadron 23 (Patrol-23) PBY out of Graciosa Bay, Ndeni Island, located four Imperial Navy cruisers and one destroyer near Ontong Java, which is approximately 300 miles northwest of Tulagi. This was VAdm Gunichi Mikawa's Covering Group, a contingent of the Outer Seas Force that had moved into position to screen RAdm Raizo Tanaka's Reinforcement Group.

Fearing that Mikawa's cruisers were on their way to bombard Henderson Field during the night, Admiral Fletcher planned to close on Guadalcanal, also during the night. As surety against a possible enemy surface attack upon his own ships, he sent RAdm Carleton Wright 20 miles ahead with a vanguard of four heavy cruisers and six destroyers drawn from the various escort formations. If no enemy ships were encountered on the way to waters off southern Guadalcanal, Admiral Wright was to return to the main body early in the morning and his ships were to rejoin their respective screen formations.

As Task Force 61 closed on Guadalcanal, the South Pacific Area commander, VAdm Robert Ghormley, ordered Fletcher and RAdm Slew McCain to cover the arrival of two cargo ships at Guadalcanal on August 22. The ships were expected to arrive off Kukum by 0300 and would be vulnerable through most of the day.

Around dusk, Fletcher radioed Ghormley with news of the Mavises downed near Task Force 61 on August 20 and 21. He told the area commander that he was sure the Japanese knew where he was. He also told Ghormley that he could not tarry too long at Guadalcanal, for he would need to refuel his ships on August 24.

♦

Ens FRED KRUEGER
USS Enterprise

Diary Entry for August 21, 1942

It has been a good day. Our scouts have begun to run into enemy units. It looks like something might be brewing. Several single units seem to be starting down this way, and it looks like we will get a crack at them after all. Everything seems to point at their trying to retake Tulagi and Guadalcanal.

On August 21, six pilots from VMF-212—five inexperienced second lieutenants and a warrant officer with years of flight time—boarded an old World War I–era destroyer-transport loaded with aviation gasoline, bombs, and bullets for the Marine fighter and bomber squadrons that had arrived at Henderson Field two days earlier. It was quite a trip. As the unescorted ship neared Guadalcanal in the afternoon and began cutting big circles in the water, several bombers appeared high overhead. The bombers no sooner passed the ship—no one aboard had any idea whose they were—than the lookout yelled, "Torpedoes!" Immediately, the little ship picked up so much speed that it went down by the bows just as a torpedo passed close astern.

It turned out that the destroyer-transport was waiting for the sun to go down so that it could sneak up to Kukum and land the munitions, fuel, and reserve pilots. After sunset, the vessel sailed along the beach for a time and then came to an abrupt stop. The six reserve pilots climbed over the side into rubber boats. All they had with them was a parachute bag apiece, filled with some clothes and their toothbrushes.

The six fresh fighter pilots did not get five yards up the beach before they heard some shooting. Dark forms grabbed the pilots and pushed them down. After the shooting stopped, the pilots were hustled into a vehicle and driven to a pitch-dark coconut grove. Sentries kept stopping the truck until someone finally told the driver he could not go any farther in the dark. The pilots settled in for the night right there, falling asleep on their parachute bags.

In the morning, it was revealed to the VMF-212 aviators that they had come ashore the night after the big battle with Col Ichiki's doomed Imperial Army force. Everyone on the island was still very jumpy, and expecting Japanese raiders to land on the beach—just as the reserve pilots had done!—or that infiltrators were trying to penetrate the coconut grove in order to get at the airplanes lined up near Henderson Field—just like the reserve pilots had done!

The first of the VMF-212 pilots flew their combat missions the next day, August 22, but they did not encounter any Japanese warplanes. They were also bombed for the first time that night when Japanese seaplanes from Rekata Bay randomly dropped bombs along the beach, runway, and coconut grove.

Chapter 18

August 22, 1942, was a busy, exciting day. The U.S. Navy cargo ships *Alhena* and *Fomalhaut* arrived off Guadalcanal well after midnight and proceeded slowly toward the anchorage off Kukum in the company of three destroyers. At about 0300, the destroyers *Blue* and *Henley* forged ahead of the other ships in order to parry any Imperial Navy destroyers that might have slipped into Lengo Channel unnoticed.

At 0355, the *Blue's* radar and sonar both picked up a single ship to starboard at a distance of 5,000 yards. Both American destroyers trained out their guns and torpedo tubes and closed on the radar contact. At 0359, with radar and sonar readings placing the target at a range of 3,200 yards, the *Blue* was struck in the stern by a torpedo that killed nine crewmen and wounded twenty-one. The Japanese destroyer was the *Kawakaze*, and she got clean away.

At dawn, the *Henley* passed a line to the severely damaged *Blue* and started towing her toward safety. But it was very slow going and would require nearly two days to reach Tulagi Harbor.

For many other U.S. Navy officers and crewmen, August 22 began with an inspirational message from Adm Chester Nimitz, commander-in-chief of the U.S. Pacific Fleet, which was published in the *Saratoga's* Plan of the Day: "Our prime objective is enemy ships. Surely we will have losses, but we will also destroy ships and be that much nearer the successful conclusion of the war."

For Task Force 61, which was approaching southern Guadalcanal from the direction of San Cristobal, a morning search undertaken by seven pairs of *Saratoga* Air Group SBDs was launched at 0600. The search areas were to the west and north of the carriers, 200 miles in the direction from which Japanese surface forces would most likely approach Guadalcanal.

None of the Imperial Navy battle forces were located, but a pair of searchers did find the *Kawakaze* about 75 miles north of Tulagi, on her way to rejoin VAdm Gunichi Mikawa's Outer Seas Force. Both SBDs attacked the lone destroyer, but neither bomb was effective.

As the negative search was under way, the carriers turned southeast at 15 knots. It was Admiral Fletcher's plan to continue on this course until noon, then turn east so as to reach the eastern side of Malaita by sunset. This would put his carrier air groups in position to strike the Japanese forces heading toward Guadalcanal from Truk.

The first big excitement of the day began when a bogey was picked up on the *Enterprise's* search radar at 1048. Immediately, the carrier's FDO vectored out a Fighting-6 Wildcat division led by Ens Red Brooks, a highly skilled former enlisted pilot. No one in Brooks's division received the message, however, because they were flying through a heavy rain squall at that moment.

The FDO next ordered Mach Don Runyon's Fighting-6 division to investigate the bogey, but neither Runyon nor his three wingmen received this message.

Finally, the FDO was able to get through to Lt Scoop Vorse's Fighting-6 division, which proceeded at 1055 on vector 270 degrees at 10,000 feet. After Vorse had flown about 15 miles, the vector was changed to 200 degrees at 8,000 feet. Moments later, the course was again corrected to 180 degrees.

Lt(jg) Slim Russell, who was monitoring the *Enterprise* fighter-frequency transmissions in the Scouting-3 ready room aboard the *Saratoga*, heard one of the fighter pilots report, "Looks like a big combination." And then, "It's a Jap Kawanishi four-engine scout P-boat." And then, "I'm going after him."

The snooper was the same Shortlands-based 14th Air Group Mavis that had located a fleet carrier south of San Cristobal on August 20. Then, the airplane had never even been noticed by U.S. Navy lookouts or radar. But now the *Enterprise's* radar had a firm fix and, though the Mavis was only 15 miles from the carriers, the crew was unable to see it because of poor visibility.

Lieutenant Vorse and his wingman, Ens Dix Loesch, climbed to deliver an overhead attack while Lt(jg) Larry Grimmell and Ens Francis Register proceeded to deliver a below-opposite attack.

Vorse executed his overhead run at 1105. He had fired only twenty-five rounds from each of his six .50-caliber wing guns when the flimsy Mavis burst into flames. He immediately pulled clear. Ensign Loesch was only just preparing to open fire when the big patrol bomber erupted in flames, so he never completed the act.

CAP Wilhelm Esders, of Torpedo-3, was returning to the task force from a morning patrol mission when he glanced to the north and saw the fighters chasing the large seaplane. Within moments, the seaplane disintegrated.

The fire started in the fuselage and quickly spread to the midwing section. A moment later, the giant parasol wings collapsed upward, and the fuselage and wings fell separately into the sea.

CAP Esders saw parts of the fuselage, wings, engines, the contents of the fuselage, and what looked like people fall from 8,000 or 9,000 feet. Esders did not see any parachutes blossom, but someone else reported seeing one man jump from the burning plane without a parachute.

Lt(jg) Slim Russell and the other Scouting-3 pilots heard Vorse's report: "Red Base [*Enterprise*] from Red-5 [Vorse]. Enemy plane shot down in flames." The scout-bomber pilots cheered and commented that the experimental radar fitted to all the American carriers was proving to be a real lifesaver.

Another Mavis out of the Shortlands briefly tracked the *Alhena* and *Fomalhaut* as they raced from the Guadalcanal area to the south, but no

Japanese searcher actually reported the presence of Task Force 61. When the downed Mavis was declared missing that night, however, the Japanese deduced that it had been destroyed by carrier fighters. So the Japanese got a good fix on Task Force 61 after all, though there was no way for them to know how many carriers were sailing in which direction.

Just as a Torpedo-8 TBF piloted by Ens J. H. Cook was nearing the *Saratoga's* bow while taking off for a stint on inner air patrol, it veered off the left side of the deck, left wing down, and plunged into the water. One crewman and a passenger got out, but Ensign Cook and his bombardier were lost when the torpedo bomber sank.

During the morning, Cdr Don Felt, the *Saratoga* Air Group commanding officer, flew to Henderson Field to assess the facilities in the event large numbers of carrier aircraft needed to land and refuel there. This was the first inkling that Henderson Field had some real strategic importance, for proper use of the base could double or even triple the range of the carrier air groups.

As Commander Felt was completing his business with Marine aviation officers, Japanese Bettys struck the field from 22,000 feet. Felt later reported to his pilots that he saw one of the Bettys trailing smoke from a 90mm antiaircraft hit as it left the area. Four Marine Wildcats were shot up trying to get to the Bettys through the Zero escort, but no Marine pilot was injured. One of the precious Marine Wildcats cracked up on landing, however. A Marine lieutenant was credited with downing a bomber, but no Japanese airplanes were lost over Guadalcanal this day.

Commander Felt's big news to the *Saratoga* Air Group troops was that a thousand-man Japanese infantry force had been defeated in a day-long battle on August 21. Felt heard that 769 Japanese bodies were piled up on the beach and along the stream guarding the eastern flank of the Lunga Perimeter.

Far to the north, 19th Heavy Bombardment Group B-17s attacked Lakunai and Vunakanau airdromes with little effect.

And at Guadalcanal, five U.S. Army Air Forces fighters arrived at

Henderson Field from Espiritu Santo. These were P-400s, an export version of the obsolescent Bell P-39 Airacobra fighter, and they belonged to the 67th Fighter Squadron, which had been serving in the French New Hebrides since March. The rest of the 67th Fighter Squadron was due to fly up to Guadalcanal as soon as the facility could handle them.

Japanese fleet units continued to move into position north of Guadalcanal. RAdm Raizo Tanaka's slow Reinforcement Group, escorted by four Outer Seas Force cruisers and three destroyers, zigzagged toward Guadalcanal at 9 knots. At noon, Tanaka was 350 miles north of Guadalcanal. He was intent upon landing the ground troops during the night of August 24.

By noon powerful Imperial Navy surface forces were guarding Tanaka's progress from rather close range. The Support Force—a battleship and three destroyers—had split up to take stations only a short distance off both of Tanaka's flanks; the main body of VAdm Nobutake Kondo's Advance Force— four heavy cruisers, two light cruisers, a light seaplane carrier, and six destroyers—was only 120 miles to the northwest; and VAdm Chuichi Nagumo's Carrier Striking Force was 200 miles to the northeast.

During the course of the day, all the warships under Kondo and Nagumo refueled at sea, and two cruisers and a destroyer from Mikawa's Outer Seas Force sailed at high speed to refuel at the Shortland Islands.

From his headquarters in Rabaul, VAdm Nishizo Tsukahara asked Adm Isoroku Yamamoto to release Nagumo's Carrier Striking Force to attack Henderson Field the next day and to provide an air patrol over Taivu Point on August 24, as Tanaka was putting troops ashore there. Tanaka supported Tsukahara's request and even expanded it by requesting that carrier aircraft cover his final approach on Guadalcanal. But Yamamoto was quite clear in his mind as to the purpose of the carriers; he would risk the *Shokaku* and *Zuikaku* air groups only in an attack against the American carriers. And only if it was demonstrated that the American carriers had withdrawn would Yamamoto authorize a strike against Henderson Field by the carrier air groups.

At 1745, August 22, the heavy cruiser *Portland,* on the starboard hand of the *Enterprise's* Task Force 16, reported that a torpedo was passing her from port to starboard. The torpedo was first seen broaching about 1,700 yards off the *Portland's* starboard beam at 240 degrees. At the same time, destroyers serving with the *Wasp's* Task Force 18 reported a sonar contact and dropped depth charges. An investigation by ships of Task Force 16 and Task Force 18 failed to produce any hard submarine targets, but it was felt that Japanese submarines were most certainly shadowing the American carriers.

At 1930, Fletcher turned Task Force 61 northwest. Malaita lay to port and open waters lay ahead. If there were Japanese carriers out there, Fletcher was ready for them. For once, Pacific Fleet Intelligence was silent on the subject of Imperial Navy carriers. The Japanese had been phasing in a new set of codes for several weeks, and the penetration of the codes was going slowly. Among the units that could not be pinpointed were the fleet carriers. As far as Pacific Fleet Intelligence could tell, the *Shokaku* and *Zuikaku* were still at the Kure Naval Base. Fletcher had no inkling that Fleet Intelligence was having trouble reading Japanese messages, but his gut told him anyway that enemy carriers were close at hand, and he was acting accordingly.

There were other complications. Fuel was a constant source of concern to Fletcher. Shortly after turning north at 1930, the task force commander sent a message to VAdm Robert Ghormley to say that he needed to fuel the carriers and their escorts on August 25, and would Ghormley please dispatch all three of the fleet oilers hovering off Efate.

No sooner had Fletcher's message gone out than a message—not a response—arrived from Ghormley. It appeared, Ghormley told Fletcher, that the Japanese might attack Guadalcanal at any time between August 23 and August 26. Pacific Fleet Intelligence had determined from deciphered messages that two battleships, ten heavy cruisers, five light cruisers, and many destroyers and submarines were moving into position in the region. Further, Ghormley's sources reckoned that eighty to one hundred bombers and more than sixty fighters were based at Rabaul. Pacific Fleet had made no mention of enemy carriers, but Ghormley stated that the presence of carriers was "possible but not confirmed." He also told Fletcher that

Pacific Fleet Intelligence did not feel that the Japanese had spotted Task Force 61 at all during the past ten days.

Given all the factors, Ghormley's message to Fletcher concluded with a recommendation that one carrier at a time be released to refuel from two fleet oilers Ghormley would dispatch from Efate in the morning.

The information in Ghormley's message was well intentioned and accurate as far as any American outside Task Force 61 knew, but it ended up doing Fletcher and Fletcher's men far more harm than good.

Chapter 19

Task Force 61 sailed northeast along Malaita's coast through the night of August 22–23. By dawn, the American carriers had achieved an excellent position from which aircraft could attack the enemy fleet components advancing on Guadalcanal to the west. During the night, VAdm Frank Jack Fletcher contacted RAdm Leigh Noyes to say that the *Wasp* task force would be released to sail south and refuel if no firm contacts were made with the enemy forces.

Before dawn the *Enterprise* Air Group, which had been on attack standby throughout August 23, launched the day's first combat air patrol. The *Saratoga* Air Group was placed on strike standby, and the *Wasp* Air Group was left to rest while awaiting word on its ship's proposed refueling run.

At 0555 the *Enterprise* launched twelve search teams composed of nine TBFs and fifteen SBDs to reconnoiter sectors from northeast to northwest at a distance of 180 miles. Next two Torpedo-8 TBFs were launched from the *Saratoga* with orders to land at Henderson Field. Riding as a passenger in one TBF—the other was an escort—was Cdr Butch Schindler, Admiral Fletcher's staff gunnery officer. He was to oversee the preparation of the land base to service a carrier air group if the need came to pass. (This was the strategic flexibility that made Henderson Field so vital; its being there increased the attack range of the Task Force 61 carrier air groups by a substantial margin.)

At 0725 Lt Turner Caldwell, the Scouting-5 commander, sighted a surfaced submarine as it bent on all speed on a due southerly course. Lieutenant Caldwell dropped his SBD's 500-pound General Purpose bomb close aboard the submarine, but he was unable to observe any results before the Japanese boat dived.

At 0815, in a nearby search sector, the Scouting-5 flight officer, Lt Birney Strong, and his wingman, Ens John Richey, surprised a second submarine running at full speed on the surface on a course a bit west of south. Once again, the American 500-pound General Purpose bombs caused no observable damage. Though this Japanese submarine also crash-dived, it surfaced twice and was strafed both times by Strong and Richey.

The Japanese battle groups known to be in the area were beyond range or in other sectors. Nevertheless, the first brush occurred at 0950 on August 23, shortly after the last *Enterprise* search team reported negative results. A Patrol-23 PBY Catalina patrol bomber based at Ndeni and piloted by Lt Leo Riester located RAdm Raizo Tanaka's transports and their Outer Seas Force escorts heading toward Guadalcanal. The sighting was reported to the tender *Mackinac,* at Graciosa Bay, and relayed to Fletcher, aboard the *Saratoga,* at 1012. Fletcher immediately ordered the *Saratoga's* skipper, Capt Dewitt Ramsey, to prepare Cdr Don Felt's *Saratoga* Air Group to strike Tanaka's troop-laden transports or, better yet, enemy carriers, if they turned up while there was still time to strike.

Lookouts aboard ships in Tanaka's Reinforcement Group and the Outer Seas Force escort first noted the presence of Lieutenant Reister's PBY at 0930, twenty minutes before Reister's first report. True to a doctrine he had helped develop, Tanaka maintained course and speed—a little west of south at 17 knots—until Reister had to return to base. As soon as the PBY was beyond visual range, at about 1040, the entire force turned a little north of east at the order of VAdm Gunichi Mikawa, who was aboard the heavy cruiser *Chokai,* in Tanaka's screen. The transports were still 300 miles from Guadalcanal, but a little foot dragging would not upset the schedule, and the turn would make the group of transports hard to find if a carrier strike force sought it out along its last known course from its last known position.

The Japanese morning searches were composed of Bettys launched from Rabaul and Mavises launched from the Shortlands. One Betty failed to return from the mission, but nothing was inferred from the loss because weather in the region was stormy. By the time all the other searchers turned for home, the Japanese had no idea where Task Force 61 was.

Farthest to the north were VAdm Nobutake Kondo's powerful Advance Force of surface warships and, only 60 miles away, VAdm Chuichi Nagumo's Carrier Striking Force. Both of these flotillas had been forging south at high speed with the intention of attacking the U.S. Navy carrier battle force on August 23 or 24—as soon as VAdm Nishizo Tsukahara's Base Air Force Bettys or Mavises located the Americans. In the meantime, it was imperative that the carriers remain out of sight and beyond the range of Allied search planes.

But time was working against the desire to cloak the presence of all or some of the Japanese carriers. The transports were scheduled to arrive off Guadalcanal during the night of August 24, and Adm Isoroku Yamamoto had made it clear that he wanted the Lunga airfield shut down by then. If the 5th Air Attack Force could not accomplish the mission, then carrier aircraft would have to. Yamamoto had also stipulated, however, that the *Shokaku* and *Zuikaku* air groups were not to get drawn into attacking land targets so long as there were American carriers to attack. This left only the small *Ryujo* Air Group, with its nine Nakajima B5N Kates and 24 Zeros.

A scheduled 5th Air Attack Force bombing attack against Henderson Field was scrubbed because of bad weather. And so it became inevitable that the *Ryujo* Air Group would be sent against Henderson Field on August 24, as soon as the little carrier and her escorts could sail within range.

Admiral Fletcher had planned to turn southeast during the late morning or early afternoon, but he altered the plan at 1140, when he received a sighting report from a V Bomber Command B-17 that had overflown Faisi in the Shortland Islands. According to the sighting report, there were two destroyers and two transports in the harbor. This was incorrect; there were only minesweepers and destroyers from Mikawa's Outer Seas Force, and they were only refueling. But to Fletcher it seemed that the Japanese were mounting a two-pronged amphibious assault against the Lunga Perimeter—exactly what every American at every level had been fearing since August 10.

First, at 1203, Fletcher conversed by blinker with RAdm Leigh Noyes, his air commander, about continuing on course to the northwest to come within striking range of Tanaka's transports. Noyes agreed that this was feasible. And then RAdm Thomas Kinkaid, the Task Force 16 commander, weighed in with a suggestion that he forge ahead with the *Enterprise* in order to deliver an attack as soon as possible. Fletcher demurred; the *Saratoga* Air Group was fresh, and he wanted the *Enterprise* Air Group to mount an afternoon search.

At 1440, thirty-one *Saratoga* Air Group SBDs and six TBFs under Cdr Don Felt headed out to locate and attack an enemy force Felt had been told was comprised of two cruisers, three destroyers, and four transports. The Japanese reportedly were then 275 miles from Task Force 61, to the north-west. Felt was also ordered to return to Guadalcanal after the attack— before sunset if possible—and to rendezvous with the *Saratoga* east of Malaita in the morning.

The estimated point of contact Commander Felt was given had been deduced from the assumption that Tanaka would hold to the course and speed he was maintaining at the time of Lieutenant Riester's PBY contact. However, Felt's initial doubts in that regard grew as his air group formed up and headed north.

Shortly after the *Saratoga* strikers left Task Force 61, the *Enterprise* launched searchers toward other quadrants. Fletcher was certain that there were Japanese carriers in the area, and he hoped that the *Enterprise* searchers would find some in time for him to redirect Don Felt's strike force against them.

The *Enterprise's* afternoon search turned up no enemy carriers or sur-face warships, but at 1530 Ens Glenn Estes and Ens Elmer Maul, both of Scouting-5, sighted and attacked a surfaced Japanese submarine as it raced on a course a bit east of south. Both airmen claimed near misses with their 500-pound General Purpose bombs, and both reported sighting a large oil slick after the submarine had disappeared from view. Though Estes and

Maul were credited with damaging the enemy boat, Japanese records do not support the claim.

The repeated sightings of enemy submarines—three for the day—were troubling, but not particularly alarming. The American carriers had been patrolling the same area for two full weeks, so it was expected that the Japanese had sent submarines to shadow or attack the American fleet.

Even as the *Saratoga* strike group was still forming up over the carriers, VAdm Robert Ghormley was getting ready to defend Guadalcanal and Tulagi. At 1431 a message from Ghormley ordered Fletcher to be ready to dispatch a surface force to deal with the Japanese transports right off Guadalcanal.

Closer to the center of the nascent maelstrom, MajGen Archer Vandegrift called in his aircraft commanders and ordered every available warplane to be launched as soon as possible against Tanaka's oncoming transports. With VMSB-232's Maj Dick Mangrum in command, Henderson Field launched nine VMSB-232 SBDs, one of the visiting Torpedo-8 TBFs, and twelve VMF-223 Wildcats. This force found no targets, only bad weather, and it returned safely to Henderson Field near dusk.

The weather facing the *Saratoga* strike force was dreadful. Visibility was poor because of rain showers and heavy cloud cover. Dead ahead of the strike force was a heavy weather front. To cope with it, Cdr Don Felt spread the strikers into a line of three-plane sections at a mere 100 feet over the sea and set their course. They flew into the weather front one hour after launch, section leaders on instruments, wingmen tucked in tight on their leaders. Because of the weather, it was difficult to maintain the integrity of the line of planes.

For Lt Paul Holmberg, a 1939 Naval Academy graduate and a relatively inexperienced member of Bombing-3, staying in formation and avoiding flying into the ocean while trying to keep track of his position and navigation was most difficult. Like many of his comrades, Holmberg flew with his cockpit open in order to see the Dauntless on which he was flying formation. It was flown by LCdr DeWitt Shumway, the Bombing-3 commander. Rain entered the open cockpit and added considerably to Holmberg's discomfort.

Even the experienced pilots were having trouble. Lt Syd Bottomley, a 1937 Naval Academy graduate, now the Bombing-3 executive officer, remarked to his rearseatman about what a nerve-wracking flight it had turned out to be, flying in formation with so many planes, in and out of showers, beneath low clouds, with poor visibility.

The pilots frequently lost sight of one another.

When the *Saratoga* strike group flew out of the weather an hour after flying into it, Commander Felt noted with considerable satisfaction and relief that everybody was still in line.

The search continued for about 275 miles with no contact—because the Japanese transports had reversed course. Finally, Commander Felt passed the word by voice radio: "Return to base," which meant Henderson Field. But the strike force still faced a flight of about 250 miles through bad weather in decreasing afternoon light. At length, the American warplanes broke out of the bad weather in three-quarters moonlight as they were making landfall on Malaita Island. When the Navy carrier bombers finally arrived over Henderson Field it was fully dark, and the pilots had to turn on their running lights. The duration of the flight was four hours, twenty minutes.

The Marine and Navy air base units servicing Henderson Field lined up several captured Japanese trucks along the edge of the runway and turned on the headlights so the *Saratoga* pilots could see where the runway was. As Bombing-3 was coming in to land, Lt Syd Bottomley's rearseatman, AMM1 David Johnson, told Bottomley that he could see fireflies in the mahogany trees to port. Lt(jg) Slim Russell, of Scouting-3, immediately understood that he was being fired on by machine guns in the trees. But Russell was strangely unconcerned. Rather, he thought about how pretty all those tracers were as they rose toward his SBD. LCdr Bullet Lou Kirn, the Scouting-3 commander, felt that the gunfire might have been the result of the tension and uncertainty that prevailed at Henderson Field—that the antiaircraft fire was from *friendly* guns. Fortunately, no damage was done, although several Navy pilots landed in the wrong direction—ostensibly to fool the gunners.

In view of the previous limited experience of a majority of the pilots under such trying conditions, Don Felt believed that his *Saratoga* Air Group had accomplished some marvelous flying. More than ever, he had complete faith in the ability of his group's experienced section leaders under extremely difficult instrument-flying conditions, and in the apparent fine discipline of all his subordinates.

On the evening of August 23, about the time the *Saratoga* strike group was landing at Henderson Field, a little drama that had begun off Guadalcanal's northern coast in the wee hours of August 22 was reaching a tragic end. The U.S. Navy destroyer *Blue* had been severely damaged by a Japanese destroyer-launched torpedo and had been under tow for more than thirty-six hours toward the safe haven offered by Tulagi Harbor. It had been slow going because the *Blue's* stern had been blown up and bent in such a way as to all but completely impede progress, but the ship was well within range of Tulagi when night fell on August 23. By then, however, the commanding officer of the destroyer division to which the *Blue* was assigned lost his nerve. He had heard that Japanese warships were about to sail unchallenged into Lengo Channel, and he feared that the *Blue* might be seized as a prize of war or sunk with crewmen aboard. So he requested permission from his superior, RAdm Richmond Kelly Turner, to scuttle the ship, and Turner assented. And so it was done. The destroyer *Henley*, which had been laboring to save the *Blue*, became her executioner. All hands were transferred to safety, and then the *Blue* was scuttled.

After launching the *Saratoga* strike force, Task Force 61 continued to sail northwest until 1800. Admiral Fletcher spent the greater part of the afternoon trying to divine the presence of enemy carriers. None could be found by his own searchers, nor by Ndeni-based PBYs. And Pacific Fleet Intelligence insisted that there were no enemy carriers south of Truk. Failing to understand how this could be so, given what was known about all previous Japanese operations, Fletcher nevertheless had to come to grips with his task force's worsening fuel situation. In the end, as the carriers turned away from their northwesterly course to get into position to recover the *Saratoga* strikers in the morning, Fletcher made his decision. At 1823 he ordered RAdm Leigh Noyes to sail with the *Wasp* and her escorts to a rendezvous with the oilers north of Espiritu Santo. At all costs, Noyes was to take only one day and then return in haste, but this all meant that the

Wasp Air Group would be beyond supporting range of the *Enterprise* and *Saratoga* air groups for at least two days. That left Task Force 61 with 153 aircraft—28 TBFs, 68 SBDs, and 57 F4Fs. VAdm Chuichi Nagumo's Carrier Striking Force had at its disposal 173 operational aircraft—45 Kates, 54 Vals, and 74 Zeros.

On the plus side of the *official* ledger, though Fletcher's instincts told him otherwise, search planes and Fleet Intelligence said that Task Force 61 and the two Marine squadrons at Henderson Field faced only two heavy cruisers, five destroyers, and four transports in two groups to the north and northwest of Guadalcanal, and only the land-based 5th Air Attack Force Bettys and Zeros at Rabaul.

After Noyes split off with the *Wasp* and her escorts (including the two Royal Australian Navy cruisers and their three American escort destroyers), what remained of Task Force 61 sailed east by south until 2200, then turned northeast until 0200, August 24, when the carriers and their escorts turned·due west. Aware that he had spent August 23 in an ideal position from which to launch a flank attack on any Japanese forces approaching Guadalcanal from the direction of Truk, Fletcher chose to tempt Fate by skirting it during the night and occupying it again, more or less, on August 24.

Admirals Nagumo and Kondo were certain that their respective battle forces had escaped detection through the day. During the evening, so as to keep pace with the Reinforcement Group, Nagumo turned north to kill time and also to remain beyond the reach of American searchers. Kondo was obliged to do the same in order to keep station on Nagumo. Both battle-force commanders planned to turn again at 0700 and dash south to cover the landing operation at Guadalcanal, which the admirals hoped would be contested by the American carriers.

When Admiral Tsukahara checked in with Admiral Tanaka to be sure the transports were on schedule, Tanaka noted that he had lost time and miles in his turn to the north to throw off American search and strike aircraft. He felt that he could not get to Guadalcanal on time, and Tsukahara concurred. The landing at Taivu Point was put off until the night of August 25.

At 2200 Adm Isoroku Yamamoto transmitted what he believed would be his final directive for the upcoming battle. In addition to as powerful an attack against Henderson Field as the 5th Air Attack Force and the *Ryujo* Air Group could muster, the surface and carrier forces under Kondo and Nagumo were to close on the American-held enclave. If morning searches failed to locate the American carriers, Kondo's and Nagumo's battle forces were to take out Henderson Field and ensure the safe passage of Tanaka's Reinforcement Group. If the American carriers were found, Kondo and Nagumo were to attack and destroy them. In the long run, Yamamoto believed, the carriers were more important. Henderson Field wasn't going anywhere; it could be ground to dust at leisure once the carriers had been put out of action.

At 0145, at Admiral Nagumo's order, the *Ryujo* was formally detached from the main carrier force and sent south to lead all the Imperial Navy fleet formations. Her escort consisted of the heavy cruiser *Tone* and the fleet destroyers *Amatsukaze* and *Tokitsukaze*. The small Detached Force, as it was named, was commanded by RAdm Chuichi Hara, who had commanded a squadron of small carriers until the Combined Fleet carrier force had been reorganized and downsized in the wake of the disastrous Battle of Midway.

Once on the ground at Henderson Field, after securing their airplanes, Lt(jg) Slim Russell and several other Scouting-3 pilots were led through a coconut grove to a tent about a mile from the runway. There Russell and the others were given a mess kit apiece piled high with stew, hardtack, peas, and pears. Though the Navy pilots were used to dining off china and being served by mess stewards aboard ship, they were all extremely glad to get at the Marines' rough but hearty fare. After eating cold Marine K-rations, Lt Syd Bottomley was able to sample a form of boilermaker consisting of a small bottle of California Lejon brandy and captured Japanese Asahi beer.

LCdr Bullet Lou Kirn, the Scouting-3 commander, was less fortunate than many of his young pilots. After seeing to the dispersal of his squadron's Dauntlesses, which had to be refueled, Kirn was unable to break for dinner until long after the Marine air group's messing facilities had closed down. All he received was some Japanese hardtack. In fact, the refueling operation went so slowly that the *Saratoga* strike aircraft could not get home before 1100, three hours after Fletcher hoped to have them back aboard.

Later that evening, Lt(jg) Slim Russell's group listened with rapt attention as their Marine hosts told stories about the August 7 landings. According to the storytellers, the Japanese had not realized that American troops were landing. When the Japanese had run for the bush just ahead of the advancing Marines, they had left their radios on, food on the tables, and fires in the stoves. Though the Marines had quickly taken control of the area around the air base, they were still having problems rounding up Japanese snipers. Russell and his fellow aviators also heard details of the heavy battle that had raged on the east flank of the Marines' Lunga Perimeter only two nights earlier.

It started raining late in the evening, but all the *Saratoga* pilots and aircrewmen had to sleep in or beside their planes in case the Japanese mounted an early-morning attack. Slim Russell could not get to sleep, so he sat around trading stories with Marines. He was surprised to learn that his countrymen slept in foxholes, which looked to Russell like graves, with only one blanket over them, a fern under them, and their clothing and helmets on.

Before the night was over, Russell learned why the Marines settled for such stark sleeping conditions: A Japanese destroyer or submarine (it was, in fact, the destroyer *Kagero)* closed on the beach at about 0200, August 24, and fired about fifteen 5-inch rounds in the direction of the parked *Saratoga* TBFs and SBDs. The shelling was close, but it did no damage. After recovering from his initial shock, Russell thought it was kind of fun to listen to the shells whistling through the air. But he slept very little the rest of the night.

The *Saratoga* Air Group was held at readiness to launch a morning strike against the Japanese transports it had missed the previous afternoon. While Marine SBDs searched northward along New Georgia Sound, between the double chain of the Solomon Islands (soon to be nicknamed The Slot), Marine groundcrewmen finished the laborious task of refueling thirty-nine Navy carrier bombers from 55-gallon fuel drums. Each Dauntless required the contents of five fuel drums, all of which had to be pumped by hand. Marine mechanics and Navy rearseatmen tinkered with engines and other systems in the waiting airplanes.

Lt(jg) Slim Russell and his buddies got up at 0700 and went down to the beach to look at dead Japanese, not yet buried though the big battle had taken place days earlier. When the pilots had seen their fill of decomposing battle-ravaged corpses, they stopped in at the base quartermaster's office, where a Marine captain gave Russell a Japanese bolt-action rifle, a new Japanese gasmask, and some chopsticks. Later, a Marine sergeant gave Russell a Japanese bayonet to fit the rifle, which was already very rusty and still full of sand. The rifle's former owner was reputed to have been bayoneted by a Marine. When Russell pulled back the rifle's bolt, he found an expended cartridge in the chamber.

While awaiting orders, Lt Syd Bottomley and several other Bombing-3 pilots were given a tour by their Marine hosts, including a look at the prisoner-of-war stockade. There, for the first time, Bottomley and the other carrier pilots saw their enemies at close range. They also visited the August 21 battlefield. Unlike many of the younger pilots, Bottomley thought "it was a sickening sight, with Japanese bodies all over the place, putrefying in the heat."

The Marine dawn air search turned up no sign of any Japanese ships. The *Saratoga* Air Group was released to return to the ship, which was nearly two hours away. To reciprocate for the hospitality and fuel it had received at Henderson Field, the Navy crews left behind all the bombs they had so circuitously lugged from the *Saratoga*.

It turned out that one of the Bombing-3 SBDs had not been fueled during the night. Its pilot, Lt(jg) Robert Elder, discovered this condition minutes after joining the formation. He could not go on, so a second Bombing-3 Dauntless was detailed to escort him back to Guadalcanal. The two were to fly to the *Saratoga* as soon as the Marines had corrected the fueling error.

Part IV

The Battle of the Eastern Solomons
August 24, 1942

Chapter 20

The Japanese and American carrier task forces were approaching to within range of one another. A clash that seemed likely to VAdm Frank Jack Fletcher seemed a certainty to VAdm Chuichi Nagumo. And so the search was on.

At 0600 Nagumo's Carrier Striking Force ended its night march to the north and turned southeast, into the wind, so the *Shokaku* and *Zuikaku* could launch the first search patrols of the day. VAdm Nobutake Kondo's Advance Force, which was 120 miles to the southeast, also turned southeast, to remain in position to guard Nagumo's eastern flank.

Beginning at 0615, the two fleet carriers launched a total of nineteen Kates on courses to the east, ranging from due north to a bit west of south and out to a distance of 250 miles. The search was considered precautionary; no one really expected to locate the American carriers, because the Japanese carriers had sailed out of range during the night and it was doubtful the Americans had dared or been able to close on them.

As soon as the searchers were away, Admiral Nagumo ordered that three strike forces comprised of all the Val dive-bombers, all the remaining Kate torpedo bombers, and many of the Zero fighters be readied for launch on short notice. Nagumo sincerely anticipated a clash with American carriers at some point during the day, so all the Japanese carrier bombers were armed accordingly. Little thought was given to an attack against Henderson Field by the *Shokaku* and *Zuikaku* air groups.

The Base Air Force advance patrol detachment in the Shortland Islands launched two Yokohama Air Group Mavises, a Yokohama Air Group Emily, and a 14th Air Group Emily at 0625. These long-range patrol bombers were vectored on courses covering a mere 10-degree arc between 092 and 122 degrees out to a range of 700 miles. The Rabaul-based Misawa Air Group launched four Betty searchers, also at 0625, on courses covering an arc from 092 to 132 degrees to a distance of 800 miles. The Base Air Force intelligence staff was absolutely certain that the American carriers would turn up east of Malaita, and they were putting all their eggs in that basket. It would be nearly noon, however, before any of the Base Air Force long-range searchers could reach the sectors in which the American carriers were most likely to be found.

The Americans were far less sure of their previous information. The last word from Pacific Fleet Intelligence was that there were no Japanese carriers within thousands of miles of the Solomon Islands, but VAdm Frank Jack Fletcher felt there were. Unfortunately, Fletcher could not go very far afield to locate or attack them; his two-carrier battle force was tethered to Henderson Field, whose air component was not yet strong enough to defend itself or its base. At dawn, after a night of sailing, Task Force 61 was still only about 170 miles east of Tulagi.

Fletcher had hoped to have Cdr Don Felt's *Saratoga* Air Group strike force back aboard by 0830, but news from Henderson Field during the wee hours spoke of a delay until around 1100. This greatly reduced Fletcher's options, for only a few bombers remained aboard his flagship, and the *Enterprise* Air Group had to mount search missions, guard its own ship, and keep something back in the way of a strike force if one was needed.

The pressure on the carrier searchers could be alleviated somewhat by Aircraft, South Pacific Force (AirSoPac) long-range PBYs based at Ndeni and B-17s based in the New Hebrides. These could cover several vital sectors to the northwest—in the direction of the last-reported sighting of RAdm Raizo Tanaka's Reinforcement Group. In response to a request to

RAdm Slew McCain from Fletcher, the advance reconnaissance detach-ment at Graciosa Bay, Ndeni, dispatched six Patrol-23 PBYs to cover sec-tors from 306 to 348 degrees to a distance of 650 miles.

Between 0555 and 0630, twenty *Enterprise* Air Group SBDs were launched in pairs to cover sectors from northwest to due east to a distance of 200 miles. Three more precious SBDs were launched from the *Enterprise* for the inner air patrol, and Wildcats from both carriers were launched on the day's first combat air patrol.

And then both sides settled back to see what their searchers were able to turn up.

The 5th Air Attack Force got away the first strike mission of the day mounted by either side. A force composed of twenty-four Bettys escorted by fourteen Tainan Air Group Zeros was dispatched against Henderson Field at 0830.

The twenty *Enterprise* searchers were destined to find no Imperial Navy warships. The last of them reported a negative search at 0947, and all of them were back aboard by 1010. By then, Task Force 61 was abuzz with news from a PBY sighting report. At 0935 the *Enterprise* radio department intercepted a message to the seaplane tender *Mackinac*, at Graciosa Bay, from the Patrol-23 PBY flown by Ens Gale Burkey, which was searching the sector between 320 and 327 degrees. According to the report, Burkey's crew had sighted a carrier, two cruisers, and four destroyers sailing due south at 04°40' south longitude, 161°15' east latitude. The *Enterprise* radiomen did not pick up Burkey's call sign, but the report was detailed enough for an accurate fix. RAdm Thomas Kinkaid personally passed the news along to Admiral Fletcher by voice radio at 0945.

An analysis of the report showed that the enemy carrier was 281 miles from Task Force 61—beyond strike range. But it was evident that at least one opposing carrier was closing, so at 1012 Fletcher ordered Kinkaid to ready a strike force.

Ensign Burkey had located RAdm Chuichi Hara's so-called Detached Force—the light carrier *Ryujo* escorted by the heavy cruiser *Tone* and two destroyers. At 0955, twenty minutes after dispatching its initial sighting report, the PBY was attacked by two *Ryujo* Zeros. At first, Burkey tried to hide in a cloud, but he was forced by persistent attacks to take refuge just above the waves—so the Zeros had to cut off diving attacks to avoid splashing into the sea. The Zeros kept it up until Ensign Burkey was able to hide in a heavy cloud formation at 1105. The PBY was not badly damaged and the crew was far from subdued, so Burkey moved to relocate and shadow the *Ryujo*. His radioman would report her position again at a crucial moment.

Next up was a sighting report intercepted by Task Force 61 at 1003 directly from an 11th Heavy Bombardment Group B-17. This crew had located a Japanese cruiser in New Georgia Sound between New Georgia and Santa Isabel, heading toward Guadalcanal.

At 1005 yet another sighting report was intercepted by Task Force 61 radiomen. This was from the Patrol-23 PBY piloted by Ens Theodore Thueson and covering the westernmost search sector, between 306 and 313 degrees. This report stated that the PBY had been attacked by three Zeros at 0900, and it caused Fletcher and his staff to surmise that the attack had been mounted by land-based fighters out of Buka. In fact, the airplanes probably were float Zeros out of Rekata Bay that were on their way to cover Tanaka's Reinforcement Group or VAdm Gunichi Mikawa's nearby Outer Seas Force. In any case, this report was seen more or less for what it was—no immediate threat or interest to Task Force 61.

At 1017 an *Enterprise* TBF filling in as part of the *Saratoga's* inner air patrol sighted a Japanese submarine running southeast on the surface at 12 knots. The submarine crash-dived before the search plane could mount an attack with its payload of depth bombs. A submarine located on the surface during the day could have been transmitting a sighting report.

The next sighting report reached Task Force 61 at 1030. It was from the Patrol-23 PBY piloted by Lt Leo Riester, the easternmost of the six AirSoPac PBYs out of Graciosa Bay. It simply said, "Attacked by aircraft planes fighting type Zero." In fact, shortly after 1000, the PBY crew had spotted two heavy cruisers and two destroyers comprising the vanguard detachment of VAdm Nobutake Kondo's Advance Force. The ships had fired on the PBY, but no damage was done until the seaplane tender *Chitose* dispatched three

Mitsubishi F1M Pete reconnaissance float biplanes to chase the reconnaissance bomber. The highly maneuverable Petes were each armed with a pair of cowl-mounted 7.7mm machine guns, which were used to attack and riddle Riester's PBY and, indeed, kill the co-pilot. However, misreported as Zeros and reported by a searchplane so far from any known Japanese land base, the aircraft that attacked the PBY seemed to Fletcher and his staff to be part of a carrier-based combat air patrol. Given the position of Riester's search sector, and its distance from Ensign Burkey's earlier sighting, the report was taken to mean that a second Japanese carrier might be out there.

At 1050 the Patrol-23 PBY commanded by Lt(jg) Robert Slater reported that "enemy planes" had attacked it. Slater's patrol sector was 334 to 341 degrees, immediately to the west of Riester's. This bolstered the Task Force 61 staff's sense that a carrier or carriers were out there, a little to the west of north of Ndeni—pretty much due north of Task Force 61.

At 1105 Lt Rodger Woodhull, the Scouting-5 exec, was on Inner Air Patrol when he found a surfaced Japanese submarine northwest of Task Force 61. The Japanese submarine, which was making full speed on a due southerly course, crash-dived while Woodhull was still three minutes away. The search pilot dropped his 500-pound depth bomb 1,200 feet along an extension of the submarine's wake, but neither he nor his rearseatman saw any signs of damage.

The next sighting report to reach Task Force 61 was an interception of a report to AirSoPac from Ens Gale Burkey's PBY, the second from this airplane. At 1110, five minutes after shaking an hour-long pursuit by two *Ryujo* Zeros, Burkey's radioman reported that a carrier, two cruisers, and one destroyer were now located at 04°40' south latitude, 161°20' east longitude, and sailing due south toward Guadalcanal. This placed the Japanese carrier only 245 miles from Task Force 61, and closing. For the first time that morning, a Japanese carrier appeared to be drawing into range.

At 1116 the *Mackinac* relayed the contents of a garbled sighting report to the *Saratoga*. It appeared that Lt(jg) Robert Slater's PBY, scouting the 334-to-341-degree sector, had located a cruiser and four other unidentified ships at 05°00' south latitude, 162°05' east latitude, on course 140 degrees. In truth, the muddled report had originated from the Patrol-23

PBY in the sector between Ensign Burkey's and Lieutenant (jg) Slater's—that of Ens James Spraggins, which was searching 327 degrees to 334 degrees. Apparently, Spraggins's crew had sighted one of the surface forces screening the *Ryujo* group.

While the Task Force 61 staff was trying to incorporate the Spraggins report into its outlook, Ens Theodore Thueson's PBY made its second report of the morning at 1125. Earlier, the westernmost patrol bomber had reported an attack by Zeros. Now it stated that two heavy cruisers and a destroyer had been sighted at 05°12' south latitude, 158°50' east longitude. These ships were on course 355 degrees (almost due north) at 20 knots. Clearly, if all the positions reported to the moment were correct, this was an entirely new force. These ships were probably rushing from a refueling stop at the Shortlands to rejoin Mikawa's Outer Seas Force.

Events appeared to be coming to a head. RAdm Thomas Kinkaid recommended an immediate attack against the known carrier revealed in two sighting reports from Ensign Burkey's PBY. But Admiral Fletcher felt there was more out there than had been definitely revealed as yet by the growing volume of sightings. And within the half-hour, the means had arrived at hand to provide many more options to the Task Force 61 commander.

Chapter 21

All of the *Saratoga* Air Group strike aircraft that had departed Henderson Field at 0830 were safely aboard their ship by 1100. The strike force's arrival had coincided with the second firm sighting report on the *Ryujo* group by Ens Gale Burkey, and RAdm Thomas Kinkaid's strong recommendation that an immediate strike be launched. Admiral Fletcher continued to resist the notion of an immediate strike, because he felt there were more Japanese carriers still to be discovered; but upon his arrival aboard the *Saratoga*, Cdr Don Felt was told, "Get ready to take off immediately. There's another enemy outfit." This was the first hard news Felt had that RAdm Raizo Tanaka's Reinforcement Group, which he had not been able to locate the day before, was not alone.

"How far away?" Felt asked. He was given the position and replied, "No. That's beyond our range. Let's just take it easy. This gang has flown all day yesterday, spent the night in their planes, and flown back here to the ship. They need just a bit of rest. Keep getting intelligence and, when those ships are within our range, we'll go get them."

The returning *Saratoga* SBDs and TBFs had all left their 1,000-pound bombs for the Marine SBDs at Henderson Field. Thus, in addition to needing to be fueled to capacity for the upcoming flight, all the *Saratoga* Air

Group strike aircraft had to be armed—1,000-pound bombs for the Dauntlesses and aerial torpedoes for the Avengers. While armorers, fueling crews, and mechanics swarmed over, under, and through each of the warplanes, the tired pilots and aircrewmen dispersed to their staterooms and berthing spaces for showers and fresh clothing. Sandwiches and coffee would be awaiting them in the squadron ready rooms.

At 1129 Admiral Kinkaid dispatched a signal to Fletcher, indicating that the *Enterprise* Air Group was ready to launch what he described as a "fighter and attack group"—twenty-five SBDs armed with one 1,000-pound bomb apiece, eight TBFs armed with two 500-pound bombs apiece, one command TBF, and twenty F4Fs. In fact, Kinkaid suggested that the eight armed TBFs and sixteen of the SBDs be sent out on a fan of ten search sectors from 290 to 90 degrees to a distance of 250 miles. But, far from being prepared to mount a full-blown strike, Fletcher was not ready to commit almost all his available search aircraft to a particular quadrant. It still seemed to him that more Japanese carriers would materialize during the afternoon. If he was truly blessed, one of the AirSoPac PBYs would locate the other carrier or carriers, and the twenty searchers Kinkaid proposed sending out could be used as strikers.

There was history in Fletcher's reluctance to expend most of the *Enterprise* bombers in searches. At the Coral Sea, in May, he had put everything on one enemy carrier, only to learn that two more carriers had arrived within range.

Responding to orders from the *Saratoga* FDO at 1143, Lt Dave Richardson, of Fighting-5, led his four-plane Wildcat division 50 miles out from Task Force 61 and encountered a four-engine Emily patrol bomber, which was heading straight for Task Force 61. As soon as the four Wildcats roared into view, the big amphibian's pilot dived for the relative safety of the surface, leveled off at 50 feet, and flew flat out toward Rabaul. The four American fighters made one firing pass apiece, chipping pieces and parts from the Emily's airframe until the inboard port engine was set on fire. The big amphibian finally fell into the waves at 1211. Its crew apparently had never seen Task Force 61; it never transmitted a sighting report.

♦

At 1158 the *Enterprise* intercepted another AirSoPac sighting report from a Ndeni-based PBY: One carrier, two heavy cruisers, and one destroyer had been sighted at 04°40' south latitude and 161°15' east longitude, heading due south. This appeared to be a repeat of Ens Gale Burkey's 1110 sighting report. In fact, the *Saratoga* received yet another repeat of this message at 1203.

The morning's action had revealed a number of things to the American leadership afloat with Task Force 61. The numerous sightings of doggedly determined *surfaced* Japanese submarines on August 23 and thus far on August 24 clearly indicated that the American carriers were being systematically shadowed. No doubt, position reports were being transmitted by the surfaced submarines to ships and bases throughout the region.

It also appeared that Task Force 61 was by then under almost constant observation by Japanese search planes. Several bogeys in addition to the downed Emily had been picked up by the *Enterprise* and *Saratoga* air-search radars during the morning. As in the fleet confrontations at the Coral Sea and Midway, these Japanese searchers appeared to be demonstrating a marked aptitude for locating and tracking an American carrier battle force virtually without being detected or, at least, directly challenged. (Indeed, all these radar contacts were erroneous; there were no Japanese search aircraft anywhere near Task Force 61 when the radar "contacts" were made.) Nevertheless, since Japanese submarines were known to be in the vicinity of Task Force 61 in the early morning of August 24, Admiral Fletcher's staff concluded that the Japanese naval commanders probably had received full and frequent reports regarding the location, speed, and heading of Task Force 61.

As the number of contacts with Japanese submarines and "search aircraft" mounted, it appeared increasingly clear that Fletcher's decision to release Task Force 18 and the *Wasp* Air Group had been ill advised. There was definitely one Japanese carrier out there, and no telling what else. If indeed a Japanese carrier or carriers meant to draw Fletcher into battle on August 24, there was a very strong probability that it or they would have closed to within range of American search—and strike—aircraft by the middle of the afternoon.

♦

At 1204 Fletcher asked Kinkaid how many and what types of aircraft the *Enterprise* would have left if the twenty searchers were dispatched, as Kinkaid had recommended. Before the reply was forthcoming, however, Fletcher at 1210 ordered the *Enterprise* Air Group to mount its second long-range search of the day "as soon as possible." The search teams would cover an arc of 10-degree sectors from 290 degrees (west-northwest) to 90 degrees (due east) out to a distance of 250 miles—precisely the mission profile recommended by Kinkaid at 1129.

A mixed bag of eight Bombing-6 SBDs, eight Scouting-5 SBDs, and seven Torpedo-3 TBFs were already spotted for takeoff on the *Enterprise's* flight deck, as were six SBDs that were to replace a like number on the Inner Air Patrol. Also, sixteen Fighting-6 Wildcats were to be launched to reinforce (not relieve) the combat air patrol already aloft. The *Enterprise* turned into the wind at 1229, and the last airplane in the launch became airborne at 1247.

At 1234 Kinkaid responded to an earlier question posed by Fletcher: After the last searcher was away and all *Enterprise* airplanes in the air had been recovered and serviced, the *Enterprise* Air Group would be able to mount an attack group of up to one command TBF, six TBFs armed with torpedoes, twelve SBDs armed with 1,000-pound bombs, and twenty Wildcats. Fletcher responded to this news at 1244: "Will hold your attack group in reserve for possible second carrier. Do not launch attack group until I direct you."

Only one minute after Fletcher sent his message to Kinkaid, the *Saratoga* FDO dispatched Lt Dick Gray's Fighting-5 division against a single bogey coming in from the south. At 1253, at a distance of 20 miles from the ship, Gray saw what at first appeared to be a B-17 hugging the waves below. Two minutes later, Lieutenant Gray reported that the bogey was indeed a Japanese bomber: It was one of the four Misawa Air Group Bettys dispatched from Rabaul at 0625. All four Wildcats went after the Betty, whose crew was unaware of their presence until the attack was under way. Gray set the Betty aflame at the outset, but all four pilots had their way with it before it crashed only 7 miles from the nearest American ships.

No one in authority in Task Force 61 believed that the Betty crew could have missed seeing and reporting the presence of the American carrier force. This certainty played large in Admiral Fletcher's mind. But the fact was that the crew of the downed Betty, like the crew of the Emily downed nearly an hour earlier, had never reported in to Rabaul. So far, despite Fletcher's and his staff's worst anxieties, Task Force 61's exact position—and composition—was still a mystery to the Japanese commanders.

Fletcher's extreme reluctance to commit the *Saratoga* Air Group against the morning's only certain carrier sighting arose mainly from the fact that the sum of all the PBY contact reports presented a vague picture and, as far as Fletcher could discern, an incomplete one. More than ninety minutes had elapsed since Task Force 61 had received any fresh news about the small carrier task force that had been found in the morning by Ensign Burkey's Ndeni-based PBY. Fletcher and most of the senior officers around him felt in their hearts that other carriers had to be lurking undetected in other quadrants; their analysis of Japanese doctrine, revealed by Japanese performance at the Coral Sea and Midway, made that surmise a virtual certainty.

On the other hand, there was the certainty that Task Force 61 had been pinpointed by the Japanese submarines and reconnaissance aircraft. Fletcher had won big at Midway by catching the Japanese air groups aboard their carriers. Indeed, the crippling destruction of the Japanese fleet carriers at Midway could be attributed largely to the presence of volatile deck-bound armed and fueled attack aircraft when the American strike force pounced. Fletcher vaguely hoped to repeat that stroke, and he undoubtedly feared being caught in a surprise attack with Cdr Don Felt's armed and fueled SBDs and TBFs on the *Saratoga's* flight deck. There was certainly no harm in trying to hit the enemy before he had an opportunity to launch his own strike.

And there was the growing lateness of the hour. The day was dwindling away. Ultimately, Fletcher knew, it would be better to dispatch the *Saratoga* Air Group strike force against the known enemy carrier group to the northwest than to do nothing at all. Felt's carrier bombers probably could be diverted if the *Enterprise* searchers located the anticipated second carrier in that general direction or to the north.

And then it simply seemed as though Time itself required a decision. So the order went out from the flag bridge. As soon as the *Saratoga* completed the launch of twelve Fighting-5 Wildcats to relieve the combat air patrol over Task Force 11, Cdr Don Felt led the *Saratoga* Air Group strike force aloft. The launch operation began at 1340.

Once Commander Don Felt's thirty SBDs armed with 1,000-pound bombs and eight TBFs armed with torpedoes had flown from sight, and until the *Enterprise* searchers reported in, the control of events had passed from Frank Jack Fletcher's hand.

An Imperial Navy Mitsubishi A6M Zero fighter. (Official USN Photo)

An Imperial Navy Nakajima B5N Kate torpedo bomber.
(Official USN Photo)

A U.S. Navy Grumman F4F Wildcat fighter making an arrested carrier
landing. (Official USN Photo)

A U.S. Marine Corps Douglas SBD Dauntless dive-bomber with a 500-pound bomb aboard. (Official USMC Photo)

A U.S. Navy Grumman TBF Avenger torpedo bomber in action. (Official USN Photo)

An LSO in Action: Lt Dave McCampbell of the *Wasp*. (Official USN Photo)

The USS *Enterprise* (CV-6).
(Official USN Photos)

VAdm Frank Jack Fletcher.
(Official USN Photo)

RAdm Sadayoshi Yamada
(Naval Historical Center)

The *Wasp* flight-deck crew respots Wildcat fighters. (National Archives)

Fighting-5 Wildcat Pilots: (l. to r.) Lt(jg) Smokey Stover, Lt Sandy Crews, Lt Pete Brown, Lt Pug Southerland, Lt Chick Harmer, LCdr Roy Simpler, and Lt Dave Richardson. (Official USN Photo)

A Fighting-Six Division: (l. to r.)
AP1 Bill Stephenson, Mach Bill Warden,
Lt Gordon Firebaugh, and Ens Bob Disque.
(Official USN Photo)

Mach Don Runyon, of Fighting-6.
(National Archives)

5th Air Attack Force G4M Betty medium bombers streak by at wave-top
height to deliver their costly August 8, 1942, torpedo attack.
(Official USMC Photo)

Shortly before this photo was taken, crewmen aboard this ditched
5th Air Attack Force Betty had been killed while firing pistols at the
destroyer USS *Bagley.* August 8, 1942. (National Archives)

Henderson Field in late
August 1942. Note the
many bomb craters.
(Official USMC Photo)

Adm Isoroku
Yamamoto.
(Imperial Navy)

VAdm Nobutake Kondo. (Imperial Navy)   VAdm Chuichi Nagumo. (Imperial Navy)

HIJMS *Ryujo.* (Naval Historical Center)

Torpedo-3 Senior Pilots: (l. to r.) Lt Johnny Myers, LCdr Charlie Jett, and Lt Rube Konig. (Compliments of J. N. Myers)

Lt Syd Bottomley (Official USN Photo)

Cdr Don Felt. (Compliments of H.D. Felt)

Enterprise sailors and Marines fire their 20mm cannon during one of the gunnery department's daily exercises. (Official USN Photo)

The *Enterprise's* port aft 5-inch antiaircraft gun group. Note the LSO platform at the edge of the flight deck. (Official USN Photo)

The USS *North Carolina*.
(Official USN Photo)

This *Shokaku* Val blows up directly over the *Enterprise's* superstructure
when a 20mm antiaircraft round apparently detonates the bomb it is
carrying. (Wartime censors have deleted all traces of the carrier's CXAM
radar from this photo.) (National Archives)

Wreckage of a pair of Vals as seen from the *Enterprise's* fantail.
(Official USN Photo)

A photographer aboard the USS *Portland* captures a Val plummeting
toward the *Enterprise* moments after the carrier's Gun Group 3 has taken
a direct bomb hit. (National Archives)

The *Enterprise's* Gun Group 3 explodes in flames as it takes a direct bomb hit. (Official USN Photo)

This dramatic view from the USS Portland shows the *Enterprise* is still capable of firing in her own defense despite the bomb hits she has sustained. (National Archives)

The third and last bomb to strike the *Enterprise* on August 24 produced a low-order explosion that nonetheless killed the photographer who took this dramatic photo. Note the ongoing blaze in Gun Group 3, at the top left. (Official USN Photo by Photographer's Mate 3d Class Robert F. Read)

Effects of the bomb that wiped out the *Enterprise's* Gun Group 3. (Official USN Photo)

Chapter 22

The Combined Fleet's carrier force was reorganized on July 14, 1942, as a result of the terrible losses sustained at Midway. For the moment, what had been five carrier divisions was two, and there were only two Imperial Navy fleet carriers left from the heady days in which six of them had ruled the seas from Ceylon to the Hawaiian Islands. When elements of the Combined Fleet sailed from home waters on August 16 to confront the reality of the Guadalcanal Campaign, only three carriers had been available for duty: the fleet carriers *Shokaku* and *Zuikaku,* and the light carrier *Ryujo.* These ships were formed into the 1st Carrier Division under the direct control of VAdm Chuichi Nagumo, who was also commander of the newly established Third Fleet (formerly the First Air Fleet).

As was the case with the other carriers, the *Ryujo* sailed with a completely reorganized air group. She had been designated a "fighter carrier" during the reorganization, so her squadron of twenty Kate torpedo bombers had been reduced to just nine airplanes, and her squadron of fifteen Zeros had been filled out to twenty-seven airplanes, a net gain in the number of airplanes but not in the striking power of the air group.

Many of the *Ryujo's* enlisted pilots had served with the air group for some time, but all the officers were new to the ship, though all were experienced combat veterans. The new *hikotaicho* and fighter-squadron commander was Lt Kenjiro Notomi, a naval officer since 1934 who had flown from the *Shoho* in the Coral Sea Battle. The fighter *buntaicho* was Lt Masao Iizuka, a naval officer since 1938 who had served with the *Kaga* Air Group until Midway. And the Kates were commanded by Lt Binichi Murakami, also a naval officer since 1938. In addition, rounding out the larger fighter squadron were two experienced warrant officers and several enlisted pilots who had served on other carriers through Midway.

At noon on August 24, the highly experienced but really quite weak *Ryujo* Air Group was 200 miles north of Guadalcanal and right on schedule to launch against Henderson Field. Spotted for takeoff were six of the nine Kates and fifteen of the twenty-seven Zeros. The Kates, which were each armed with six 60-kilogram "land" bombs, were under the command of the squadron leader, Lieutenant Murakami. The Zeros were divided into two uneven *chutai*—six escorts commanded by WO Katsuma Shigemi and a nine-plane "raiding force" commanded by the *hikotaicho*, Lieutenant Notomi.

Before the takeoff commenced at 1220, deck crewman had to remove four tall radio masts that impeded the Kates on the tiny carrier's narrow flight deck. The fighters took off first, and then the light bombers. After the last Kate was safely off, the ship launched three more Zeros to cover the minuscule Detached Force.

It is difficult to understand what the Japanese thought the strike force was going to accomplish with thirty-six 60-kilogram bombs and the bullets and cannon shells carried by nine Zero strafers. Moreover, unknown to Admiral Hara or anyone else riding in his Detached Force warships, the 5th Air Attack Force Bettys and Zeros launched from Rabaul at 0830 had run into extremely bad weather en route to Henderson Field. The land-based strikers had no choice but to return to their base, and they were all safely on the ground by 1130. Thus, the entire air effort against the Lunga Perimeter came down to just six Kates and nine Zeros assigned to attack ground targets. Indeed, all the bombs aboard the Kates were to be expended against antiaircraft batteries, and not even the vital runway. As far as the

Ryujo airmen knew, they were assisting Rabaul-based Bettys that shortly would be mounting a crippling blow against Henderson Field itself.

From the moment of their arrival at Henderson Field only five days earlier, the Guadalcanal-based Wildcat pilots of VMF-223 had been totally dependent upon coastwatcher sighting reports to place themselves in good position at ample altitude to intercept strikes by Rabaul-based bombers. Extremely slow climbers, the heavy Wildcats had to be given enough time between takeoff and the appearance of the incoming strike to attain an initial altitude advantage over the attackers. If the slow-climbing Marine fighters arrived on the scene only a minute or two late, they might not be able to launch attacks against the bombers—or penetrate phalanxes of swifter defending Zeros—until after the bombs had already fallen.

Since there was no working radar as yet at Lunga, and coastwatcher sightings had proven to be something less than completely reliable, LtCol Charlie Fike, the Marine Air Group 23 executive officer, had taken to spotting a Wildcat division or two aloft every day at Tojo Time—between about 1100 and 1500, the times most likely for an incoming strike to appear. At 1415 on August 24, there was one division of Marine Wildcats in the air and about a dozen Wildcats and 67th Fighter Squadron P-400s on alert, more or less ready for launch. The division in the air was commanded by Capt Marion Carl, the third-ranking VMF-223 pilot and a blooded veteran of Midway. With Carl was 2dLt Fred Gutt, VMF-212's Marine Gunner Tex Hamilton, and TSgt Johnny Lindley.

By 1420, the *Ryujo* Kates and Zeros were streaking toward Guadalcanal from the direction of Florida and Malaita. All the carrier planes were at nearly 10,000 feet (3,000 meters, in fact). The Kates under Lieutenant Murakami and the six-plane escort under Warrant Officer Shigemi were in one large formation, and the attack Zeros under Lieutenant Notomi, the *hikotaicho*, were at the same level, about 1,600 feet (500 meters) to the right of the bombers. The Kates were arrayed in the tight arrowhead formation from which they would execute a mass drop of all their bombs on signal from Lieutenant Murakami, who was piloting the lead carrier bomber.

Captain Carl spotted the strike force as it cleared Florida, more or less over Tulagi. As he wheeled his lone division into position, Carl radioed the air-operations center at Henderson Field, and this precipitated a wild scramble of fighter pilots to all the available Wildcats and a further scramble of all the manned Wildcats down the main runway. The idea was to take off in order of divisions and sections behind the flight leader. In practice, however, everyone rushed to get the altitude advantage over the incoming bombers. Since some of the fighters could outperform others, the system of elements and divisions invariably broke down, and everyone usually just joined up on whomever was closest. Leading the dash was Capt Rivers Morrell, the VMF-223 executive officer. In addition, Capt Dale Brannon, the 67th Fighter Squadron commander, hurtled aloft in a P-400, and one other P-400 followed on his wing.

Capt Marion Carl peeled off from his division at 1423 and led the way down on the *Ryujo* strike force from 12,000 feet. To Carl's eye, there was nothing but bombers to choose from. He lined up his sights on six airplanes in the larger Japanese formation—Shigemi's six escort Zeros—and then selected one of them. Firing from overhead and diving through the formation with Technical Sergeant Lindley glued to his wing, Carl felt certain he had set fire to one of the "bombers." Indeed, it was his first victory over Guadalcanal and his second of the war.

Close behind Carl and Lindley, Gunner Hamilton and Lieutenant Gutt opened fire on the same formation. Hamilton was drawn into a protracted dogfight with three escort Zeros, but Gutt was able to fire on at least one of the Kates and dive through the Japanese formation behind Carl and Lindley, who became separated as they used the speed and power of their dives to regain altitude for a follow-up attack. By then, the Kates were directly over the beach at Lunga, lining up on the four 90mm antiaircraft guns of Battery E, 3d Defense Battalion. At 1428 the 90mm guns opened fire on the Kates, and the Kates released their thirty-six 60-kilogram bombs at 1430. The overexcited gunners claimed a "Betty," but they actually hit nothing. Neither did the bombs; there was no damage on the ground even though the bombs detonated on either side of Battery E.

Lieutenant Notomi's ground-attack Zeros had better hunting. Attacking in *shotai* formations from three directions just as the bombs were dropped, the Zeros strafed the runway and facilities with impunity. Indeed, Notomi's *shotai* caught up with a Wildcat that had just taken off and shot it up in a flash. The Marine pilot was wounded in the head and shoulder, but he managed to keep the airplane aloft for a bit and ditch reasonably well off Florida. He was destined to be rescued by islanders the following day and returned to the Marine base at Tulagi.

The last American fighters to get airborne during the attack were the two 67th Fighter Squadron P-400s—a Lend Lease version of the thoroughly inadequate Bell P-39 Airacobra. Five of the long-nosed P-400s—which were armed with four .30-caliber and two .50-caliber wing-mounted machine guns and a 20mm cannon that peered out from the center of the propeller spinner—had flown into Henderson Field from the New Hebrides on August 22. The interception of the August 24 raid was the combat debut of the P-400 and the Army Air Forces' 67th Fighter Squadron over Guadalcanal.

The 67th Fighter Squadron's skipper, Capt Dale Brannon, and his regular wingman, 2dLt Deltis Fincher, had earlier seen the black Condition I flag go up over the air-operations radar van at Henderson Field, and both had immediately dashed for their fighters. By the time the P-400s' engines had been started, both Army Air Forces pilots thought they could hear the drone of aircraft engines overhead. Bombs began hitting the ground as Brannon and Fincher turned off the taxiway and raced in echelon along the wide main runway. As the two lifted off and retracted landing gear, a Zero swooped in front of them, apparently to strafe the runway but in fact to evade ground fire while already strafing. It was a bad move. Brannon and Fincher pounced. They turned into one another and let fly with everything—a total of eight .30-caliber machine guns, four .50-caliber machine guns, and two 20mm cannon. The Zero disintegrated.

After flying through the debris, Brannon and Fincher continued to race aloft, but they were attacked in turn by the *shotai* leader and wingman of the Zero they had just destroyed. The Japanese made one pass and disappeared. Bullets from Fincher's guns damaged one of the Zeros, and both P-400s were hit by 7.7mm bullets, but Brannon and Fincher were undeterred. Nevertheless, they missed out on the main action because of a previously unperceived altitude limitation imposed by their squadron's inability to charge the high-pressure British oxygen systems that had been installed in the fighters in anticipation of their being shipped to Britain. The P-400s got to 16,000 feet, but both pilots became woozy and had to drop back down to 14,000 feet to fully regain their senses.

Three Wildcats took on a handful of retiring ground-attack Zeros at low altitude over Lengo Channel. In a running fight, VMF-212's 2dLt Bob McLeod got good hits on a Zero, which he claimed as destroyed. The pilot of this Zero, Lieutenant Notomi's wingman, was able to nurse his stricken fighter back over Guadalcanal, where he crash-landed and was eventually recovered. In return for McLeod's victory, however, VMF-223's 2dLt Elwood Bailey was shot down. Bailey was seen as he descended in his parachute toward the water near Tulagi, but he never made it home.

After dropping their bombs, Lieutenant Murakami's Kates executed a wide formation turn to the north and attempted to retire from the area. At 1433 Captain Carl executed what observers called "the most beautiful over-head pass" and he downed a Kate on the left side of the formation. Lindley and Gutt also executed overhead passes and fired on the Kates. As they did, the reinforcements began arriving. Capt Rivers Morrell, probably fly-ing the best Wildcat in the lot, led the way, followed by five second lieuten-ants. All six newcomers attacked the five remaining Kates and the five remaining escort Zeros from below. As they did, two of the ground-attack Zeros arrived to help ward off the Wildcats. In his first pass, 2dLt Ken Frazier destroyed a Kate on the right side of the formation, and then Carl shot a Zero off Lindley's tail—but did not destroy it, as was claimed. An-other Zero shot up 2dLt Fred Gutt's Wildcat and wounded Gutt in the left arm and left leg, but Gutt made it back to Henderson Field. Lieutenants Rex Jeans and Red Taylor teamed up to disable a Kate, but Taylor, a VMF-212 pilot, was immediately shot down and killed by another Zero. And, last of all, VMF-212's 2dLt John King fired on a Kate that simply blew up. After King's victory, the Wildcats withdrew. Later, a bullet-riddled Kate—

probably the one shot up by Lieutenants Jeans and Taylor—dropped out of formation. It crash-landed on a small island north of Malaita, and the crew was rescued the next day by an Imperial Navy destroyer.

Altogether, the VMF-223 claimed twenty confirmed victories—twelve Kates, a "Betty," and seven Zeros—but the Japanese lost only four Kates (including the one that crash-landed) and three Zeros, including the one that fell to the Army P-400s. Capt Marion Carl, who was credited with four victories in this action, including a Betty, was immediately feted as the first Marine Corps ace in history. This he would become two days hence, but for the moment he was in fact two kills shy of the honor.

At 1430, Cdr Tameichi Hara's destroyer *Amatsukaze* picked up a message from Lt Binichi Murakami, whose *Ryujo* Kate was the only one equipped with a radio. In this message, Lieutenant Murakami claimed that the Guadalcanal bombing had been successful, but Commander Hara wondered just how effective the six-plane raid could have been.

Capt Tadao Kato, the *Ryujo's* captain, recorded that his six carrier attack planes and fifteen fighters "delivered a strong attack on the airfield at Guadalcanal, destroying fifteen enemy fighters in the air, bombing antiaircraft and machine-gun emplacements, and silencing them." More to the point, Captain Kato's combat report claimed that "having been thoroughly deceived by this maneuver, the enemy believed this small force to be our main strength."

In fact, the *Ryujo* Kates and ground-attack Zeros caused negligible damage on the ground. In the air, three Marine Wildcats had been downed and two of their pilots had been killed. This was hardly the crippling blow from the sky that Adm Isoroku Yamamoto had ordered up in support of the Imperial Army and Imperial Navy troops slowly approaching aboard RAdm Raizo Tanaka's transports.

Chapter 23

As the last of three combat-air-patrol Zeros left her flight deck following the launch of her strike force against Lunga, the *Ryujo* turned north. RAdm Chuichi Hara, the Detached Force commander, had considered a run out of range, in which case the strike force could have made for Buka after hitting Guadalcanal. But he had merely floated this possibility to the *Ryujo's* Capt Tadao Kato. An experienced officer who had earned his wings in 1921, Kato would have no part in leaving his carrier pilots; he convinced Admiral Hara to tarry in the area until they returned. But that return was four hours off, and it had surely penetrated that the PBY chased off and shot up by two of the *Ryujo* Zeros between 1000 and 1100 had had an opportunity to report the ship's position.

At 1320 the *Saratoga's* CXAM air-search radar had been able to track and follow a large group of airplanes as they made their way from almost due north of Task Force 61 at a distance of 112 miles. The gaggle was clearly on course away from the American carriers, heading toward Guadalcanal. Though the gaggle soon faded from the *Saratoga's* radar, there could have been little question as to what it was, what it was doing, or where it had originated. The last hard sighting of the *Ryujo* force had been at 1105, as Ens Gale Burkey's Patrol-23 PBY was departing for Graciosa Bay. Strangely, this data was not relayed to Cdr Don Felt, whose *Saratoga* Air Group strike force was launched only twenty minutes after the radar sighting was made.

Even as the American strike force was becoming airborne, Detached Force lookouts noticed that a PBY was once again shadowing their ships. This time it was the Patrol-23 PBY piloted by Lt Joseph Kellam, which had flown out on the 313-degree line and was now returning to Graciosa Bay on the 320-degree line—the same line Ensign Burkey had followed out hours earlier. Lieutenant Kellam's crew saw the Japanese ships, too. At 1405 the PBY's radioman broadcast a sighting report, indicating that a carrier, two cruisers, and two destroyers were at 05°40' south latitude, 162°20' east longitude on course 140 degrees.

It appeared to the Task Force 61 senior officers that Kellam's crew had spotted the same carrier that Burkey's had more than two hours earlier, but the difference in positions—60 miles—was just enough to cause everybody to think that *perhaps* this was a second carrier. Worse, Don Felt's strike force was going to the wrong coordinates. It was a long enough flight to begin with, but the new sighting, if it was correct, was 60 miles from the coordinates Felt had been given—an extra 120 miles of flight. There was nothing Fletcher could do beyond transmitting the new coordinates to Felt. This was done, but there was no reply.

LCdr Charlie Jett, the Torpedo-3 commander, and Ens Bob Bye, also of Torpedo-3, had been dispatched at about 1230 to search to the northwest of Task Force 61, on the 320- to 330-degree search sector. Everyone seemed to feel that this was the most promising direction for finding the Japanese carrier pinpointed by the morning PBY searches out of Graciosa Bay. Jett was convinced that he and his young wingman really would find the carrier.

Shortly after Jett and Bye took off from the *Enterprise*, ARM2 Dewey Stemen, Bye's radioman–turret gunner, spotted a Japanese plane, probably an E13A Jake reconnaissance floatplane off an Imperial Navy cruiser. For a few moments, since the TBF was still climbing toward its search altitude of about 1,500 feet, Stemen thought that Bye was trying to intercept the snooper. Apparently the Japanese pilot thought the same thing—and that the TBFs were F4Fs, which looked nearly the same but were smaller. In any case, the snooper was soon lost in the clouds as he climbed away from Bye and Jett.

The barely wavering drone of the single huge engine had been numbing the edge of LCdr Charlie Jett's mind for what seemed like eons, and the gray haze blurred the image of the sea below as far as his hooded, steel-blue eyes could see. The crow's-feet at the edges of his eyes pulsed as he squinted into the uneven gray light. The sweaty, rubber-cushioned earphones constraining his close-cropped light brown hair snapped and whined at odd and infrequent intervals, but they had uttered no words since take-off. His eyes, aching from the watchfulness, darted across the horizon in long, practiced sweeps, mentally counting the whitecaps to test the speed and course of the otherwise unperceivable wind.

They could be there, Jett thought: The enemy carriers he had been stalking since the word reached him in San Diego that December Sunday eight months earlier. If they were there, he mused . . . well, he'd report back and then attack them, hit them. Likely die trying. There seemed to be no other alternative. They were out there. The carriers. Somewhere. In this sector, or the next one.

Charlie Jett quickly glanced aft, over his right shoulder. Ensign Bye was still there, holding formation. Another young kid, as prepared for the war as any of Charlie Jett's aged-seeming contemporaries. Bye, the wingman, had it a tad tougher, Jett knew; he had to search as well as hold formation on his squadron commander. But these new Grumman airplanes were good, responsive, forgiving of the gaffes the ensigns who filled Jett's torpedo-bomber squadron were prone to perform. Hot kids, Jett knew; fighter pilots, most of them, dragooned to the torpedo squadrons to help make good the astounding losses sustained at Midway. God, Jett thought, so many dear friends lost in a matter of minutes!

Today was going to be the day Charlie Jett paid the killers back in kind. Not the actual killers, Jett knew; most of them had been lost in June, along with the torpedo crews with whom he had cruised and trained and partied in peacetime. But the same *kind* of killer was out there: the enemy carriers and the men who flew from them.

He looked once more to the left as he planned far in advance his turn across the end of the search sector and the long, fruitless flight back to the friendly carriers. And that's when he thought he saw them, looming gray shapes hundreds of feet down and to the left—roughly to the west. All he could see were their foaming wakes streaking the dull gray surface of the ocean.

It was 1440.

Within seconds, Jett was certain that one of them was a carrier, but for the moment he was unable to identify the other two or three ships.

The flight commander looked over at Bye, who was on his right wing. He was fairly certain the younger pilot had seen the ships, too. Bye stayed right with Jett, who flew on straight ahead while his radioman, ACRM I. H. Olson, broke radio silence to report the sighting—what Jett took to be a carrier, three destroyers, and two cruisers—and Jett's best reckoning of his position. It was the searchers' main job to report back.

Jett's first thought after reporting to base was that he controlled four 500-pound bombs—two in Bye's bomb bay and two in his own. He figured they were already out there, so he and Bye might as well try to damage the carrier. Jett was sure that the searchers in neighboring sectors would be vectored over to his sector to pick up the trail or mount attacks.

After the two torpedo bombers had observed the Japanese force for a while, ARM2 Dewey Stemen, Bye's radioman, transmitted an amplifying report to base. Stemen thought the TBFs would return to Task Force 61, so he was surprised when he noticed that they were still climbing and had turned toward the enemy ships. As Stemen was pondering these events, his earphones crackled as Bye informed the bombardier, AMM3 W. E. Dillon, that the bombers were going to attack the enemy carrier. Stemen riveted his attention to the quadrants behind his airplane, looking for Japanese fighters.

The TBFs could not go in low, as they would have if they had torpedoes aboard. Charlie Jett knew that the best altitude for a level bombing attack was 8,000 feet. He continued flying northward, slowly climbing all the way to conserve fuel.

Cdr Tameichi Hara, commander of the destroyer *Amatsukaze*, had just finished eating his lunch on the bridge at 1455 when one of his lookouts called, "A plane, looks like the enemy, coming from 30 degrees to port." Through binoculars, Hara indeed saw an airplane slipping in and out of the distant clouds. Immediately, signal flags went up, ships' whistles blew, and antiaircraft guns were trained out to track the American airplane.

As the first airplane approached RAdm Chuichi Hara's Detached Force, a second one emerged from the clouds. Cdr Tameichi Hara turned toward the *Ryujo* and stared openmouthed, for the carrier was taking no precautionary action whatsoever.

Commander Hara ordered his ship's antiaircraft guns to open fire. However, the American carrier bombers—which Hara believed to be B-17s— were much higher than the gunners believed. The heavy cruiser *Tone*, the Detached Force flagship, and the destroyer *Tokitsukaze* also began firing, too—no doubt in reaction to the *Amatsukaze's* lead.

After what Commander Hara felt was an interminable delay, three Zero fighters and a Kate took off from the *Ryujo*—the Zeros to defend the carrier against air attack and the Kate to hunt for submarines. No other Japanese planes were aloft.

As LCdr Charlie Jett finally neared bombing altitude at about 1455, he curved back around toward the carrier, and west of it. This placed him in a favorable up-sun position relative to the *Ryujo*, which he could now see was a very small carrier.

As the TBFs began their bomb run, all four ships turned toward the torpedo squadron commander to present the smallest possible targets. The *Tone* and the two destroyers also spread out to nearly three miles from the *Ryujo*, thus providing the carrier with very little protection. When Jett and Bye got within range, all four ships were shooting at them. Despite the fire, Jett rigidly led Bye along the bombing line.

Jett was fairly certain he saw other airplanes a long way off during the early part of the bomb run, but he was also surprised that he had not encountered a Japanese combat air patrol. If there had been fighters up, he would never have had a chance to drop his bombs, for he and his bombardier-tunnel gunner would have had their hands full defending themselves.

ARM2 Dewey Stemen, Ensign Bye's radioman-gunner, was also surprised that he had not seen any enemy aircraft during the climb or initial
approach on the *Ryujo*. As Stemen peered beyond the intense but very
inaccurate antiaircraft fire, he noticed that there were no airplanes on
the carrier's flight deck. He thought the absence of aircraft around the
Japanese task force was very strange until he realized that the *Ryujo*
had probably already dispatched an attack force—presumably against Task
Force 61.

Jett began his bomb run from 12,200 feet. His bombardier, AMM2
Herman Calahan, was manning the Norden bombsight, which was located
forward in the airplane, right beneath and behind the flight deck. Calahan,
who by then had lined up the crosshairs of the bombsight on the carrier's
deck, was in charge; he directed Jett on the final approach. Jett assumed
that Bye was still with him, but he had no attention to divert from the target.

The antiaircraft fire from all four Japanese warships remained heavy,
but it was all well below the two Avengers.

As soon as Calahan released the bombs, at 1458, Jett dived away from
the carrier at full power. The *Ryujo* turned sharply to starboard as soon as
the bombs were released. Charlie Jett saw all four bombs—Bye's and his
own—simultaneously burst in the wake of the ship, about 150 feet astern
and very close together.

Jett kept diving away from the gunfire and leveled off again at full
speed—about 250 miles per hour—at about 150 feet. He had done his job,
and then some; it was time to head for home.

The three Zeros launched minutes earlier by the *Ryujo* climbed rapidly
toward Jett and Bye while the two were preparing to drop their bombs,
but when the withdrawing TBFs flew into some clouds, these fighters gave
up the chase and flew back to take up defensive positions directly over
the *Ryujo*.

Commander Hara was astonished at the *Ryujo's* lack of aggressiveness
in her own behalf. He was both worried and furious at the lackluster performance of the carrier's captain and the three fighter pilots. He felt that the
Ryujo would be helpless in the event of a full-blown American air strike, so

he wrote out a note and gave it to his signal officer to transmit to the carrier by semaphore flags: "From Cdr Tameichi Hara, *Amatsukaze* CO, to Cdr Hisakichi Kishi, *Ryujo* executive officer: Fully realizing my impertinence, am forced to advise you my impression. Your flight operations are far short of expectations. What is the matter?"

The message was extraordinarily rude and audacious for a Japanese officer. Indeed, Commander Hara was certain he was the first Japanese naval officer ever to have sent such a message during an operation. He had addressed the message to Commander Kishi because the two had been classmates at the Eta Jima Naval Academy. Hara knew that his classmate was not responsible for the *Ryujo's* flight operations, but he wanted to make his feelings and fears understood; he was reasonably sure that Kishi would wield his influence with the carrier's master, Capt Tadao Kato.

The response was quickly transmitted by semaphore flags from the *Ryujo's* bridge: "From Kishi to Commander Hara: Deeply appreciate your admonition. We shall do better and count on your cooperation." Minutes later, the *Ryujo* launched two more Zeros.

Lt Johnny Myers, the Torpedo-3 executive officer, was flying with Mach Harry Corl, also of Torpedo-3, in the 300- to 310-degree search sector—two sectors to LCdr Charlie Jett's left. The two had clear weather in their sector, so Myers had elected to conduct his search from about 9,000 feet. It thus is quite possible that unperceived wind conditions at the higher altitude caused the two to drift off course well to the north of their intended route.

Lieutenant Myers did not hear Charlie Jett's position report at 1440. He and Machinist Corl had already turned on the cross leg of their search pattern, and they were about to turn again for the return leg. As they did, Myers spotted a Japanese heavy cruiser. That was at about 1500 hours. He first saw the *Tone* from a distance of about 8 miles at about one o'clock on his starboard bow. There was a cloud bank in the direction of the ship, which was zigzagging.

Myers ordered his radioman to break radio silence and report the enemy position to the *Enterprise*. Meanwhile, though the two Avengers were already at 9,000 feet, Myers and Corl spiraled higher, to 10,000 feet, to get above the antiaircraft fire. The fire from the cruiser was accurate and rising in steps from 7,000 to 9,000 feet. Myers absently noted that the cruiser sported five antiaircraft batteries—two on the port side, two on the starboard side, and one forward. There was no antiaircraft fire aft. The cruiser herself was a bit strange in that all four of her 8-inch gun turrets were forward of the bridge.

As Lieutenant Myers and Machinist Corl started their horizontal bombing run on the *Tone*, Myers's radioman-gunner reported at least three Zeros overhead. With that hint in mind, it was only a moment or two before Myers spotted the carrier and what appeared to be two destroyers.

As one Zero attacked Corl head-on, another Zero approached Myers's TBF from the port quarter, rolled over on its back, and fired. It missed, but moments later two Zeros—the first one and the one that had attacked Corl—dived on Myers's starboard beam. They both fired, but their tracers were low. With that, one of these Zeros departed to take on Corl again, but the other persisted and finally convinced Myers to leave the area.

Myers radioed Corl to tell him to take independent evasive action and try to take cover in a cloud bank in the direction of the surface force. Corl was ahead of Myers. After the head-on attack by one of the Zeros, he had dived through the clouds to evade. When Myers called, Corl was just above the surface and his radioman was trying to transmit a sighting report to the *Enterprise*. He never heard Myers's warning and his report was not picked up.

Myers reached the safety of the clouds and made a position report to the *Enterprise*, which was picked up. Then he tried to radio Corl with orders to rendezvous for their return to base, but Corl did not respond. Myers's gunner told the pilot that he believed Corl's plane had been hit but that he was not sure. Further attempts to contact Corl failed, so Myers had his radioman transmit his last position to the *Enterprise*. Then he turned for home alone. No one knew for sure what happened to Mach Harry Corl's TBF until April 1943, when ARM3 Delmer Wiley, the radioman-gunner, was picked up from a remote island by an Allied coastwatcher and returned to Guadalcanal. According to Wiley, Corl and his bombardier-gunner perished when their airplane was hammered into the sea by two Zeros.

♦

Ens Harold Bingaman, of Torpedo-3, and Ens John Jorgenson, of Scouting-5, were flying together in the 310- to 320-degree sector, to the west of and immediately adjacent to LCdr Charlie Jett's sector. Ensign Bingaman was supposed to have flown with another TBF, but it had been grounded with a mechanical problem and Jorgenson's SBD had been substituted.

ARM3 Paul Knight, Bingaman's radioman-gunner, spotted a carrier and "three destroyers" at about 1510. However, Bingaman descended to about 500 feet and to within about 5 miles of the enemy ships before ordering Knight to transmit a position report. Knight, who was scanning the entire sky from his power turret, saw no other airplanes in the area, but someone in the two-plane section, probably Jorgenson, later reported seeing two TBFs make a horizontal bombing run and two other Avengers being chased by a Zero. After Knight transmitted his report, Bingaman and Jorgenson turned back for the *Enterprise*.

The last search team to find the *Ryujo* was composed of two Dauntlesses flown by the Scouting-5 flight officer, Lt Birney Strong, and Ens John Richey. As Strong led Richey down the inbound leg of their 330- to 340-degree sector at 1,500 feet, he saw at least three ships about 15 miles ahead and to starboard. That was at about the same moment that Myers and Corl were being attacked by Zeros, and Bingaman and Jorgenson were approaching the *Ryujo* for a better look.

Strong led Richey in a shallow dive to investigate. As the two SBDs flew through the haze, Strong counted three surface warships. He did not at first see the *Ryujo*, but the haze before him shifted a bit as he came to within 5 miles of the Japanese task force. There was the *Ryujo!*

Immediately, Strong's radioman, ARM2 Gene Strickland, flashed a message to the *Enterprise*: "Position lat[itude] 06-25S, longi[tude] 161-20E, course 180, speed 15 [knots]." Though Strickland repeated the message over and over in plain language for six straight minutes, the *Enterprise* did not acknowledge.

With that, Lieutenant Strong and Ensign Richey turned for home.

A total of five TBFs and three SBDs flew at least to within sighting distance of RAdm Chuichi Hara's Detached Force. At least five separate sighting reports were transmitted by the American searchers beginning at 1440. However, the first report—Jett's—did not reach VAdm Frank Jack Fletcher until 1500. The reasons for the delay were purely technical: During the period of the numerous *Ryujo* sightings, the fleet fighter directors were making heavy use of the frequency they shared with the searchers and local radio disturbances were created whenever the fleet had to operate at high speed to launch or recover aircraft, as it was doing throughout that hour.

Chapter 24

The third and last Japanese searchplane to locate Task Force 61 on August 24 was the charm. Though VAdm Frank Jack Fletcher and his staff believed that their ships had been under surveillance all morning by Imperial Navy submarines, and that one or both of the multiengine searchers downed at noon and 1300 by U.S. Navy fighters had reported the presence of the *Enterprise* and *Saratoga* to higher authorities, nothing of the sort had occurred; the surfaced submarines had filed no reports regarding Task Force 61's presence, and neither had the downed Emily out of the Shortlands or the downed Betty out of Rabaul. For the entire morning, and longer, the Japanese were as much in the dark as to Fletcher's presence as he was in the dark about the presence of the *Shokaku* and *Zuikaku*.

The moment of truth arrived on the wings of an Aichi E13A Jake twin-float reconnaissance biplane launched by the heavy cruiser *Chikuma* at 1100 as part of a precautionary search pattern by VAdm Hiroaki Abe's surface Vanguard Force. The very fact that this Jake was even launched on the search was miraculous, for it had been added at the very last minute to a late-morning search pattern that would otherwise have missed Task Force 61 by scores of miles to the northeast.

The Jake was picked up as a bogey at 1338 by the *Enterprise* CXAM air-search radar, and Lt Hank Rowe, the fighter director on duty, immediately advised the two *Enterprise* Wildcat divisions then aloft of its presence. At 1341, after checking for more bogeys, Rowe dispatched all eight fighters against the Jake. Under Rowe's guidance, the Wildcats, which were at 15,000 feet, got ahead of the Jake, which was at 3,000 feet and roughly northwest of the *Enterprise*. Lt Lou Bauer, the Fighting-6 commanding officer, was unable to see the intruder against the waves below; but at 1355, Ens Douglas Johnson, the number-four man in Mach Doyle Barnes's division, said he saw it. At that moment, the Jake was at 3,000 feet and directly over Stewart Island, just 35 miles from the *Enterprise*, and closing. At 1356 Machinist Barnes announced, "The bogey is a bandit, apparently a slow seaplane type." With that, Barnes's division attacked. But the Jake was skillfully piloted. It first entered a cloud, then maneuvered in such a way as to throw off the swift Wildcats. In his second pass at the Jake, Gunner Chuck Brewer, Barnes's section leader, killed the rear gunner with a well-aimed burst, and then, at 1400, Barnes set the floatplane on fire and knocked it into the sea just 28 miles from the *Enterprise*. But the kill was late. Though all three Japanese airmen perished, they had more than done their duty, for they had transmitted *the* crucial sighting report of the day: "Spotted large enemy force. Being pursued by enemy fighters." VAdm Chuichi Nagumo had Task Force 61's position in his hands at 1425. Though it gave no coordinates and did not specifically mention carriers, Nagumo knew it for what it was. Given the Jake's search sector, "enemy fighters" could only refer to carrier fighters. And given that the Jake's route and speed were known to Nagumo's staff, it was nothing to determine where those carriers were. As soon as the calculations were in hand, Nagumo ordered the *Shokaku* and *Zuikaku* to get their deckloads of waiting strikers off without delay. By the staff's best estimate, the American carriers were 260 miles away on a bearing of 153 degrees. With luck, the strike force would be over the enemy decks by 1630.

Only a continuation of the early afternoon's run of ill luck prevented Fletcher from receiving a double dose of information every bit as crucial as that which Fate had placed in Nagumo's hand. For, in addition to the four

Enterprise Air Group search teams that located the *Ryujo* between 1440 and 1510, two other *Enterprise* search teams located new targets and transmitted important information to Task Force 61.

Air searchers normally went out 200 miles, flew a cross leg, and then flew back 200 miles to base. On August 24, however, Lt John Lowe, the Bombing-6 executive officer, and Ens Bob Gibson, also of Bombing-6, were ordered to fly out 50 miles farther than usual in the 350- to 360-degree search sector. Lowe and Gibson flew at 1,000 feet and navigated by dead reckoning.

The two were nearing the tail end of their extended search sector at about 1430 when they ran into what appeared to be five heavy cruisers and three destroyers heading due south at 20 knots. The position was almost due north of the spot from which Lowe and Gibson had been launched from the *Enterprise*. And there appeared to be other ships far to the northwest.

Lowe's radioman immediately transmitted a contact report. When he received no response, Lowe led Gibson up to a higher altitude and tried to send the report again. Still no answer.

Next the two Dauntlesses circled to the east—up-sun and away from the cruiser force—and climbed to 11,000 feet. Lowe had decided to bomb the largest cruiser in the vicinity.

The U.S. Navy dive-bombers pitched over into their dives at 1445. As they dived, the cruiser turned her beam to them. As they neared the end of the dive, the cruiser abruptly swung to starboard and skidded around to reverse course. Most of the antiaircraft fire was falling away well short of the dive-bombers.

Lowe and Gibson both released their 500-pound bombs from 2,500 feet, glided the rest of the way down to 20 feet off the water, and retired to the south at full throttle. On the way down, Lowe's rearseatman saw his bomb strike the water about 20 yards off the cruiser's port quarter. Ensign Gibson's bomb hit within 25 feet of the cruiser's port bow; its blast sprayed seawater over her bows, but it did no apparent damage.

Lowe had the impression the cruiser fired her main guns at him as he was leaving the area with Gibson.

Lowe and Gibson had attacked the heavy cruiser *Maya*, which was sailing with the main body of VAdm Nobutake Kondo's Advance Force.

Elements of Kondo's Advance Force already had been located shortly after 1000 by the Patrol-23 piloted by Lt Leo Riester. But the PBY crew had then reported only that their airplane was under attack by a Zero fighter— when in fact it was under attack by several F1M Pete reconnaissance floatplanes from the seaplane carrier *Chitose*. At the time, Riester's report had led the Task Force 61 senior staff to surmise the presence of a carrier or carriers in the area, and Lowe and Gibson had been sent there to confirm the sighting, as much as anything else. The fact that they did not locate a carrier, but only surface ships, turned out to be of no value at all to Task Force 61, for, as Lieutenant Lowe feared when he failed to receive a response from any friendly station, neither of his sighting reports ever reached Task Force 61. Nevertheless, this failure in communications was not nearly as crucial as the next.

Lt Ray Davis, the Bombing-6 commander, and his wingman, Ens Bob Shaw, were flying a 250-mile search in the 340- to 350-degree sector. They were at 1,500 feet and proceeding on the outbound leg of the search when they both sighted a large Japanese task force at 1515. Initially, Davis saw only cruisers and destroyers, and he decided to attack one of two vanguard "light cruisers," which in fact was a destroyer. As Davis's radioman-gunner, AOM1 John Trott, transmitted the sighting report, the Dauntlesses went into a steep, spiraling climb to about 14,000 feet. The target was VAdm Hiroaki Abe's Vanguard Force, which was just 40 miles ahead of Nagumo's carriers, both screening the Carrier Striking Force and poised to dash ahead to attack the American carriers with gunfire.

During the climb to get into position to attack Abe's force, Lieutenant Davis detected a carrier of about 20,000 tons trailing another screen of "light cruisers." And then Davis saw that a second carrier was a little farther off. As the near carrier—Davis correctly identified it as the *Shokaku*— had a flight deck full of planes, she instantly became Davis's priority target.

AOM1 Trott's sighting report to the *Enterprise* identified two large carriers with full flight decks, four heavy cruisers, six light cruisers, and eight destroyers on course 120 degrees—east-southeast—at a speed of 25 knots.

As yet unseen by Japanese lookouts or patrolling Zeros, Davis and Shaw began their dives from upwind and down-sun at 1545. Davis noted that the target carrier was turning to starboard when he began his dive. In the time it took Davis and Shaw to drop from 7,000 feet to 2,000 feet, the carrier completed a 60-degree turn.

By this time, the *Shokaku's* experimental air-search radar had made the first contact ever by a shipborne Japanese radar with an enemy airplane. But it took long minutes for the report to reach the hands of the carrier's captain, for the Japanese had not begun to hammer out a procedure for handling or disseminating such information. More important for the American airmen, no one told the combat air patrol.

Meanwhile, heavy antiaircraft fire from many ships was bursting at all levels up to and beyond the diving Dauntlesses. The larger caliber fire seemed to be inaccurate, but many of the smaller weapons seemed to be right on target. As Ray Davis was bounced all over the sky by near misses, he felt he would be extraordinarily lucky to survive.

The *Shokaku* was in a very tight turn to starboard when the American pilots released their 500-pound bombs from 2,000 feet and followed through into standard low-level pull-outs. They used the high speed accumulated in their dives to withdraw more or less in the direction of the easternmost "light cruiser."

AOM1 Trott reported to Lieutenant Davis that his bomb hit no more than 5 feet off the carrier's starboard side, aft of amidships. Shaw's bomb was thought to hit no more than 20 feet off the carrier's starboard quarter, close to Davis's. Both SBD gunners saw two splashes of water where the bombs struck, and a single column of smoke. In fact, Davis's bomb struck the water only 10 meters from the side of the ship, and Shaw's struck only 10 meters beyond that. The detonation of Davis's bomb killed six crewmen but caused little damage.

Shaw's radioman-gunner, AOM2 Harold Jones, observed eight airplanes amidships and a dozen more spotted aft on the carrier's flight deck.

The ordeal was far from over. Accurate antiaircraft fire from the easternmost "light cruiser" struck both dive-bombers as they passed over that ship. And there now appeared to be seven or eight planes in the air over the carrier. One Zero began a run on the retiring Dauntlesses. Davis was sure it was downed by friendly guns, but it apparently pulled up short in the face of the heavy, indiscriminate fire.

AOM1 Trott and AOM2 Jones repeatedly broadcast contact reports as Lieutenant Davis and Ensign Shaw fled back to the *Enterprise*. Neither the *Saratoga* nor the *Enterprise* picked up any of the contact reports, but several screening vessels did, and the news was immediately relayed to the *Saratoga's* flag bridge. Unfortunately, the same radio-reception problems that had delayed and garbled reports from *Enterprise* Air Group searchers over the *Ryujo* played the same sort of havoc with the reports transmitted by Trott and Jones. About all Task Force 61 copied was the presence of two carriers—but not their position or course, not the potentially revealing identity of the searchers, and certainly not the fact that both carrier decks were full of airplanes that appeared ready to launch.

And there was another bit of vital information that the U.S. Navy warships did not pick up from the search team that had discovered the whereabouts of the *Shokaku* and the *Zuikaku*—a bit of vital information that had been denied Lieutenant Davis and his team by a bit of unfortunate timing: Starting at 1450, twenty-five minutes after receiving the sighting report from the downed *Chikuma* Jake and twenty-five minutes before Davis and Shaw arrived over VAdm Chuichi Nagumo's Carrier Striking Force, the two Japanese fleet carriers dispatched a strike force against Task Force 61—a total of twenty-seven Vals and fifteen Zeros from both carriers. All of the strikers had departed the vicinity of the carriers just minutes before Davis and Shaw happened on the scene. The deckloads of airplanes the searchers had seen on the carriers were to mount a *second* strike against the *Enterprise* and *Saratoga*.

The unsettling discovery of their carriers by the two aggressive American searchers set the Japanese on edge. As far as they knew, two deckloads of American strike aircraft might be only minutes away. By 1530, there were twenty-nine Zeros in the air, covering the carriers, a total that included five *Shokaku* Zeros recalled in a moment of panic from the strike group already on the way to attack Task Force 61. At 1550, Admiral Nagumo ordered Admiral Abe's Vanguard Force to surge ahead and attack the American carriers with gunfire by nightfall. And, finally, between 1550 and 1600, the *Shokaku* and *Zuikaku* launched all the aircraft on their flight decks, as much to clear the decks of volatile airplanes as to mount a planned follow-up blow against Task Force 61. Like the first strike force, the new launch was composed of twenty-seven Vals from both carriers, escorted by nine Zeros, also from both carriers. These were the last of the Vals, but each carrier still had eighteen Kate torpedo planes aboard and a small reserve of Zeros.

If nothing untoward occurred, the second Japanese strike force would arrive over Task Force 61 at about 1800.

Chapter 25

Soon after launching, and not many miles away from the *Saratoga*, S1
Bob Hansen, a radioman-gunner serving with Scouting-3, became
aware of a worsening stomachache and shooting pains in his groin.
Hansen at first thought he had come down with appendicitis, or something
worse, and he became extremely agitated about his possible fate, not to
mention the unrelieved discomfort. The pains increased until he became
too uncomfortable to sit still or concentrate on scanning his dive-bomber's
rear quadrants for enemy fighters. Soon Hansen found himself conducting
an internal debate about whether he should ask his pilot, Ens Jim Sauer, to
turn back because he was too ill to go on. While trying to arrive at a decision, Hansen continuously squirmed around in his seat trying to contrive a
position that would permit him to relieve the stress in his guts. He could
not decide if he should ask Sauer to turn back on a combat hop the pilot
had been looking forward to during two years of training and operational
flying, or if he should suffer in silence until his Dauntless returned to the
Saratoga hours later.

Somewhere along the line, as Seaman Hansen shifted around in search
of a comfortable position, he unbuckled the leg straps of his constraining
parachute harness to give himself a little added freedom. Immediately, he

noticed a marked improvement in the aches and pains, so he began searching for the secret of such welcome relief. After almost completely recovering from the distress, he realized with immense private embarrassment that, in his haste to put on his parachute, he had unwittingly strapped his left testicle to his left leg.

Ensign Sauer was permitted to undertake his maiden combat flight without interruption. The only strike plane to abort was one of eight Torpedo-8 TBFs, which had an engine malfunction.

At 1518, Cdr Don Felt's radioman intercepted a contact report stating that one carrier, one cruiser, and two destroyers had been located at 06°25' south latitude, 161°00' east longitude on course 270 degrees at a speed of 20 knots. Felt immediately shifted his heading northward to make for the indicated position. But when the *Saratoga* strike bombers did not make contact as expected, Felt turned back to a westerly heading. At this point, Felt's command radio receiver failed, and he had to turn the lead over to LCdr Bullet Lou Kirn, the Scouting-3 commander.

RAdm Chuichi Hara's Detached Force was sighted by the *Saratoga* strike group at 1605 near 06°32' south latitude, 160°40' east longitude. The *Ryujo* and her escorts were on a southwesterly course and running at high speed. At the time of the sighting, the SBDs were at 14,500 feet, the TBFs were at 11,500 feet, and all were southeast of the *Ryujo*. High scattered clouds bordered the enemy task force. The surface wind was estimated to be 8 knots from out of the southeast.

As the strike force closed on the Detached Force, Commander Felt directed that Scouting-3, the 1st Division of Bombing-3, and five of the seven remaining Torpedo-8 TBFs attack the *Ryujo*. Bombing-3's 2d Division and the two remaining TBFs were to attack the heavy cruiser *Tone*.

Upon the order "Execute," the dive-bombers climbed away to the north and began the final approach from the northeast at 16,000 feet. During the climbing approach, the *Ryujo* was observed turning into the wind and launching two Zeros. None of the Americans had yet spotted the five Zeros and one Kate that were already aloft.

♦

While the *Ryujo* was launching the last of her ready fighters, her surface escort—*Tone* and the destroyers *Amatsukaze* and *Tokitsukaze*—moved to protect the minuscule carrier with a ring of antiaircraft fire. One of the destroyers took up station nearly 3 miles (5,000 meters) off the carrier's starboard beam, the other destroyer was the same distance ahead on the port bow, and the *Tone* was ahead on the starboard quarter and also about 3 miles away. At the same time, the *Ryujo* frantically radioed her returning Guadalcanal strike force to order the Kates and Zeros to fly directly to the Buka emergency strip.

Scouting-3's attack commenced at 1550 from 14,000 feet, with dives initiated from the northwest quadrant. Several Japanese planes were observed circling the carrier at low altitude, and light, ineffective antiaircraft fire from the carrier was encountered by the diving dive-bombers. No Zeros were anywhere near the strike aircraft.

LCdr Bullet Lou Kirn's own five-plane 1st Division of Scouting-3 was the first to push over into near-vertical dives. Kirn was the leader. All five pilots dropped their 1,000-pound bombs from about 2,500 feet, but they scored no hits.

Next up was Scouting-3's 2d Division, led by the squadron executive officer, Lt Robert Milner. Lt(jg) Bill Henry's rearseatman told Henry that his bomb landed close to the ship, inside the carrier's turn.

Another member of Milner's division, Ens Roger Crow, had mastered a unique dive-bombing technique while training earlier in the war. When Crow's dive-bomber—number S-13—went over into the dive, Crow not only flipped open the dive flaps, he also flipped the adjacent landing-gear control. So, instead of diving at a rather breathless 240 knots, he went down at about 160 knots. With the wheels and dive flaps slowing Crow, all the trailing Scouting-3 bombers soon passed him.

Crow's airplane was shaking violently, something he had not learned to overcome in his ongoing experiments. When he looked at the deck of the carrier and saw all the ships shooting at him, he naturally thought he was being hit. He looked around for fighters, but he did not see any.

While Ensign Crow hung as if suspended in midair, the four members of Scouting-3's 2d Division who had started out behind him dropped their

1,000-pound bombs—and missed. The five Dauntlesses of Scouting-3's 3d Division, led by Lt Ralph Weymouth, also passed Ensign Crow in their dives.

Ens Jim Sauer called back to his radioman-gunner, S1 Bob Hansen, over the phones: "Are you ready, Hansen?"

"Ready as ever."

"Here we go, then."

Their SBD assumed the vertical.

In all dives, the rearseatman dives backward. His primary purpose is to protect the pilot and plane from enemy fighters. Thus, Seaman Hansen caught only a fleeting, furtive look over his shoulder at the target. The flight deck was painted a dull orange color. Near the bow was a large red circle; he presumed it was for identification purposes. Hansen thought the sight of the colorful warpaint contrasting with the bright blue of the water and the foaming, silvery-white wake was rather pretty. As far as he was concerned—war or no war—the Japanese had built a beautiful ship.

Sauer's and Hansen's dive was uneventful. Their Dauntless was not hit by antiaircraft fire, and the anticipated Zeros did not materialize. After Ensign Sauer released his 1,000-pound bomb, he pulled out of his dive, which allowed Seaman Hansen to take a good, long look at the beautiful warship. As Sauer leveled off just above the water, Hansen saw bullets kicking up tiny fountains of spray alongside the airplane, and an occasional burst of antiaircraft fire from the *Tone* soared over their heads, but without effect.

Lt Syd Bottomley, whose Bombing-6 division was flying into position to attack the *Tone*, watched in amazement as Dauntless after Dauntless dived on the *Ryujo*—as 1,000-pound bombs fell all around her without any direct hits. The *Ryujo* was circling at high speed, a tactic Bottomley had seen Japanese destroyers use with astounding success at Midway.

Lt Gordon Sherwood, a senior member of Bottomley's division, also watched in amazement as all those dive-bombers peppered the water all around the carrier with their bombs. Like Syd Bottomley, Sherwood attributed the misses to the *Ryujo's* speed and her seemingly endless skidding turn.

♦

All but one of the Scouting-3 bombers assigned to hit the *Ryujo* had released their 1,000-pound bombs and missed. The last man to reach drop altitude was Ens Roger Crow. Because of his slow speed, he had a dead easy shot at the carrier.

Dive-bomber pilots normally gauged their bomb drops on the leader's bomb. When Crow saw where the bombs of every man in front of him missed, he made the needed correction. It was good enough. Crow was certain his 1,000-pound bomb went straight down the *Ryujo's* forward elevator shaft.

S1 Bob Hansen was riding Ens Jim Sauer's Scouting-3 Dauntless away from the *Ryujo* when he definitely saw Crow's bomb strike the carrier. Smoke and debris ascended several hundred feet in the air, and an open fire broke out. That was Scouting-3's only hit.

As the Scouting-3 Dauntlesses ran from the immediate vicinity of the *Ryujo* and her escorts to a predetermined rendezvous point, LCdr Bullet Lou Kirn's radioman-gunner, ACRM C. E. Russ, was certain he saw a Zero destroyed when it flew over an exploding bomb on the water. When there was a moment to look back, Kirn himself saw that the *Ryujo* was smoking heavily from Ensign Crow's solitary hit.

Bombing-3's 1st Division, led by the squadron commander, LCdr DeWitt Shumway, made diving attacks on the *Ryujo* from 15,000 feet. The Dauntlesses dived from various directions in an attempt to counteract the expert ship handling that had thrown off the aim of all but one of the preceding Scouting-3 pilots.

Lt Paul Holmberg, who was following Shumway at about a 10-second interval, had difficulty picking up the carrier in his bombsight because the dive-bomber division was badly out of position for making a good dive on the carrier. The *Ryujo* was steaming in a tight circle and Holmberg noticed that the *Tone* was in a bigger circle 3 miles out from the carrier. Holmberg had to rotate his airplane's wings counterclockwise about 60 degrees and pull up the nose a little to move the crosshairs in his 1x bombsight "on top" of the carrier's flight deck. Holmberg saw Shumway's bomb leaving his aircraft at about 2,000 feet, and he could see that it was going to miss the target. As a result of this observation, Holmberg tried to skid his airplane around to get his bomb to hit, or at least drop closer to the target than Shumway's. He did so by depressing his left rudder pedal. Holmberg did not see his bomb hit the *Ryujo*, but shortly after he pulled out of the dive, he looked back and thought he saw a tall geyser of water alongside the starboard quarter of the carrier. How much damage Holmberg's near miss caused is problematic.

Though hits were claimed by several members of Bombing-3's 1st Division, it is virtually certain that, of twenty-one 1,000-pound bombs dropped thus far, only Ens Roger Crow's had actually struck the *Ryujo*.

While the twenty-one Scouting-3 and Bombing-3 SBDs assigned to attack the *Ryujo* were mounting the main attack, Bombing-3's seven-plane 2d Division, under the squadron exec, Lt Syd Bottomley, was on its way northward to get into the best position from which to attack the *Tone*. Bottomley deliberately took his time getting lined up for his dive against the cruiser because the antiaircraft fire was light and he could locate only three or four fighters in the air. An extremely skilled veteran dive-bomber leader, Bottomley felt he had all the time in the world to do it right.

Farther out, the leader of Bottomley's second section, Lt Gordon Sherwood, could see a pair of TBFs circling near the edge of a cloud, waiting until Bottomley's division began its attack so they could begin their own runs against the *Tone*.

At length, Bottomley's Dauntlesses arrived in position to dive on the cruiser. As Bottomley pushed over, he kept the *Ryujo* in sight out of the corner of his eye. Dauntlesses were still diving on her, but there were still no hits. At last, after losing several thousand feet of altitude in his dive, Lieutenant Bottomley precipitously pulled out and closed his SBD's dive brakes. He radioed Lieutenant Sherwood: "Hey, Gordon, belay that. Come over and hit the carrier."

At just that moment, Cdr Don Felt noted that nothing better than very close misses was being obtained by the first ten dive-bombers, so he radioed Bottomley to countermand his original order. Everything was to be put on the carrier.

When what Felt thought was the last dive-bomber had gone into its dive, he too pitched over and attacked the *Ryujo*. According to Felt's radioman-gunner, who took a photograph as they pulled out of the dive, Felt obtained a hit slightly to the left and aft of the center of the *Ryujo's* flight deck. As Felt pulled out, he took a quick look back and then strafed a destroyer that suddenly loomed in his gunsight.

As Commander Felt was making his solitary dive, Lt Syd Bottomley's seven-plane Bombing-3 division picked up a little of its lost altitude as it got into position to get the carrier.

Prior to a combat dive, there were several things to be taken into consideration. The most important was the direction of the surface wind. It was preferable for the dive-bombers to work their way upwind of the target to a point where their angle to the target from the horizontal was about 70 degrees. This diminished the effect of the wind in deflection errors, right or left. On the other hand, it steepened the dive toward the vertical if they were diving downwind, and increased the possibility of throwing the bomb over the target. It was much more difficult to hit a target if the wind moved the dive-bomber right or left and if the path of the plane turned into a corkscrew. Diving upwind flattened the dive, which lessened the vertical speed and kept the bomber in its dive longer.

The speed and direction of the carrier was a factor that was best compensated for during the dive by estimating where the helpful red ball at the *Ryujo's* bow was going to be at the time the bomb would hit. As far as Syd Bottomley was concerned, this was the factor that would separate a hit from a near miss.

With the carrier slightly forward of the beam, Bottomley waggled his wings and peeled out of the formation, followed by his wingman and the rest of his division. As Bottomley pushed over for the second time in a matter of minutes, he vowed to himself to flame the carrier with his bomb or plummet all the way into the flight deck. Fortunately, the only opposition was from reasonably light antiaircraft gunfire; not one Zero had approached in Bottomley's sector at altitude.

As the nose of Bottomley's SBD tipped all the way over, he acquired the carrier's flight deck in his electric bombsight. He opened the dive brakes and throttled the engine back, pushing the fuel-mixture control forward to "automatic rich" while putting the propeller in low pitch and the blowers—air intakes—in "low." He could still adjust the trim tabs as needed and concentrate on the dive maneuver.

Bottomley pointed the electric-sight crosshairs at the position at which he expected the carrier to move and momentarily held them there to see how the wind was affecting the dive and whether the target was moving as he had estimated.

On the way down, while the carrier was still in her turn, Bottomley tried to visualize the advance and transfer vector that the carrier's bridge was making. He twisted his airplane toward the projected aiming point.

Bottomley's rearseatman, ARM1 David Johnson, sang out the altimeter readings as they descended. Bottomley constantly corrected all the way down. He knew that he had to be steady on by 4,000 feet; last-instant corrections before hitting the release point were futile.

Shortly after Johnson called out "3,000 feet," Bottomley felt he was in position. He pressed the electric bomb-release button on the top of his stick to release his 1,000-pound bomb. Immediately, he reached forward under the instrument panel to pull the manual bomb release—just to make sure. Due to altimeter lag, he knew he must have been at about 1,200 to 1,500 feet when the heavy bomb fell away.

Lt Gordon Sherwood saw Syd Bottomley's bomb strike the *Ryujo* squarely amidships.

Due to the excitement of the pull-out—closing dive brakes, putting on full throttle, getting down on the water, heading for the nearest opening between the screening ships, jinking and turning to avoid antiaircraft fire—Bottomley was unable to see what followed. But his rearseatman, ARM1 Johnson, could. He reported at least three more hits or very near misses before he was no longer able to follow the action.

Lt Gordon Sherwood carefully watched his altimeter before releasing his bomb. His rearseatman and others saw it hit a little behind Bottomley's. As Sherwood pulled out, he saw Lt(jg) Roy Isaman get a hit, too.

By this time, the *Ryujo* was smoking badly. Flames were soaring out from beneath the flight deck on both sides and down her entire length.

As S1 Bob Hansen's Scouting-3 Dauntless ran from the Japanese task force, Hansen's only thought was to look for fighters. He scanned the sky and water for aircraft. Since all Hansen could see was clear sky except for two friendly torpedo bombers that were just going into the attack, he peeked at the carrier:

> The ship appeared as though in black silhouette. Heavy black smoke was curling from the sides and rolling over the deck in a streaming curtain. An occasional lick of flame appeared from amidships. The water cut by the bow was high enough to attract my attention from the ship itself. I surmised that her skipper was turning his speed up to full. From out of the smoke near the after end, flickering spurts of rapid-fire antiaircraft were showing. I marveled at the pluck and downright guts of the gunners sticking to their tasks against such strong and horrible odds.

Cdr Tameichi Hara, captain of the destroyer *Amatsukaze,* saw nearly the same sights as Seaman Hansen:

> Two or three enemy bombs hit [the *Ryujo*] near the stern, piercing the flight deck. Scarlet flames shot up from the holes. Ominous explosions followed in rapid order. Several more bombs made direct hits. Water pillars surrounded the carrier, and it was engulfed in thick, black smoke. This was no deliberate smoke screen. Her fuel tanks had been hit and set afire.

The TBFs of Torpedo-8 were up next.

Many of the seven Avenger pilots over the Detached Force had personal scores to settle that day. Torpedo-8 had been virtually wiped out at Midway, all but one attacking pilot slaughtered in a suicidal torpedo attack. Several of the TBF pilots stalking the *Ryujo* had survived Midway largely because they were not in on the massacre strike. Rather, several had been detailed to bring new TBFs out to the Pacific from the States to replace the slow Douglas TBD-1 Devastators in which the main body of Torpedo-8 had flown to its death at Midway. The new TBFs and their crews had arrived too late to depart for the battle aboard their carrier, so they had flown to the Midway airstrip. From there, several had delivered an attack on the Japanese fleet. Of that contingent, only Ens Corwin Morgan and his crew had survived. Morgan was leading the two-plane element assigned to attack the *Tone*.

The larger Torpedo-8 contingent—the five TBFs initially assigned to launch an attack against the *Ryujo*—began encountering antiaircraft fire while gliding downward through 12,000 feet. Despite the gunfire, the flight leader, Lt Bruce Harwood, proceeded with the attack. The bulk of the anti-aircraft fire was behind the Avengers, which employed their high speed and jinking maneuvers to evade it. However, most of the seven Zeros aloft in the vicinity of the carrier were spotted between sea level and 7,000 feet.

As the TBFs passed through 2,000 feet, they were attacked by several Zeros. Ens Gene Hanson, Harwood's second-section leader, was facing Zeros for the first time; he found them to be very fast and maneuverable. Two or three of them attacked Harwood, but they did not stay with his section very long. One of them started to make a run on Ensign Hanson, who ordered his turret gunner, ARM3 Joseph Godfrey, to track him. As Hanson saw the Zero above start to dive on his TBF, however, he pulled the huge carrier bomber up on its tail and headed straight for him. The Zero immediately veered away. ARM3 Godfrey got off a couple of rounds at him as he went by and later reported the Zero as destroyed. Ens Aaron Katz, who was behind Hanson, radioed to say that the Zero's bullets went way above Hanson's airplane. For some reason, Ensign Hanson alone was singled out for attack by the Zeros. He was strafed three more times, but succeeded each time in scaring the enemy fighters away.

The truth is that the *Ryujo* fighter pilots did not press their attacks with much determination. Many of the TBF gunners reported hitting the Zeros, but only ARM3 Godfrey claimed a kill. In fact, the Zero survived.

The Zeros disappeared altogether when the torpedo bombers broke into two sections ahead of the *Ryujo* to deliver simultaneous hammer-and-anvil torpedo attacks against both of the carrier's bows. At that point, Ens Gene Hanson noted, the carrier, cruiser, and destroyers were throwing every-thing they had at the TBFs. He was sure that the antiaircraft fire was the major factor in the withdrawal of the Zeros.

Lieutenant Harwood's section of three TBFs took the starboard bow, and Ensign Hanson went after the port bow along with Ensign Katz.

The Scouting-3 attack, which had been going on throughout the approach of the torpedo bombers, was by then concluded. It was necessary for both Harwood and Hanson to postpone their attack three separate times due to the smoke obscuring the carrier from Ens Roger Crow's hit, and perhaps Cdr Don Felt's as well. There was a large fire amidships coming from beneath the flight deck. During one abortive approach, the TBF pilots saw at least three more definite bomb hits on the carrier—all by Lt Syd Bottomley's Bombing-3 division.

In that time, Lt Bruce Harwood estimated, the carrier made two complete circles. When he could finally see her again with some clarity, she was still moving, but slowly—at less than 10 knots—and apparently losing speed fast. At that moment, the *Ryujo* was broadside to Harwood's approach and in an ideal position for a torpedo run. Harwood released his torpedo.

On the opposite bow, Ens Gene Hanson had identical difficulties getting into a good attack position. By the time he did, the *Ryujo* appeared to be completely ablaze from bomb hits. Hanson released his torpedo at about 1,200 yards, but he was unable to see if he had scored as he immediately made a left turn to dodge the heavy antiaircraft fire.

S1 Bob Hansen, of Scouting-3, saw a huge column of water appear from the far side of the ship—Ensign Hanson's side. He was certain that at least one of the torpedo bombers had scored a hit. Moments later, S1 Bob Hansen, in the rear seat of Ens Jim Sauer's withdrawing SBD, saw several more columns of water, more smoke, and more debris rise all around the *Ryujo*.

Nearby, Cdr Don Felt's radioman-gunner observed a torpedo hit on the starboard bow of the carrier—Harwood's side. It lifted the bow out of the water and set it over to the left.

Lt Gordon Sherwood, of Bombing-3, saw one perfect torpedo hit, which threw water high into the air. To Sherwood, it appeared that the carrier was jarred from her course upon impact.

Struck soundly in the starboard side aft by one torpedo, the *Ryujo* lost her engine room and fire room in the blast. She quickly lost headway and soon lay dead in the water.

Torpedo-8 claimed one certain and two probable hits on the *Ryujo*. In fact, just the one torpedo had detonated against her hull. However, it is possible—even probable—that still other torpedoes had struck the light carrier's hull but failed to detonate.

The attack on the *Tone,* as originally ordered by Cdr Don Felt, was to have been a coordinated attack by Lt Syd Bottomley's Bombing-3 division and two TBFs under Ens Corwin Morgan, the Midway survivor. The attack order was countermanded by Commander Felt, but the TBFs did not receive the countermand order and proceeded with their attacks on the cruiser.

During the final approach on the *Tone,* Ensign Morgan's wingman, Ens Robert Divine, was repeatedly attacked by Zero fighters. Divine's plane was struck by bullets from one Zero while he was making his torpedo run, but he persisted in his attack. Morgan and Divine released their torpedoes on the starboard quarter, but, though a hit was claimed, both missed.

Cdr Tameichi Hara of the destroyer *Amatsukaze* watched in stupefaction as the long lines of American bombers turned from the *Ryujo* and headed for the carrier's three surface escorts: "All guns opened fire as the planes swooped on us. My ship was making 33 knots and zigzagging frantically. Tremendous bow waves kicked up by the speeding destroyer drenched me on the bridge."

If Commander Hara was made to feel uncomfortable by the American airmen, it was more or less unintentional. All the U.S. Navy pilots and aircrewmen had one basic impulse once their bombs and torpedoes had been expended: Escape!

Ens Bill Behr, a Bombing-6 pilot who had been swept into Scouting-3 for the strike, had been the third American pilot to release his bomb over the *Ryujo.* Behr was pulling out at 1,200 feet when a pair of Zeros took up station on his SBD, one on each side. Sensing that the Zeros were about to initiate simultaneous firing passes on his plane, Behr turned his highly maneuverable dive-bomber into the right-hand fighter. But he was a little too late; fourteen 7.7mm rounds fired by the left-hand Zero struck the evading Dauntless. Ensign Behr next pushed the control stick in his right hand all the way to the firewall and dived away from the Zeros, which completed several more firing passes apiece before they drew off. After turning toward the *Saratoga,* Behr climbed back to 1,000 feet, where he met three more Zeros. Without waiting for any prompting, Behr pointed his Dauntless's nose back toward the waves. The Zeros followed, but they could not get in any good firing passes so close to the water, and they soon departed.

As Lt(jg) Bill Henry, of Scouting-3, pulled out of his dive low on the water, he passed too near a Japanese destroyer. Henry was sure the destroyer's gunners would fill his SBD with antiaircraft rounds, but the gunfire seemed to be passing him in favor of another target farther to the right. Henry nervously glanced in the direction of the heaviest fire and saw that Ens Roger Crow was flying with his wheels down and was the main target for all the antiaircraft gunfire.

The Japanese were apparently concentrating on Crow because he was the slowest target in the sky. By the time he got his speed up, the gunners had him zeroed in, so they kept after him. All the gunfire was hitting the water close to Crow's SBD Number S-13, but instead of turning tail—as he would have been expected to do—he flew up through the funnels of bullets. As long as the gunfire hit the water, he knew, he could safely gain altitude to miss the deadly trajectories. It was a good theory; he did not get a single hole in the airplane. After a long solitary escape, Crow caught up with the rest of his squadron.

After pulling out of his dive, Lt Paul Holmberg, the second member of Bombing-3 to drop his bomb, saw a Japanese fighter up ahead making a pass at LCdr DeWitt Shumway's airplane. Next the Zero turned to make a pass at Holmberg, who turned toward the fighter in such a way as to force him to turn into a tighter circle if he expected to shoot Holmberg down. Apparently, the Zero pilot was out of ammunition or did not want to wrap up in a tight turn that close to the water—they were at less than 100 feet—so he broke off the attack.

After getting clear of the screening vessels, Lt Syd Bottomley headed for Bombing-3's rendezvous point and made one or two orbits to allow other members of his squadron to join on him. Then they headed straight for Task Force 61.

Scouting-3's Lt Fred Schroeder claimed a Kate destroyed. This was the lone antisubmarine patrol plane launched by the *Ryujo* as the first

Enterprise searchers had been sighted nearly an hour earlier. In fact, the Kate later turned up at the Buka emergency strip.

AOM1 Ervin Wendt, Lt Bruce Harwood's TBF tunnel gunner, could not use his gun until after Harwood had dropped his torpedo, made a left turn, and swung away from the *Ryujo*. At that point, Wendt was free to strafe the burning ship's flight deck, which he did.

As Harwood was retiring, one Zero followed him. Harwood managed to turn his large but highly maneuverable torpedo bomber under the nimble Zero. Then ACRM G. J. Sullivan drew a bead with his single turret-mounted, power-operated .50-caliber machine gun and let fly. The Zero pulled out before coming close enough to hurt Harwood's airplane, although Harwood saw bullets hitting the water ahead of his wing. When the Zero returned for another pass, AOM1 Wendt looked up through ACRM Sullivan's turret in time to see the Japanese attack from overhead at a 45-degree angle. Wendt saw Sullivan's tracer rounds fall into the Zero's nose and knock off part of the engine cowling. Then the evasive motion of the TBF caused Wendt to lose sight of the Japanese plane, which did not make another attempt to duel Chief Sullivan.

As Ens Gene Hanson was retiring in the direction of the *Tone*, his TBF was hit in the tail by a small-caliber explosive round, which tore loose part of the vertical fin and peeled off a large portion of fabric from the rudder.

The last sight most of the American pilots and aircrewmen had of the *Ryujo* was a huge pillar of oily black smoke billowing skyward and spreading across the horizon.

As the American warplanes flew from sight, RAdm Chuichi Hara signaled from the *Tone*, "Destroyers, stand by the *Ryujo* for rescue operation." Belatedly, at 1600, Capt Tadao Kato sent a message to Lt Kenjiro Notomi, the *Ryujo* Air Group *hikotaicho*, to lead the Guadalcanal strike force to Buka. But it was too late; the strikers were too far from Buka to get there on the fuel remaining in their tanks.

Cdr Don Felt stayed back, all alone, to be sure the little carrier was as good as dead. He loitered in the clouds until 1620 and would eventually write in his report of the attack: "Carrier continued to run in circles to the right, pouring forth black smoke which would die down and belch forth in great volume again."

The surviving *Ryujo* strike aircraft returned from Guadalcanal on schedule. Without a carrier deck to land on, the raid survivors joined the remaining patrol Zeros and circled overhead. The only *Ryujo* airplane with enough fuel aboard to reach Buka was the antisubmarine Kate. It flew off alone and eventually set down safely at the emergency strip.

Hours passed as the *Ryujo's* crew fought for the life of their crippled ship. There was little the three escort warships could do except circle the stricken carrier and prepare to mount a rescue effort.

Cdr Tameichi Hara's *Amatsukaze* was approaching the burning carrier when three airplanes suddenly popped out of the clouds. As they drew nearer, they were identified as *Ryujo* fighters. The Zeros circled slowly over the burning carrier, then one of them slowly glided toward the water and ditched beside the *Amatsukaze*. Commander Hara did not see what became of the other Zeros—they ditched near the *Tokitsukaze*—for he was obliged to redirect his attention to rescuing the pilot of the first Zero. All three pilots were rescued, but their fighters had to be abandoned in the water, there being no means for hoisting them aboard the destroyers.

The rescue of the three ditched patrol pilots took valuable time from setting up the rescue of the survivors among the *Ryujo's* seven hundred–man crew. It seemed to Commander Hara that the light carrier would sink at any moment, but the flame-engulfed, smoke-shrouded ship with many gaping holes remained afloat. In time, the flames subsided—possibly, Commander Hara surmised, because of the thousands of tons of seawater flowing into her. When the fires had abated, the *Tokitsukaze* eased in beside the carrier to help with the wounded.

After picking up several more ditched aviators, the *Amatsukaze* was closing on the *Ryujo* again at 1810 when a new alert brought Cdr Tameichi Hara's attention skyward once again. Two large airplanes emerged from the clouds. Hara correctly identified them as U.S. Army Air Forces B-17s, but he failed to see a third B-17 in the 11th Heavy Bombardment Group formation commanded by Maj Ernest Maniere.

The alert obliged the *Tone* and the *Amatsukaze* to zigzag away from the crippled carrier at high speed lest the heavy bombers engulf them in their anticipated pattern of bombs. The *Tokitsukaze* had to back away from the *Ryujo* at high speed in order to gain sea room. As the surface warships scattered, all three opened fire at the heavy bombers with all the antiaircraft guns that could bear. The three B-17s over the Detached Force dropped strings of 300-pound bombs from high altitude. One hit was claimed, but the bombs all fell into the sea wide of any targets. One of the B-17s was shot up by three Zeros, which erroneously claimed a kill. However, on return to Espiritu Santo, one of the undamaged airplanes crashed while landing, and its pilot and four crewmen were killed.

It was dusk when the B-17s flew from sight. There was barely enough light left for the destroyers to conduct the long-overdue rescue operation.

The *Ryujo* was still afloat, but she had no power. As the *Amatsukaze* drew near, Commander Hara was struck by the amount of damage he could see. The fires had gutted the vessel. Hideous, grotesque corpses were strewn everywhere. The carrier had a 40-degree list to starboard and was visibly sinking farther into the sea with each passing minute.

Hara saw one of the light carrier's signalmen waving semaphore flags, which read: "We are abandoning ship. Come alongside to rescue crew." Commander Hara ordered his destroyer to close on the *Ryujo's* lower starboard flank, though he knew he was risking the loss of his ship if the heavier carrier suddenly heeled over and locked the *Amatsukaze* in a death grip.

Long rolling waves caused the *Ryujo's* canted superstructure to brush against the *Amatsukaze's* exposed bridge, which sent a trickle of cold sweat down Commander Hara's back. Many of the destroyer's strongest seamen were sent to the port side of the ship and outfitted with long poles with which they tenuously held the *Amatsukaze* off the *Ryujo*. Long planks were run out to link the two vessels and, soon, the first of three hundred wounded and able-bodied survivors filed across to the *Amatsukaze's* deck. Among those killed in the bombing attack had been Commander Hara's Eta Jima classmate, Cdr Hisakichi Kishi.

Suddenly, as the flow of survivors waned to a trickle, the *Ryujo's* list dramatically increased. She was definitely about to go under. "Evacuation finished?" Commander Hara shouted.

An officer at the end of the plank nodded and answered, "Yes, sir! Please cast off. It's getting dangerous."

The *Amatsukaze's* powerful turbine engines roared to full power, and the lithe warship pulled away from the *Ryujo's* flank. The destroyer had bounded forward barely 500 yards when the *Ryujo* slipped beneath the surface.

The *Amatsukaze* immediately joined the *Tokitsukaze* and *Tone* to help rescue swimmers. As wounded, oil-stained survivors clambered aboard the surface vessels, the last of the surviving Kates and Zeros had to ditch. All the pilots and aircrewmen were saved, but all the warplanes were lost.

As the last rays of sunlight receded in the west, the *Tone*, *Tokitsukaze*, and *Amatsukaze* turned east. They had been ordered by VAdm Chuichi Nagumo to rejoin the screen of his Carrier Striking Force.

Chapter 26

The defense of U.S. Navy aircraft carriers in mid-1942 was conducted across three interlocking spheres. The first defense was by carrier-based fighters, whose primary mission it was to intercept and engage incoming enemy bombers as far from the friendly carrier deck as possible. Next, any incoming bombers that got past the fighters were to be engaged by relatively long-range heavy-caliber antiaircraft gunnery put up by the carrier herself and the warships accompanying her. The final defense lay in the hands of gunners manning medium- and light-caliber automatic weapons aboard the escorts and the carrier herself.

Task Force 61's first line of defense—the distant fighters—was controlled by fighter direction officers (FDOs) based aboard the two carriers. Throughout 1942, the FDOs had access to radar sets, which were the key to the system. On August 24, 1942, the most experienced FDO in the United States Fleet was LCdr Ham Dow, of the *Enterprise*. Dow was the 1926 Naval Academy graduate and veteran pilot who had overseen the defense of his carrier at Midway. Assisting and trading shifts with Dow on August 24 was Lt Hank Rowe, a 1937 Annapolis graduate and also a pilot who had been seconded to the Royal Air Force in 1941 specifically to learn the rather eclectic art of controlling fighters at a distance by means of radar.

Rowe had attended all the British schools on the subject and, because the British were the world's leading experts in radar-guided fighter direction, Rowe was considered one of the U.S. Navy's leading lights. He had helped establish the U.S. Navy Fighter Direction School in Hawaii directly under Pacific Fleet auspices and then had been temporarily assigned as a working evaluator to the *Enterprise* fighter-direction staff for the Guadalcanal invasion.

Given the combined expertise of Ham Dow and Hank Rowe, the *Enterprise* was the obvious choice to serve as the central clearinghouse for radar-assisted fighter direction on August 24. Thus, the combat air patrols and ready fighters of both Fighting-6 and Fighting-5 came under the *Enterprise's* direction at 1502, the moment the air-search radar picked up a bogey approaching Task Force 61 at low altitude from a bearing of 340 degrees.

Hank Rowe had the duty when the bogey was picked up on the radar, and he immediately vectored out Lt Dick Gray's Fighting-5 division to look it over and take appropriate action. At 1514 Gray reported in: "Bogey appears to be a PBY." This was highly unusual, especially because it appeared to Gray that the PBY was trying to close on Task Force 61. Lieutenant Rowe directed Gray to trail the questionable airplane while, at 1530, he directed Lt Scoop Vorse to close on the PBY with his Fighting-6 division. Vorse reported in at 1535 that the bogey was indeed a PBY. But Rowe had heard that several PBYs had been captured by the Japanese earlier in the year in the Netherlands East Indies. He told Vorse to take a good look, and Vorse did so. At 1540, he reported to Rowe that the PBY "looks okay."

Indeed it was. The pilot, Patrol-23's Lt Joseph Kellam, was on what he considered to be a vital mission to deliver information to Task Force 61. Earlier, Kellam's PBY had been flying the patrol sector between 313 and 320 degrees. On its return from an otherwise uneventful flight, the crew had spotted a Japanese carrier and several surface ships. A sighting report had been transmitted at 1405, and then the PBY had flown on toward its base at Graciosa Bay. But doubt had gnawed at Lieutenant Kellam; he had no way of being sure his vital message had reached the friendly carriers. So he decided to pay Task Force 61 a visit in order to personally deliver the information.

Escorted by Scoop Vorse's division, Kellam's PBY eased up the

Enterprise's wake while the radioman sent a message by blinker tube: "Small enemy carrier bearing 320 True distance 195 miles." The course and speed of the carrier were likewise transmitted, and so was some completely new information. According to the PBY's blinker report to the *Enterprise*, Kellam's crew had also spotted a cruiser, two destroyers, and three transports just 50 miles from the small carrier and its escort force. Though nearly two hours old, this was the first news Task Force 61 had received on August 24 regarding RAdm Raizo Tanaka's Reinforcement Group.

Lieutenant Kellam and the *Enterprise* signalmen concluded their business, and the PBY lumbered off toward Graciosa Bay, its crew proud that it had gone the extra mile this day. Kellam's entire report was passed along to the *Saratoga's* flag bridge, but Fletcher and his staff were not convinced that the PBY or the message were authentic. An inquiry was transmitted to the *Mackinac* at Graciosa Bay, but the delay brought about a missed opportunity with regard to the Tanaka troop convoy.

Even while the PBY was being tracked by two fighter divisions, Fletcher and RAdm Thomas Kinkaid were reaching an agreement regarding the strike aircraft the *Enterprise* and *Saratoga* still had aboard. Fletcher had been holding firm for hours against Kinkaid's entreaties to launch a second strike against the *Ryujo*, but by 1530 he was growing concerned that keeping the strikers in hand while waiting for news of more Japanese carriers was risking their potential effectiveness entirely. At 1536, before Lieutenant Kellam's PBY reported by blinker tube, Fletcher for the first time hinted to Kinkaid that the small force of *Enterprise* strikers might indeed be dispatched against the *Ryujo*. He transmitted a second hint at 1543, but not an actual order. However, recognizing that his boss was working toward a decision, albeit a reluctant one, Kinkaid ordered through channels that the *Enterprise* air boss make ready to send off all the available strikers.

Other factors were coming together in favor of a launch. Many fighters had been aloft on combat air patrol for a long time, and several divisions were now reaching the limits of their fuel supplies. The *Enterprise* had been effectively out of service for landings since the reserve strike force had been spotted aft hours earlier. The *Saratoga's* flight deck also needed to be cleared for launching her ready fighters and taking aboard many other fighters that were low on fuel.

At 1600 Fletcher ordered Task Force 11 to turn into the wind so the *Saratoga* could launch sixteen Fighting-6 Wildcats that earlier had landed aboard for refueling. As soon as these fighters were away, the *Saratoga* air boss ordered that five Torpedo-8 TBFs and two Bombing-3 SBDs be taxied forward so the ship could begin taking aboard twelve Fighting-5 Wildcats that were reporting very low fuel states.

And then, at 1602, Task Force 61 ran out of time.

The radar-assisted fighter-direction capability of the day was both experimental and crude. Indeed, it was Lt Hank Rowe's mandate to act as a participating observer as a means for finding specific ways to improve sighting, tracking, communications, control, and interception techniques— all of which needed work, according to findings following the Coral Sea and Midway battles.

The system was based on the experimental CXAM air-search radars, which had been built by RCA only since mid-1941. Since the operating end of the device looked to many like a bedspring, sets in use aboard ships of the United States Fleet were familiarly known as "bedspring" radar.

The FDOs were assigned to a small compartment known as Radar Plot, which was located on the third deck of the carrier's island structure. Armed with only a microphone on a long cord, the lead FDO—LCdr Ham Dow— stood over a plotting table. On the far side of the table were two junior FDOs—two of the six trainees who comprised the backup pool of FDOs aboard the carrier. The two assistants were equipped with earphones and chest-supported sound-powered microphones connected to the radar communications frequency. The radar repeaters and their operators were located in an adjacent compartment, so information was passed to the junior FDOs only by means of their sound-powered battle phones. Their job was to plot the progress of the incoming enemy flights, along with the relative positions of gaggles of friendly fighters, on the polar chart located on the table. A fourth member of the team was the gunnery liaison officer, who coordinated moves by fighters with the ship's gunnery department—hopefully to help fighters stay clear of friendly fire. The gunnery liaison officer was the only member of the team who had access to eyeball information from outside the windowless Radar Plot compartment. Lt Hank Rowe was also squeezed in around the table, where he would serve as an immediate backup for Dow as well as an evaluator of the system.

Three radiomen and their radio receivers were also crammed into Radar Plot; one each of the radios was devoted to incoming traffic from the torpedo bombers, scout bombers, and fighters, all of which usually operated on separate frequencies. A fourth radio was used to monitor talk between the task force commander and all his ships. These radios were the FDOs' only means for following the changing scene of the battle outside on the constantly revised and updated polar chart.

In theory the fighter-direction operation provided a controlling influence over defensive fighter operations, which tended to become diffused as enemy aircraft drew nearer and combat action eventually erupted. Just as the landing signal officer's observations outweighed even those of the pilot making arrested landing, so the FDO's instructions were to outweigh the on-the-spot deployment decisions of the fighter leaders—up to the point at which the battle was actually joined. In essence, the FDO was the commander of fighters and the orchestrator of defensive fighter tactics.

That was the theory. The reality was that the crude CXAM had limited range, and there were gaps in its vista.

Though the CXAM was designed to "see" a single airplane 50 miles out in any direction, it was known that it could pick up larger formations of incoming aircraft at ranges of up to 90 miles—if the airplanes were high enough and if the air was humid enough. (Moist air is a better conductor than dry air.)

As soon as the first radar sighting was made, the CXAM—rotating high atop a special mast over the island superstructure—was to be routinely stopped for a better fix and then rotated some more to search for other targets. All that the enlisted radarman answering to the FDO had to go on was a fuzzy sort of inverted v-shaped interruption in an otherwise level horizontal white line running the width of his radarscope. The bearing of the target was easily determined by a gyro-controlled bearing indicator located right over the radarscope.

As soon as the radar sighting, bearing, and time of sighting had been confirmed, the information was fed via sound-power telephone to the junior FDOs, who marked each sighting report on the large polar chart. The center of the chart represented the carrier, and each new mark represented the progress of various groups of aircraft. Enemy aircraft or unidentified "bogeys" were marked x and friendly aircraft were marked o. The progress of each group was represented by lines drawn between each new time-annotated mark and the previous time-annotated mark. The polar chart was calibrated by means of degree-marked radii emanating from the center of the chart and concentric distance-marked circles.

The only way to separate enemy aircraft from friendly ones was by means of the IFF (identification, friend or foe) transmitter carried aboard every U.S. carrier-based fighter or bomber. Whereas each group of enemy or unidentified aircraft on the radarscope registered above the line as an inverted v, IFF registered as a v below the line.

The size of a gaggle of incoming airplanes had to be estimated from the size of the v. Exhaustive testing had been run over the preceding year, and the experienced radarmen manning the scopes aboard the *Enterprise* and *Saratoga* were considered so well versed in their arcane trade that their judgments were not questioned. As a matter of fact, their estimates proved to be remarkably accurate.

The speed of radar-monitored aircraft was easily determined by the time it took the incoming or passing airplanes to get from one point on the polar chart to another.

The only variable that had to be purely estimated was the altitude of the incoming gaggles. Until incoming airplanes flew to within the 12-mile range of standard gunnery radars, there was no way to provide hard information regarding that vital statistic. The CXAM had no means for providing an explicit altitude reading. It had been noted, however, that there were reliably permanent gaps in the readings of each individual radar set. These gaps had been calibrated by exhaustive use of friendly target planes flying at known altitudes and distances from the ship. Thus, each time a bogey disappeared, the "fade" chart that had been specially prepared for each radar was supposed to yield a confirmatory altitude. Because the charts had been drawn up in calm seas, however, any roll experienced by the ship heavily influenced the accuracy of the implied readings. In fact, the *only* way to be certain that friendly fighters had an altitude advantage over the incoming enemy was to direct the Wildcats to sufficient altitudes without recourse to radar estimates. It was easier for fighters to dive from above than to try to climb from below.

Another dangerous gap in the system was the inability of the CXAM to spot low-flying bogeys at distances in excess of 12 miles. This was caused simply by the effect of the curvature of the earth upon a line-of-sight technology.

The next radar sighting after Lt Joseph Kellam's PBY was picked up at 1502 was a very large bogey that appeared on the *Enterprise* radarscope precisely an hour later, at 1602. LCdr Ham Dow was back on duty by then, and he swung into action as soon as the *Enterprise's* radar sighting had been confirmed by the *Saratoga's* radar. First, Dow took stock of all the fighter assets arrayed on the polar chart. He had to decide whom to send where, and whom to hold back in reserve. Such variables as time aloft—which is to say fuel supply, which is to say range, which is to say duration of fighting ability—and who was leading what division had to be factored into the equation.

Almost as soon as the initial sighting had been made and evaluated, all the incoming airplanes faded from the radarscopes.

The large bogey—indicating many unidentified aircraft—was spotted 88 miles from the *Enterprise* and 112 miles from the *Saratoga* on a bearing of 320 degrees—a straight line from Task Force 61 back to VAdm Chuichi Nagumo's Carrier Striking Force. The target faded at 85 miles from the *Enterprise,* which, when everything was factored into the equation, yielded an estimated altitude of 12,000 feet—which was very much on the low side.

Lieutenant Commander Dow began positioning the fighters he had aloft, and both carriers moved to launch numerous reserve fighters, which took off at 10-second intervals until, by 1636, a total of fifty-three Wildcats—twenty-five from Fighting-5 and every one of Fighting-6's twenty-eight operational fighters—would be clawing for altitude over Task Force 61 or moving to the northwest, toward the periphery of the arena.

If ever there was a time to clear carrier flight decks of fueled and armed airplanes, this was it. If for no other reason than to make the carriers just that much more fireproof, Task Force 61 *had* to launch all its ready strikers. Having been talking to Kinkaid all afternoon about a second strike against the *Ryujo*, and still without confirmation from the *Mackinac* that Lt Joseph Kellam's PBY was the genuine article, Fletcher completely overlooked Kellam's news about Tanaka's Reinforcement Group. As soon as the moment of truth was upon him, Fletcher released all the *Saratoga* and *Enterprise* strikers for a second attack against the *Ryujo*.

The *Saratoga* strike reserve consisted of just five Torpedo-8 TBFs that had not gone out against the *Ryujo* with Cdr Don Felt's strike force. The launch of the little *Saratoga* reserve strike force was precipitous. The Avenger pilots were given a vector, but there was no opportunity for them to collect charts or flight gear; they simply started going as soon as the order arrived.

The Torpedo-8 skipper, Lt Swede Larsen, initially missed out on claiming an airplane from the five that were available because he was at first told that the TBFs would simply orbit out of range to the southeast. When he heard that the torpedo bombers were being launched against a carrier, he dashed to the ready room to collect his gear and reemerged on the flight deck as the very last available TBF was taxiing into the launch position. Larsen, who had commanded Torpedo-8's land-based TBF contingent at Midway, was not about to miss this strike. He sprinted to the moving airplane and stopped the launch. He then unceremoniously ejected the TBF's veteran enlisted pilot and climbed behind the controls.

The last flyable strike aircraft left aboard the *Saratoga* were two Bombing-3 SBDs. These were in the care of Lt(jg) Robert Elder, who had had fueling problems at Henderson Field in the morning, and Elder's wingman, Ens Bob Gordon. The two had arrived home too late to rearm and refuel in time to launch with Commander Felt's strike group. As soon as Swede Larsen's TBFs were away, Elder and Gordon were called to the flight deck to taxi their armed and fueled dive-bombers forward to make room aft for returning fighters. The next thing either of them knew, they were motioned into taxi position and showed terse chalkboard notes that provided them with little more than a vector. Then they were launched. Neither pilot had his navigation board nor charts of any sort. As soon as Elder and Gordon were airborne, they raced to catch up to Larsen's TBFs, whose guidance would mean life or death for the SBD pilots and rearseatmen.

As the *Saratoga* Air Group TBFs and SBDs formed up on the run, Swede Larsen was ordered to join the *Enterprise* Air Group strikers that were about to be launched.

Initially, the *Enterprise* Air Group strike force was composed of eleven SBDs that had taken part in morning searches and air patrols. The pilots—some of whom had flown grueling morning searches, and the rest of whom were on the day's "battle bill" as reserve attack pilots—were hurriedly briefed on the *Ryujo's* last known position and course, and prepared for launching.

The first SBD off the *Enterprise's* flight deck was piloted by Lt Turner Caldwell, the Scouting-5 commander. The remaining Dauntlesses—a total of eight from Scouting-5 and three from Bombing-6—were launched in haste because the large bogey was quickly approaching. The SBDs joined up on Caldwell as they arrived, without much concern for organization by rank or formal division assignments. The three Bombing-6 pilots, who had received no briefing at all, joined up wherever they could.

As soon as Lieutenant Caldwell's SBDs—recorded in the Air Operations log as Flight 300—had cleared the *Enterprise's* deck, seven pilots from Torpedo-3 were called from their squadron ready room and ordered to taxi their TBFs forward to make room for fighters in need of fuel and afternoon searchers, who were due back within minutes.

Lt Rube Konig, the Torpedo-3 flight officer and senior member of the small contingent of ready TBF pilots, was preparing to taxi forward when he heard the flight-deck loudspeaker blare, "This is a launch." Konig was also advised that, since the task force's future course could not be remotely predicted, the torpedo pilots should try to land at Henderson Field. Saying so and doing so were two different things, however, for neither Konig nor any of the other Avenger pilots had their mapboards or charts with them. The dismay was just setting in when Konig saw a flight-deck crewman approach his airplane and hold up a chalkboard reading, "Enemy bearing

330. Approx. distance 300 miles." With that, Konig and the other five Torpedo-3 pilots hurled themselves into the air and an uncertain future.

The last bomber pilot to launch was LCdr Max Leslie, the *Enterprise* Air Group commander, who was flying a long-range TBF that he had had specially modified with extra fuel tanks and radios to serve as a strike-control airplane. Because of the weight of the extra fuel, Leslie had to begin his launch from the after elevator. By the time he reached the launch position, the *Enterprise* was zigzagging at high speed to throw off incoming Japanese dive-bombers. Leslie was set to go, but at the last moment he was ordered to cut his engine and stand by. He had no idea why. A few moments later, without explanation for the delay, the *Enterprise* Air Group commander was ordered to take off.

The launch was smooth, but upon making the normal left turn, Leslie found himself facing a sky full of outgoing antiaircraft gunfire. His earphones crackled, full of sighting reports and tally-hos from the fighters. Many of the screening surface warships were obviously firing at Leslie's fuel-laden Avenger. The air group commander dived toward the water and weaved around the battleship *North Carolina* as her antiaircraft gunners filled his right wing with shrapnel holes. Once free of friendly fire, Leslie shaped course for the reported enemy carrier and flew alone far behind the SBDs and TBFs, which had by then receded from sight. He had no way of knowing if he would have a ship to come home to.

Chapter 27

For Lt Sandy Crews of Fighting-5, August 24 had started out rather tamely. Crews was the second-section leader in a four-plane division led by Lt Chick Harmer, the Fighting-5 exec. Harmer's division had been launched on an early combat air patrol in which not a thing had happened and not a word had been spoken. The four Wildcats routinely landed after three hours and ten minutes in the air.

Harmer's division was again launched on a routine combat air patrol a little after 1400 and climbed to 20,000 feet. As the uneventful patrol entered its fourth hour, Sandy Crews began thinking it was time to return to the *Saratoga* for the day, but Chick Harmer sensed that a sudden upturn in radio traffic might lead to an exciting delay.

The issue was decided when the *Saratoga's* FDO asked Harmer if his division could delay landing for a while. The communications were terrible, but Harmer was able to gather from the transmission fragments that the radars had just picked up a large bogey at some distance. Harmer's four Wildcats each had an average of only 70 gallons of fuel remaining at that moment, but the division leader felt it was enough to warrant their remaining aloft. When positioned by the *Enterprise* FDOs, Harmer's Fighting-5 division was quite near the *Enterprise* at 10,000 feet.

◆

Mach Howell Sumrall was the second-section leader in the Fighting-6 division led by Lt Scoop Vorse. In an unusual departure from routine, Vorse placed Sumrall at the tail of the division formation in order to provide some extra protection for the two relatively inexperienced wingmen. Vorse's division was initially dispatched north-northwest, somewhat away from the big enemy gaggle, to investigate a small bogey coming in low at an estimated 1,500 feet.

In addition to Vorse's division, Lt Hank Rowe had already dispatched seven Fighting-6 Wildcats and three Fighting-5 Wildcats, organized into three uneven divisions, after the same bogey. At 1608, with the bogey approaching to within 30 miles of the *Enterprise*, Rowe sent four more Fighting-6 Wildcat divisions—sixteen airplanes—that had just been launched under the command of Lt Lou Bauer.

The bogey, which Scoop Vorse got to first at 1615, turned out to be a pair of Torpedo-3 TBFs approaching Task Force 61 with their IFFs turned off. The friendly bombers were very likely flown by Lt(jg) Weasel Weissenborn and Ens Fred Mears, the first afternoon search team to have turned for home. Whomever they were, they had drawn thirty of the forty-six Wildcats then in the air away from the main enemy formation at a critical moment.

At the same time this chase was going on, the *Enterprise* and *Saratoga* began launching all their ready bombers, to be followed by all the ready fighters on both decks.

As soon as the small bogey was reported as friendly, Hank Rowe began to reposition his fighter force against the big formation. Just before the Japanese strikers had flown into the radar blind spot at 85 miles from the *Enterprise*, the entire formation had made a slight course correction. It seemed to Rowe that this correction was the beginning of a larger swing to begin the attack on the *Enterprise* from due west rather than from the northwest. Accordingly, he swung the sixteen Fighting-6 Wildcats under Lt Lou Bauer to intercept the large bogey as far to the west of the carriers as possible. Rowe also vectored Scoop Vorse's division and seven other Fighting-6 Wildcats away from the TBFs toward the large bogey by the most direct route. But lacking a clear radar fix, he had no way of knowing that only Vorse's division had a remote chance of intercepting the enemy force.

The big bogey reappeared in the *Enterprise* radarscope at 1618. Its range was firmly fixed at 44 miles, half the initial distance to Task Force 61 at which it had originally been sighted sixteen minutes earlier. LCdr Ham Dow used the brief minutes remaining to reposition Lou Bauer's four Fighting-6 divisions directly against the large formation's newly revealed track, but it remained to be seen if these Wildcats could get into position in time to intercept the large bogey. If it happened at all, it would be close.

Ens Bob Disque, of Fighting-6, was a member of the division led by Lt(jg) Dick Gay, which had also flown a four-hour morning mission before being recovered by the *Saratoga* at 1530. While Gay's Wildcats were being refueled, the pilots first heard that friendly scouts had sighted a Japanese carrier and had made uncoordinated bombing attacks with unobserved results.

Gay's Fighting-6 division, and others from both Fighting-6 and Fighting-5, began launching after the last of the reserve strike TBFs and SBDs had been cleared from the flight deck. By the time Bob Disque was airborne at about 1624, radio silence had been broken, and everyone was chattering on the air.

Meantime, with little time remaining, the Fighting-5 division led by LCdr Roy Simpler landed aboard the *Saratoga* at 1625 because the Wildcats were critically low on fuel. It was a dangerous compromise, but the refueling operation would be accomplished in record time and the vital deck would be clear before the enemy strike force was within range.

Also at 1625, the *Enterprise* launched the last seven Wildcats she had aboard and ready to go. But because these Wildcats had originally been slated to accompany the reserve strike bombers against the *Ryujo*, their radios were tuned to the strike frequency. This meant that their pilots would not be able to hear the FDOs.

LCdr Mamoru Seki, the *Shokaku hikotaicho* and overall strike commander, spotted a carrier—the *Enterprise*—and her ring of surface escorts at 1620. The ships were 40 miles dead ahead beneath absolutely clear skies. Several minutes later, Seki also spotted a second carrier— the *Saratoga*—and her escorts, which were about 25 miles beyond the *Enterprise*.

At 1627 Seki's observer transmitted the signal, "Assume attack formation." Immediately, the four *Shokaku* Zeros comprising an "air control" force surged ahead of the Val formation to take on American fighters defending the near carrier. There had been nine Zeros in this formation when the strike force departed for the attack, but five of them had been sent back to defend the *Shokaku* when it came under attack by Lt Ray Davis and Ens Bob Shaw.

The advance of the "air control" force to take on the American fighters left only six *Zuikaku* Zeros with the twenty-seven Vals.

LCdr Roy Simpler's four Fighting-5 Wildcats, hurriedly landed aboard the *Saratoga* at 1625 to refuel, were the last American fighters launched—at 1636. By then, communications between the FDOs and the fighters were in a state of total chaos. To Simpler's immediate and immense chagrin, his division was vectored away from the enemy strike force to intercept a bogey flying in from the southeast at about 12,000 feet.

Chapter 28

The first Wildcat pilots to actually see any Japanese aircraft were Mach Doyle Barnes and members of his Fighting-6 division, one of four separated Fighting-6 divisions under the direct command—but not the direct control—of Lt Lou Bauer. The sighting was made 25 miles from the *Enterprise* at 1629, and the quarry—ahead of Barnes's division and to the right—was a *chutai* composed of nine *Zuikaku* Vals commanded by Lt Reijiro Otsuka.

Lieutenant Otsuka's Vals were the left element of LCdr Mamoru Seki's strike force of twenty-seven *Shokaku* and *Zuikaku* Vals, and the six *Zuikaku* Zeros remaining as escorts. When the Vals were spotted by Barnes and members of his division, the Japanese strike force was letting down in a shallow descent from an initial altitude of 16,400 feet (5,000 meters).

The first voice-radio report from Barnes's division was from Gunner Chuck Brewer, the second-section leader. He gave the position of the *Zuikaku* Val *chutai* relative to the *Enterprise*, as well as its altitude and heading.

Even as Brewer was reporting, Machinist Barnes was leading the division in a frantic climb toward the dive-bombers. But the Wildcats started the climb from 12,000 feet, and soon they had to reverse course beneath the Vals and give chase while climbing slowly toward them. There was, in fact, no way Barnes's division could catch the speedy Vals in a tail chase, especially since the Vals were letting down and thus picking up speed. But the Wildcat pilots gave it all they had.

In the meantime, Lt Lou Bauer and the eleven other Wildcat pilots under his command saw nothing. They had missed all of the Vals and were out of position to intercept.

At 1631 Gunner Brewer reported that enemy aircraft, probably Zeros, had just passed overhead but had disappeared. The enemy aircraft were in fact the four *Shokaku* "air control" Zeros, which were commanded by Lt Yasuhiro Shigematsu and manned by skilled veteran carrier pilots with solid combat experience in earlier battles. When spotted by Chuck Brewer, they already had a division of Fighting-6 Wildcats in their sights.

Lt Scoop Vorse's Fighting-6 division, which had been at 2,000 feet following its contact with the friendly TBFs, was the lowest of all the Wildcat divisions sent to examine the bogey. However, the four Wildcats had been sent climbing and racing by LCdr Ham Dow's frantic follow-up order: "Vector three-two-zero, angels twelve, distance thirty-five [miles]. Buster [immediately]."

As the division climbed through 8,000 feet at 1633, Vorse spotted all thirty-six brown-and-tan Vals arrayed against the clear blue sky in a classic vee-of-vees formation. The aggressive division leader yelled "Get in back of them; let's go get them!" into his throat mike and climbed steeply toward the approaching Japanese dive-bombers.

At 1634, as Mach Howell Sumrall hung his tail-end Wildcat on its propeller to match Vorse's full-throttle climb, he spotted what he took to be a dozen Zeros—actually only Lieutenant Shigematsu's four *Shokaku* "air control" Zeros. To Sumrall's eyes, from three to six Japanese fighters appeared to be using their considerable altitude advantage to close on the Wildcat division.

The Wildcats weaved and maneuvered as they climbed toward the Vals. So did the Zeros, but the Japanese pilots declined to attack. For the moment, Shigematsu was content to interpose his fighters between the Wildcats and the Vals, but not to be drawn into a dogfight. Indeed, he carefully and skillfully remained out of effective range.

Soon Sumrall noticed that the last man in the Japanese formation was getting very restless; he continued to roll upside down to look at Sumrall, who was flying the tail-end position, which was usually the realm of the least qualified junior pilot. Sumrall guessed that the Japanese pilot was hoping he would straggle, so he accommodated him by dropping back. As the Wildcats climbed through 10,000 feet, the rear Japanese pilot waggled his wings to indicate he was attacking, a foolish and unnecessary display.

While the Zero was losing altitude, Sumrall kicked full right rudder, pulled his fighter's nose as high as possible, and fired a short burst to make the Zero pilot steepen his dive. The Japanese pilot obliged and dived away underneath Sumrall. The veteran U.S. Navy pilot dropped the Wildcat's nose and fired. His .50-caliber bullets blew off the rear end of the Zero's belly tank and passed through the Zero's fuselage. The burning fighter entered a long, shallow glide and flew all the way into the ocean. Ens Francis Register, Howell's wingman, who was actually leading Sumrall throughout the action, also fired at the Zero and thought he hit it. He followed the burning fighter down despite orders from Sumrall to rejoin, and he saw the pilot bail out at 6,000 feet. The Japanese pilot survived and was later rescued.

As Sumrall was drawing off his Zero, Scoop Vorse and his wingman, Ens Dix Loesch, matched altitude with the nearest nine-plane Val *chutai*. As Vorse reversed his heading to climb into the Vals, he and Ensign Loesch were deserted by the three remaining Zeros, which raced to catch up with the receding Vals. The Zero pilots soon spotted Machinist Sumrall, however, who was climbing to rejoin Vorse and Loesch.

As Lieutenant Shigematsu and one wingman continued to close on the Vals, the other wingman broke formation to attack Sumrall. Scoop Vorse decided to attack the attacker. The Japanese pilot opened fire at great range and continued to fire bursts as he closed, but Sumrall held his course because he saw that Vorse was closing in behind the lone Zero. Vorse, who had to be reminded by Dix Loesch to drop his belly tank, executed a low-side attack on the Zero. Flames streamed out behind the Zero's cockpit for a moment, then nearly died out. The Zero climbed, but Vorse and Loesch both shot at it. The Zero fell away—intentionally, as it turned out—and Vorse and Loesch followed it down to 1,000 feet before climbing away again to try to get back into the fight. The Americans claimed a victory, but the Zero and its pilot survived.

Sumrall rejoined Vorse and Loesch during their climb, but they were prevented from overtaking the Vals when Lieutenant Shigematsu and his wingman broke up the formation with a diving attack. Vorse's division was out of the fight, and the two remaining Zeros made haste to rejoin the attack at low altitude.

Scoop Vorse's 1633 sighting report on the Vals was the last clear radio transmission of the battle. Immediately, the fighter-direction channel manned by LCdr Ham Dow was literally squelched off the air as the additional direct sightings of Japanese aircraft were reported by overexcited Wildcat pilots. Since the American combat-air-patrol fighters were obliged to operate on the single fighter frequency available to Dow, it was absolutely assured that two or more of them would be transmitting at the same moment—and that caused a painfully audible squeal to be emitted across the entire network. At those odd intervals where the squeal abated, the elated cries of "Tally ho" and worried warnings of "There's a Zero on your tail" thoroughly cluttered the airwaves.

Within minutes, as the first U.S. Navy fighters pitched into the oncoming Japanese formations, Ham Dow was bathed in sweat as he vainly expended physical and psychic energy to try to reestablish needed radio discipline. The fighter-direction system fell apart when the communications link was utterly overwhelmed at the outset of the defensive fighter attacks.

Fighting-5's Lt Dave Richardson had been launched from the *Enterprise* at about 1545 with Lt Marion Dulfiho and Ens Leon Haynes, neither of whom usually flew with Richardson. During the launch preparation, Richardson had been briefed on a mission to escort a strike force against Japanese carriers, but as the three Wildcats moved into position to launch, he was ordered by means of a chalkboard message to simply climb to 10,000 feet and orbit until contacted. At 1608, the three Fighting-5 Wildcats had been vectored after what turned out to be the Torpedo-3 TBFs, and then they had been dispatched against the large bogey the FDOs thought at the time was changing course to attack the *Enterprise* from due west.

At 1638, after flying all out and searching high and low for many minutes, the three *Saratoga* Wildcat pilots spotted the attack waves of Vals at a great distance and much higher altitude as they passed through 15,000 feet on their way toward the *Enterprise*. Dave Richardson immediately executed a climbing turn toward the dive-bombers, but all three Wildcats of his makeshift division, which were flying in loose echelon, were simultaneously bounced by all six of the *Zuikaku* escort Zeros, which were commanded by Lt Saneyasu Hidaka.

Ensign Haynes, a Coral Sea veteran, reflexively turned in to meet a direct attack from astern by two of the Zeros, which passed him and then turned to engage again from head-on. Both Zeros passed Haynes yet again, and then one reversed to match speed and open fire from dead astern the Wildcat. Haynes had no option but to dive away, but he recovered, climbed back into the fight, and opened fire at the first Zero he could bring into his sights. This airplane fell away and was last seen diving through 6,000 feet.

Meanwhile, Dave Richardson evaded the two Zeros that attacked him from ahead and above, then turned into them to give chase. The Zeros disappeared, but Richardson dropped down to 4,000 feet before he was sure they had not gotten on his tail. He climbed back to find Haynes and Dulfiho, and perhaps go after the Vals again. But only Ensign Haynes joined him, and the bombers were out of range by then.

The third member of the Richardson trio, Lt Marion Dulfiho, an extremely well seasoned veteran with two August 7 kills to his credit, disappeared without a trace. Apparently he was downed by the third pair of *Zuikaku* Zeros.

This melee was witnessed and joined by Fighting-5's Lt Dick Gray and Ens Frank Green, who had been launched as a pair from the *Enterprise* at 1445. Earlier, with an attack imminent, the two had been turned away from a fueling stop aboard the *Saratoga*. Though low on fuel, they had climbed to the northwest to greet the incoming attackers, and it was during the climb that they spotted the Vals. As Green continued in a climbing turn toward the dive-bombers, Gray, who earlier in the day had overseen the downing of a Japanese four-engine patrol bomber—arrowed toward the swirling fighter-versus-fighter action already in progress between Dave Richardson's Fighting-5 trio and the six *Zuikaku* Zeros. Richardson was drawn into a series of aerobatic maneuvers aimed, for his part, at getting into firing position on a lone Zero that attacked him from above. Though no one definitely saw Gray's victim crash, he got so many rounds into the Zero at such close range that he was able to see the pilot slump forward. The last he saw of the Zero, it was spinning away, violently out of control. Gray was given credit for killing the pilot and, thus, for destroying the Zero. However, when a second Zero attacked, Gray dived away from 10,000 feet, an action that took him out of the battle altogether.

The four *Shokaku* "air control" fighters and the six *Zuikaku* escort fighters did their duty—they prevented all the American Wildcats that might have reached the Vals on the outer limits of Task Force 61 from doing so.

At 1638, as the fighter battle was being joined, LCdr Mamoru Seki passed the final order to his Val commanders by way of a Morse code message from his observer: "All forces attack." Upon transmission of the coded order and a waggle of Seki's wings, all eighteen *Shokaku* Vals under Seki's immediate command opened out into line-astern formation and followed the leader in a sharp turn to the south, directly toward the *Enterprise*. At the same moment, Lieutenant Otsuka's nine *Zuikaku* Vals opened into line-astern formation and continued on their original course in order to skirt the Task Force 16 antiaircraft umbrella and attack the more distant *Saratoga*. Both attacks would be launched from 11,480 feet (3,500 meters) as soon as each lead Val reached its optimal attack position.

Chapter 29

Ens Bob Disque, a member of Lt(jg) Dick Gay's division of Fighting-6, began hearing reports from fighters farther out that flights of nine or twelve Val dive-bombers were coming in at about 17,000 feet. Frequent reports of "Splash one" were heard. There were also quite a few excited calls of "Zero on your tail." A quick look down revealed that the ships beneath Disque's Wildcat had begun taking evasive maneuvers. Disque was able to see their long curving white wakes on the dark blue water. Soon, he saw orange flashes brighten the gray outlines of the ships, and black puffs appeared in the bright blue canopy over the task force.

The antiaircraft fire erupting from the ships was an indication that LCdr Mamoru Seki's eighteen *Shokaku* Air Group Vals were nearly at their dive point over the *Enterprise*. There were very few Wildcats standing between the dive-bombers and the carrier, and very few of them were in anything remotely like a position to attack the Vals. But the Vals were far from getting a free punch.

Lt Chick Harmer, the Fighting-5 exec, never did receive a vector from the *Enterprise* FDO because the volume of traffic on the fighter channel was so great—almost a steady roar—that Harmer could not make out a complete message to or from anybody. What galvanized Harmer to take independent action was the sight of Lieutenant Commander Seki's line-astern formation silhouetted against the backdrop of a large cloud on the opposite side of the task force from his patrol station. Without asking or telling anyone, Harmer headed up for the intercept at full bore from 5,000 feet.

When Harmer first spotted them, the *Shokaku* Vals were still 15 to 20 miles away from the *Enterprise,* not yet at their dive position. The four Fighting-5 Wildcats and the Japanese warplanes were heading directly toward each other, with the Japanese to Harmer's right. As far as Harmer could see, the Japanese were not under attack by any American fighters.

The lead Japanese formation was the nine-plane *chutai* led by Lieutenant Commander Seki, which Harmer's division eventually joined almost right over the *Enterprise.* Indeed, Seki started his dive from over the turning carrier's port bow at 1641, just as Harmer started his attack approach from above Seki's own three-plane *shotai.*

At this point, in Harmer's view, his pilots blew everything that they had been trained to do. Instead of following the division leader against the lead Val *shotai,* they broke formation and went off on their own. Harmer was closing on Seki's Val when his wingman, Ens John McDonald, overtook him and opened fire on Seki, a move that forced Harmer to fall back and not open fire, lest he hit McDonald as well as Seki.

McDonald followed Seki down from 8,000 feet through intense antiaircraft fire from the *Enterprise* and many of her escorts. It is doubtful that McDonald's fire damaged the *hikotaicho's* dive-bomber, but it definitely rattled the veteran pilot's concentration. As the *Enterprise* twisted through a tight starboard turn, Seki was unable to precisely follow his aiming point. His 250-kilogram bomb, dropped from only 1,500 feet, missed the carrier to port. *Enterprise* gunners reported that the lead Val plunged into the sea, but Seki got away at very low level, and so did the overly aggressive Ensign McDonald, who faced as much danger from antiaircraft guns as any of the Val crews.

After relinquishing the Japanese leader to his wingman, Chick Harmer latched onto the second Val, which was about 300 feet behind Seki's, and followed it right through the beginning of its vertical dive. The Japanese observer-gunner fired several 7.7mm bursts at Harmer, but he was evidently silenced by the initial burst from Harmer's six machine guns. Though the Val did not burn, as Harmer was sure it must if it had sustained fatal damage, it suddenly steepened its dive. There was no way Harmer's Wildcat could match the dive, so Harmer pulled out. The Japanese pilot dropped his bomb too high, and it missed by a wide margin.

Despite Harmer's misgivings about his subordinates, Lt Sandy Crews managed to attach himself to the back of the third Val and give it two or three good bursts that struck the wings, fuselage, cowling, and engine. Crews was unable to see anyone in the Val's rear seat, and there was no return fire. As with Harmer's Val, Crews's target did not begin to burn by the time the antiaircraft fire from the *Enterprise* and supporting warships got too thick to breast. Crews pulled out at about 3,000 feet, but his target Val's bomb was released too high, and it fell into the water 200 yards off the carrier's port quarter. The Val, which started burning after Crews pulled out, spiraled into the water 600 yards off the *Enterprise's* port beam. It is possible that Crews's bullets seriously or even fatally injured the pilot, thus causing the bad drop and subsequent crash.

After pulling up out of his dive at 3,000 feet, Lieutenant Crews climbed back toward the stream of incoming dive-bombers. He was able to make one opposite-course pass at another Japanese plane, but without any observed results.

Ens Benjamin Currie, Crews's wingman, could not get a piece of any of the twisting Vals entering the cone of heavy antiaircraft fire. He dived alone toward the water in the hope of finding a target.

The lead *Shokaku shotai* scored no hits for three tries and lost one of its number to Lt Sandy Crews's guns—despite at least one other claim by Ens John McDonald and ships' gunners. No Wildcats opposed the next four Vals—the lead *chutai's* middle *shotai* and the lead Val of the lead *chutai's* rear *shotai*. Nevertheless, all four bombs missed the *Enterprise*. These four Vals pulled out low in the direction of the destroyer *Grayson*, off the carrier's port quarter, and the battleship *North Carolina*, dead astern.

Following a long, climbing tail chase from the outer edge of the fighter screen, the four-plane Fighting-6 division led by Mach Doyle Barnes finally caught up with the nine Vals of the second *Shokaku chutai* as they went into their dives over the *Enterprise*. At 1640 Barnes yelled over the radio, "Okay, let's go give them hell!" It was one of the few clear messages on the fighter channel during this crucial phase of the attack.

Machinist Barnes and his wingman, Ens Ram Dibb, attacked dive-bombers at the rear of the second *chutai* formation that were still waiting in line to dive. Dibb, whose altimeter read 14,000 feet, quickly hit a Val and drew smoke, but this Val did not fall to Dibb's fire, as he thought. Dibb surged ahead through friendly antiaircraft fire to try to get into position to fire on another Val, but he pulled up short and did not try to follow any of the dive-bombers into the friendly fire.

Barnes did follow the Vals down. At 1642, as he did, his Wildcat was hit dead-on by a 5-inch shell that blew off its wings and tail. The fuselage, with Barnes in it, plunged into the water 2,000 yards off the destroyer *Balch's* port quarter.

Gunner Chuck Brewer, the second-section leader, overshot the entire rear *chutai* as he roared down from 15,500 feet and overtook the two rear Vals of the lead *chutai's* rear *shotai* just after the two had simultaneously pushed over. Brewer's guns definitely set the next-to-rear Val on fire, which caused the pilot to jettison his bomb too high. The bomb detonated off the *Enterprise's* starboard bow, and the Val struck the water 1,000 yards from the carrier.

Next Brewer shifted his guns against the other Val, the rear lead-*shotai* dive-bomber. As he did, the pilot maneuvered to give the observer-gunner a better shot. Brewer returned the fire and fatally damaged the Val, but he was forced off the quarry at 4,000 feet by extremely heavy antiaircraft fire. The Val, now burning from nose to tail, continued to dive toward the tightly turning *Enterprise*. The pilot dropped the bomb from 2,000 feet and stayed in the dive, probably in the hope of crashing into the carrier's flight deck. LCdr Orlin Livdahl, in Sky Control, tucked his head into his shoulders as this flaming dive-bomber sharply dived to within what he was certain was only 20 feet of his perch. The bomb missed just to starboard and the Val screamed in only a short distance away. Both hits were so close, and so close together in time, that many Japanese observers credited the crew with crashing into the *Enterprise* with the bomb still aboard.

Back at 14,000 feet, Brewer's wingman, Ens Douglas Johnson, made a firing pass at one of the rear Vals in the rear *chutai,* missed, and came back around to execute a high-side pass on the same Japanese bomber, now at 10,000 feet and picking up speed in its dive. Johnson followed the rear *Shokaku* Val *shotai* all the way down.

This phase of the attack looked completely different from various vantage points aboard various ships—the *Enterprise* and her surface escorts.

As a case in point, to officers and men on the deck and bridge of the destroyer *Balch,* Gunner Chuck Brewer's second victim, with Brewer still in hot pursuit, appeared to twist directly toward their ship. The *Balch's* guns immediately trained on the Val and appeared to riddle it. Apparently unable to get lined up again on the *Enterprise,* this Val seemed to be coming down on the *Balch,* which was more or less dead ahead of the carrier. Observers occupying numerous vantage points saw the Val stagger in midflight under the impact of rounds from the *Balch's* guns and then alter course as if to crash into the *Enterprise's* flight deck, which it barely missed.

Only minutes into the Japanese attack, U.S. Navy fighter pilots operating close in to Task Force 16 were facing columns of antiaircraft fire from the water to 20,000 feet and 5 miles out from the *Enterprise.* It was an awesome display, and most of the converging Wildcat divisions kept their distance.

This gave all nine Vals of the rear *Shokaku chutai* a much better chance to hit their target. The antiaircraft fire was intense and deadly, but there were no more attacks by fighters to break the concentration of these pilots.

Chapter 30

AMM2 Bernard Peterson, a member of the Torpedo-3 ground crew, had been on the *Enterprise's* flight deck watching the distant opening air battle when his section chief suggested they head for the protection of the hangar deck. Once below, the two joined a group of sailors in the open boat pocket and continued to eye the air battles, which seemed to be closing in.

From his vantage point about 1,800 yards off the *Enterprise's* starboard quarter, Lt(jg) George Hamm, the destroyer *Monssen's* first lieutenant, saw the sunlight glint off a glass canopy as the lead Vals emerged from a puff of high cumulus cloud at about 1640. First one tiny dot appeared, then another. Within moments, Hamm saw six or seven of the Vals lined up in single file. At first, they moved so slowly that they appeared to be hanging in midair.

The first man aboard the *Enterprise* to actually *see* one of the Japanese dive-bombers was 1stSgt Joseph Schinka, commander of a Marine-manned four-gun battery of 20mm cannon located on one of the catwalks around and just below the portside edge of the carrier's flight deck. In accordance with standing orders, 1st Sergeant Schinka immediately gave the order to open fire.

It was 1641—thirty-nine minutes after the *Enterprise's* first radar contact. Seconds after 1st Sergeant Schinka's sighting, the *Enterprise's* loudspeakers boomed the warning: "Enemy aircraft overhead."

The *Enterprise's* gunnery department, which was essentially devoted to antiaircraft gunnery, oversaw three types of weapons. The most powerful and longest-ranged were eight 5-inch, .38-caliber dual-purpose guns (hereafter referred to as "5-inch" guns) arrayed in pairs of mounts at each corner of the flight deck. Four medium-range quadruple 1.1-inch pom-poms were located in pairs at flight-deck level just ahead and just aft of the superstructure, and a fifth quad 1.1-inch mount was located at the bows just beneath the leading edge of the flight deck. Finally, thirty 20mm cannon on stanchions—with several .50-caliber machine guns thrown in—were located on the catwalks just below and virtually all the way around the flight deck.

The gunnery department was in the hands of the carrier's gunnery officer, LCdr Orlin Livdahl, a 1926 Naval Academy graduate. His key assistant, the antiaircraft gunnery officer, was LCdr Benny Mott of the Annapolis class of 1930.

All defensive fires were formally coordinated by the gunnery and antiaircraft gunnery officers and their assistants from Sky Control, which was atop the island, 110 feet above the waterline. They all acted on the basis of what they saw for themselves, or from reports from the gunnery liaison officer manning the polar chart in Radar Plot, or from the 105 officers and sailors of L ("Lookout") Division, who were manning posts all around the flight deck and throughout the tall island structure on the starboard side of the flight deck. L Division was an integral part of the gunnery control system. Its lookouts had been painstakingly trained to keep their eyes riveted to particular sectors—no matter what was going on elsewhere.

Gunnery control was exercised largely by means of sound-powered battle phones once the sound of gunfire drowned out the ship's loudspeakers. Each battery had at least one talker connected to the primary and secondary gun-control centers. The gunnery officer's and antiaircraft gunnery officer's talkers could cut into any fire-control circuit by means of a rotary switch. When the various battery officers or lookouts reporting to them saw airplanes approaching, they deployed their forces in proportion to the threat and tried to hold something back for new threats. If no battery was firing at a new target, the gunnery officers, from their Sky Control vantage points, ordered particular batteries to switch targets.

Since the start of the war, Lieutenant Commander Livdahl and Lieutenant Commander Mott had been unrelenting in their quest for perfect defensive gunnery. An analysis early in the war had revealed to Livdahl that 96 percent of all rounds fired fell behind the target. His reaction was to train his gunners to lead their targets—to take into account the forward momentum of the target and to visualize a point ahead where the line of flight and the line of tracers would converge. In addition, he spread the word that the pointer of any gun who missed astern of a target would be replaced. This, more than anything, assured a climbing rate of hits. When the rate of hits among formally assigned gun pointers rose to near perfect, Livdahl concentrated on cross-training every other member of every gun crew and then raising their accuracy to near-perfect levels. Whenever possible—most days—gunners aboard the *Enterprise* spent the noon hour firing at target sleeves towed by airplanes.

One dubious advantage Orlin Livdahl counted on was the probability that the *Enterprise* would be the main focus of most or all of the Japanese attackers. If that was so, he reasoned, the task of his gunners would be made easier, for there would be no need to lead airplanes that were heading straight for them.

A real problem with the gunnery program lay in the fact that only a relatively small percentage of the gun crews were composed of full-time gunners, who were also primarily responsible for maintaining the guns. The majority of sailors and Marines assigned to the gun crews normally worked at a wide range of jobs in the ship's company or the various air departments. Shooting and learning to shoot was a vital but secondary duty.

There were many problems inherent in the system, not the least of which were the possible speed and accuracy of the 5-inch and 1.1-inch guns. Early in the war, a full-time gun captain in charge of one of the quad 1.1-inch mounts had been asked by LCdr Benny Mott how he would go about shooting down an airplane. The gunner's mate replied that he would quickly traverse the mount back and forth and quickly raise and lower the four barrels to put out a lethal area barrage that incoming aircraft would have to fly through. Since the ship's five 1.1-inch mounts were entirely hand-operated and without any automatic guidance system, the gunner's answer was about the best Mott was going to get at that time. Mott was certain that a lethal dose of 1.1-inch ordnance would be more a matter of luck than skill. In fact, in training exercises conducted in the days before the August 24 action, the 1.1-inch guns had merely fired at target sleeves pulled along at low speed by TBFs. All the guns around the island— sixteen barrels—had fired at once, and, though the sleeve had been hit, no one considered the exercises to be remotely realistic.

The 1.1-inch guns and their projectiles aboard the *Enterprise* were crude and outmoded. Each round's point detonator, which was armed as soon as it emerged from the gun barrel, was so sensitive that it could be detonated by a raindrop. Gunners on other ships had been killed or maimed by the sensitive rounds going off too close to them, and the 1.1-inch gunners aboard a cruiser recently had even refused to man the weapon following a fatal accident.

Keeping the gun on target was the job of the pointer, who was assisted in this task, as well as in target selection, by the battery officer, who was responsible for two mounts, and the gun captain, who was responsible for just one mount. The 1.1-inch pom-poms and their ammunition, which were designed and built at U.S. Navy arsenals, were so crude that a "tracer" effect for each round was gained by attaching a small strip of silk, which was ignited by the detonation of gunpowder when the round was fired.

The job of the loaders for each 1.1-inch mount was to extract empty magazines and replace them with full magazines. The chamber serving the four guns in one mount held two magazines, so quick loaders could ensure that the guns were always armed. Old ammunition frequently jammed, however, and had to be extracted by hand, thus appreciably slowing the real rate of fire, or silencing the mount altogether.

The 5-inch guns were more reliable, but they were hampered by a much slower rate of fire. Each round, with its premeasured powder charge, had to be loaded by hand. Though the guns were aimed and fired at long range and high altitude by a relatively sophisticated radar-assisted battery director, the system was fairly crude and quite slow in its own right. At low altitude and short range, the guns went on local control, which slowed them even more. About the best a 5-inch crew could hope for was a near miss that blossomed into a lethal burst of shrapnel in proximity to a diving or oncoming airplane.

The last line of defense lay in the hands of the 20mm gun crews. Each of these rapid-fire cannon was manned by two trained gunners. One, the senior gunner, was strapped into a shoulder harness right behind the gun. The other, the loader, worked at his shoulder and stood ready to take over the firing if the gunner was injured or killed. The gun was fixed on a highly flexible stanchion mount that was welded to the flight-deck catwalk; it operated as an extension of the man to which it was mated. Capable of putting out many rounds in short bursts, the 20mm cannon—which were grouped in four-gun batteries—were far more responsive and reliable than the 1.1-inch guns and generally a more useful weapon than either the 5-inch or 1.1-inch guns.

One important innovation undertaken by Lieutenant Commander Livdahl was the transfer of Marines from their traditional station manning the 5-inch guns to the 20mm cannon. Livdahl felt that Marines had the basic know-how to make the best use of the lighter weapons, which had to be fired with great reliance upon precisely the sort of hand-eye coordination they had mastered on rifle ranges during and after boot camp. But since there were not enough Marines to go around, sailors manned many of the 20mm cannon.

Of course, the *Enterprise's* fate was also largely in the hands of gunners aboard the six destroyers, one light antiaircraft cruiser, one heavy cruiser, and one battleship assigned to Task Force 16 on August 24. All of these surface vessels had gone into a circular defensive deployment around the carrier at the first news of the incoming air strike.

The best antiaircraft gunship in the array around the *Enterprise* was the light cruiser *Atlanta,* a swift new vessel that had been specially designed for a fleet antiaircraft role. The *Atlanta* did a superb job of following the *Enterprise* through her radical turns, but since she was sailing off the carrier's starboard beam or bow and the Vals were attacking from port, her sixteen radar-controlled 5-inch rapid-fire guns mounted in eight dual mounts could not provide cover at intermediate or low altitudes. The best the *Atlanta* could do was fire across the *Enterprise* at the Vals as they entered their dives or wait until retiring Vals flew past the carrier. The *Atlanta* was further prevented from making the most of her deadly guns because friendly vessels kept showing up in her sights.

The heavy cruiser *Portland,* which maintained station more or less off the *Enterprise's* port bow, had better clearance for her 5-inch secondary batteries, but she had only four such guns on each side. These were controlled by slow, antiquated gun directors and took far longer to get rounds out than the *Atlanta's* modern batteries. Thus, although the *Portland's* numerous lighter weapons engaged many of the Japanese dive-bombers, she was not the best ship in the best spot.

Closing on Task Force 16 from the southwest, observers and ready gunners aboard the *Saratoga* and her Task Force 11 surface escorts were mildly elated to see that the full weight of the air strike was falling elsewhere. Though Task Force 11 was only 10,000 yards from Task Force 16, and firing in support of it, the Japanese pilots were apparently intent upon crippling one carrier before going after the other.

Though the destroyer *Grayson,* which was 1,800 yards off the *Enterprise's* port quarter, had no firm targets in sight, she also opened fire at 1641, as soon as the *Enterprise's* 1st Sergeant Schinka set off the antiaircraft conflagration. The first view the *Grayson's* gunners actually had of the Vals was when the dive-bombers were ahead of and high over the *Enterprise.* Thus, all of the *Grayson's* guns, including the four in her 5-inch main battery, were redirected from a bearing on the starboard quarter—up-sun—to port and well ahead. All the other destroyers in the Task Force 16 screen—the *Benham, Monssen, Balch, Maury,* and *Ellet*—also opened fire within seconds of 1st Sergeant Schinka's reaction to the airplanes overhead. None of this fire was coordinated; it just filled the sky over the carrier and around the task force with deadly ordnance.

The *North Carolina,* a thoroughly modern "fast" battleship, brought up the rear of the formation. As soon as the action started, she had increasing amounts of difficulty keeping station or keeping up. Rated for 27 knots, she was fast for a battleship, but she was slower than any of the carrier's other escorts, and even the *Enterprise* was able to grind out 30 knots of speed once she got going.

The battleship's antiaircraft firepower was awesome. LCdr John Kirkpatrick, the antiaircraft gunnery officer, personally controlled forty .50-caliber machine guns, forty 20mm cannon, four quad 1.1-inch mounts, and twenty 5-inch twin-mount dual-purpose guns. As had LCdr Orlin Livdahl aboard the *Enterprise*, Kirkpatrick, a 1931 Naval Academy graduate who had served in the Reserves from 1935 until recalled in 1941, had overseen a strict training program that had brought his gun crews to high proficiency for their first battle.

The first time the *North Carolina* fired off her entire antiaircraft array at once was when the first Vals arrived in attack position over the *Enterprise*. Even Lieutenant Commander Kirkpatrick was shaken by the volume of noise, smoke, heat, and smell of burning materials. As did many others aboard the *North Carolina*, Kirkpatrick briefly wondered if all that gunfire had set the battleship ablaze. It seemed so as well to Lt(jg) George Hamm, who was abeam the *North Carolina* aboard the destroyer *Monssen*. Indeed, the Task Force 16 commander, RAdm Thomas Kinkaid, radioed from the *Enterprise* at the height of the attack to inquire if the *North Carolina* was on fire.

Just as the dive-bomber attack began, LCdr Max Leslie, the *Enterprise* Air Group commander, passed close to the *North Carolina*, and his command TBF was struck by a round from the battleship's very first antiaircraft salvo. Leslie was lucky to survive the ordeal and fly clear, for the fire was utterly indiscriminate.

The *Enterprise's* crew had been on duty since an hour before sunrise. By the time the Japanese strike force appeared on the carrier's CXAM radar, the sailors on deck—who were *not* told of the new development—were bored and restless.

BM2 Arthur Davis, the *Enterprise* Air Group master-at-arms, was just leaving an hours-long game of acey-deucey—he was the big loser—when he decided to share a dire premonition with BM1 Al Gabara, captain of the Number-4 1.1-inch gun mount, the carrier's sternmost medium-caliber weapon. Though distant air battles and infrequent loudspeaker reports had alerted the crew that *something* was up, it was by no means certain that a major air strike was closing in from the northwest. Thus, Davis simply told Gabara that he had a "bad feeling" and bet that an attack against the *Enterprise* herself would soon be mounted. Gabara told Davis that, in that event, he would finally have an opportunity to fire his guns, to get paid off for the long hours of training and the many longer hours of unrelieved boredom.

No sooner said than 1st Sergeant Schinka sighted a glint of sunlight off LCdr Mamoru Seki's lead Val as it tipped over against the port side of the ship. Davis and Gabara turned toward Schinka's voice, and Davis shouted, "Here they come!" as he pointed skyward.

Immediately, all the guns that could bear were trained around to the port side of the ship and fired—whether or not the gunners had targets in sight.

For all the boredom they had endured, the officers and sailors on and around the flight deck could at least react to what they could see with their own eyes. Sailors and officers below decks, busy or not, had to rely upon other senses, and that tended to raise the levels of anxiety and fear in closed areas.

AM3 Ed Krzeminski was on the hangar deck when the guns over his head began firing. Since Krzeminski could not see anything, he reflexively dropped to the steel deck in a little passageway with a ladder leading up to the island. There was little more he could do than hope for the best. Suddenly, a great wash of seawater all but carried him away from his place at the foot of the ladder. The great ship had swerved so radically that seawater had been washed up as high as the hangar deck. Thoroughly rattled, Krzeminski crawled out onto the deck of the cavernous hangar and lay on his stomach near the forward elevator. Better, he felt, to be exposed in the open than drowned—or worse—in a tight little steel vault.

From his vantage point about 1,800 yards out, Lt(jg) George Hamm of the destroyer *Monssen* felt that he was looking down upon the carrier's flight deck from a great height, so far did the great ship heel over in her turn.

High up on the third deck of the *Enterprise's* island, the force of the hard turn to port and an attendant 28-degree list were magnified to awesome proportions. The five officers huddled around the FDO's polar chart in Radar Plot were sure the big ship was capsizing. Consequently, the battle was momentarily abandoned by a rather panicked exodus toward the nearest hatchway. LCdr Ham Dow was so rattled that he grabbed the D-rings on his Mae West lifejacket and inflated the vest before leaving the table. The two junior FDOs threw their pencils on the polar chart and executed smart about-faces, but they came up short when the gunnery liaison officer blocked the route to the outside. Ens George Givens was brought back to earth when he heard the grinning gunnery liaison officer, who was the only one of the group with outside communications, announce that all was well with the ship. All hands sheepishly returned to their work.

High above, in Sky Control, LCdr Orlin Livdahl noticed that the butterflies that had been plaguing him since the first radar sighting at 1602 had suddenly flown away. He was dead calm.

Lt(jg) Weasel Weissenborn and Ens Fred Mears of Torpedo-3 returned to the task force in clear skies at about 1640 and made a recognition signal before completing their approach on the *Enterprise*. All of a sudden, without any warning, Mears saw the light antiaircraft cruiser *Atlanta*, which was guarding the *Enterprise's* starboard flank, become immersed in a great cloud of gray-black smoke. Mears was at first sure the cruiser had been struck by something—a bomb or a torpedo—but he quickly realized that she had opened fire with her antiaircraft batteries. Farther on, directly astern the *Enterprise*, the mighty *North Carolina* lit up from stem to stern as all her light, medium, and heavy antiaircraft batteries seemed to open fire at once.

As all the ships turned in unison to match the *Enterprise's* turns, Ensign Mears looked up and saw three Vals, lined up one after the other, slowly dive on the nearby carrier. At the same instant, Mears's earphone crackled with an urgent warning: "All friendly planes keep clear during the attack."

The two TBFs turned away and circled beyond the rim of the fight. Mears became so engrossed in watching the colorful action that he all but forgot to fly his Avenger. There were masses of flame as burning airplanes dodged in and out of the antiaircraft cloud. Nearby, shrapnel from bursting 5-inch antiaircraft rounds was falling in patches like heavy rain. Mears saw great white or brown geysers mark the spots where Japanese 250-kilogram bombs detonated among the waves near the *Enterprise*.

The *Enterprise* was making 27 knots when the first *Shokaku* Val *chutai* started down on her port side and port quarter at 1640. The first Vals that survived the fighter onslaught spiraled down from about 18,000 feet, entered steeper dives at about 15,000, and finally dropped their bombs from between 2,000 and 1,500 feet. The Val pilots clearly attempted to follow the carrier through her radical evasive maneuvers in the last seconds before releasing their bombs, but every one of them was off the mark.

From his vantage point in Sky Lookout Forward, more than 100 feet above the flight deck, directly above the captain's bridge, Ens Ross Glasmann, the L Division junior officer, clearly saw the Vals passing through 15,000 feet and heading straight toward him from off the port bow. At that instant, a Val with a Wildcat firmly attached to its tail flitted into view. As the Val tried to dive away from the pursuing U.S. Navy fighter, Glasmann saw its twin cowl-mounted 7.7mm machine guns wink at him. He instinctively ducked as a stream of bullets buzzed close by Sky Lookout Forward and fell far below to the surface of the ocean. When Glasmann looked back around for the Val, all he could see was a flaming wreck falling into the sea. A moment later, a Wildcat descending through the heavy antiaircraft fire also burst into flames and knifed straight into the water.

Glasmann turned his gaze to another Val just as it swung from off the port bow to off the port beam to release its bomb. From his high vantage point, he was able to follow the bomb as it fell toward the flight deck, narrowly missing the ship.

Adding immeasurably to the excitement were streams of 7.7mm machine-gun bullets fired by Val pilots in their dives or Val observer-gunners retiring from the vortex of the attack. One Marine loader had a full magazine of 20mm rounds blown up in his hands by a 7.7mm round. Live rounds cooked off in all directions, but no one, not even the loader, was hurt.

◆

Each near miss caused the ship's stern to slewaround and staggered Marine Pfc Robert Lee, who was manning the portside stern 20mm cannon. Several bombs fell close enough to the ship to dash cold seawater over Lee, his loader, and the nearby gunners. The noise of the gunfire was so overwhelming that it continued to ring in Lee's ears even when he momentarily ceased firing so his loader could change ammunition drums.

Burning airplanes seemed to be falling all around the *Enterprise*. More than 100 feet above the waterline, in Sky Lookout Forward, Ens Ross Glasmann and his lookouts felt the heat of flames on their upturned faces as a Val—probably the first one shot down by Fighting-6's Gunner Chuck Brewer—faltered right over them and then plunged into the sea.

Another flaming Val—no doubt Brewer's second victim—dived obliquely past Sky Lookout Forward and straight into the water, almost on top of its own bomb. The double impact threw up a huge geyser of water and a smelly black substance that fell over Sky Lookout Forward, one of the highest points on the nearby carrier.

As the attack developed and the ship continued her tight turn to starboard, the string of Vals moved clockwise from the port bow and on down the starboard side. LCdr Benny Mott, the antiaircraft gunnery officer, was initially elated because the carrier's greatest array of firepower was concentrated on the starboard side. But the ship continued to swing around, and the Vals were soon diving on the ship from astern, and then from the port quarter.

Pfc Robert Lee, manning one of the portside stern 20mm cannon, immediately felt that his first exposure to combat was much easier than the long hours of training he had endured over many months. The plunging Vals obliged by diving straight at him. All Lee had to do was lean back in his harness, flex his knees to tilt the barrel of the gun straight up, draw a bead, and put out a few tracer rounds to see how close to the target he could come. The zero-deflection corrections from that point were simple. Lee had been trained to concentrate on one target at a time, until it dropped its bomb, disappeared from his ring sight, or blew up.

All nine Vals of LCdr Mamoru Seki's lead *Shokaku chutai* had attacked the *Enterprise*, and all had failed to score a single hit. Three of the Vals had been destroyed by fighters, possibly with assists from antiaircraft gunners, who certainly had also destroyed Mach Doyle Barnes's Wildcat and killed Barnes.

As the destroyer *Monssen* was radically shifted from the *Enterprise's* starboard quarter to her port beam as a result of the carrier's continuing wild evasive maneuvers, it looked to Lt(jg) George Hamm like the bomb from the very next Val would certainly strike the carrier.

Chapter 31

Even as Gunner Chuck Brewer was swatting down the last two Vals of the lead *Shokaku chutai,* the lead *shotai* of the rear *Shokaku chutai* was already diving toward the twisting carrier below, its Vals arrayed at 300-foot intervals. The commander of the *chutai* was Lt Keiichi Arima, the *Shokaku* Bomber Squadron *buntaicho,* who was riding as the observer behind pilot PO1 Kiyoto Furuta.

Starting his dive over the port quarter of the turning *Enterprise,* Petty Officer Furuta expertly guided his dive-bomber through intense antiaircraft fire, following the target in a twisting turn of his own, designed to throw the gunners below off their mark. The 250-kilogram semi-armorpiercing bomb was released at low altitude, and Furuta recovered smoothly almost on the surface. Lieutenant Arima, riding in the rear seat, saw a definite hit.

Indeed. The first bomb ever to strike the *Enterprise* did so at precisely 1644. The delayed-action bomb angled into the teak flight deck at the forward starboard corner of the after elevator and penetrated 42 feet through three steel decks before detonating in the chief petty officers' quarters. The entire ship whipsawed from the shock of the blast, which jerked hundreds of sailors and Marines from their feet.

AMM2 Bernard Peterson owed his life to a prescient warning from his section chief. Peterson, among many other onlookers, had been standing in the open hangar-deck boat pocket when the bombing attack began. The section chief warned the dozen-odd sailors to stand clear only an instant before the bomb exploded below decks and only 20 feet away. The explosion caused the entire after section of the hangar deck to bulge upward, and that actually popped several onlookers clear up to the overhead. Most of the men in the area suffered flash burns and shrapnel wounds, but none was as seriously injured as they all might have been had they remained in the exposed boat pocket.

The immediate area of the detonation, including the chiefs' quarters and a metal shop, was devastated. An entire damage-control party, an ammunition-handling detail, and the detail manning the elevator pump room were instantly gutted. Thirty-five men were killed outright and as many as seventy were injured. The steel deck beneath the detonation was left with a 24-foot crater, and the overhead had a bulge 24 feet in diameter. The flight deck, three levels up, was left with a 2-foot-high bulge and the after elevator was rendered inoperable—fortunately while flush with the flight deck. Several large storerooms at or just below the waterline were holed, and several of the holes were 6 feet in diameter.

Two factors probably prevented the ship from being rapidly engulfed in flames: Flammable paint had been chipped from the compartments around the impact zone, and, moments before the attack, Mach Bill Fluitt, the ship's gasoline officer, oversaw the draining and venting of nearby aviation fuel lines, which were all filled with inert carbon dioxide moments before the bomb struck.

The steeply angled path of the bomb had carried it through the sponson supporting Lt John Williamson's Gun Group 3—the aft starboard pair of 5-inch guns—where it started several small fires. Lieutenant Williamson secured the entire crew of Number-5 5-inch gun to fight the fire.

The ship settled on a minor starboard list as fires broke out in all the affected berthing and storage areas. As the flames quickly spread through mattresses, clothing, and stores, thick, blinding smoke choked off the entire area. Several key electrical cables and mains were destroyed or shorted out, and water pressure in nearby fire-fighting mains dropped off to useless levels.

There was no time to recover from Furuta's and Arima's bomb. The second Val in Arima's lead *shotai* was 30 seconds behind Arima, and its contact-fused 242-kilogram "land" bomb struck the after flight deck only 15 feet away from the first hit, only 11 feet from the starboard edge of the flight deck.

Each of the *Enterprise's* eight 5-inch gun mounts was manned by a crew of twenty-four, including one officer, and each of the two-mount gun groups was under the supervision of one battery officer. Thus, there were forty-six enlisted sailors and three officers manning Lt John Williamson's Gun Group 3—the two after starboard 5-inch mounts. In addition, the after-battery troubleshooter, GM1 William Powell, had run over to Gun Group 3 from the port aft 5-inch guns when the first bomb set off the ready powder. Powell had just dropped into the gun gallery from the flight deck when the second bomb detonated at deck level and right on top of the guns.

Observers on other ships or elsewhere on the *Enterprise*—including a Navy movie cameraman who caught the whole thing on film—noticed that the bomb blast was instantly followed by a secondary blast of very large magnitude. The secondary blast was the sympathetic detonation of Gun Group 3's ready powder casings—perhaps as many as sixty-five that early in the action. Tremendous heat coupled with the shattering explosion and release of a huge orange ball of flame and voluminous black smoke ensured the instantaneous death of forty-one of Gun Group 3's fifty gunners and officers—including Lt John Williamson and GM1 William Powell. All of the surviving gunners and at least four bystanders were severely injured. Indeed, all of the fatalities who were not ripped to shreds by the force of the blast were burned beyond easy recognition; many were little more than small, grotesque charcoal caricatures of the men they had once been.

The terrific blast threw large chunks of metal and pieces of human bodies out as far as the destroyer *Monssen,* which was roughly a mile off the carrier's starboard quarter, endeavoring to follow the larger ship through her radical turns. As debris struck the destroyer and the water around her,

Lt(jg) George Hamm saw that someone aboard the *Enterprise* had had the presence of mind to throw out a smoke marker and life rafts in the event that live crewmen had also been blown overboard.

Early on, when Ens Ross Glasmann, more than 100 feet above the waterline in Sky Lookout Forward, realized that many of the Vals were bound to recover right over his station, he had drawn his .45-caliber automatic pistol, held it in both hands at arm's length, and deliberately squeezed the trigger in the hope of placing at least several rounds into the cockpit area of each passing dive-bomber. Glasmann was only 30 or 40 feet from each of the passing dive-bombers. He felt collected and in full control, even when he found himself staring right into the eyes of a passing Val pilot who appeared to be growing a beard. Glasmann saw one of his rounds hole the cockpit right in front of the bearded pilot, and this Val peeled off to the left and plunged into the ocean. As Ensign Glasmann fired, he was completely oblivious to the angry taunts that he shouted at the passing dive-bombers, and would be quite taken aback by his outspoken enmity when one of his lookouts later commented on it.

A Val that still had its bomb aboard—the third member of the lead *shotai* of Lieutenant Arima's rear *Shokaku chutai*—was plummeting toward him in flames from directly overhead when Ensign Glasmann saw a 20mm round from one of the surface escorts strike the nose of the lethal projectile the Val was carrying between its fixed landing gear. There was a terrific dark blast right over Sky Lookout Forward, and slivers of the bomb and parts of the vaporized Val rained down on the tiny exposed nest. Several large pieces and numerous tiny pieces struck the helmets of men in exposed positions throughout the island, but no one was noticeably injured. Fortunately, the momentum and path of the diving Val impelled the worst part of the detonation out over the water.

Well before Ensign Glasmann's ears cleared from the blast, he returned his attention to sighting in on other passing Vals with his automatic pistol. Two more targets dived past his high perch after dropping their bombs. Glasmann could plainly see numerous tracer-marked streams of 20mm and .50-caliber rounds from many sources enter the wings, fuselage, and cockpit area of each passing dive-bomber. He knew his pistol rounds, fired at very close range, were striking home, but he had few illusions as to their effectiveness. Glasmann fired off two eight-round clips in about three minutes.

The first two Vals of the second *shotai* of Lieutenant Arima's rear *Shokaku chutai* both missed the *Enterprise*, but one of the pilots placed his bomb close enough to the starboard side of the big ship to drench officers and men on the high island structure. Also, despite numerous reports of their demise, both Vals survived the gauntlet of fire and recovered low on the water.

The third Val in Arima's second *shotai* was hit dead-on several times as it reached its release point. Many observers saw the Val stagger in the air and simply fall apart. Its bomb fell free, however, and glided down toward the flight deck below.

It was coming up on 1646. BM1 Al Gabara, the Number-4 1.1-inch gun captain, happened to be looking at his friend, BM2 Arthur Davis, when the bomb from the demolished Val was stopped by a structural member of the after elevator. This 242-kilogram "land" bomb was fused to detonate on impact; it went off at flight-deck level in a relatively low-order detonation incorrectly judged by many observers to be the result of a defect. BM2 Davis, who was standing in the open next to the Number-2 elevator, was simply blown apart by the full force of the blast. A large chunk of him landed in the after 1.1-inch gun pointer's lap.

BM1 Gabara went into shock for a few seconds, until one of the loaders yelled into his ear, "Gabby, you're hit!" He did not feel a thing, but he followed the loader's gaze until he found that a steel sliver had holed his right arm just below the elbow. He also found that he had spent a few lost moments absently sweeping shell casings from the mount.

PhoM3 Robert Read, one of three still photographers who had been charged with recording the defense of the carrier on film for later study, was standing tall in an exposed vantage point on the island as he followed the third bomb in his viewfinder all the way to impact. Read got his superb shot, but shrapnel from the blast killed him.

S1 Willie Bowdoin, a member of the Number-3 1.1-inch gun crew, was wounded in the leg and posterior by tiny steel shards and knocked to the flight deck. When Bowdoin recovered his senses, he saw that a small fire had broken out behind the gun, so he moved to grab a fire extinguisher to put it out. He was arrested in his tracks by the screams of S1 Joyce Lamson, the Number-3 gun pointer, who had also been thrown to the deck. Lamson's abdomen had been torn open by bomb shrapnel and his intestines were exposed. One of his legs also appeared to be shredded. Almost without thinking, AMM2 Joe Greco and another aviation groudcrewman gingerly lifted Lamson and carried him to the aid station located just beneath the flight deck.

Meantime, S1 Willie Bowdoin fought the fire, and won.

As BM1 Al Gabara's circle of attention widened beyond his own injuries, he saw that every man in his gun crew had been peppered and slightly injured by flying steel slivers. It took several more moments for Gabara to notice that the starboard after 5-inch gun gallery was a smoking ruin.

Though the 27-knot *North Carolina* continued to fall farther and farther behind the 32-knot *Enterprise,* her guns were able to bear on many Vals as they recovered from dives on the carrier.

At 1645, just as the *North Carolina* was struck by several errant antiaircraft rounds from other ships, she became the exclusive target of the last three Vals of Lieutenant Arima's *Shokaku chutai,* which lagged behind the rest of the carrier bombers and thus could not get into effective position over the *Enterprise.* It is also possible that this *shotai* was thrown off the mark by the last-minute attack by Mach Doyle Barnes's Fighting-6 Wildcat division. In any case, these dive-bombers detached themselves from the main *Shokaku* Val force and dived head-on to the lagging battleship. Along with the three Vals, firing bursts as he came, was Fighting-6's Ens Douglas Johnson, who moments earlier had attacked the rear *Shokaku* Val *shotai* at 10,000 feet and then followed it into the remainder of its dive.

Two bombs missed to port, and the third missed to starboard. The Val pilots and gunners also strafed the battleship's deck and upper works as they dived and recovered.

The *North Carolina's* own 5-inch, 1.1-inch, and 20mm guns downed the lead Val 1,500 yards off her starboard quarter. And the second Val was shot down, too, either by converging antiaircraft fire from the *North Carolina* and the *Atlanta,* or by Fighting-6's Ens Douglas Johnson, who claimed and received a full victory credit. The wings of Johnson's Wildcat were also struck by shell fragments from below, and the radio antenna was shot away, but Johnson himself was unscathed. Also, the third Val was able to recover and withdraw from the immediate vicinity of Task Force 16.

Of eighteen *Shokaku* Vals in on the attack, five had been downed over the *Enterprise* by fighters or antiaircraft fire, and two had been downed over the *North Carolina*, also by a fighter or antiaircraft fire. Of eight Fighting-5 and Fighting-6 Wildcats that had intercepted the attack, one had been downed by antiaircraft fire. *Shokaku* airmen who survived the battle claimed six hits on the *Enterprise*, but they had scored only three, which was plenty.

Chapter 32

At 1638, two minutes before the air action began over the *Enterprise*, Lt Reijiro Otsuka had led his nine-plane *Zuikaku* Val *chutai* toward the *Saratoga*, which, with her entire ring of surface escorts, was then about 10 miles beyond the *Enterprise* and closing. Initially, Lieutenant Otsuka's *chutai* had been guarded by Lt Saneyasu Hidaka's six *Zuikaku* escort Zeros. All the fighters had been drawn into early combat with Lt Dave Richardson's three-plane Fighting-5 division, however, and had thus fallen far behind Otsuka's Vals when the crunch came.

As had the two *Shokaku* Val *chutais* on their way to attack the *Enterprise*, the *Zuikaku chutai* opened into a line-astern formation as it began letting down from 16,400 feet (5,000 meters) on its way to the dive point. Just as the Vals opened out, they were attacked by a three-plane Fighting-5 division commanded by Lt Hayden Jensen that had been climbing at top speed since first spotting the entire Val formation at 1632. These Wildcats had gotten themselves into an excellent position to attack Otsuka's *chutai*; when they opened their attack, the three Fighting-5 Wildcats were ahead of the Vals at 20,000 feet.

Lieutenant Jensen initiated his diving attack against the center *shotai* and arrived in firing range just as the Val formation opened out. He executed a high-side run on one of the Vals and claimed a victory when he saw the dive-bomber fall out of the formation in flames. The fight became a melee as Jensen and his two wingmen, Ens John Kleinman and Lt(jg) Carlton Starkes, made several independent passes at the Val formation, claiming many hits and victories to a total of seven Vals destroyed in the air.

Less than a minute behind Jensen and his wingmen, Mach Don Runyon's four-plane Fighting-6 division joined the fight against Otsuka's *Zuikaku* Vals from 20,000 feet and out of the sun following a long chase from the outer limits of the early fighter cordon. Apparently, the arrival of Runyon's quartet convinced Lieutenant Otsuka that his formation stood very little chance of reaching the distant *Saratoga*. As Runyon's Wildcats pitched in, the *chutai* leader edged toward the nearer *Enterprise*, and his entire formation dutifully followed. Meanwhile, as with Jensen's division, the four Fighting-6 Wildcats made repeated runs at the Vals, and Runyon claimed two definite victories as well as, in his mind, forcing two Vals to break off the attack and turn for home.

As Runyon's division continued to attack the Vals with single-minded diligence, they were jumped by four *Zuikaku* Zeros fresh from the fight with Lt Dave Richardson's Fighting-5 trio. It is possible that one of the Zero pilots downed Runyon's second-section leader, Mach Bill Reid, for Reid did not emerge from the melee and was never seen again. In addition to possibly downing Reid, the four *Zuikaku* Zeros were largely responsible for breaking up the one-sided Wildcat attacks on the Vals. Lt Hayden Jensen had to dive away in a hurry, and both of his wingmen, Starkes and Kleinman, had to divert their attention to defending themselves and other Wildcats, including Jensen's. Runyon also had to divert from the bombers to take on a Zero, which he claimed.

The next Wildcat to enter the melee was a single flown by Ens Frank Green, of Fighting-5. Moments earlier, Green had broken off from his leader, Lt Dick Gray, when Gray went to the aid of Dave Richardson's division in its fight with the *Zuikaku* Zeros. He attacked a Val that he had watched during his climb into the fight as it was attacked by three other Wildcats. While attacking this Val from dead astern, Green saw it emit smoke and then fall flaming from the formation. He attacked another Val and then was forced to dive away when yet another Val opened fire on him with its cowl guns.

The last Wildcats to enter the fight against the *Zuikaku* Val *chutai* was a three-plane Fighting-5 division led by Lt Jim Smith. This division was strictly an ad hoc affair of convenience brought about by the last-minute launch to clear the *Saratoga's* flight deck in the face of the incoming attack. Smith's wingmen were Ens Horace Bass and Ens Ike Eichenberger.

The three made contact as the *Zuikaku* Vals reached their pushover point, which is to say in the midst of the antiaircraft umbrella over the *Enterprise*. Ensign Eichenberger followed one of the Vals right into the antiaircraft umbrella. Eichenberger's two partners, Lieutenant Smith and Ensign Bass, apparently dived into the friendly fire, too, but neither pilot emerged from the cauldron and neither was seen again. Observers aboard several escort vessels saw a Wildcat spin out of control into the ocean and a flaming Wildcat dive from great height straight into the water about 2 miles from the destroyer *Balch*. No one on any of the ships suggested that either Wildcat had been hit by friendly fire, but it is a distinct possibility despite the presence of Lieutenant Hidaka's *Zuikaku* Zeros.

As near as anyone can tell, despite more victory claims than there were Vals or Zeros, only two Vals were downed by the fifteen Wildcats that attacked the *Zuikaku chutai*—Lieutenant Otsuka's and one other dive-bomber. On the other hand, the U.S. Navy fighters broke the integrity of the Val formation and forced four of the dive-bombers so far out of position that they would be unable to attack the damaged and smoking *Enterprise*.

As the new attack unfolded, AOM2 Lester Tucker and other members of the *North Carolina's* aft 20mm gun batteries spotted six aircraft flying up the battleship's wake. Four were *Zuikaku* Vals and two were Fighting-6 Wildcats piloted by AP1 Howard Packard and Ens Dutch Shoemaker, the two wingmen from Don Runyon's division. Beginning at 1645, Packard attacked the line-astern Val formation from rear to front—three times— and reported that he had seen smoke being emitted from one of the Vals before he had to pull away once and for all. Shoemaker swooped down after one of the Vals, but he passed it in the dive, briefly fired at another Val, and pulled up before entering the cone of fire from the *North Carolina's* after 20mm batteries.

By the time Packard and Shoemaker left the scene, the four Vals were too low and out of position to complete a true dive-bombing attack; they elected to execute a much shallower glide-bombing approach, and did so as the *North Carolina* turned hard to port—either to evade the imminent attack or to follow the *Enterprise* into an evasive turn. One group of the battleship's starboard twin 5-inch mounts dropped their barrels from high-altitude targets, but the big guns were prevented from firing at the oncoming Vals because the gun-target line passed right through the stern catapults, each of which sported a fully fueled OS2U observation floatplane armed with light bombs. Thus, the only opposition the *North Carolina* could offer was from several aft 20mm guns.

The glide-bombing technique pretty much uses the momentum of a shallow dive to throw the bomb at the target. It is an inexact science requiring immense skill. The Japanese gliding down on the *North Carolina* were not sufficiently skilled, or perhaps they were rattled by all the shocking events leading up to their attack. At 1646, within the minute, all four bombs missed the huge ship, either to port or to starboard, but one struck abreast the port catapult close enough to knock down gun crews, dent the side of the ship above the waterline, and raise a column of seawater that drenched several of the port aft 20mm gun crews.

As the Vals were passing overhead, AOM2 Lester Tucker's loader became mesmerized by the sights of the battle and forgot to replace the gun's expended ammunition drum. Tucker pulled himself from his harness to give the awestruck loader a swift kick in the rear. Just as the surprised loader turned, a passing Val unleashed a twin stream of 7.7mm bullets. One round barely missed the loader's head before passing between Tucker's legs and on into a bag of expended 20mm cartridges, which spilled out over the deck. Another 7.7mm round from the same burst passed through the abdomen and out the back of AMM3 George Conlon, the loader on the next gun forward. Conlon, who had just made his rate that morning, sat down heavily on the deck behind his gun and fell over backward.

One of the last *Zuikaku* Vals to dive on the ship recovered and flew down the starboard side, close enough for FC3 Larry Resen—in Sky Control, 120 feet above the water—to see the pilot's face. Resen was certain that the pilot wanted to carry home detailed information about the first modern U.S. fast battleship to weather combat in the Pacific. When AOM2 Tucker and nearby gunners saw the last Val fly by only 150 feet away with its canopy thrown back and the pilot and observer intently staring at them, they took revenge for George Conlon by blasting it with everything they had. The gunners claimed a kill, but as with so many other claims by shipborne gunners, it just wasn't so. All four Vals managed to recover and pass beyond the range of Task Force 16's antiaircraft umbrella.

AMM3 Conlon was carried by stretcher to the aid station set up in the aviation storeroom by the fantail aircraft catapults, but he expired before the corpsmen could begin treating him. He was the battleship's only fatality of the day.

That left just three *Zuikaku* Vals, and they all attacked the *Enterprise*. One of the Vals attacked alone. The other two were the fallen Lieutenant Otsuka's wingmen—very likely the same pair that Mach Don Runyon thought he had chased from the scene. These two flew completely over the *Enterprise* at altitude and reversed to attack from the southwest. When they plunged together toward the carrier from 12,000 feet at 1647, they were followed into the maelstrom by Fighting-5's Ens Ike Eichenberger, the sole survivor of the ad hoc trio led by Lt Jim Smith.

Moments before the final attack began, a 20mm gunner on the twisting carrier's after catwalk complained aloud that he had something in his eye and needed relief. AMM2 Bernard Peterson had qualified as a TBF .50-caliber turret gunner, and friends among the 20mm gunners had given him a little practice on their weapons, so he strapped into the harness and immediately began firing at a diving Val. *Bonk . . . Bonk . . . Bonk.* Peterson was at first surprised by the 20mm gun's low rate of fire, but he quickly settled in. A real sense of power suffused him as his gun's bright popcorn balls of tracer seemed to stitch the Val's body and the airplane appeared to blow up. Before Peterson could swivel onto a new target, a second Val appeared to be swiped from the air by other guns. Then Peterson's tracer joined with others against yet another Val, and that also appeared to fall out of the sky.

In fact, none of the three *Zuikaku* Vals succumbed to fire from below. The first one, attacking alone, missed the great ship, recovered low, and cleared the task force formation. The second Val, with Ensign Eichenberger attached to its tail and firing bursts from 12,000 feet on down to 4,000 feet, near-missed the ship and also recovered low.

Lt Robin Lindsey, the *Enterprise's* senior landing signal officer, was on the tiny LSO platform at the port after corner of the flight deck when the second Val's 250-kilogram bomb raised a huge geyser of seawater almost directly beneath his feet. Lindsey jumped down to the walkway next to the exposed LSO platform and yanked out his .45-caliber pistol—more a totem to salve his frazzled nerves than a suitable weapon for staving off enemy dive-bombers. Nevertheless, Lindsey sighted down the barrel of his automatic pistol and cranked off several rounds at the departing Val observer-gunner, who was firing at the ship.

Lt(jg) Ed DeGarmo, the 20mm battery officer nearest to the blast that unnerved Robin Lindsey, was painfully wounded by a hot sliver of steel deep in his right foot, but he refused relief. One of his gun captains took a sliver of steel that would render him blind in one eye, but he too refused to relinquish his battle station. And a 20mm gun loader was lifted right out of the aft sponson and tossed up onto the flight deck. He was so dazed that he climbed down to the 20mm gun nearest his resting place and reloaded it before realizing it was not his own.

This very-near miss severely dented the carrier's hull, but no holes were blasted, no seams were sprung, and no lives were lost.

The last bomb aimed at the *Enterprise* this day was dropped almost at the same instant as the near miss. It raised a geyser of seawater 300 yards to port. The Val that dropped it recovered low and made for the nearest exit.

The middle Val, whose bomb had nearly hit the ship, was the same airplane that had been followed most of the way down by Ens Ike Eichenberger. As it recovered and headed out between the *North Carolina* and the *Grayson*, it was attacked by Fighting-6's Ens Ram Dibb, the departed Mach Doyle Barnes's wingman. After attacking the *Shokaku* Vals earlier, Dibb had stayed out of the antiaircraft umbrella, but he had been forced to dive in when attacked by one of the *Zuikaku* escort Zeros. Extremely lucky to have survived the attack—and the wrath of countless indiscriminating friendly gunners—he happened to be in the right place when the middle *Zuikaku* Val came off its attack on the *Enterprise*. Dibb fired on the Val and, with many other observers, saw it fall into the water 500 yards off the *Grayson's* port bow. And indeed it did—the only recovering Val to be downed within Task Force 16's ring of fire. Of course, gunners on several nearby ships also claimed the kill, and all were awarded credit.

Ensign Dibb also fired at another departing Val, but he ran out of ammunition in the midst of his attack and bent on all speed to clear the task force formation before the friendly gunners could swat him from the sky.

The attack of Task Force 16 was over by 1648. All ships ceased firing between 1649 and 1650. For most of the officers and men topside in Task Force 16, the abrupt silence was almost painful.

Chapter 33

Nearly all of the eleven *Shokaku* Vals and six *Zuikaku* Vals that survived their dives on the *Enterprise* and the *North Carolina* were pretty much obliged to recover along a path directly between the destroyer *Grayson* and the *North Carolina*. All of these Japanese airplanes remained at very low altitude but flew at the top speed they could muster.

The first recovering Val—LCdr Mamoru Seki's—crossed over the destroyer from starboard to port at an altitude of about 300 feet. The *hikotaicho* incurred the wrath of all hands aboard the destroyer by opening fire with his cowl-mounted 7.7mm machine guns. A shower of bullets struck the *Grayson's* Number-3 5-inch gun, an adjacent 20mm battery, and the aft torpedo mount, and eleven destroyermen were wounded. The *Grayson's* after 20mm gun groups trained onto the passing Val and poured out a heavy concentration of fire. It was claimed by the ship's crew that Seki's Val staggered and fell away into the water off the destroyer's port bow, but it is doubtful that it was even so much as hit.

The next three Vals to get away from the *Enterprise* flew up the *Grayson's* starboard side. The first was claimed by the *North Carolina's* port 5-inch guns, but it actually got clean away. The second Val drew the wrath of the *Grayson's* starboard 20mm battery, which reported repeated hits at close range that apparently caused it to sideslip and crash 100 yards off the *Grayson's* port bow. But no such ending occurred; this Val also flew clear of Task Force 16. And the third Val was engaged by only one 20mm gun, because all the destroyer's other starboard guns had been directed against distant targets high over the *Enterprise*. This Val jinked away from the *Grayson's* lone gun and flew directly into the immense cloud of low-level fire the *North Carolina's* port batteries were putting out. It was claimed by the battleship as a definite kill, but it also cleared Task Force 16.

One other Val was seen banking sharply away from the *Enterprise* before it pulled out of its dive just a few feet above the water and zoomed right over the destroyer *Monssen*. In that fleeting instant, Lt(jg) George Hamm managed to look the begoggled Japanese pilot right in the eyes. As Hamm turned to follow the Val's progress, he looked straight down the barrel of a 20mm gun that was also tracking the warplane. Many streams of 20mm tracer crossed behind, ahead, and apparently right through the receding dive-bomber. This airplane briefly smoked and streamed a flame, but Hamm saw the fire go out as the Val flew from sight.

More kills were claimed by various ships than there ever were Vals over the task force, but the fact is that every one of the six lead *chutai* Vals to survive the bombing attack on the *Enterprise* cleared Task Force 16 and flew safely from the range of its many antiaircraft guns. In fact, of the eleven *Shokaku* Vals and seven *Zuikaku* Vals that dropped their bombs and recovered from their dives, only one was downed on the way out of the Task Force 16 circle, and that was the *Zuikaku* Val credited to Fighting-6's Ens Ram Dibb and about a half-dozen surface ships.

Carrier pilots in the air over their own flight decks are motivated at several levels: There is the thrill of the hunt, which itself tends to block out a lot of other matters; there is the sense of duty to the living souls stranded in the friendly ships, which is a powerful motivational force; and there is the pragmatic realization that a severely damaged or sunken flight deck cannot be used for a safe landing.

These three motivations are precisely the forces that carried so many Wildcat pilots against the diving Vals—and on into the cones of friendly antiaircraft fire. At least one, and possibly four, of the five Wildcat pilots lost in the opening melees over Task Force 16 were brought down by friendly fire.

The motivation for the hard fight the Wildcat jocks—and other U.S. Navy pilots—gave the retiring Vals was pure revenge.

After the Japanese dive-bomber leader dived away from Lt Chick Harmer, the Fighting-5 exec peeled out of his own dive and found another Val in his sights. This Val appeared to Harmer to have already dropped its bomb, but Harmer followed it anyway, though his Wildcat sustained several hits while trading bursts with the Val's rear gunner. Harmer fired at close range from above and behind the dive-bomber, and probably killed the gunner. But before Harmer could direct his bullets at the pilot or the Val's vulnerable fuel tanks, the Val suddenly pulled up right in front of the Wildcat—it looked like the pilot was trying to loop—and Harmer had to pull out in a steep right bank to avoid colliding with it. As the fighter-squadron exec completed a 180-degree turn, he saw a huge splash below the wings of his fighter. He was thus credited with a probable kill. Harmer was by then at less than 500 feet, and not another F4F was in sight; all the other aircraft he could sight were Japanese. He had evidently flown into their rendezvous area.

Chick Harmer immediately lost interest in the last Val's possible crash sight when a blast of tracer passed his fighter. He was certain he had a Zero on his tail, but it was a Val.

Harmer tried to out-turn or out-climb the enemy airplane, but the Imperial Navy dive-bomber was able to hang quite comfortably on Harmer's tail and follow his every evasive maneuver while letting the Wildcat have it with repeated 7.7mm bursts. One burst penetrated the Wildcat's canopy, struck the instrument panel, and injured Harmer in both legs. The Wildcat pilot did the only thing he had left in his bag of tricks—he turned the armor-plate in the back of his seat to the Val's guns and did his level best to keep it there. He could hear and feel the gunfire for long, long seconds, but then it abruptly stopped. Harmer had no idea what spared him as he rather gingerly flew from the area.

While Chick Harmer was going it alone at the Vals' rendezvous point, his wingman, Lt(jg) John McDonald, also dove to the surface, where he immediately got on the tail of one of the recovering Vals. As McDonald attempted to move into firing position, the Val pilot led him through a series of S-turns at an altitude of 50 feet, but McDonald stayed with him and eventually fired into the Val at full-deflection—a difficult 90-degree shot. McDonald reported that the Val was last seen heading down in flames, and he was given credit for this, his second kill of the day.

A third member of Harmer's Fighting-5 division, Ens Benjamin Currie, also met up with a Val at low altitude. Currie claimed the enemy bomber as it turned and withdrew in a northerly direction.

Also catching the Vals near the surface was Fighting-5's Lt(jg) Carlton Starkes. As he pulled level at 1,000 feet after diving from altitude, Starkes found himself directly in front of a three-plane *Shokaku shotai* that was heading out in formation. Starkes maneuvered around for an attack, fired at one Val, saw hits, and pulled away in the belief that he had probably downed it.

After actually downing a Val from the rear *Shokaku shotai* before it could attack the *Enterprise*, Ensign Ram Dibb, a member of the Fighting-6 division that had been commanded by Mach Doyle Barnes, dived all the way through the vast cone of friendly fire at what he thought was a Zero. Despite Dibb's initial advantage, the enemy airplane twice maneuvered into superior attack positions from which Dibb emerged following violent evasive maneuvers. The last successful evasion carried Dibb almost to the surface, where he opportunistically shot up a Val as it was recovering from its bombing run. At that point, Dibb had to leave the fight because his Wildcat's engine was struck by small-caliber bullets. Also, as it turned out, there were holes caused by antiaircraft shrapnel in the carburetor intake and exhaust manifold of Dibb's Wildcat. Dibb was given credit for downing two Vals, but he had downed only one for certain.

Gunner Chuck Brewer, the heroic leader of Machinist Barnes's second section, was on the surface, looking for departing Vals when he spotted one of the *Shokaku* dive-bombers low on the waves. As Brewer lined up on this Val, he was attacked from behind by a Zero. With cool detachment, Brewer shot up the Val before turning sharply to evade the Zero. Then, with utter precision, he chopped the throttle, pulled up, and headed around to engage the Zero in a head-on attack. The two fighters passed one another, apparently without harm, and then both turned to reengage. Brewer was the first to fire. He shot up the Zero with a difficult full-deflection burst that seemed to finish it off. In all, Brewer was credited with two Vals and the Zero.

One of the day's most surprising engagements took place as Lt Rube Konig's tiny strike force of six Torpedo-3 Avengers circled around Task Force 16 to gain altitude and locate the mixed group of eleven Scouting-5 and Bombing-6 SBDs sent out following their last-minute launch from the *Enterprise*. The SBDs never joined up. As Konig finally turned north, toward the *Ryujo's* last-known position, a lone Val joined up on his formation. Clearly, the Japanese pilot was looking for some help navigating home, though it is doubtful he initially realized he had joined a U.S. Navy formation.

In the second or two it took the U.S. airmen who noticed the intruder to figure out what to do, the Japanese pilot woke up and opened fire on Mach John Baker's TBF from 500 yards astern and off Baker's port quarter. Immediately, Baker's turret gunner, ARM3 Carl Gibson, returned the fire. The first burst, a short one, struck the Val's fuselage. A longer second burst fell between the Japanese warplane's cockpit and engine. According to Gibson, the Val, which had been closing on him, dropped away in flames and appeared to dive all the way into the ocean.

Lt(jg) Dick Gay's unengaged Fighting-6 division, which had been among the last Wildcats to launch from either carrier, climbed away from Task Force 16 and was just executing a climbing turn through 14,500 feet when Gay noticed three Zeros chasing a lone Wildcat at about 12,000 feet. As Gay led his division down, the menaced Wildcat pilot, Fighting-6's Ens Francis Register, managed a tight wingover that placed the Zero dead ahead of his Wildcat. The Japanese pilot rolled to the left to evade Register, but he came out right in front of Gay's diving Wildcats. The Zero pilot tried to evade Gay's fighters by executing a climbing turn to the right, but this only put him into Register's sights again. Register fired a full-deflection burst at the Zero at close range, but the Japanese pilot evaded in a maneuver Register described as a cartwheel! But Dick Gay was by then on top of things, and he nailed the Zero despite its skilled pilot's best efforts. So did Gay's wingman, Ens Charles Lindley. And Register thought he had killed the Zero, too. In fact, all three Wildcat pilots were given full credit for the one airplane.

Meanwhile, Ens Bob Disque, Gay's tail-end Charlie, went into a tight turn to follow the other three Wildcats in his division down to help Ensign Register. As Disque prepared to follow his section leader, Mach Joe Achten, after a second Zero, he heard what sounded like someone throwing a handful of gravel against the side of a tin barn. At that, he instinctively knew that his fighter had been hit by a third Zero he had yet to see. He pulled into a tight turn and scrunched up his tall body to present as small a target as possible to the next burst. But the next burst did not come. This Zero was chased off (but not caught) by Machinist Achten, who gave up pursuit of his own quarry in order to save Disque.

Ensign Disque continued around in his tight turn and, within seconds, came upon the Zero Joe Achten had been chasing. He poured bullets into the Japanese fighter in an almost head-on pass. Before Disque pulled away, black smoke was pouring from the Zero, which rolled over and fell away toward the surface. Disque claimed this as a victory, but, though this *Zuikaku* Zero was certainly damaged, it survived.

Though four claims were made for the one *Zuikaku* and two *Shokaku* Zeros that had been menacing Ensign Register, only one, the *Zuikaku* fighter, was actually shot down—almost certainly by Lt(jg) Dick Gay.

By the time Ensign Disque completed his pullout from the head-on firing pass, he found himself alone in the sky. His fighter had a multitude of neat, clean holes in both wing roots, a number of grooves in the covering for the oxygen bottle down by the right rudder pedal, and two holes in the canopy track by the pilot's right shoulder. Though severely chastened, Disque silently gave credit to the Japanese pilot, whom he felt had to be a superb marksman to have put his entire burst right into the Wildcat's cockpit area at nearly a 90-degree angle. Disque would later learn that his

Wildcat had been hit by about 110 rounds in the cockpit and wing-root area. It all happened so fast, there had been no time for Disque to think about it.

As Ensign Disque flew alone around the edge of the main action, he saw a TBF low on the water, banking and turning, trying to evade a Zero that was making repeated firing passes at it. This was the Torpedo-3 search plane flown by Ens Harold Bingaman.

Bingaman had returned to the task force in the company of an SBD flown by Ens John Jorgenson, who had accompanied him on the search hop. Moments after sighting Task Force 16, which appeared to be under attack, Bingaman's TBF was attacked by three Zeros, and Jorgenson's SBD disappeared from sight, perhaps because it was also attacked.

Ensign Bingaman, a fighter pilot who had been dragooned into torpedo bombers following the Midway massacre, allowed his killer instincts to prevail over his good sense. He immediately began challenging the three Zeros by maneuvering into direct head-on passes. This effectively negated the defensive capabilities of his two crew gunners—AMM3 Calvin Crouch, who was manning the TBF's .30-caliber tunnel stinger, and ARM3 Paul Knight, who was manning the .50-caliber power-turret gun.

Finally, after what seemed like ages to the gunners, Bingaman leveled off right over the sea and flew straight ahead at top speed. Apparently, the now-certain kill was left to just one of the Zeros, which made a rear approach ARM3 Knight saw as being right out of the gunnery school manual. At the precise moment the Zero flew into range, Knight plinked out a short burst and saw his tracer going just a hair over the Zero's starboard wing. Knight also saw a thin wisp of yellowish smoke curl back over each of the Zero's wings—the telltale signature of 20mm cannon fire.

From Ens Bob Disque's high vantage point, the Zero and TBF appeared to be so close to the surface of the ocean that the Zero's 7.7mm and 20mm rounds were kicking up a visible pattern in the water.

ARM3 Knight nudged his power turret over just a hair and resumed firing. It was a long burst. Knight was gratified to see that his tracers were falling right across the top of the Japanese fighter's engine cowling.

At this moment, Ensign Disque dropped down and caught the Zero from behind.

ARM3 Knight did not see the friendly Wildcat, but he saw essentially the same thing Bob Disque saw from his totally different vantage point: The Zero dropped its right wing, as if peeling off to the right, and flew straight into the water.

Though Disque passed close to the TBF, Knight never saw him. He had other matters to contend with. At the precise moment the Zero staggered to the right in its death throes, a 20mm cannon round—or perhaps a .50-caliber round from one of Disque's guns—struck the Plexiglas power turret. Everything seemed to explode in Knight's face.

Seconds later, before Knight could recover, Ensign Bingaman announced that he was ditching the bullet-riddled TBF. AMM3 Crouch climbed out of the gun tunnel and strapped into a seat facing the rear of the crew compartment right behind the cockpit. Knight, who was strapped into his turret seat, merely braced himself for the shock of the imminent contact.

The Avenger slid into the water at fairly high speed and came to an abrupt stop, the shock from which momentarily knocked Paul Knight unconscious. When Knight fully regained his senses, he found that the airplane was well down by the nose and that he was in the process of ejecting the side escape hatch. As the radioman-gunner attempted to crawl through the hatch, however, he felt something holding him back by the left ankle. There was a momentary fit of panicked kicking, which freed the foot, and Knight left the airplane.

By the time Knight left the sinking Avenger, Bingaman and Crouch had deployed a life raft. Knight kicked across the few yards of water separating him from the raft, and was helped aboard by his crewmates. It was only then discovered that the explosion in the power turret had left Knight with lacerations in the forehead, face, left leg, and left hand.

Moments later, the TBF sank.

Shortly after helping to knock down the Zero that had been menacing Ensign Bingaman's TBF, Ens Bob Disque sighted another Zero low on the water, apparently headed for home. He approached the fighter from above and camped on its tail before firing every .50-caliber round he had left. Then Disque had to watch the Zero slowly pull away and disappear over the horizon.

◆

Lt Walter Clarke led his five-plane Fighting-5 division around the friendly antiaircraft fire, but Lt(jg) Smokey Stover and his wingman, Ens Mortimer Kleinmann, separated from Clarke—more or less accidentally—and started to enter the snarling Wildcat-versus-Zero melee at the top of the antiaircraft curtain. Immediately, a Zero zoomed them. Stover and Kleinmann gave chase and repeatedly fired at the Zero, but with no apparent results. The two U.S. Navy pilots chased the swifter Imperial Navy fighter for five minutes but could not gain on it even after dropping their belly tanks. Kleinmann fired all his ammunition during the chase but could not even claim damage on the Zero.

No member of Clarke's five-plane division claimed a victory.

LCdr Roy Simpler's Fighting-5 division was launched from the *Saratoga* at 1636, the last Wildcats to be sent aloft before the attack. In the excitement following the first collision of American and Japanese warplanes, however, the FDOs forgot to call or could not get through to Simpler or anyone in his division, which they had vectored out after a bogey in the opposite direction of the Japanese air strike just before the start of the action. Simpler took his division high to chase after what was probably a flight of three 11th Heavy Bombardment Group B-17s on their way to attack the *Ryujo*. However, before Simpler's division could get to altitude, it was deterred by an impressive wall of antiaircraft fire that, in Roy Simpler's vivid description, looked like "black air." For all that, however, Simpler dutifully remained on his original heading for more than a half-hour before he was able to break into the communications net with a request for new instructions. The FDO with whom he spoke ordered his immediate return to Task Force 61.

By the time Simpler reached Task Force 61, all the attackers were retiring at high speed and low altitude. The Fighting-5 commander immediately flew down to low altitude near Task Force 16, but the fight there was pretty much over by the time he and his division arrived. However, as this division let down to take on any Vals that had not yet retired, Ens Wayne Presley spotted a parachute shroud just over the water at some distance. He led Ens Mel Roach out to investigate, and they were accosted at low altitude along the way by a lone Val that attacked Presley from dead ahead

The Val and the Wildcat traded shots with each other until the Val dove straight into the sea.

After he landed, LCdr Roy Simpler let it be known in rather strong terms that he was furious with the foul-up that had kept him from the fight.

Lt Lou Bauer, the Fighting-6 commander, had launched with his division from the *Saratoga* at 1600 and had also been vectored away from the fight during the brief period the FDOs had had control of the fighter deployment. As the battle over the *Enterprise* heated up, Bauer led his division around to intercept an anticipated Japanese follow-on strike force, if there was one, or to block the escape routes he felt would be used by retiring Vals and Zeros. The move paid off at 1645 when Bauer found a lone Val speeding northward, away from Task Force 61, at 2,000 feet. Leaving two Wildcats high to provide cover, Bauer set up a high-side attack in which both he and his wingman, Ens Wildon Rouse, put many rounds into the Val before it stalled out in a climbing turn and crashed.

Moments after the Val crashed, Bauer led Rouse to higher altitude to rejoin the high section. On the way, a lone Zero passed close enough to attract Bauer's attention. This Zero took absolutely no evasive action as Bauer fired into it for some moments. Then, trailing a stream of gasoline from a punctured tank, the Zero flew to wave-top altitude and put on enough speed to outrun Bauer. Ens Jim Halford, the leader of Bauer's second section, spotted the Zero from great height and dove to intercept. Halford fired a burst at maximum range, and this rattled the Zero pilot into making evasive S-turns, which only allowed Halford to close the range. It took Halford ten minutes to catch up with the Zero, and then he pounded it into the sea—a certain kill that was witnessed by Lou Bauer.

Lt Vince de Poix's section of Lt(jg) Hal Rutherford's Fighting-6 combat-air-patrol division was at 17,000 feet when it arrived in the vicinity of the departing strike aircraft—a bit late because it had been tied down guarding a distant sector. Casting about for some sort of target, de Poix spotted a lone Zero passing in the opposite direction at what he estimated to be 12,000 feet. As de Poix dived at full speed after the Japanese fighter, he saw markings on the Zero's tail slowly resolve themselves into a

pattern that seemed to identify the pilot as a *buntaicho*, a fighter leader. At that, de Poix poured on so much power that his Wildcat began vibrating. So intent was he upon scoring against a senior Japanese pilot that he entered the awesome curtain of antiaircraft gunfire the *North Carolina* was still putting out. The Zero disappeared without de Poix's having an opportunity to fire, and de Poix roared into a turn to avoid the sheets of gunfire that were rising to meet him.

The Fighting-5 and Fighting-6 Wildcats were by no means the only U.S. warplanes operating in proximity to Task Force 16 during the fateful minutes of the Japanese attack. In addition to the *Enterprise* SBDs that were conducting routine air patrols when the Japanese began their approach, Fate conspired to bring numerous *Enterprise* scouts back home in time to watch or become embroiled in the swirling action.

Ens Howard Burnett, Ens Glenn Estes, and Ens Walton Austin, all piloting Scouting-5 Dauntlesses, got back to the *Enterprise* only minutes after she had launched the last of her fighters and several minutes before the Japanese attack started. Burnett was in the landing pattern when his gunner, ARM2 Harold Wilger, saw the pilot of one of the other SBDs point up over the carrier. Wilger turned in his seat to see what was going on just as the first two Vals completed their dives. This was also the first Wilger saw of the rising antiaircraft curtain.

With the other two Dauntlesses trailing, Ensign Burnett immediately broke away from the traffic circle, rolled over, and dived for the surface. The plan was to intercept low-flying torpedo bombers to the north of the task force, but Burnett's recovery brought him right onto the tails of two by-then retiring Vals. Burnett decided to go for the trailing Val first, and he opened fire with his two cowl-mounted .50-caliber machine guns as soon as he could lay his sight on the target. The Val burned and fell away, and Burnett raced to catch up with the lead Val. ARM2 Wilger, who was looking back over his gunsight for other enemy airplanes, saw the stricken Val send up a great plume of water as it skidded into the sea.

Ensign Burnett flew right up the tail of the second retiring Val and followed it in a 60-mile chase, but he could not get close enough to hit the Japanese dive-bomber. Task Force 61 was long out of sight when Burnett decided to break off. He saw a small island on the horizon, from which he took a bearing, and turned back to join numerous other U.S. Navy warplanes milling around the edge of the fight. By then, ARM2 Harold Wilger's biggest fear was that he would not have a ship to go home to. He had served with Scouting-5 aboard the *Yorktown* at the Coral Sea, where she had been damaged, and at Midway, where she had been sunk.

As Ensign Burnett departed the task force in pursuit of his second Val, Ens Glenn Estes found himself running head-on toward another recovering Val. When the Japanese dive-bomber pulled up to avoid a collision, Estes saw bullets from his own cowl guns go into its belly, but then he passed it by and lost sight of it.

LCdr Charlie Jett, the Torpedo-3 skipper, and Ens Bob Bye, Jett's wingman, did not quite have Task Force 61 in sight when they heard the order to bombers to keep clear of the area. Jett led Bye in a gentle, climbing turn to 3,000 feet to circle well away from the action. The antiaircraft barrage could be seen clearly by the crews of both TBFs; and ARM2 Dewey Stemen, Bye's radioman-gunner, saw several Japanese bombs near-miss or actually strike the *Enterprise*. Stemen also noticed that the *Saratoga's* Task Force 11 was slowly putting distance between itself and the Japanese main effort.

At length, two retiring Vals approached the two search TBFs low on the water and made abrupt firing passes, which caught both Avenger crews by surprise. Charlie Jett was not sure the Avengers could put out enough fire to scare off the Vals, but he knew that the TBF's big wings made for slower, tighter turns than any other warplane in the air. It was possible for the TBF pilots to chop speed back to a grindingly slow 70 knots at low altitude, well below the stalling speed of the Vals. So, unable to outgun the Vals, Jett led Bye around in an effort to outmaneuver them.

While the TBF pilots tried to outfox the Vals, the TBF gunners tried to shoot them down. ARM2 Dewey Stemen, who was manning Bye's turret-mounted .50-caliber machine gun, tracked and fired at two Vals in quick succession as they passed overhead from nose to tail. Stemen locked on to a third dark blur—and barely held his fire when it registered as a Dauntless dive-bomber. The stray SBD briefly joined up on Bye's wing, but it soon flew off on its own. Bye was particularly incensed by the SBD's departure; he and Jett needed the extra firepower the dive-bomber's twin-.50-caliber and twin .30-caliber guns could have provided. He testily asked Stemen if he had noted the airplane's number, which he intended to report, but Stemen had not.

ARM2 Stemen went back to searching for approaching Vals and picked one up as it came storming in directly from starboard. This was the best target Stemen had had thus far. He took his time getting his gunsight on the largest feature, the engine cowling. Bye was moved by the long silence to urge Stemen to open fire, but the gunner would not be rushed, even when the Val's guns twinkled with red-and-yellow flame. When Stemen was finally set, he fired, but all his tracer rose to a point just over the Val's starboard wing root—a shade high and a shade to the left. The Val veered away around and below Bye's tail and then came up right into the notch between the TBF's tail and starboard wing—just a hair too low and too close to be endangered by the TBF's turret or tunnel guns. ARM2 Stemen stared at the Japanese pilot and rear gunner in stark disbelief until the Val dropped down and away. Stemen was so nonplused by the close encounter that he did not get his turret around in time to fire so much as a parting salute.

Neither side drew blood, and all the Japanese warplanes soon left. By that time, however, Bye had become separated from Jett. Unable to locate any other American airplanes, he flew on alone until he encountered three more Vals. Another of the many fighter pilots who had been sent to reman the torpedo squadrons after Midway, Bye reflexively selected the Val whose pilot seemed the least aware of the goings on around him and approached from starboard. The Val pilot saw Bye at the last instant and foolishly maneuvered directly into the TBF's line of fire. Bye pressed the gun-button knob on his control stick and activated the single .30-caliber popgun mounted on the cowling in front of the cockpit. As soon as Bye completed the burst, he turned his big torpedo bomber back toward the two remaining Vals and fired his nose gun at medium range into the port beam of one of them. Then Bye turned away again to pursue his first target, which he shot full of holes from dead astern. By then, however, three other Vals had swarmed over Bye to protect their comrade. Bye and the Vals broke off the action by tacit mutual consent.

♦

Late in the action, the bomber command channel resounded with a fierce order: "SBDs: Attack the torpedo planes."

Though he was flying a TBF, Ens Fred Mears of Torpedo-3 reacted to this order by leaving his section leader, Lt(jg) Weasel Weissenborn, and flying straight toward the *Enterprise*, into the circle of fire. On the way, he met two Japanese warplanes recovering from steep dives. At first Mears was convinced that he was being bounced by Zeros, which was a severe jolt, but a second look convinced him that he had luckily encountered a pair of Vals. Chastened, Mears banked away from the Vals, as much to give his turret gunner an easy shot as to rejoin Weissenborn in the safe zone. But the Vals followed the Avenger and opened fire. By the time Mears found Weissenborn again, Weissenborn had joined up on the wing of LCdr Charlie Jett, who had been searching for his own lost wingman, Ens Bob Bye.

As Mears nudged up beneath Jett's left wing, one of the pursuing Vals prudently withdrew. The other, however, flipped in a fast head-on firing pass at Mears, who could easily see the long streamers of yellowish smoke curling back from the twin cowl-mounted 7.7mm machine guns. As the Val was about to pass over the top of Mears's TBF, Mears pulled up and fired his single cowl-mounted .30-caliber machine gun. But then the Val was gone, chased off by the Avenger formation's three turret-mounted .50-caliber machine guns.

Lt Johnny Myers, the Torpedo-3 exec, who had lost his wingman, Mach Harry Corl, to Zeros over the *Ryujo*, made it to within 25 miles of the *Enterprise* when he was bounced by a lone Zero, which made a wide sweep from port before passing from sight astern. Four of the Zero's 20mm cannon rounds detonated on or in Myers's previously damaged TBF—one in each wing, one in the fuselage, and one in the rudder. And at least fifty 7.7mm rounds also struck the Avenger. When the smoke cleared, Myers discovered that his radioman-gunner and bombardier had both been hurt.

Myers fought his sluggish controls and turned away from the battle to find a safe place to hide out until it was time to land—or ditch, whichever came first.

◆

Lt Carl Horenburger, of Bombing-6, was approaching the fleet in the quadrant assigned for recognition of friendly warplanes when he first noticed the heavy volume of antiaircraft fire rising from over the horizon. Horenburger prudently aborted his approach and began cutting lazy circles in the air well beyond the intensifying action. One lazy pass brought him within sighting distance of four Vals, which were circling at 200 to 300 feet prior to retiring to their own carriers.

Horenburger roared after the four Vals, but his efforts to place the fire of his twin cowl-mounted .50-caliber machine guns was significantly hampered by the weight of the 500-pound bomb he had lugged on his long search flight and which he was loath to jettison just yet. Sheer persistence brought Horenburger's laden Dauntless within range of the Vals. He saw his tracers strike at least one of them, but he felt 7.7mm rounds strike his own airplane before the Vals completed their rendezvous maneuvers and rapidly drew away from the slower SBD.

Bombing-6's Lt Ray Kline returned to Task Force 16 from an uneventful solo search mission at about 1655, just in time to spot five Vals as they were retiring from the scene. Kline jerked his Dauntless into a pass at the rear Val, but he could not keep the Japanese bomber in his gunsight long enough to get off a shot. At length, Kline's rearseatman, ARM1 Edward Garaudy, was able to fire a burst with his twin .30-caliber guns, and he saw a number of his tracers strike the Val. By then, however, Kline was far from home and low on fuel, so he gave up the chase.

Among the first *Saratoga* Air Group strike bombers back from sinking the *Ryujo* was a section of three SBDs led by LCdr DeWitt Shumway, the Bombing-3 skipper. The three, and several others strung out farther behind in loose formation, sighted the position of Task Force 16 while there was still plenty of antiaircraft fire in the air, so Shumway led the way a bit to the north to ride out the storm.

After a long look at the conflagration over the *Enterprise*, Lt Paul Holmberg glanced across at the airplane flying off Shumway's other wing and was stunned to see two fixed-gear dive-bombers—Vals!—slip into formation with Shumway's other wingman. Holmberg immediately grabbed his intercom microphone and ordered his rearseat gunner, ARM2 C. W. Albright, to fire at them. Albright was apparently focusing on the big show over the *Enterprise*, so he did not bring his guns to bear in time. No doubt embarrassed and frightened when they noticed their egregious error, the two Japanese broke off and dived away from the Dauntlesses.

At 1655 LCdr Bullet Lou Kirn, the Scouting-3 commanding officer, was leading a mixed formation of twelve other *Saratoga* Air Group dive-bombers back from the *Ryujo* strike at 500 feet. Now only 75 miles from Task Force 61 and well-informed as to the scope of the attack on the *Enterprise*, Kirn was not overly shocked when he noticed a formation of what he took to be Japanese dive-bombers and fighters flying along on the same heading at 8,000 feet. Sensing that his formation had not yet been spotted by the other formation, Kirn ordered his radioman, ACRM C. E. Russ, to break radio silence to warn the friendly vessels of a possible impending follow-on strike. The message was repeated twice more.

The large formation was indeed a follow-on strike force composed of twenty-seven *Shokaku* and *Zuikaku* Vals and nine Zero escorts. This force did not know where the American carriers were, however, and, failing to spot Kirn's returning strikers, could not locate Task Force 61 by tagging along. Soon the two bomber forces drew apart without the Japanese ever having seen the *Saratoga* SBDs.

At 1707 Bullet Lou Kirn was again the first American pilot to spot other airplanes at a distance. These turned out to be 11th Heavy Bombardment Group B-17s that had been sent out from Espiritu Santo to join the search for Japanese ships. The B-17s approached the starboard quarter of Kirn's group from the southwest. Kirn assumed the recognition was reciprocal until, at a range of only 500 yards, the nose gun of one of the B-17s was seen to open fire. The fall of the tracer indicated that the stream of bullets was well short, but the carrier bombers took evasive action and flew on.

At 1710 several of Kirn's pilots simultaneously spotted four Vals slightly to starboard and racing on an opposite heading at 1,000 feet—500 feet higher than the SBDs. Once again, ACRM Russ sounded the alarm, while Lieutenant Commander Kirn maneuvered to get directly beneath the Vals.

Then, as the Vals passed right over Kirn's section of Dauntlesses, the American pilots lifted their noses to climb in unison and simultaneously fire their twin .50-caliber cowl guns. All the rearseatmen who could bring their guns to bear also fired straight up at the passing Vals.

As the Vals—three *Shokaku* dive-bombers led by Lt Kazuo Yoshimoto, plus one *Zuikaku* straggler—flew by overhead, Lt Ralph Weymouth, Ens Alden Hanson, Lt(jg) Bob Campbell, and Lt(jg) Alan Frank left Kirn's formation to deliver individual attacks on them. All four SBD pilots claimed kills, Bullet Lou Kirn counted three burning pyres on the surface, and someone reported that a smoking Val flew from sight. But none of these Vals was actually downed.

One of the last clear orders LCdr Ham Dow had been able to transmit from the *Enterprise* before the attack went to the Fighting-6 division led by Ens Red Brooks, a recently commissioned former enlisted pilot with many years of carrier flying experience. While most attention was firmly riveted on the rapidly approaching high-altitude Val and Zero formations, Dow's radarman had noticed a small bogey approaching virtually at wave-top height. Ensign Brooks was ordered to investigate just before Dow's fighter-direction channel was overwhelmed by a flood of radio calls.

Brooks's division—which picked up a fifth member, a stray Fighting-5 Wildcat piloted by Ens Mark Bright—flew out 100 miles along its north-westerly vector before Brooks decided that he had missed seeing the enemy aircraft. Shortly after turning for home at 1715, the fighter pilots spotted eight aircraft, which Brooks believed to be a mixture of Vals and Kate torpedo bombers. In fact, he had spotted four retiring Vals as they were being chased by the four *Saratoga* SBDs.

As Red Brooks led his division down after the bombers from 11,000 feet, the SBDs turned back for home, and so there were only the four Vals when the Wildcats came within firing range. The Wildcat division leader immediately delivered a high-side run on one of the Vals and thought he hammered it down into the water from an altitude of only 50 feet. In addition to being wrong about the victory claim, Brooks was wrong about the type of airplane he thought he had downed. He claimed a Kate. As Brooks pulled up, he found himself directly on the tail of one of the Vals, which sustained numerous solid hits from Brooks's six .50-caliber wing guns. Brooks's wingman, Ens Harry March, who confirmed Brooks's claim for a Kate and a Val, fired up every last round in his ammunition boxes—1,440 .50-caliber rounds in all—without fatally damaging the "Kate" he had in his sights.

RE Tommy Rhodes, Brooks's second-section leader, executed a high-side run on what he correctly took to be a Val—a lone, straggling *Zuikaku* Val, as it turned out. Ens Mark Bright opened fire on the same airplane, but his guns jammed before he could get strikes on the target. Ensign Bright recharged his guns and was turning in for a second pass at this Val when he saw it spin out to the left and crash into the water.

AP1 Paul Mankin dived straight down upon another *Zuikaku* Val that was just arriving in the vicinity of the melee. He pulled up almost dead astern of the Japanese carrier bomber and poured in bullets until it went down in flames.

Several other Japanese aircraft were claimed by the five Wildcat pilots, but it is certain that only two *Zuikaku* Vals were actually downed—by Rhodes and Mankin—although Mankin and Bright might have downed yet another straggler. Three of the four Vals originally under attack by the *Saratoga* SBDs comprised the *Shokaku* section led by Lt Kazuo Yoshimoto, and they all escaped. No Kates had been dispatched against Task Force 61, but claims by Red Brooks and Harry March, coupled with the expectation that Kates would have been sent, led to some pretty wild stories claiming that Brooks's division had turned back an entire torpedo squadron.

Finally, at 1744, three Vals were spotted to the starboard of LCdr Bullet Lou Kirn's returning SBD strikers at a distance of 5 miles. These three were led by the *Shokaku's* Lt Keiichi Arima, who with his wingman had remained at the rendezvous point to aid any remaining stragglers. Only one other Val joined Arima, and then the three were driven away to the west by four Wildcats. Arima's little formation was striking for home when several of the *Saratoga* SBDs under Lieutenant Commander Kirn broke formation to chase them.

The Vals highballed away from the Dauntlesses on a long, curving course. Ens Roger Crow, one of the pursuers, knew that he could not catch the Vals in a tail chase, so, while the other Dauntless pilots tried to overtake the

Japanese from astern, he flew across the cord of the Vals' curving course, directly to the point at which he anticipated the Vals would straighten out. The result was that Crow's S-13 beat the other SBDs to the Vals.

Crow positioned himself up-sun and high in such a way as to force the Vals to come at him from the port side. Certain he had not been seen, he alerted his gunner, ARM3 T. H. Miner, that a target would soon appear low and to port and that "You better get it." In the end, although they fired every bullet in their ammunition cans, neither Crow nor Miner actually got any of the Vals. Crow was given official credit for a probable, however.

The 25-mile chase left Ensign Crow and his fuel tanks thoroughly drained. When Lt Ralph Weymouth pulled up alongside, Crow signaled that he needed an escort. The two SBDs turned toward the *Saratoga* at a fuel-conserving speed and, when they arrived, Weymouth signaled the ship that Crow needed to make an immediate landing. Crow was recovered without incident on the last of his fuel.

In all, U.S. Navy fighter pilots, bomber pilots, bomber gunners, and gunners from every ship in Task Force 16 claimed seventy of the twenty-seven Vals as confirmed kills, as well as many more Zeros than had been in on the strike. And there were even claims for two Kates.

The real total of kills—shared by many—was ten of eighteen *Shokaku* Vals, seven of nine *Zuikaku* Vals, one of four *Shokaku* Zeros, and three of six *Zuikaku* Zeros—twenty-one of thirty-seven strike bombers and escort fighters. The downed *Shokaku* Zero pilot was eventually recovered. Also, one *Zuikaku* Zero and one *Shokaku* Zero ditched due to fuel starvation, but both pilots were rescued; one *Zuikaku* Val ditched near a friendly cruiser, which rescued the crew; and one *Zuikaku* Val that became lost ditched near Malaita, where the pilot and airplane commander joined a band of Japanese coastwatchers. In all, then, only eight *Shokaku* Vals, two *Shokaku* Zeros, and two *Zuikaku* Zeros landed safely.

Returning Japanese pilots made outlandish claims, too. They reported hitting two carriers with bombs and leaving both burning and sinking. They also claimed hits on a battleship, which was also left burning. Zero pilots reported downing many more than the five Wildcats and one TBF that were actually shot down. As it was, at least one of the downed Wildcats—and perhaps as many as four—succumbed to friendly fire from surface warships.

Chapter 34

Ships at sea that are on fire are in mortal danger. From the standpoint of fire alone, the *Enterprise* had sustained about the worst sort of bomb hit imaginable. The only factors that saved her from immediately blowing up were the timely flooding of vulnerable aviation-fuel lines with inert carbon dioxide gas, the sangfroid of a sailor who jettisoned into the sea a huge detachable tank of low-octane fuel, and the actions of a dazed storekeeper who emerged from the eye of the blast and made his way to the paint and pyrotechnic storerooms to set off the system that smothered both compartments with carbon dioxide.

As it was, however, the first bomb had detonated in a berthing compartment, with its ample bedding and clothing to feed the flames, and in a metal shop, where tiny pieces of scrap could become molten harbingers of the ultimate fate of the rest of the steel ship. The blast threw out or severed electrical circuits that controlled lighting and firefighting pumps, and several key water mains serving that part of the ship were also destroyed or disabled. Moreover, most members of the nearest damage-control party— Repair IV—were killed or injured in the blast.

Deaths and destruction notwithstanding, nearby damage-control teams from Repair III, the midships repair party, swung into immediate action toward the vortex of the 500-kilogram bomb blast. First, an investigation team from the nearest surviving damage party—men who had been trained for the eventuality of key fatalities—felt its way along intervening passage-ways and compartments. It arrived almost before the effects of the initial blast had dissipated.

Upon inspecting the damage, the team reported via its sound-powered battle phone to the ship's first lieutenant, LCdr Herschel Smith, and his assistant, Lt George Over, who were running the damage-control effort out of a compartment beneath the island known as Central Station. Smith already had a pretty good idea that the damage-control party in the imme-diate vicinity of the blast had been gutted; he had not been able to estab-lish contact with it. After checking with other damage parties nearby, Smith swung his resources into action. Initially, Smith and Over pored through engineering diagrams of the ship to find and suggest useful alternatives to men on the scene for the best ways to reestablish communications, electri-cal power, and water pressure in the bomb-damaged sectors. As soon as Smith had definitive reports, he would place the orchestration in Lieuten-ant Over's hands and proceed to the scene of the major conflagrations to personally assess damage to the ship and directly control firefighting and repair efforts.

The first task was to contain and control the fires that were in danger of consuming the innards of the ship. Electricians ran out emergency power cables for lighting, and firefighters ran hoses aft from the nearest undam-aged water main forward of the blast site. Sailors wearing gas masks and wielding flashlights headed into the murk at the outer edges of the smoky blaze and felt their way inward toward the center, checking and reporting on damage as they moved. They could not go far, however, because the gas masks could not filter out suffocating smoke and fumes. To advance farther, they needed rescue breathing apparatus (RBA) vests, which filtered and refiltered air sealed from outside contamination.

Right behind the scouts were corpsmen, also rigged out in gas masks and carrying flashlights in addition to medical-aid bags. If there were liv-ing men in the shambles, the corpsmen would carry them out and treat them. There were in fact ninety-five officers and sailors who needed treat-ment for everything from smoke inhalation to traumatic amputations of limbs.

♦

Before the repair parties below decks could even begin to deploy to fight the fires in and around the chiefs' quarters and metal shop, the second bomb took out Gun Group 3. In its way, the blast on the after starboard quarter was as threatening to the *Enterprise* as the fires below decks.

As had happened below, damage parties immediately converged on the conflagration, though the danger from exploding ordnance was acute and approaches were made with a good deal of extra caution. LCdr Slim Townsend, the carrier's flight-deck officer, took charge of the topside damage-control efforts. Townsend's immediate concern, beyond controlling the intense blaze in Gun Group 3, was to repair the flight deck so the *Enterprise* could begin landing warplanes at a moment's notice.

Ens Jim Wyrick, a junior gunnery officer, was among the first men into the conflagration. Together with three enlisted firefighters, Wyrick heaved burning and flammable material right over the side of the ship. The heat around the quartet was so intense that they would have succumbed had not a nearby firefighter sprayed a stream of water directly on them.

Lt Robin Lindsey, the ship's senior LSO, first realized that there was something amiss when he heard an unusual crackling sound from Gun Group 3, which was located directly across the flight deck from the catwalk beneath the LSO platform on which Lindsey had taken cover. Once the thought of a fire penetrated Lindsey's numbed brain, he sprang to action with nearby sailors and helped haul a hose hooked up to a fulmite fire-retardant generator across the after flight deck to the fiercely burning 5-inch gun gallery. The smoke in the gun gallery obscured all sights, and the heat was intense. Lindsey was certain that he would be roasted alive when the ready ammunition detonated.

As the smoke slowly dissipated, Lieutenant Lindsey looked down and found that one of his feet was firmly implanted in the open stomach cavity of a roasted sailor; ribbons of guts were spread in all directions. Though sickened, Lindsey carried on.

Moments later, the sailor with whom Lindsey was controlling the high-pressure nozzle of the fulmite hose blurted out, "I can't hang in any longer. Do you think you can handle the hose?" Lindsey said he could, and the sailor left. Immediately, the LSO was knocked off balance by the pressure from the hose and thrown up against a bulkhead at his back. He could barely move until someone stepped in and helped.

Meantime, Ens Jim Wyrick had discovered a locker filled with unexploded 5-inch rounds and powder charges. He quickly organized a fifteen-man detail from among volunteers and oversaw the jettisoning of every potentially lethal round into the sea.

One ongoing problem was a jet of flame shooting out one side of the gun gallery that no amount of fulmite could quell. It later was revealed that the bomb had nicked a steel line carrying hydraulic oil to the after elevator. The oil was under 820 pounds of pressure, so the tiny tear had the effect of a blowtorch. Until the chief machinist's mate in charge of the after elevator came topside to see if his elevator was flush with the deck, no one knew what the source of the dangerous blast of flame might be or how to defeat it.

The third bomb, a 250-kilogram device that struck at 1646, was of relatively low order, a land bomb set to detonate on impact. Withal, it blew a 10-foot hole in the flight deck and shut down the midships elevator. The area was sprayed down, and ship fitters went right to work fashioning a metal plate to cover the yawning gap.

One of the top men on the scene of the firefighting below decks was CSF Jim Brewer, of the Construction and Repair Department. As each new compartment in the vicinity of the below-decks blast was reached, Brewer was among the first—if not *the* first—to enter. His job was to locate the source of each individual blaze and to tell hose teams the best means for beating it down. If equipment or supplies had to be removed from the compartment, Brewer pointed it out and allocated the manpower to undertake the job. In time, Brewer was overcome by smoke and heat and had to be ordered from the scene by the ship's executive officer. His loss was felt, but there were other good men to take his place.

While the fight to save the *Enterprise* was focused on the metal shop and chiefs' quarters, CMM Reuben Fisher took charge of a hose that had been brought aft from a working water main. With the hose, he entered a storeroom that led directly to an ammunition hoist loaded with 5-inch powder charges on the way up to Gun Group 3 from the magazine. If the fire reached the ammunition, Chief Fisher knew, there was no telling what lethal chain of events might be set off.

As Chief Fisher opened the door to the compartment, he was met by heat, smoke, and flame. The fire hose was trained into the compartment and the fire was slowly beaten back. The hose team advanced behind Fisher into the darkened space, where smoldering racks of dry provisions were sprayed and sprayed again. The ammunition hoist was reached in due course, and the dangerously hot powder cans were cooled with water from the hose.

A fire in the highly flammable parachute loft was also quickly extinguished, as was a blaze that threatened the torpedo storage magazine.

Fulmite foam, oil from ruptured tanks, blood, seawater, and debris made footing particularly precarious in unlighted, smoke-filled compartments. Often, ventilation fed fires as much as it cleared smoke. Portable blowers had to be used to selectively ventilate numerous blind spaces, and gasoline-fueled handy-billy portable pumps had to be used to reduce water levels in others. The work was treacherous and tiring—generally a threat to the lives and health of the firefighters, ship fitters, and carpenters who moved directly in their wake.

By the glow of emergency lights, several carpenters had to wade into armpit-deep water to caulk a number of gashes—the largest was 6 by 2 feet—left by the bomb below the waterline. Using emergency supplies of heavy lumber stored in strategic locations throughout the ship, the carpenters built a cofferdam to contain the flooding. Then they used wire mesh to bind bedding and pillows into the tears in the carrier's side. Once the cofferdam was filled with the bedding and wedged in place, emergency pumps went to work, emptying flooded and partially flooded compartments. Nearly 250 tons of seawater were pumped from one large storeroom alone.

At 1749—sixty-five minutes after the first bomb tore its way into the *Enterprise's* innards, and while firefighting and repair efforts frantically continued below—the carrier majestically turned into the wind at 24 knots and began the routine recovery of her warplanes.

Chapter 35

All four Wildcats of Lt Scoop Vorse's intact Fighting-6 division were on reserve fuel when the fight over Task Force 16 ended, so they headed for the undamaged *Saratoga*, which was amply protected from the brunt of the Japanese attack by concealing low clouds. Three of the Wildcats safely landed aboard the big steel-decked carrier at 1710, but Lieutenant Vorse ran out of fuel as he flew up the groove, and he had to settle for a neat water landing, right in the carrier's wake. He was picked up by a guard destroyer after only moments in the water.

Following two contacts at the start of the Japanese air strike, Lt Sandy Crews of Fighting-5 chased after a few airplanes, but they all turned out to be friendlies. The sky was full of bursting antiaircraft shells and burning and exploding planes, and airplanes and bombs were crashing into the water. The Fighting-5 section leader could not help musing that real life this day was just like in the movies.

All the diving, twisting, turning, and shooting Crews had done since spotting the first *chutai* of Vals on its way toward the *Enterprise* had long ago separated him from the rest of Lt Chick Harmer's division, and his wingman had long ago gone his own way. Crews's fuel supply was critically low, so he headed back to the *Saratoga* and made a wide approach to the carrier with his wheels down, because he knew a lot of people were trigger-happy; the last thing he wanted was to look like a Japanese plane to ships' gunners. Crews's approach was made without incident, and he landed on the last of his fuel at about 1710. He had been in the air three hours and forty minutes.

Wounded and alone in his battered Wildcat following a scary engagement with an aggressive Val crew, Lt Chick Harmer, the Fighting-5 exec, could easily see the smoke from the burning *Enterprise* as he searched for a safe place to land. He quickly spotted the *Saratoga*, which was about 10 miles farther on. He passed the burning carrier, even though she appeared ready to take on airplanes, and flew on at 1,000 feet, intent upon landing aboard his own ship.

When he arrived, Lieutenant Harmer saw that his was the only airplane in the *Saratoga's* landing pattern. He made an approach he felt was a really good one, but just as he leveled his wings in anticipation of receiving the "cut," the LSO, Lt Walter Curtis, gave him a "come on" followed an instant later by the expected "cut." The little extra throttle Harmer had to give in response to the "come on," along with his airplane's being light because it was nearly out of fuel and ammunition, sent Harmer into a thoroughly embarrassing barrier crash that flipped his fighter over on its back. Harmer was not hurt, but his F4F was wiped out—along with his pride.

It turned out that the leg wounds Harmer had acquired in his last fight with a Val were minor, but the doctor routinely gave him a jolt of morphine and sent him to bed.

At 1726 the destroyer *Grayson* was ordered to sail 40 miles to the northwest to stand by to pick up returning scouts and strike aircraft that were by then running low on fuel. She was to remain on station overnight and catch up with the departing Task Force 16 around noon the next day, August 25. The *Grayson* turned to her new heading only one minute after receiving the order and proceeded from sight at a speed of 25 knots.

The returning *Enterprise* Air Group scouts, which had been aloft far longer than any other U.S. Navy warplanes, were made especially vulnerable to the rigors of ditching, because they were kept from landing aboard either carrier while the fighters of both air groups were given priority when the *Enterprise* resumed full landing operations at 1749.

Lt John Lowe, the Bombing-6 exec, and his wingman, Ens Bob Gibson, returned from their encounter with the Japanese surface Vanguard Group while the Japanese air attack was still under way. Lowe thought that the *Wasp* might be undergoing her refueling close enough to Task Force 61 to risk a flight south to find her. But the *Wasp* was well beyond range, as Lowe eventually realized, and he and Gibson returned to their own task force on the last of their fuel. Gibson was just turning upwind at 1740 to begin his approach on the *Saratoga* when his SBD's engine died. He ditched dead ahead of the heavy cruiser *Minneapolis*, and he and his rearseatman climbed out onto one wing. Both airmen were neatly plucked from the water by the destroyer *Farragut*. Lieutenant Lowe landed aboard the *Enterprise* without difficulty at 1800.

When Lt Carl Horenburger, of Bombing-6, approached the *Enterprise* following his inconclusive duel with rendezvousing Vals north of the task force, he joined up with numerous fighters and bombers that were forced to wait patiently while the battle damage was repaired. Fuel was getting to be a problem for Horenburger, who had been on a long search hop and had used a great deal of it attempting to engage several Vals at high speed. He used the last of the fuel in his SBD's four 50-gallon tanks and was well into his 18-gallon reserve when the "Charlie" landing-signal flag was hoisted over the damaged carrier at 1749. When Horenburger's turn to land finally came and he was entering the groove off the *Enterprise's* stern, another carrier bomber broke in from the starboard quarter—a highly unorthodox approach, to say the least. Horenburger stubbornly held to his course; he was angry at the intruder and did not feel he had enough fuel left to go around again. The intruder veered off and made a water landing just as Horenburger safely reached the ramp and took the "cut" from the carrier's senior LSO, the incomparable Lt Robin Lindsey.

Six Torpedo-3 searchers had managed to join up on the squadron commander, LCdr Charlie Jett, by the time the *Saratoga* was ready to begin landing the large torpedo bombers. First, the Avengers were ordered to jettison their bombs. Only four of the seven still had their bombs aboard; the other three—Jett, Ens Bob Bye, and Lt Johnny Myers—had all dropped theirs on the *Ryujo* hours earlier. Lieutenant Myers, whose TBF had been riddled by Zeros over the *Ryujo* and again close to home, was the first of the group to land aboard the *Saratoga*. Indeed, he signaled that his would be an emergency landing; his controls had been damaged by Japanese 7.7mm and 20mm rounds, and Myers was not sure they or he would withstand the demands of a precision carrier recovery.

While warplanes on the *Saratoga's* flight deck were being respotted to accommodate Myers's damaged TBF, Ens Fred Mears of Torpedo-3 and Ens Robert Divine, a member of the Torpedo-8 group that had struck the *Ryujo,* opted to fly 25 miles to the *Enterprise,* which had no planes in her landing pattern just then. LCdr Charlie Jett followed Mears and Divine aboard the *Enterprise* a few minutes later.

Lt Johnny Myers made his approach gingerly and managed to get aboard the *Saratoga* on his first pass, which was fortunate. As soon as the tired pilot gave his engine a bit of throttle to clear the arresting wires, the engine died. The TBF was out of gas.

Ens Bob Bye, who had used up a great deal of fuel keeping station on LCdr Charlie Jett's wing during the long afternoon patrol—a wingman's occupational hazard—and still more fuel in a series of running fights with Vals, could not keep his TBF airborne long enough to take his turn landing aboard the *Saratoga*. He flew off to the side of the big carrier at 1802 and told his aircrewmen to prepare for a water landing. ARM2 Dewey Stemen, who was manning the turret gun, locked up the turret armor plate, put his feet on the footrest, and leaned back hard into his seatback, praying he would not be knocked unconscious by the sudden stop and thus left to go down with the airplane. The sea was dead calm, and Bye made a smooth water landing—only two or three little bounces. As the Avenger settled in, Stemen popped the turret's port escape hatch and climbed out onto the wing, from which he slipped and fell into the water. By the time Stemen climbed back aboard the wing, the bombardier, AMM3 W. E. Dillon, was at work on the other wing, trying to release the life raft from its outside compartment. Stemen opened the compartment from his side and pushed the raft bundle while Dillon pulled. When the raft was free, Stemen crawled over the top of the fuselage to join Dillon. They inflated the raft and then went forward to find out why Ensign Bye had not joined them. The pilot was in the cockpit, busily attending to a last-minute scavenger hunt. As soon as Bye had retrieved everything he wanted—and at the insistent urging of his crewmen—he climbed to the wing. The three airmen jumped into the raft just as the TBF slipped beneath the waves. In time, Bye, Stemen, and Dillon were rescued by the destroyer *Balch*, which sank their trusty life raft with machine-gun fire.

At 1805 the main body of Cdr Don Felt's *Ryujo* strike force—which had not lost a single airplane during the strike or in several air battles—began landing aboard the *Saratoga*.

RE Werner Weis of Torpedo-3 had been launched from the *Enterprise* with Lt Rube Konig's tiny strike team just before the start of the Japanese air strike, but he had been unable to retract his landing gear and had therefore dropped out. Weis was not molested as he circled out of range of the fight, and he eventually joined up on the group of Torpedo-3 searchers led by LCdr Charlie Jett. He landed safely aboard the *Enterprise* at 1808.

At 1809 Ens John Jorgenson, who had flown wing in his SBD on Ens Harold Bingaman's TBF during the afternoon search, ran out of fuel in the *Enterprise* landing pattern. After ditching, he and his rearseatman were picked up by a destroyer.

Lt Ray Davis, the Bombing-6 skipper, who had found and attacked the Japanese fleet carriers, was forced to buzz around during a very long delay and wound up landing aboard the *Enterprise* at 1809 with a mere 4 gallons of fuel remaining in his reserve supply. Davis was the last of the main group of *Enterprise* searchers to land.

Evening was coming on and fuel supply was getting low when Ens Bob Disque of Fighting-6 dropped down into the landing pattern to go aboard the *Enterprise*. As he flew alongside his ship, he saw for the first time that she had been heavily damaged. Huge steel plates covered several large holes in the after flight deck; starboard-aft gun positions were twisted and burned; and only three of the normal twelve landing wires were deployed. Ensign Disque's Wildcat came aboard fast at 1810 with inoperative landing flaps, because the stainless steel vacuum tank that controlled them had been holed by the Zero that had gotten 110 rounds into his fighter. In fact, Disque wound up on his back in the barrier. A bit dazed by the unanticipated impact and his sudden inversion, Disque automatically released his safety belt—and dropped to the flight deck, right on his head. Disque was pulled clear, and his fighter was pushed aside in time for three Dauntlesses from the antisubmarine patrol to begin landings at 1811—only one minute after the barrier crash.

Right after Bob Disque landed, the *Enterprise* shut down landing operations so her deck handlers could respot and launch five Fighting-6 Wildcats for a combat air patrol. The frantic deck crews and pilots got the fighters aloft in under three minutes.

At 1813, immediately upon completing her twenty-fifth recovery—Ens William Behr's battle-damaged Bombing-3 SBD—the *Enterprise* sharply veered from her course, far to the left. The astonished helmsman shouted at Capt Arthur Davis, "Lost steering control, sir." A returning fighter right over the ramp responded to the LSO's wave-off and roared across the turning deck.

Instantly, the TBS ("Talk Between Ships") radio network was filled with dire warnings, and the huge carrier sounded several blasts on her siren. Another siren sounded from deep within the bowels of the ship to indicate that the steering control room could not control the huge vessel as she cut a 24-knot swath through Task Force 16.

When the massive rudder had gone as far to the left as it could, it began swinging back to the right. Farther and farther it went, crazily bending the carrier's wake in a sharp S-turn until the ship's massive bows were bearing directly down upon the destroyer *Balch*.

The rudder jammed 20 degrees to the right as the *Balch's* stack emitted a puff of black smoke to signify that she was on full emergency power. The *Enterprise* missed the tiny plane-guard destroyer by fewer than 50 yards.

Once the *Balch* was clear, all the attention of Captain Davis and the bridge watch could be placed on slowing the runaway carrier and safely guiding her between more-distant obstacles—or, rather, on warning the more-distant obstacles to stand clear—and to finding and correcting the cause of the steering problem.

First Captain Davis tried to correct the sharp rightward swing by cutting power to the port engine and increasing power on the starboard engine. But that only endangered the massive engines, so Davis belayed the effort. All he could do was cut speed to 10 knots and get the rudder fixed.

As the *Enterprise* helplessly circled within a moving stockade of destroyers, cruisers, and a battleship, her air-search radar picked up a large bogey approaching from the north—a Japanese follow-on strike launched from the *Shokaku* and *Zuikaku* following the departure of the last U.S. Navy searchers from the vicinity of VAdm Chuichi Nagumo's Mobile Force. Suddenly, miraculously, the bogey veered around from the north to the west of Task Force 61. Exceptionally nervous air-search radar operators monitored the large bogey on the radar repeaters and called out new readings to the junior FDOs manning Radar Plot. Hurriedly refueled fighters were launched in makeshift divisions from the *Saratoga* and stationed in a northerly to westerly arc around Task Force 61. Soon—and still miraculously—the large bogey described a 50-mile arc to the south, around the American task force. The U.S. Navy fighters were held on a tight leash—no one wanted to attract attention while the *Enterprise* was helpless. In time the Japanese strike force disappeared altogether from the radar repeaters.

Meanwhile, the *Saratoga* carried the full burden for both air groups. Following Lt Chick Harmer's upset in the barrier, she had resumed the recovery of returning *Saratoga* strikers and sundry fighters at 1805, and she did so nonstop until 1855, when a Fighting-6 Wildcat closed down flight operations by flipping over in the barrier.

As the situation aboard the involuntarily circling *Enterprise* came clear, it was discovered that she had lost steering control due to a freak accident in her steering control room, a tiny metal box located hard against the rudder and one deck beneath the waterline. The room contained a control panel and two large electric motors—one online and one spare—which were used to respond to steering orders automatically signaled from the bridge helm. It was also possible to steer the ship from the steering control room by means of a compass, a wheel, and orders passed from the bridge by sound-powered phone.

The tiny blind compartment, its two motors, and it complement of three electrician's mates, three machinist's mates, and one quartermaster were cooled by means of a long ventilator shaft that began at the starboard after gun gallery, topside. The ventilation was routinely and briefly shut down—so the fresh air would not feed a fire—during General Quarters. Thus, it was not unusual during such periods for the temperature in the room to rise to 120 degrees.

One of the bombs that struck the *Enterprise* went right through the starboard after gun gallery—Gun Group 3. There it tore apart the ventilation shaft leading to the steering control room. When the 500-kilogram bomb finally detonated three decks down, it did so right above and ahead of the steering control room. Thick black smoke immediately entered the blind compartment by means of the local engine-cooling system. At the same time, hot water sprayed out of the starboard-engine cooling jacket. The seven-man crew quickly shut off the fans that were pulling in the smoke and sealed their end of the large ventilator shaft. The room was thus effectively proofed against air—fresh *and* smoky—from outside compartments.

Soon, because compartments all around were on fire, the temperature in the tiny room soared to more than 140 degrees, and then it continued to rise toward 160. Several of the sailors lost consciousness, and the rest were on the verge of doing so.

As firefighters attacked the blazes in adjacent compartments, an automatic safety system reopened the ventilator shaft. Immediately, thick clouds of black smoke again entered the overheated compartment along with a goodly supply of water and fulmite fire retardant that had entered the vent shaft through splinter holes and ruptured seals from as high up as the bomb-damaged gun gallery. The hot water shorted the control panel, which in turn caused the steering motor to reverse. The ship's huge rudder ran out of control all the way to the left, reversed again, and came to rest at 20 degrees right rudder.

When the steering alarm sounded, only one of the seven steering control room inmates, MM2 William Marcoux, had enough strength left to attempt to switch over to the undamaged port motor. He got partway through the drill just as the *Enterprise* knifed past the *Balch*. Then he was felled by the 170-degree heat.

There was one man aboard the *Enterprise* who could be considered an expert in every aspect of the vast ship's machinery. He was ChMach Bill Smith, a diminutive, curly headed blond man who had set something of a record in putting on rank since he had enlisted in the Navy in 1925. He had become the Navy's youngest chief machinist's mate and had gone on to become its youngest chief warrant machinist. There were many engineering officers who outranked Smith, but not one of them could run the machine that was the *Enterprise* the way Bill Smith and his hand-picked team of chief machinist's mates could.

As soon as the emergency siren sounded, Chief Machinist Smith dropped whatever else he was doing and headed toward the source of the trouble. First he placed a call by sound-powered phone to the blind compartment and explained to dopey, overheated CEM Alex Trymofiev how he could draw fresh air into the compartment by switching the vent baffles. Trymofiev passed out after removing only the first of a number of screws.

Smith's only alternative then was to rush through burning, smoke-filled sectors and enter the vital compartment himself. He buckled on an RBA vest and proceeded forward. This particular vest had been modified by one of Smith's leading acolytes, CMM Murell Twibell, to provide added breathing power. It had a safety line attached to the back in case Smith fell along the way and had to be pulled out in a hurry. Smith also grabbed a number of wrenches he thought he would need once he reached the vital smoke-filled compartment.

Smith made it only halfway to the steering control room on the first try. He fell to the burning deck and had to be pulled clear. Following a quick breather, he entered the smoky realm once again, this time in the company of MM1 Cecil Robinson.

By the time Smith and Robinson started toward the compartment together, it had already been breached by F3 Ernest Visto, a huge man, quite capable of carrying other men great distances. Visto had left his battle station without permission as soon as he learned there were men trapped below. He attached himself to a rescue party descending by way of a trunk from the chiefs' quarters above. The trunk was too narrow for Visto and his

RBA, so he traded the breather in for an ordinary gas mask. Visto could do nothing for the steering gear, which was beyond his ken, so he latched onto the nearest fallen body and dragged it up the escape trunk. In the end, he carried or cajoled all seven men—whose condition ranged from groggy to unconscious—to safety from the by-then 180-degree heat. As the last man was carried from Visto's arms, the big fireman uttered a weak apology and collapsed.

Six of the seven rescued men survived.

Meantime, ChMach Bill Smith and MM1 Cecil Robinson reached the compartment, but both were felled by the heat and had to be hauled to safety for a breather. They went back through the smoke yet again, and this time entered the abandoned compartment after undogging the water-tight door.

Smith quickly surveyed the situation and went to work. With Robinson assisting, he completed the transfer of power to the port motor and got the steering system back online.

High above, the bridge helmsman reported to Captain Davis, "Steering control regained, sir."

It was 1853. Steering control had been lost for forty of the longest minutes anyone involved would ever remember. But the *Enterprise* had resumed recovery operations as early as 1820, when two Wildcats from her combat air patrol landed without incident. The flight deck was down for only seven minutes.

The Japanese follow-on strike force remained on American air-search radars until 1827, when it was 70 miles southwest of Task Force 61. As with so many awry American plans and opportunities throughout the long day, a communications foul-up lay at the heart of this failure by the Japanese strikers to locate the U.S. carriers. The strike commander failed to receive two vital contact reports. The first was from a scout launched by the heavy cruiser *Chikuma* that broadcast a precise fix on the American carriers at 1650, and the second was a rebroadcast at 1730 of a contact and position report filed by LCdr Mamoru Seki, leader of the first strike. Both reports were picked up by other aircraft in the second strike group, but not by the strike commander. And no one took the initiative to signal him that something might be wrong with his radio receiver.

The Japanese strikers searched the empty sea well to the south of Task Force 61 until dusk, and then they turned for home. Arriving over their own carrier force well after dark, the strikers had more than their share of troubles—as if narrowly missing the vulnerable American carriers was not enough. One of the returning Vals ditched, and its crew was rescued by a destroyer, but one entire Val *shotai* and one other Val were never seen again.

Chapter 36

he flight of five Torpedo-8 TBFs commanded by Lt Swede Larsen,
which had launched from the *Saratoga* at 1605, succeeded in joining with the pair of SBDs flown by Bombing-3's Lt(jg) Robert Elder
and Ens Bob Gordon at 1655. Though all the *Saratoga* pilots maintained a
lookout for the two small *Enterprise* SBD and TBF strike elements, no contact was made during the flight north into darkness.

Lieutenant Larsen's mixed group found a target at 1735, just before
dusk. Several ships, 15 miles to the west-northwest, were seen as they
sailed away to the southeast at a speed of 15 or 20 knots. Within a minute
or two, the U.S. Navy airmen were able to count an estimated four heavy
cruisers, six light cruisers, and six or eight destroyers. This was clearly
VAdm Nobutake Kondo's Advance Force—combined with VAdm Hiroaki
Abe's Vanguard Force—which appeared to be rushing to catch up with
Task Force 61.

At the time of the sighting, the five TBFs were at 7,000 feet and the two
SBDs were at 9,000 feet. Lieutenant Larsen led his contingent of torpedo
bombers in a great circle to the north to set up a torpedo attack. As soon as
the TBFs flew within range, the Japanese ships fired heavy antiaircraft
concentrations at them.

"Get the nearest big one," Swede Larsen ordered. They were the only words anyone said during the entire attack.

The path of the diving torpedo attack carried the TBFs into a cloud. When they emerged into the face of antiaircraft fire, they were coming up on the port quarter and port bow of a clump of cruisers and destroyers. The antiaircraft fire was so heavy that all the torpedo-bomber pilots had to take independent evasive action.

The best targets were several cruisers sailing in line abreast and dead ahead of the Avengers. Larsen led his tiny strike force over the tops of the first line of light cruisers, for he was intent upon getting the biggest ship around—a distant heavy cruiser.

Drops were made by all five torpedo bombers at roughly the same moment. Each pilot then pulled away in gut-wrenching twists and turns, and all five TBFs retired to the west.

At 1750, at more or less the same instant the TBFs were dropping into their attack run, the SBDs piloted by Elder and Gordon were diving from 12,500 feet on what both perceived in the fading light to be a battleship they had discovered by accident 7 miles to the north.

The "battleship" was really the seaplane tender *Chitose*, an important enough target in her own right. Moments earlier, she had been dead in the water, recovering observation seaplanes, but when first seen by Elder and Gordon she was picking up speed, seeking the protection of intervening clouds, and steaming with her protective ring of destroyers in tight counterclockwise circles to evade the dive-bombers. Very heavy antiaircraft fire from the warships barred the way. Bombs were released at 2,000 feet. During the recovery and retirement, both Dauntless pilots observed what appeared to be a direct hit on the "battleship." In fact, the *Chitose*, which had virtually no armor protection, was severely damaged by a pair of near misses, and several search planes she had aboard were set afire. Plates loosened on her port side led to flooding, and her port engine room had to be shut down, but the *Chitose* was able to retire toward Truk.

Pursued by three unperceived scout planes, Elder and Gordon ran southward to join on the TBFs. They arrived in time to see what looked in the fading light like a massive explosion beside one of the heavy cruisers. The rendezvous was something of a shock, for only three Avengers and the two Dauntlesses joined up for the flight home.

At a point about 40 miles south of the Vanguard Force, Larsen and the others were overtaken by a Japanese twin-float airplane. The Japanese pilot made a single firing pass at the TBF section and then followed the flight for two or three minutes before flying off into the darkness.

The three TBFs and two SBDs under Lieutenant Larsen landed safely aboard the *Saratoga* beginning at 1940.

As its crew searched the sky for their mates, the missing TBF piloted by Lt(jg) Frenchy Fayle was attacked by a pair of *Shokaku* Zeros that were covering Kondo's force. Though the right wing, fuselage, and Plexiglas turret were holed by 7.7mm bullets, Fayle was able to maintain control and the turret gunner, ARM3 Edward Velasquez, was able to down the lead Zero. The second Zero pilot claimed the TBF as a kill, but seems not to have attacked it at all. Fayle continued to grope through the lowering darkness near the Japanese surface force for some time before proceeding south in the hope of reaching Henderson Field. The TBF was forced down when its tanks ran dry. On the last of his nervous energy, Frenchy Fayle managed a good water landing off tiny Nura Island, but he had to be dragged into the life raft by his equally exhausted crewmen.

The second lost TBF, piloted by Lt John Taurman, got as far as San Cristobal before its fuel was exhausted. Taurman made one low pass across a moonlit beach to see if he could draw fire. The place appeared to be deserted, so he completed a superb water landing just off the strand and led his two aircrewmen ashore.

Four 11th Heavy Bombardment Group B-17s that had taken off from Espiritu Santo at 1305 located VAdm Hiroaki Abe's Vanguard Force, some 30 miles ahead of VAdm Chuichi Nagumo's main body, at 1750. Led by Maj Allan Stewart, all four B-17s dropped their bombs over the destroyer *Maikaze*, but failed to score any hits. Then the four heavy bombers flew on to the north, where their crews were able to see the *Shokaku*, the *Zuikaku*, and their many surface escorts. The bomber formation was attacked by twenty-three Zeros, but little damage was sustained by any of them. The bomber gunners claimed five Zeros destroyed, but none actually were. The heavy bombers returned to Espiritu Santo without incident.

♦

Lt Rube Konig was one of the most worried airmen alive by the time Task Force 61 faded from sight following Konig's late launch as leader of seven Torpedo-3 strike aircraft. After the TBF piloted by RE Werner Weis aborted because of a landing-gear problem, Konig missed a rendezvous with the eleven-plane *Enterprise* SBD flight led by Lt Turner Caldwell. Fearing an attack by Japanese fighters—the TBFs had already been shot at by a Val—Konig finally severed his ties with Task Force 61 at the height of the Japanese air strike and shaped a course to the north to find the damaged *Ryujo*.

The things that really worried Rube Konig were that he had already seen the *Enterprise* sustain at least one bomb hit, he had not been given a good fix on his target, he had not been given a good fix on his own task force, and he had no charts, no radio call sign, no frequency-change schedule, and no way of monitoring news of changing conditions anywhere in the wide Pacific.

After about an hour's flight along the northward track, Ens Ed Holley reported by radio that his engine had developed a major oil leak and that his Avenger's windshield was covered with goo. It was beginning to get dark, so Konig advised Holley to maintain his position in the formation for as long as possible; if he had to land in the water, Konig would do his best to get a fix on the spot.

The minuscule strike element was about 250 miles from home when Konig spotted what he thought might have been the moonlit wake of an enemy warship. He immediately gave the signal to attack, and the Avengers split into two groups of three to deliver coordinated anvil attacks on either bow. Each group fanned out in line abreast formation.

Moments before coming up on the release point at a mere 50 feet over the water, one of the pilots exclaimed that the target was a round reef and the "wake" was the surf pounding against it. This was Roncador Reef, 100 miles northwest of Santa Isabel. The TBFs joined up, climbed, and carried on along their original northward heading.

They were about 300 miles from home when Rube Konig announced that they would fly 30 miles farther before heading for what he hoped—but secretly doubted—would be the place the friendly ships were waiting.

The distant point was reached without a sighting, so Konig led the formation to the west for 50 miles. Nothing there. The next turn was for home. They were 50 miles along the return leg when Konig decided to conserve fuel. He ordered everyone to jettison their heavy torpedoes. At that instant, a stream of tracer passed close to Konig's cockpit from the rear. There was a moment of stunned silence, and then Lt(jg) Fred Herriman's abashed voice came up on the radio: "Sorry, Konig. I pressed the wrong button."

After a little inner battle, Konig announced to the group that he felt they did not have enough fuel to take them to Henderson Field—even if anyone knew where it was. A straw poll revealed that everyone felt they had to find the carriers. Konig told the other pilots that if one plane had to ditch, they would all ditch together.

The flying was grueling. Ens Ed Holley's oil line had not ruptured, but it was not difficult to imagine the pressure he felt during the long flight; his engine might freeze on him at any moment, and only God knew where on earth he was.

After five hours in the air, Konig felt that his fuel supply was getting dangerously low. Typically, the flight leader used less fuel than following aircraft, which expended a certain extra margin to remain in formation. If Konig's tanks were nearly dry, it was only a matter of time before one of the others completely ran out.

At about 2115, Konig's radioman, ARM2 David Lane, announced on the intercom, "Mr. Konig, I think I hear an 'N.' "

If Lane had indeed heard the single faint Morse code signal—for no one else in the flight did, and Lane did not hear it again—Lt Rube Konig and the others were back from the dead. It could only have been the carrier homing signal, no doubt received at extreme range.

Konig led the flight 45 degrees to the right, the correct move for the "N" signal. (Other letters would have indicated other headings.) Fifteen minutes after the single faint contact, at 2130, the tiny TBF group found Task Force 16. Konig easily identified the huge moonlit silhouette of the *Enterprise*, which was already turning into the wind to recover the Avengers.

Mach John Baker landed first without incident. Next up was Ens Ed Holley. It was a dark night, Holley had oil all over his windshield, and he was physically, mentally, and emotionally drained. He came in way too fast and way too high; he did not see the LSO wave him off. He missed all the arresting cables and the barrier, and flew right into the carrier's island. The heavy torpedo bomber flopped straight onto the deck on its three wheels and literally fell apart around its three-man crew. Holley suffered a minor laceration on his forehead, but the radioman and bombardier both emerged without a scratch.

The *Enterprise's* flight deck was effectively closed down by the stunning crash, so Lieutenant Konig and his fellows were ordered by signal lamp to proceed to the *Saratoga*. Of the four TBFs that landed aboard the flagship, two ran completely out of fuel as soon as they were down. These had to be pushed out of the way by the plane handlers. When the fuel level in Lt Rube Konig's tanks was measured with a dipstick, he learned that he had not had enough fuel aboard to go around again if he had been waved off.

No one in Lt Rube Konig's TBF force had spotted Lt Turner Caldwell's eleven *Enterprise* Air Group SBDs, but they had occupied pretty much the same volume of air as the TBFs, at least until sunset. Caldwell's Dauntlesses were much higher than Konig's TBFs, and they were no doubt farther ahead, but they flew up the same heading as Konig's TBFs, toward the last known position of the *Ryujo*.

The Dauntless force—designated Flight 300—found nothing in the darkness. With far less fuel than the Avengers, and far less hope of finding their way home, the SBDs were in serious straits. Several pilots were truly worried about the future by the time Caldwell announced that he was shaping a course for Henderson Field.

The grueling flight into the unknown ended when Caldwell saw in the vague moonlight what he thought was a familiar strand of coastline. He had seen Guadalcanal only during the strikes he had led over Tulagi on August 7 and 8. Neither he nor any of the Scouting-5 and Bombing-6 pilots behind him had ever landed on the crude coral-and-earth runway of Henderson Field.

The intruders' identity was established by signal lantern to the satisfaction of Marine antiaircraft gunners manning everything up to 90mm antiaircraft batteries on the beach and around the runway. After Marine groundcrewmen had set out flashlights to mark the extremities of the runway, Caldwell attempted to raise the tower by voice radio. There was no reply; air-ground communications were down.

The Flight 300 pilots were released from the squadron formation and ordered to land, every man for himself. Nine of the eleven, with Caldwell leading, made standard individual approaches from the landward end of the runway, and all landed safely. Two individualists made straight-in approaches from seaward, which began an exciting interlude due to an undisclosed, unperceived high stand of palm trees at the seaward end of the dirt-and-coral strip. Nevertheless, all eleven Flight 300 SBDs landed, precious bombs and all, without damage or injury.

Friendly Marine groundcrewmen helped the Navy pilots and gunners secure the airplanes in tree-lined revetments. Then the twenty-two exhausted Navy airmen were led into the nearby coconut grove, where they were fed and billeted in tents.

The last airplane to return from the precipitous late U.S. Navy strike launches just before the Japanese strike force appeared was piloted by LCdr Max Leslie, the *Enterprise* Air Group commander. Leslie had flown off alone in his modified TBF command bomber and had tried—vainly, as it turned out—to catch up with the small Dauntless and Avenger groups that had been sent north only minutes earlier.

When Leslie had flown as far as he dared without once seeing a friendly airplane, he came upon what looked like the wake of a ship. Though he had only two 500-pound bombs aboard, the air group commander—who had been cheated out of an opportunity to hit a Japanese carrier at Midway—reflexively followed the telltale marker toward its source.

There was no source. A trick of the waning light had made waves breaking over an isolated submerged reef—Roncador Reef, again—seem to Max Leslie's eager eyes to be an enemy ship. The air group commander broke off his useless attack, took a bearing, and reluctantly headed for Point Option, the spot on the ocean at which Task Force 61 was supposed to be.

The command TBF flew to within radar and radio range of Task Force 16 at 1842, but Leslie was unable to see any ships in the pitch blackness.

He transmitted a radio signal he hoped would be answered, but it was not, though it was picked up and an attempt was made by a friendly destroyer to answer it. Leslie doggedly flew on down the course heading he hoped would carry him over a friendly flight deck or two. All the while, he was wondering if either of the carriers had survived the pounding he had seen in the making as he flew flat-out for the horizon as the first Vals were entering their dives.

By now at extremely low altitude, Leslie thought he saw a small ship—perhaps two small ships—pass beneath his wings. It was a good sign for a lost aviator. Then it occurred to Leslie that they might be Japanese destroyers. He flew on. There was no choice.

Finally, the silence was broken. Leslie's earphones crackled with the sound of a familiar voice: "Max, this is Ham Dow. Keep coming. Get some altitude."

Leslie flew on into the darkness, the icy grip of fear around his heart melting with each passing minute. Several more terse messages arrived from Lieutenant Commander Dow, who refused to leave the *Enterprise's* Radar Plot compartment as long as a friendly airplane was still aloft. Besides, Max Leslie was a Naval Academy classmate, a fellow naval aviator, and a close personal friend.

Leslie had not had much schooling in the use of new fangled radar in his long flying career. He was aware of its potential, but until that midnight ride he had never considered it to be a lifesaving tool.

At long last, a big full moon peeked out from behind dark clouds. The vista below was of many ships trailing silvery wakes. To make matters better, Ham Dow announced that the *Saratoga* would flick on her deck lights at the last minute. This was an enormous concession, and Leslie was humbled by the risk his fellow sailors were taking in his behalf.

Leslie's experience flying the new TBF was minimal, and he had never done so at night. Indeed, this was also the first time he would be landing a TBF aboard a carrier; until a week or so earlier, he had been flying only SBDs.

The lights went on at just the right moment, and Leslie completed a perfect landing at 2303.

♦

With the recovery of LCdr Max Leslie's command Avenger, Task Force 61 was free to sail from the scene of the battle. This was indeed VAdm Frank Jack Fletcher's reasonable response to the facts he had at hand. The two most important facts were that he had a damaged carrier and the Japanese had at least two *un*damaged fleet carriers within range. So at Fletcher's order Task Force 61 turned south to join the *Wasp's* battle group beyond the range of the potentially onrushing Japanese carriers.

For their part, the Japanese were content with honoring reports from returning strike pilots that they had left two U.S. Navy carriers burning and sinking off the Stewart Islands. Believing that the American battle fleet was withdrawing beyond range at high speed, VAdm Chuichi Nagumo decided to head north after recovering various patrol fighters and the second-strike bombers and fighters. However, VAdm Nobutake Kondo's Advance Force joined VAdm Hiroaki Abe's Vanguard Force for a dash south to engage the American battle fleet. The Japanese surface force was attacked between 1735 and 1750 by Lt Swede Larsen's TBFs and two SBDs, and the *Chitose* was damaged. Nevertheless, Kondo pressed southward, but the chase was abandoned at midnight following a fruitless high-speed search.

After Kondo and Abe turned north, the only piece remaining on the board was RAdm Raizo Tanaka's Reinforcement Group, which was still charged with delivering seven hundred Imperial Army infantrymen and eight hundred Imperial Navy infantry bluejackets to Guadalcanal.

Chapter 37

Agood deal of confusion reigned in both camps the night of August
24 and throughout August 25. During the night, on the Japanese
side, was the conviction that LCdr Mamoru Seki's strike force had
left two American fleet carriers burning off the Stewart Islands. Based on
contacts with American carrier aircraft very late in the day, however, the
Japanese felt they might still be facing a third American carrier with an
unscathed air group.

Taken against the facts that the *Ryujo* had been sunk and its small air
group destroyed, and that the *Shokaku* and *Zuikaku* air groups had been
seriously depleted both over the American carriers and by way of numerous operational losses later on, VAdm Chuichi Nagumo had withdrawn early
in the evening toward the base at Truk, as much for the need to refuel as for
any fear of counterstrikes on August 25. The *Shokaku* and *Zuikaku*, though
unharmed, had nonetheless been temporarily neutralized by their aircraft
and aircrew losses as well as low fuel supplies.

Similarly, the powerful Japanese surface force had been neutralized
during the wee hours by the conviction that the American carriers still had
some bite left. And so VAdm Nobutake Kondo had withdrawn out of range

at midnight, following his abortive search for the crippled American carriers. In addition, as was the case with the Japanese fleet carriers, Kondo's ships needed to refuel.

VAdm Gunichi Mikawa, the Eighth Fleet commander, had followed the action throughout August 24 and during the night, and what he heard had disheartened him. Initially, he ordered RAdm Raizo Tanaka's Reinforcement Group to withdraw from range of Guadalcanal-based light bombers. As the night wore on, however, Mikawa became convinced that the American carriers had been severely damaged and that perhaps there was a window of opportunity to land the reinforcements charged to his and Tanaka's care. Tanaka was ordered south once again, although Mikawa failed to provide any additional cover from his force of cruisers and destroyers.

An equal if different view prevailed on the American side. Based on reports from his carrier airmen, VAdm Frank Jack Fletcher allowed himself to be convinced that as many as seventy Japanese carrier bombers and fighters had been destroyed over Task Force 16 on August 24, and that the *Ryujo's* entire air complement had been wiped out. In addition, American stations monitoring Japanese radio traffic during the late evening concluded that many or even most of the Japanese aircraft deployed for the second strike had become lost in the dark and had ditched or crashed at sea. By the wee hours of August 25, the American admirals and their advisers counted three Japanese carriers as being out of the picture—the *Ryujo* by virtue of having been sunk, and the *Shokaku* and *Zuikaku* by virtue of their having been stripped of fighters and bombers.

For all that, Fletcher was unable to muster a killing blow. Though her captain claimed much greater flexibility, the *Enterprise* was severely restricted in her ability to conduct flight operations from a battered deck and with two marginal elevators. Nevertheless, her air group, and the *Saratoga's*, had suffered minor losses on August 24 and, combined, they were indeed the dominant air force in the region on the morning of August 25. But this did nothing to allay Fletcher's concern about the *Enterprise's* damage, nor his perennial worry about fuel supplies. In the end, he opted to withdraw from range of any and all Japanese bases, afloat or ashore, in order to save the *Enterprise* and refuel the *Saratoga* and all their surface escorts. There was some talk of pursuing the withdrawing Japanese with the *Wasp* and her air group, but Task Force 18 had not completed its refueling at sea until the afternoon of August 24 and could not arrive at Task Force 61's former position off the Stewart Islands until well after midnight. Even at that, the *Wasp's* power plant was considered too fragile to undertake a protracted high-speed pursuit.

After midnight on August 25, the *Enterprise* and Task Force 16 passed east of the *Wasp* and Task Force 18 on the way toward the New Hebrides. And shortly thereafter, the *Saratoga* and Task Force 11 arrived in the refueling area. Thus all three U.S. Navy carriers were well beyond the range of effective pursuit by or against the withdrawing Japanese carriers. This effectively ended the carrier phase of the Battle of the Eastern Solomons, although a number of tender- and cruiser-based Japanese search planes would be encountered and knocked down by *Wasp* aircraft on August 25.

In the end, the job of stopping or even destroying RAdm Raizo Tanaka's troop-laden transports fell to the rather weak air establishment based at Guadalcanal's Henderson Field. But mustering the VMSB-232 and Flight 300 Marine and Navy dive-bombers for a killing blow was no easy task.

Shortly after midnight, while airmen and groundcrews were busily arming and fueling the mixed bag of Marine and Navy Dauntlesses and Marine Wildcats, three Japanese destroyers sailed into Lengo Channel and bombarded the Lunga area. The interlude was exciting for both sides, but no real harm was done.

Maj Dick Mangrum, the commander of VMSB-232, led two other Marine SBDs aloft in an effort to get at the destroyers. Night-bombing techniques in mid-1942 being rather basic, all three of the extremely brave Marine pilots missed their targets.

A second three-plane strike—this one composed of newly arrived Dauntlesses from Lt Turner Caldwell's *Enterprise* Flight 300—was mounted at 0330. The Navy airmen found the trio of Imperial Navy warships retiring past Savo Island, but again no hit was scored. Indeed, Ens Walter Brown lost his way in the dark and ultimately ditched his precious dive-bomber off Malaita.

Following the withdrawal of the Japanese destroyers, MajGen Archer

Vandegrift, the Marine commanding general, received a message from South Pacific Area headquarters that enemy carriers were closing on Guadalcanal and might launch strikes against Henderson Field at daylight from a position off northern Malaita. To underscore this gloomy and wildly inaccurate warning, five seaplanes launched from Admiral Mikawa's cruisers bombed the Lunga area at 0340. Once again, no harm was done, but nerves were frazzled all around.

At 0430 on August 25, General Vandegrift finally received a message, filed at 2015 the previous evening by a VP-23 PBY, that one carrier and six other vessels had been sighted 180 miles north of Guadalcanal, proceeding south at 17 knots. This was certainly Tanaka's Reinforcement Group, and it is understandable that in the dark the PBY crew mistook the largest transport for a carrier.

Believing that a carrier strike might obliterate his tiny air force and leave the Lunga Perimeter and Henderson Field vulnerable to a feared counterinvasion, General Vandegrift decided upon the only course of action that was really open to him: Attack the carrier at dawn. At 0600, five VMSB-232 and three Flight 300 SBDs under Maj Dick Mangrum and ten VMF-223 Wildcat escorts under Capt John Lucien Smith were launched against the carrier force.

Of course, there was no carrier; only Tanaka's three transports, one light cruiser, four destroyers, and three troop-laden patrol boats were in range of Henderson Field. At 0740 the three Eighth Fleet destroyers that had shelled Lunga after midnight joined and were added to the screen. And by 0800, the entire Reinforcement Group was within just 150 miles of Henderson Field. Tanaka's plan was to land the troops at night, bombard Henderson Field, and be out of range by dawn on August 26.

Maj Dick Mangrum's little land-based strike group spent two hours searching for the carrier that was not there—continuing on alone after the Wildcats, which were not equipped with belly tanks, had to turn for home on what remained of their fuel. On the way home, the Wildcats crossed the path of a Yokohama Air Group Mavis long-range reconnaissance bomber out of the Shortland Islands, and two of the Marine pilots attacked. The

Marines claimed a victory, but the severely damaged airplane, with one mortally wounded crewman aboard, made it to the Shortlands, where the pilot ran it aground to prevent a total loss. This was to be the only fighter action of the day.

Second Lieutenant Hank Hise, who was flying off Major Mangrum's right wing, was getting a stiff neck from constant craning to watch for trouble and keep station on the flight leader. Endless columns of puffy white clouds could be seen marching across the vast emptiness of sea and green-hued islands—but there was no carrier, no surface warships, no nothing. The short-legged Wildcats had long since turned for home. Suddenly, at 0805, as Hise looked off to port from an altitude of 12,000 feet, he spotted three columns of ships sailing in a southwesterly direction, toward Guadalcanal. The strain of long hours of flying instantly dissipated.

Without prior planning, the American airmen broke off to go after the largest warship, the light cruiser *Jintsu*—Admiral Tanaka's flagship. Lieutenant Caldwell chose to lead his wingmen after the largest transport, the *Kinryu Maru*—the ship the PBY crew had mistaken for a carrier.

Major Mangrum executed a classic dive-bombing attack, approaching from east to west, 90 degrees to the direction in which the ships were traveling. Then he waggled his wings, broke the flight off to the left, and pitched over his left wingman, 2dLt Larry Baldinus. When Baldinus went, Hank Hise kicked his airplane up and over, dropped flaps, eased back on the throttle, and rolled on the left trim tab to overcome the lack of torque. As the young Marine pilot swung on his seat harness, fighting to keep down the bile rising in his throat, he instinctively looked around for the biggest ship; he was determined to go out in a blaze of glory.

Baldinus and Hise plummeted toward the *Jintsu*. It was over within seconds. Hise reached his release point, dropped his bomb, came back on the stick, and added power. All emotions were overcome by the pull of gravity on the blood supply to his brain. An instantaneous gray mind-numb vaporized.

Unable to bear missing the result of his first combat dive, Hise broke a cardinal rule. While he was closing his dive flaps, he eased off to the right to look back at the target. The anticipated ball of fire did not emerge, but

Hise did see his bomb explode in the water beside the *Jintsu's* hull. He advanced his throttle to full power, got his flaps all the way up, and joined on Baldinus, thankful to be with someone he was certain would know the way home. The two were surprised to see Mangrum execute a second dive. The squadron commander's bomb had not released during the first dive, so he had hauled it back up to 10,000 feet and gamely tried again. His bomb narrowly missed the troop-laden *Boston Maru*.

Baldinus's 500-pound bomb was planted between the *Jintsu's* forward gun mounts. No one was surprised by Baldinus's success. Though this was his first combat drop, Baldinus was a former enlisted pilot with many years' experience. The blast from Baldinus's bomb knocked RAdm Raizo Tanaka unconscious.

Following Baldinus's superb drop, the two remaining Marine SBD pilots, 2dLt Charles McAllister and 2dLt Leland Thomas, both near-missed the light cruiser.

Lt Turner Caldwell led his two wingmen, Ens Jesse Barker and Ens Chris Fink, after the *Kinryu Maru*. Fink, who was the last man in the Navy formation, saw Caldwell's 500-pound bomb miss the target, but he did not have time to track Barker's 500-pound bomb—which also missed—because he quickly arrived at his own release point. As Fink was pulling out, he heard his rearseatman shouting over the intercom that his 1,000-pound bomb had hit the transport dead amidships. Fink quickly glanced back and saw smoke rising and debris settling out of the air. He also saw that the *Jintsu* was aflame.

All eight American dive-bombers made a running rendezvous while heading south for home. As soon as the Navy Dauntlesses were clear of the action, Lieutenant Caldwell signaled his wingmen to check their fuel situation. Fink had 40 gallons remaining; Caldwell and Barker each had only 25. All three—and all the Marine airmen—safely reached Henderson Field and went right to work refueling their airplanes, a job that consisted of straining aviation gasoline from 55-gallon drums through chamois skin into 12-quart buckets that were then emptied into the airplane fuel tanks.

When the fueling had been completed, all ten of the Navy SBDs were ordered out to find Tanaka's force once again. All of the Navy pilots except Ens Chris Fink were able to get airborne.

♦

Shortly after RAdm Raizo Tanaka came to, after narrowly escaping death in the vortex of 2dLt Larry Baldinus's 500-pound bomb, he transferred his flag to one of the destroyers and sent the damaged *Jintsu* back toward Truk under her own power. After seeing to the damaged *Kinryu Maru*, Tanaka intended to go on.

The *Kinryu Maru*, which was carrying most of the rear echelon of an elite Imperial Navy infantry landing battalion, was definitely sinking. The destroyer *Mutsuki* went alongside to begin taking off the crew and the naval infantrymen.

At 1015 four 11th Heavy Bombardment Group B-17s commanded by Capt Walter Chambers arrived on the scene from Espiritu Santo. The *Mutsuki's* captain felt safe where he was; horizontal bombing against ships was known by everyone to be highly inaccurate. The man was blown into the water when five of forty-four 500-pound bombs dropped by the heavy bombers blanketed his ship, which immediately sank.

As the remaining destroyers and patrol boats stopped at once to pick up survivors from the sunken destroyer and sinking transport, tough, resolute RAdm Raizo Tanaka felt that it was past time to depart the scene. He ordered all his ships to make for Rabaul as soon as survivors from the *Mutsuki* and *Kinryu Maru* were aboard.

Early that sunny afternoon, the crew of the *Enterprise* conducted a memorial service for her crewmen and airmen killed in the August 24 action. Altogether, seventy-four bodies were buried at sea. Several other dead sailors and officers had been blown overboard in the bombing raid, and, of course, several airmen never returned to the ship.

A strike force composed of nine Flight 300 Dauntlesses under Lt Turner Caldwell went looking for Admiral Tanaka in the afternoon, but it found just one Japanese destroyer, the *Mochizuki*, about 150 miles northwest of Henderson Field. Six of the Dauntless pilots were ordered to attack, but the rest were held in reserve pending the discovery of the Japanese main force.

Ens Hal Buell, a Scouting-5 veteran of the Coral Sea and Midway, was the third man in the string. He saw the first two bombs miss by a fair margin, and he saw a good deal of antiaircraft gunfire rising to meet him. The lithe destroyer was well into a hard starboard turn when Ensign Buell released his 500-pound bomb at what he felt was just the right instant. His rearseatman reported only a near miss to starboard, however. The fourth and fifth pilots dropped their bombs close aboard the destroyer's port side, but the last man was not even close. Nevertheless, the *Mochizuki* appeared to have been amply damaged.

After tooling around for a while, using up precious fuel, the Navy pilots returned to Henderson Field.

The *Wasp* Air Group also tried its hand at locating and attacking the reduced Reinforcement Group. LCdr Wallace Beakley, the air group commander, was launched at 1326 with twenty-four SBDs and ten Avengers from a position near southeast Malaita. The launch was disrupted a bit by the arrival of a 14th Air Group Emily amphibious patrol bomber, but the intruder was driven off and shot down by four VS-71 SBDs.

The *Wasp* strike group searched a wide area centered on Tanaka's last known position, but no Japanese ships were found. Commander Beakley then led the strikers to Santa Isabel's Rekata Bay in the belief that a seaplane tender was running air searches from there. But the bay was empty, it was getting late, and fuel was getting low, so Beakley decided to return home. After shaping the most-direct course and jettisoning bombs and torpedoes as a fuel-conservation measure, the strike force arrived over the *Wasp* at 1737 and was fully recovered by 1806. As soon as her combat air patrol had landed, the *Wasp* and Task Force 18 turned south to join the *Saratoga* and Task Force 11 well out of range of land- and carrier-based enemy aircraft.

By then the *Enterprise* was well on her way to Tongatabu Island for emergency repairs, and a large part of her air group, including most of Fighting-6, had been transferred to the *Saratoga* Air Group. Also, the battleship *North Carolina*, the light antiaircraft cruiser *Atlanta*, and four destroyers were stripped from Task Force 16 to bolster Fletcher's two remaining carrier task forces.

Task Force 11 completed the refueling at 2330 and sailed north to join

Task Force 18 southeast of Malaita. When joined, the two carriers would wait to see if the Japanese mounted a follow-on effort against them or Henderson Field.

In fact, there had been a brief flurry of activity on the Japanese side during the day. Following sightings of an American carrier task force by two fleet submarines during the night of August 24–25, Adm Isoroku Yamamoto had ordered the *Zuikaku* and three destroyers to reverse course to the southwest to screen Admiral Tanaka's Reinforcement Group against a possible carrier-based attack. And the Combined Fleet commander-in-chief had sailed southeast from his position off Truk aboard his flagship, the super battleship *Yamato,* in the company of two destroyers and the *Taiyo,* an escort carrier with only a few Zeros aboard. These forces came no closer than 400 miles to Guadalcanal before turning northeast to join Admiral Kondo's Support Force, and they posed no threat to any American ships or installations.

The last air action of August 25 was undertaken by seven 11th Heavy Bombardment Group B-17s from Espiritu Santo, which found a large unidentified Japanese vessel being towed by a much smaller vessel. The two were presumably a destroyer and the seaplane tender *Chitose,* which had been damaged the evening before by Lt(jg) Robert Elder and Ens Bob Gordon, of Scouting-3. All seven of the heavy bombers made individual runs against the larger vessel, and several hits were claimed. The *Chitose* did not herself report any new damage, however.

Epilogue

Ens Harold Bingaman, AMM3 Calvin Crouch, and ARM3 Paul Knight had safely ditched their disabled TBF and scuttled aboard their life raft, but they had been left behind by the departing task force. Bingaman had suffered a small laceration between his eyes, and Knight had also suffered a throbbing blow to the head as well as a painful, swelling ankle injury.

Fortunately, Ensign Bingaman had spotted a not-too-distant island—Stewart Island, in fact—and he and Crouch rowed the raft to it over the eight-hour period from 1645 on August 24, until somtime after midnight on August 25. Once during the long, lonely hours before dawn, the hum of multiple airplane engines sounded overhead, but the three marooned airmen were afraid to attract attention to themselves.

At sunrise on August 25, Bingaman and Crouch left the injured Knight in a concealed spot on the beach and went off to explore the island. After an interminable period alone with his worst fears, Knight saw four islanders approaching him. He cocked his heavy .45-caliber automatic pistol, though it was of dubious value after its immersion in saltwater. Thankfully, one of the islanders waved and smiled, and all four carried Knight to their village, where he was reunited with Bingaman and Crouch. More than three hundred islanders lived in the village, and they had ample food to share with the castaways. One islander was permanently assigned to care for Knight's head wound and swollen ankle, which he constantly washed.

Late in the afternoon of the third day, the isolation was shattered by the hum of PBY engines. Ensign Bingaman fired a flare into the sky, and that attracted the attention of the friendly airmen. The VP-11 PBY piloted by Lt(jg) George Clute landed in the lagoon, and the entire village transported itself and its guests to the amphibian bomber in outrigger canoes. ARM3 Knight was passed through one of the open waist-gun blisters, and Crouch and Bingaman climbed aboard under their own power. As the canoes pulled away, the PBY crewmen passed out packs of cigarettes to the castaways.

The flight to Espiritu Santo was made without incident. The three TBF crewmen were treated for their various ills and injuries aboard the seaplane tender *Curtiss*.

Two Torpedo-8 TBFs had ditched north of Guadalcanal during the night of August 24. Lt John Taurman and his crew were rescued from San Cristobal on August 28, and Lt(jg) Frenchy Fayle and his crew were rescued from tiny Nura Island by a U.S. Navy destroyer on August 29.

That left ARM3 Delmer Wiley, who had survived the destruction of Mach Harry Corl's VT-3 search TBF near the *Ryujo*. Wiley's life raft drifted to the northwest for fifteen days and then grounded on tiny Carteret Island, only 40 miles from the Japanese airstrip at Buka. Wiley would endure an adventure-filled seven months before he finally reached Guadalcanal on April 11, 1943.

And that ended the Battle of the Eastern Solomons.

Order of Battle

August 23–25, 1942

SOUTH PACIFIC FORCE
VAdm Robert L. Ghormley

TASK FORCE 61
VAdm Frank Jack Fletcher

Task Force 11	VAdm Frank Jack Fletcher
Saratoga (CV) (FF)	Capt Dewitt C. Ramsey
Air Group	Cdr Harry D. Felt
VF-5	LCdr LeRoy C. Simpler
VB-3	LCdr DeWitt C. Shumway
VS-3	LCdr Louis J. Kirn
VT-8	Lt Harold H. Larsen
Task Force 11 Screen	RAdm Carleton H. Wright
Minneapolis (CA) (F)	
New Orleans (CA)	

Destroyer Squadron 1
  Phelps (DD)
Destroyer Division 2
  Farragut (DD)
  Worden (DD)
  MacDonough (DD)
  Dale (DD)

Task Force 16   RAdm Thomas C. Kinkaid
  Enterprise (CV) (F)   Capt Arthur C. Davis
  Air Group   LCdr Maxwell F. Leslie
    VF-6   Lt Louis H. Bauer
    VB-6   Lt Ray Davis
    VS-5   Lt Turner F. Caldwell
    VT-3   LCdr Charles M. Jett

  Task Force 16 Screen   RAdm Mahlon S. Tisdale
    North Carolina (BB)
    Portland (CA) (F)
    Atlanta (CLAA)
    Destroyer Squadron 6
    Balch (DD)
    Maury (DD)
    Ellet (DD)
    Benham (DD)
    Destroyer Division 22
    Grayson (DD)
    Monssen (DD)

Task Force 18   RAdm Leigh Noyes
  Wasp (CV) (F)   Capt Forrest P. Sherman
  Air Group   LCdr Wallace M. Beakley
    VF-71   LCdr Courtney M. Shands
    VS-71   LCdr John Eldridge, Jr.
    VS-72   LCdr Ernest M. Snowden
    VT-7   Lt Harry A. Romberg

Task Force 18 Screen   RAdm Norman Scott
    San Francisco (CA) (F)
    San Juan (CLAA)
    Salt Lake City (CL)
  Destroyer Squadron 4
    Selfridge (DD)
  Destroyer Squadron 12
    Farenholt (DD)
    Aaron Ward (DD)
    Buchanan (DD)
  Destroyer Division 14
    Lang (DD)
    Stack (DD)
    Sterett (DD)

TASK FORCE 63
(Land-based Aircraft)
RAdm John S. McCain

Marine Air Group 23   LtCol Charles L. Fike, USMC
  (at Guadalcanal)
    VMF-223   Capt John L. Smith, USMC
    VMSB-232   Maj Richard C. Mangrum, USMC
11th Heavy Bombardment Group   Col La Verne Saunders, USA
  (at Espiritu Santo)
67th Fighter Squadron   Capt Dale D. Brannon, USA
  (at Guadalcanal)
Elements of VP-11 and VP-23
  (at Ndeni)

♦

COMBINED FLEET
Adm Isoroku Yamamoto

GUADALCANAL SUPPORT FORCE
VAdm Nobutake Kondo
(CinC 2nd Fleet)

Advance Force   VAdm Nobutake Kondo
Cruiser Division 4
Atago (CA) (FF)
Maya (CA)
Takao (CA)
Cruiser Division 5
Myoko (CA) (F)
Haguro (CA)
Destroyer Squadron 4
Yura (CL) (F)
Asagumo (DD)
Yamagumo (DD)
Hayashio (DD)
Koroshio (DD)

Support Group
Mutsu (BB)
Murasame (DD)
Harusame (DD)
Samidare (DD)

Seaplane Group   RAdm Takaji Joshima
Chitose (CVL) (F)
Natsugumo (DD)

MOBILE FORCE

VAdm Chuichi Nagumo
(CinC 3rd Fleet)

Shokaku (CV) (F)	
Air Group	LCdr Mamoru Seki
Fighter Squadron	Lt Hideki Shingo
Bomber Squadron	LCdr Mamoru Seki
Attack Squadron	LCdr Shigeharu Murata
Zuikaku (CV)	
Air Group	Lt Sadamu Takahashi
Fighter Squadron	Lt Ayao Shirane
Bomber Squadron	Lt Sadamu Takahashi
Attack Squadron	Lt Shigeichiro Imajuku

Akigumo (DD)
Kazegumo (DD)
Shikinami (DD)
Uranami (DD)
Yugumo (DD)

VANGUARD FORCE

VAdm Hiroaki Abe

Battleship Division 11
  Hiei (BB) (F)
  Kirishima (BB)
Cruiser Division 7
  Suzuya (CA) (F)
  Kumano (CA)
  Chikuma (CA)
Destroyer Division 10
  Nagara (CL) (F)

Akizuki (DD)
Hatsukaze (DD)
Maikaze (DD)
Nowaki (DD)
Tanikaze (DD)
Yukikaze (DD)

CARRIER STRIKING FORCE
RAdm Chuichi Hara

Ryujo (CVL)[sunk]   Lt Kenjiro Notomi
  Air Group   Lt Kenjiro Notomi
    Fighter Squadron   Lt Binichi Murakami
    Attack Squadron
Tone (CA) (F)
Amatsukaze (DD)
Tokitsukaze (DD)

OUTER SEAS FORCE
VAdm Gunichi Mikawa
(CinC 8th Fleet)

Reinforcement Group   RAdm Raizo Tanaka
  Escorts
  Jintsu (CL) (F)
  Yayoi (DD)
  Kagero (DD)
  Uzuki (DD)
  Mutsuki (DD) [sunk]
  Kawakaze (DD)
  Isokaze (DD)
  Suzukaze (DD)
  Umikaze (DD)

Transports
  Kinryu Maru [sunk]
  Boston Maru
  PB-1
  PB-2
  PB-3

Covering Group   VAdm Gunichi Mikawa
  Chokai (CA) (F)
Cruiser Division 6
  Aoba (CA) (F)
  Kinugasa (CA)
  Furutaka (CA)

Submarine Group
  I-121, I-123, RO-34

LAND-BASED AIRCRAFT

Base Air Force (Eleventh Air Fleet)   VAdm Nishizo Tsukahara
  5th Air Attack Force (26th Air Flotilla)
    2d Air Group (A6M, D3A)
    4th Air Group (G4M)
    14th Air Group Detachment (H8K)
    Misawa Air Group (G4M)
    Tainan Air Group (A6M)
    Yokohama Air Group Detachment (H6K)

ADVANCE EXPEDITIONARY FORCE
VAdm Teruhisa Komatsu
(CinC 6th Fleet)
Submarine Force
  I-9, I-11, I-15, I-17, I-19, I-26, I-31, I-174, I-175

Bibliography

BOOKS

Belote, James H., and William M. Belote. *Titans of the Seas: The Development and Operations of Japanese and American Carrier Task Forces During World War II*. New York: Harper & Row, 1975.

Burns, Eugene. *Then There Was One: The USS Enterprise and the First Year of the War*. New York: Harcourt, Brace and Company, 1943.

Carl, MajGen Marion E., with Barrett Tillman. *Pushing the Envelope: The Career of Fighter Ace and Test Pilot Marion Carl*. Annapolis: Naval Institute Press, 1994.

Craven, Wesley F., and James L. Cate (eds.). *The Army Air Forces in World War II*, vol. IV: *The Pacific: Guadalcanal to Saipan, August 1942 to July 1944*. Chicago: University of Chicago Press, 1950.

Dull, Paul S. *A Battle History of the Imperial Japanese Navy, 1941–1945*. Annapolis: Naval Institute Press, 1978.

Feuer, A. B. *Coast Watching in the Solomon Islands: The Bougainville Reports, December 1941–July 1943*. New York: Praeger, 1992.

Hammel, Eric. *Aces Against Japan*, vol. I: *The American Aces Speak*. Novato, Calif.: Presidio Press, 1993.

————. *Aces Against Japan II*, vol. III: *The American Aces Speak*.
Pacifica, Calif.: Pacifica Press, 1996.

————. *Guadalcanal: Starvation Island*. Pacifica, Calif.: Pacifica Press,
1992.

————. *Guadalcanal: The Carrier Battles*. New York: Crown Publishers,
1987.

Hara, Tameichi, with Fred Saito and Roger Pineau. *Japanese Destroyer
Captain*. New York: Ballantine Books, 1961.

Knott, Richard C. *Black Cat Raiders of WWII*. Baltimore: Nautical &
Aviation Publishing Company of America, 1981.

Lundstrom, John B. *The First Team: Pacific Naval Air Combat from Pearl
Harbor to Midway*. Annapolis: Naval Institute Press, 1984.

————. *The First Team and the Guadalcanal Campaign*. Annapolis:
Naval Institute Press, 1994.

Mears, Lt Frederick. *Carrier Combat*. Garden City: Doubleday, Doran
and Co., Inc., 1944.

Miller, Thomas G., Jr. *The Cactus Air Force*. New York: Harper & Row,
1969.

Mondey, David. *Concise Guide to American Aircraft of World War II*.
London: Temple Press, 1982.

————. *Concise Guide to Axis Aircraft of World War II*. London: Temple
Press, 1984.

Morison, RAdm Samuel Eliot. *History of United States Naval Operations
in World War II*, vol. V: *The Struggle for Guadalcanal*. Boston: The
Atlantic Monthly & Little, Brown & Co., 1962.

Okumiya, Masatake, and Jiro Horikoshi. *Zero!: The Inside Story of
Japan's Air War in the Pacific*. New York: E. P. Dutton & Co., 1956.

Olynyk, Dr. Frank J. *USMC Credits for the Destruction of Enemy Aircraft
in Air-to-Air Combat in World War II*. Aurora, Ohio: Frank J. Olynyk,
1982.

————. *USN Credits for Destruction of Enemy Aircraft in Air-to-Air
Combat: World War II*. Aurora, Ohio: Frank J. Olynyk, 1982.

Porter, Col R. Bruce, with Eric Hammel. *Ace!: A Marine Night-Fighter
Pilot in World War II*. Pacifica, Calif.: Pacifica Press, 1985.

Potter, E. B. *Nimitz*. Annapolis: Naval Institute Press, 1976.

Reynolds, Clark G. *The Fast Carriers: The Forging of an Air Navy.* New York: McGraw-Hill, 1968.

Roscoe, Theodore. *United States Destroyer Operations in World War II.* Annapolis: Naval Institute Press, 1953.

Rust, Kenn C. *Fifth Air Force Story.* Temple City, California: Historical Aviation Album, 1973.

Sakai, Saburo, with Martin Caidin and Fred Saito. *Samurai!.* New York: E. P. Dutton, 1957.

Sherrod, Robert. *History of Marine Corps Aviation in World War II.* San Rafael, Calif.: Presidio Press, 1980.

Stafford, Cdr Edward P. *The Big E: The Story of the USS Enterprise.* New York: Random House, 1962.

Stover, E. T., and Clark G. Reynolds. *The Saga of Smokey Stover.* Charleston, S.C.: Trad Street Press, 1978.

Tillman, Barrett. *The Dauntless Dive Bomber of World War II.* Annapolis: Naval Institute Press, 1976.

———. *The Wildcat in WWII.* Baltimore: Nautical & Aviation Publishing Company of America, 1983.

Toland, John. *The Rising Sun: The Decline and Fall of the Japanese Empire.* New York: Random House, 1970.

Toliver, Raymond F., and Trevor J. Constable. *Fighter Aces of the U.S.A.* Fallbrook, Calif.: Aero Publishers, Inc., 1979.

Weiland, Charles Patrick. *Manuscript Found in a Battle: A Marine Fighter Pilot's Story.* Beaufort, S.C.: CAVU Press, 1993.

Wolfert, Ira. *Torpedo 8.* Boston: Houghton Mifflin Company, 1943.

PERIODICALS

"Capt Robin M. Lindsey, USN (Ret): The Last Cut for an LSO." *The Hook* (Summer 1984).

Gates, Thomas F., "Track of the Tomcatters: A History of VF-31, Part 2: Fighting Six at Guadalcanal." *The Hook* (Winter 1984).

Hammel, Eric, "Bogies At Angels Twelve." *World War II* (March–April 1986).

Lundstrom, John B., "Saburo Sakai Over Guadalcanal." *Fighter Pilots in Aerial Combat* (Fall 1982).

Lundstrom, John B., with Henry Sakaida, "Saburo Sakai Over Guadalcanal, Part II." *Fighter Pilots in Aerial Combat* (Winter 1983).

Poulos, George, "Recollections of a VP Pilot." *Naval Aviation News* (September 1982).

Southerland, Lt J. J., II, USN, "One of the Many Personal Adventures in the Solomons." *U.S. Naval Institute Proceedings* (April 1943).

Tanaka, VAdm Raizo, "Japan's Losing Struggle for Guadalcanal, Parts I and II." *U.S. Naval Institute Proceedings* (1956).

Toyama, Saburo, "Lessons from the Past." *U.S. Naval Institute Proceedings* (September 1982).

Index

Achten, Mach Julius A. (Joe), 71, 73,
 282
Adams, Lt Dudley H., 67–69
Aircraft carrier operations, 26–35
Aircraft descriptions
 Aichi D3A Val carrier bomber, 13
 Bell P-39/P-400 Airacobra fighter,
  189
 Consolidated PBY Catalina amphib-
  ian patrol bomber, 14
 Curtiss SOC Seagull scout-
  observation floatplane, 14
 Douglas SBD Dauntless dive-
  bomber, 11
 Grumman F4F Wildcat fighter,
  9–11
 Grumman TBF Avenger torpedo
  bomber, 11–12
 Kawanishi H6K Mavis amphibian
  patrol bomber, 14–15

Kawanishi H8K Emily amphibian
 patrol bomber, 14–15
Mitsubishi A6M Zero fighter, 12–13
Mitsubishi G4M Betty medium
 bomber, 15
Nakajima A6M2-N Rufe floatplane
 fighter, 14
Nakajima B5N Kate torpedo
 bomber, 13–14
Albright, ARM2 C. W., 292
Allied Air Forces, 82, 83
Alligator Creek, Guadalcanal, 135–
 139, 142–143, 145
Arima, Lt Keiichi, 263, 265, 266,
 267, 268, 294
Austin, Ens Walton A., 287
Aviation Cadet Act of 1935, 20

Bailey, 2dLt Elwood R., 190
Baker, Mach John R., 281, 316

Baldinus, 2dLt Lawrence, 130–131, 325–327

Balenti, Ens Robert, 128

Barker, Ens Jesse T., 326

Barnes, Mach Doyle C., 203, 240–241, 248, 249, 262, 268, 275, 280

Bass, Ens Horace A., Jr., 272

Bauer, Lt Louis H., 55–56, 203, 237, 240, 241, 286

Beakley, LCdr Wallace M., 67, 328

Behr, Ens William A., 220–221, 306

Bingaman, Ens Harold L., 200, 283–284, 305, 331–332

Bismarck Archipelago
  Japanese occupation, 39

Blair, Ens Foster J., 59–63, 66, 149

Block Four Village, Guadalcanal, 144

Boston Maru, 326

Bottomley, Lt Harold S. (Syd), 165, 168, 170, 212, 214–216, 219–221

Bougainville Island, 54

Bowdoin, S1 Willie C., 267–268

Braitmeyer, GySgt Nelson, 142

Brannon, Capt Dale D., 188–190

Brewer, Gunner Charles E., 203, 240–241, 249–250, 261, 263, 280, 281

Brewer, CSF James J., 299

Bright, Ens Mark K., 86–87, 293–294

Brodecki, Pvt Andrew, 141

Brooks, Ens George W. (Red), 154, 293–294

Brown, Lt Herbert S., Jr. (Pete), 55–56, 59-60, 66

Brush, Capt Charles A., 134–135

Buell, Ens Harold L., 327–328

Buin, Bougainville, 105

Buka Emergency Strip, 53, 81, 176, 211, 222

Buka Island, 79, 105

Burkey, Ens Gale C., 175–179, 181, 183, 193

Burnett, Ens Howard R., 287–288

Bye, Ens Robert J., 193–195, 197, 288, 290, 304–305

Calahan, AMM2 Herman K., 197

Caldwell, Lt Turner F., 161, 234, 315, 317, 318, 323, 325–327

Campbell, AOM2 Alfred D., 112, 113, 114, 116, 132

Campbell, Lt(jg) Robert K., 293

Cape Esperance, Guadalcanal, 46, 48

Carl, Capt Marion E., 187–188, 190–191

Carmichael, LtCol Richard N., 82

Carrier air group organization and doctrine
  Imperial Navy, 17–19
  U.S. Navy, 16–19

Carteret Island, 332

Caruthers, AMM2 Herman H., 69

Case, 1stLt Leo B., 146

Cates, Col Clifton, 135, 141, 143

Chambers, Capt Walter, 327

Clarke, Lt Walter E., 48, 285

Clemens, Capt Warren F. M. (Martin), 135, 136

Clute, Lt(jg) George S., 332

Coastwatchers, 40, 54, 93, 105

Codrea, 2dLt George, 139

Coit, Ens Harlan J., 129

Conlon, AMM3 George, 273–274

Cook, Ens Earl W., 89, 91

Cook, Ens J. H., 156

Coral Sea Battle, 7, 21, 41, 42, 124, 126, 180, 181, 183, 186, 244, 288, 327

Corl, Mach Harry L., 198–200, 290, 332

Corpus Christi (Texas) Naval Air Station, 21

Cresswell, LtCol Lenard B. (L. B.), 143, 144, 146

Crews, Lt Howard W. (Sandy), 236, 248, 301, 302

Crouch, AMM3 Calvin, 283, 284, 331–332

Crow, Ens Roger C., 211–214, 219, 221, 294–295

Currie, Ens Benjamin F., 248, 280

Curtis, Lt Walter, 302

Daly, Ens Joseph R., 59–63, 66

Davis, Capt Arthur C., 306, 307, 310

Davis, BM2 Arthur J., 257–258, 267

Davis, Lt Ray, 205–207, 239, 305

Davy, Ens Charles D., 86–87

DeGarmo, Lt(jg) Edward F., 275

De Poix, Lt Vincent P., 71–73, 286–287

Diamond, Cpl LeRoy, 138

Dibb, Ens Robert A. M. (Ram), 249, 275, 278, 280

Dillon, AMM3 W. E., 195, 304–305

Disque, Ens Robert M., 74–76, 78, 238, 246, 282–284, 305–306

Divine, Ens Robert A., 220, 304

Doolittle Tokyo Raid, 44

Dow, LCdr Leonard J. (Ham), 226–227, 229–230, 232, 238, 241, 243, 259, 293, 319

Dulfiho, Lt Marion W., 86–87, 243, 244

Edmundson, Maj James V., 115

Efate Island, 109, 114, 158, 159

Egawa, Lt Renpei, 54, 56–57, 61, 71, 83

Eichenberger, Ens Charles E. (Ike), 272, 274–275

Elder, Lt(jg) Robert M., 170, 233, 312–313, 329

Eldridge, LCdr John, Jr., 67, 68–69

Elliott, ARM3 Harry E., 68

Escher, Ens Robert A., 147–148

Esders, CAP Wilhelm G., 155

Espiritu Santo Island, 106, 108, 157, 314, 332

Estes, Ens George G. (Glenn), 163–164, 287–288

Eta Jima Naval Academy, 22

Fairchild, Pvt Elmer, 142

Faisi, Shortland Islands, 116, 162

Fayle, Lt(jg) Edward L. (Frenchy), 314, 332

Felt, Cdr Harry D. (Don), 49, 91, 156, 161, 163–164, 174, 179, 183–184, 193, 210, 214–215, 219, 220, 222–223, 233, 305

Fiji Islands, 39

Fike, LtCol Charles L., 130, 187

Fincher, 2dLt Deltis H., 189–190

Fink, Ens Christian, 326

Firebaugh, Lt(jg) Gordon E., 73, 75–79

Fisher, CMM Reuben, 299–300

Fletcher, VAdm Frank Jack, 42, 54, 80, 89, 93, 99, 106—108, 126,

Fletcher, VAdm Frank Jack *(cont.)*
    147, 150, 154, 158–160, 162,
    163–164, 166–168, 173–175,
    177–180, 182–183, 193, 201–203,
    228–229, 320, 322, 328
Florida Island, 44, 47, 113
Fluitt, Mach William E., 264
Frank, Lt(jg) Alan S., 293
Frazier, 2dLt Kenneth D., 190
Fujita, Lt Bakuro, 97, 98
Furuta, PO1 Kiyoto, 263, 265

Gabara, BM1 Alfred, 257–258,
    267–268
Garaudy, ARM1 Edward J., 291
Gavutu Island, 44, 47, 90
Gay, Lt(jg) Theodore S., Jr. (Dick),
    71–73, 238, 246, 281–282
Ghormley, VAdm Robert L., 106–108,
    150, 158–159, 164
Gibson, ARM3 Carl L., 281
Gibson, Ens Robert D., 69–70, 107–
    108, 204, 303
Givens, Ens George P., 259
Glasmann, Ens Ross C., Jr., 260–261,
    266–267
Godfrey, ARM3 Joseph, 218
Gordon, Ens Robert M., 233, 312–
    313, 329
Graciosa Bay, Ndeni, 147, 150, 161,
    175, 176, 193, 228
Gray, Lt Richard, 48, 85–86, 149,
    182, 227, 244, 245
Greater East Asia Co-Prosperity
    Sphere, 118
Greco, AMM2 Joseph F., 268
Green, Ens Frank O., 244, 271

Guadalcanal Island, 106, 118
    Japanese airfield, 40, 42, 50,
    see also Henderson Field
    Lunga airfield, 103–104, 106–107,
    118, 120
Gutt, 2dLt Fred E., 187, 188, 190

Halavo, Florida Island, 47
Halford, Ens James A., Jr., 286
Hamilton, MG Henry B. (Tex),
    187–188
Hamm, Lt(jg) George S., 251, 257–
    258, 262, 266, 278
Hancock, Sgt James, 142
Hansen, S1 Robert W., 209–210,
    212–213, 216–217, 219
Hanson, Ens Alden W., 293
Hanson, Ens Eugene R., 218–219,
    222
Hara, RAdm Chuichi, 168, 175, 186,
    192, 196, 200, 210, 222
Hara, Cdr Tameichi, 191, 195–198,
    217, 220, 223–224
Harmer, Lt Richard E. (Chick), 236,
    246–247, 279–280, 301–302,
    307
Harmon, MajGen Millard F., 107
Harwood, Lt Bruce L., 218–219, 222
Hayashitani, Lt(jg) Tadashi, 97, 98
Hayes, Maj Charles, 111, 131
Haynes, Ens Leon W., 243–244
Henderson Field, Guadalcanal, 108–
    109, 111–112, 114–115, 121,
    125, 130, 133, 147–148, 150,
    152, 156–157, 160–162, 164–
    168, 170, 174–175, 179, 186–
    189, 234, 314, 317–318,
    323–324, 326–328

see also Guadalcanal, Japanese
　airfield
Henderson, Maj Lofton R., 108
Henry, Lt(jg) William E., 113, 211,
　221
Herriman, Lt(jg) Fred C., 316
Hidaka, Lt Saneyasu, 244, 270, 272
HIJMS *Akagi*, 6–7
HIJMS *Amatsukaze*, 168, 191, 195–
　196, 211, 220, 223–225
HIJMS *Chikuma*, 202, 207, 310
HIJMS *Chitose*, 122, 176, 205, 313,
　329
HIJMS *Chokai*, 161
HIJMS *Hagikaze*, 115
HIJMS *Hiryu*, 6–7
HIJMS *Hosho*, 6–7
HIJMS *Jintsu*, 325–327
HIJMS *Kaga*, 6–7
HIJMS *Kagero*, 169
HIJMS *Kawakaze*, 153–154
HIJMS *Maikaze*, 314
HIJMS *Maya*, 204
HIJMS *Mochizuki*, 327–328
HIJMS *Mutsuki*, 327
HIJMS *Ryujo*, 6–7, 122, 168, 175–
　176, 179, 185, 191–192, 196–
　201, 204, 207, 210–224, 225,
　228, 233, 238, 281, 285, 290,
　291, 304, 317, 321, 322, 332
HIJMS *Shoho*, 7, 186
HIJMS *Shokaku*, 7, 122, 158, 173,
　185, 202–203, 205–208, 239,
　314, 321–322
HIJMS *Soryu*, 6–7
HIJMS *Taiyo*, 329
HIJMS *Tokitsukaze*, 168, 196, 211,
　223–225

HIJMS *Tone*, 168, 175, 196, 198–
　199, 210–214, 218, 220, 222–
　223, 225
HIJMS *Yamato*, 119, 133, 329
HIJMS *Zuiho*, 7
HIJMS *Zuikaku*, 7, 122, 158, 173,
　185, 202–203, 207–208, 314,
　321–322, 329
Hise, 2dLt Henry W., 130–131,
　325–326
HMAS *Canberra*, 99, 106
HMS *Furious*, 3
Holley, Ens Edward B., 315–317
Holmberg, Lt Paul A., 164, 213–214,
　221, 291
Holt, Lt(jg) William M., 59–63, 66
Horenburger, Lt Carl H., 69, 291, 303
Horsman, Pvt Harry, 139, 142
Howard, Lt(jg) Robert L., 95–96

Ichiki, Col Kiyano, 122, 136–137,
　140, 146, 152
Iizuka, Lt Masao, 186
Imperial General Headquarters, 118
Imperial Japanese Army, 109, 114,
　120, 134
　7th Infantry Division, 146
　28th Infantry Regiment, 122, 146
　35th Infantry Brigade, 133
　Ichiki Butai, 135+136, 139, 140,
　　143, 146, 148, 152, 156
　Southeast Area Command, 109
Imperial Japanese Navy
　First Air Fleet, 185
　1st Carrier Division, 185
　2d Air Group, 81–83, 85–88
　Second Fleet, 119
　Third Fleet, 119, 185

4th Air Group, 52, 54, 56, 58, 61,
  62, 74–76, 78–79, 81, 83, 92,
  95-98, 100, 148
5th Air Attack Force, 52, 54, 80–81,
  83, 91, 93, 95, 99, 104–106,
  108, 114, 119, 132, 148, 162,
  167, 168, 175, 186
Eighth Fleet, 322, 324
Eleventh Air Fleet, 104
14th Air Group, 129, 155, 174, 328
Advance Expeditionary Force, 122
Base Air Force, 104, 123, 162, 174
Combined Fleet, 22, 39, 42, 119–
  121, 123–124, 126, 127, 168,
  185, 329
KA Advance Force, 121, 133, 157,
  162, 168, 173, 204–205, 312,
  320-322
KA Carrier Striking Force, 157, 162,
  167–168, 173, 205, 207–208,
  225, 232, 314, 321
KA Covering Group, 150
KA Detached Force, 168, 175, 179,
  186, 192–200, 210–225
KA Guadalcanal Support Force, 121,
  157, 329
KA Reinforcement Group, 122,
  132–133, 148, 150, 157, 161,
  163–164, 167–168, 174, 176,
  179, 191, 228, 233, 320, 322–
  329
KA Seaplane Group, 122
KA Support Group, 121, 133
KA Vanguard Force, 122, 202, 205,
  207, 303, 314, 320
Kaga Air Group, 186
Misawa Air Group, 83, 92, 95–96,
  98, 100, 148, 174, 182

Mobile Force *(Kido Butai)*, 122,
  307
Outer Seas Force, 119, 122, 150,
  154, 157, 161, 162, 176, 178,
  324
Ryujo Air Group, 162, 176–177,
  185–192, 197, 222–223,
  321–322
Shokaku Air Group, 157, 162, 174,
  208, 238–241, 245–250, 260–
  261, 263, 265–270, 275, 277–
  278, 280, 282, 292–295, 307,
  314, 341
Southeast Area, 122
Special Naval Landing Force
  (rikusentai), 114–115, 120
Tainan Air Group, 53–56, 68, 74,
  78–79, 81–83, 92, 96, 98, 100,
  106, 112, 148, 175
Yokohama Air Group, 149, 174, 324
Yokosuka 5th Special Naval Landing Force, 122
Zuikaku Air Group, 157, 162, 174,
  208, 239–240, 244–245, 270–
  278, 282, 292–295, 307, 321
Innis, Ens Donald A., 59, 66
Inoue, Lt Fumito, 82, 84–88, 90
Isaman, Lt(jg) Roy M., 216
Iwaoka, PO2 Minoru, 85

Jachym, 2dLt John J., 134–135,
  143–144
Jacksonville (Florida) Naval Air
  Station, 21
Jacobs, Pvt Whitney, 138
Jeans, 2dLt Cloyd R. (Rex), 190–191
Jensen, Lt Hayden M., 85, 87–88, 270
Jett, LCdr Charles M., 193–198, 200–
  201, 288–290, 303–305

Johnson, AMM1 David F., Jr., 165, 216
Johnson, Ens Douglas M, 203, 249–
    250, 268–269
Jones, AOM2 Harold L., 69–70, 206–
    207
Jorgenson, Ens John H., 200, 283,
    305

KA Operation
    organization and planning, 121–
    127, 166–168, 185
Kakimoto, PO2 Kenji, 69–70
Kato, Capt Tadao, 191–192, 198, 222
Katz, Ens Aaron, 218
Kawai, Lt Shiro, 55, 59, 68, 71, 74,
    77, 148
Kellam, Lt Joseph M., 193, 227–228,
    232–233
Kenney, MajGen George C., 82, 83
Kephart, Lt(jg) William P., 67–68
Kimura, PO3 Yutaka, 96
King, Adm Ernest J., 107
King, 2dLt John H., 190
Kinkaid, RAdm Thomas C., 147, 163,
    175, 178–180, 182, 228, 233,
    257
Kinryu Maru, 325–327
Kirkpatrick, LCdr John E., 257
Kirn, LCdr Louis J. (Bullet Lou), 165,
    168, 210–211, 213, 292–294
Kishi, Cdr Hisakichi, 198, 224
Kleinman, Ens John M., 271
Kleinmann, Ens Mortimer V., Jr., 285
Kline, Lt Raymond P., 291
Knight, ARM3 Paul W., 200, 283–
    284, 331–332
Kokumbona, Guadalcanal, 114–115

Kondo, VAdm Nobutake, 119, 121,
    132–133, 157, 162, 167, 173,
    176, 204–205, 312, 320–321,
    329
Konig, Lt Ruben H., 234–235, 281,
    305, 315–317
Kotani, Lt Shigeru, 92, 95–97
Krueger, Ens Fred J., 151
Krzeminski, AM3 Edmund, 258
Kukum, Guadalcanal, 46–47, 50–51,
    108, 151, 153
Kure Naval Base, Japan, 119, 158

Lae, New Guinea, 54, 82, 104
Lakunai Airdrome, Rabaul, 54, 70,
    79, 82, 92, 106, 156
Lamson, S1 Joyce W., 268
Lane, ARM2 David H., 316
Larsen, Lt Harold H. (Swede), 233–
    234, 312–313, 320
Lee, Pfc Robert E., 261
Lengo Channel, 153, 166, 323
Leslie, LCdr Maxwell F., 55, 56, 235,
    257, 318–320
Lindley, Ens Charles W., 282
Lindley, TSgt Johnny D., 187–188,
    190
Lindsey, Lt Robin M., 275, 298–299
Livdahl, LCdr Orlin L., 249, 252,
    253, 255, 259
Loesch, Ens Richards L., Jr. (Dix),
    155, 242–243
Lowe, Lt John T., 204–205, 303
Luckey, Maj Robert B., 140, 141
Lunga Perimeter, Guadalcanal, 112,
    114–115, 134–136, 147, 163,
    169, 186, 324
Lunga, Guadalcanal, 43, 46, 47, 48,
    50, 51, 105

Lupo, S2 Lawrence P., 96–97

MacKenzie, Lt Hugh, RAN, 111, 112
MacNair, Lt M. P., 128
Makambo Island, 44, 47
Malaita Island, 154, 160, 323
Mangrum, Maj Richard C., 130–131,
    164, 323–326
Maniere, Maj Ernest, 223
Mankin, AP1 Lee P. (Paul), 74–76,
    78, 294
March, Ens Harry A., Jr., 88, 294
Marcoux, MM2 William N., 308–309
Marshall, Gen George C., 107
Mason, PO Paul, RAN, 54, 105
Maul, Ens Elmer, 163–164
McAllister, 2dLt Charles, 326
McCain, RAdm John S. (Slew), 108–
    110, 147, 150, 175
McClanahan, 2dLt James, 142
McDonald, Ens John B., Jr., 247–248,
    280
McLeod, 2dLt Robert F., 190
Mears, Ens Frederick, 30, 33, 237,
    259, 260, 290, 304
Mester, Lt(jg) Charles H., 147
Miami (Florida) Naval Air Station, 23
Midway Battle, 10–11, 22, 40, 41, 42,
    44, 108, 117, 124, 125, 126,
    130, 168, 181, 183, 186, 187,
    194, 217, 229, 233, 289, 327
Mikawa, VAdm Gunichi, 119, 122,
    150, 154, 157, 161–162, 176,
    322, 324
Milner, Lt Robert M., 211
Miner, ARM3 T. H., 295
Morgan, Ens Corwin F., 218, 220
Morrell, Capt Rivers J., 188, 190

Mott, LCdr Elias B., II (Benny), 252–
    254, 261
Murakami, Lt Binichi, 186–187,
    190–191
Myers, Lt John N., 198–200, 290,
    304

Nagle, Mach Patrick L., 89, 91
Nagumo, VAdm Chuichi, 119, 122,
    132–133, 157, 162, 167, 173,
    185, 203, 207, 225, 232, 307,
    314, 320–321
Nakagaki, WO Seisuke, 87–88
Nakajima, LCdr Tadashi, 53–55, 57,
    59, 62, 71, 74, 76, 83
Nakamoto, S1 Seiki, 85
Nakamura, PO1 Asayoshi, 61
Naval Aviation Reserve Act of 1939,
    21
Naval Disarmament Conference of
    1922, 3
Ndeni Island, 174
Netherlands East Indies
    Japanese invasion, 54
New Caledonia Island, 39, 106
New Georgia Sound (The Slot), 105,
    169, 176
New Hebrides Islands, 40, 157, 174
Nimitz, Adm Chester W., 107, 153
Nishiura, PO1 Kunimatsu, 78
Notomi, Lt Kenjiro, 186–187, 189–
    190, 222
Noumea, New Caledonia, 106
Noyes, RAdm Leigh, 90–91, 94, 108,
    147, 160, 163, 166
Nura Island, 314

O'Neill, GM2 James J., 95–96

Oahu, Hawaii, 110
Olson, ACRM I. H., 195
Ontong Java, 150
Ota, WO Gengo, 84, 85, 88
Otsuka, Lt Reijiro, 240, 245, 270–
    272, 274
Over, Lt George R., 297

Packard, AP1 Howard S., 87–88, 272
Paretsky, Ens Jacob S., 67–68
Parker, Pvt Ray, 140
Pearl Harbor attack, 7, 39, 126
Pearl Harbor, Oahu, 107
Pease, Capt Harl, Jr., 83
Pellesier, Ens R. E., 113
Pensacola (Florida) Naval Air Station,
    20–21, 44
Peterson, AMM2 Bernard W., 34, 251,
    264, 274
Philippine Islands
  Japanese invasion, 39, 54
Pilot training
  Imperial Navy, 22–24
  U.S. Navy and U.S. Marine Corps,
    20–24
Poliny, Pvt Andrew, 144–145
Pollock, LtCol Edwin A. (Al), 135,
    139–141
Port Arthur Battle (1904), 124
Port Moresby, New Guinea, 82–83,
    108, 118, 120
  Japanese invasion attempt, 41
Powell, GM1 William K., 265
Presley, Ens Wayne C., 285
Price, Ens Robert L., 59, 66

Rabaul, New Britain, 40, 104–105,
    109, 123

Rabi Airdrome, New Guinea, 52
Ramsey, Capt Dewitt W., 90–92, 161
Read, PhoM3 Robert F., 267
Read, Sub-Lt Jack, RAN, 93, 105
Register, Ens Francis R., 155, 242,
    281–282
Reid, Mach Beverly W. (Bill), 271
Rekata Bay, Santa Isabel, 123, 152,
    176, 328
Resen, FC3 Larry, 273
Rhodes, RE Thomas W., 74–78, 294
Richardson, Lt David C., 86–87, 180,
    243–244, 270–271
Richey, Ens Gerald S., 107–108
Richey, Ens John F., 161, 200
Riester, Lt Leo B., 161, 163, 176–
    177, 205
Rikusentai, see IJN, Special Naval
    Landing Force
Rivers, Pvt John, 138
Roach, Ens Melvin C., 285
Robinson, MM1 Cecil S., 309–310
Rodenburg, Ens Eldor E., 69
Roncador Reef, 315, 318
Rouse, Ens Wildon M., 94, 97–98,
    286
Rowe, Lt Henry A., 203, 226–227,
    229–230, 237
Royal Navy, 5
Runyon, Mach Donald E., 87–88, 94,
    97–98, 154, 271, 274
Russ, ACRM C. E., 213, 292
Russell Islands, 57
Russell, Lt(jg) Allard G. (Slim), 46–
    48, 50–51, 65–66, 99, 105–106,
    110, 128–129, 154–155, 165,
    168–170
Rutherford, Lt(jg) Harold E., 286

Sakai, PO1 Saburo, 63–65, 68–70, 74, 79

Sakimoto, PO1 Yoshiyuki, 58, 61–62, 72

Samoa, 39

Sampson, Lt William, 108

San Cristobal Island, 114, 130, 154, 155, 314

Santa Cruz Islands, 147

Santa Isabel Island, 74, 83, 91

Sasai, Lt(jg) Junichi, 55, 57, 59–60, 63, 68, 74, 76

Sato, PO3 Seiji, 87

Sauer, Ens F. J. (Jim), 209–210, 212–213, 219

Savo Island, 88, 323

Savo Island Battle, 99, 109, 119

Schindler, Cdr Walter G. (Butch), 160

Schinka, 1stSgt Joseph R., 251–252, 256, 258

Schmid, Pvt Albert, 138–139

Schroeder, Lt Fred J., 221

Seki, LCdr Mamoru, 238–240, 245–247, 258, 261, 277, 310–311, 321

Shands, LCdr Courtney, 47, 94

Shaw, Ens Robert C., 69–70, 205–207, 239

Shea, Cpl John, 140

Sherwood, Lt Gordon, 212, 214, 216, 219

Shigematsu, Lt Yasuhiro, 241, 242

Shigemi, WO Katsuma, 186–188

Shoemaker, Ens Joseph D. (Dutch), 87–89, 94, 98, 272

Shortland Islands, 81, 88, 105, 123, 129, 149, 155, 157, 174, 324

Shumway, LCdr DeWitt W., 164, 213–214, 221, 291

Simpler, LCdr Leroy C., 48, 94, 149, 238, 239, 285–286

Simpson Harbor, Rabaul, 108

Slater, Lt(jg) Robert E., 177–178

Smith, LCdr Herschel A., 297

Smith, Lt James C., 272, 274

Smith, Capt John L., 130, 148, 324

Smith, ChMach William A., 309–310

Snowden, LCdr Ernest M., 91

Solomon Islands
    Japanese occupation, 39

South Pacific Area, 107, 150, 324

South Pacific Force, 106
    Aircraft, South Pacific (AirSoPac), 108, 110, 174, 176, 180–181

Southerland, Lt James J., II (Pug), 55–59, 61–66, 68, 72, 74, 108

Southwest Pacifica Area, 82

Sowa, Pvt Adam, 144

Spillane, Cpl John, 139

Spraggins, Ens James A., 178

Starkes, Lt(jg) Carlton B., 86–87, 271, 280

Stemen, ARM2 Dewey A., 193, 195, 197, 288–289, 304–305

Stephenson, AP1 William J., Jr., 74–78

Stevenson, 1stLt Nikolai, 144

Stewart Island, 331

Stewart Islands, 203, 320–323

Stewart, Maj Allan, 314

Stover, Lt(jg) Elisha T. (Smokey), 43–49, 51, 112, 116, 131, 132, 148, 149, 150, 285

Strickland, ARM2 Eugene C., 200

Strong, Lt Stockton B. (Birney), 161, 200

Sullivan, ACRM G. J., 222

Sumrall, Mach Howell M., 71–73, 237, 241–243

Suva, Fiji, 109

Tabberer, Lt(jg) Charles A., 59, 66
Taivu Point, Guadalcanal, 115, 157
Takahashi, PO2 Koji, 85, 88
Tanaka, RAdm Raizo, 122, 132, 133, 148, 150, 157, 161, 163, 167, 174, 176, 179, 228, 320, 322, 324–327, 329
Tanambogo Island, 44, 47, 91
Taurman, Lt John, 314, 332
Taylor, 2dLt Lawrence C. (Red), 190, 191
Tenaru River Battle, 137–146, 156
Tetere, Guadalanal, 134
The Slot, *see* New Georgia Sound
Thomas, LtCol Gerald C., 143
Thomas, 2dLt Leland E., 326
Thueson, Ens Theodore S., 176, 178
Tinian, Mariana Islands, 83
Togo, VAdm Heihachiro, 124
Tongatabu Island, 328
Townsend, LCdr William E. (Slim), 298
Townville, Australia, 54
Trott, AOM1 John W., 205, 207
Truk Atoll, Caroline Islands, 122, 132, 133, 154, 321, 329
Trymofiev, CEM Alex, 309
Tsukahara, VAdm Nishizo, 104, 110, 122–123, 132–133, 148, 157, 162, 167
Tucker, AOM2 Lester B., 272–273
Tulagi Harbor, 153, 166
Tulagi Island, 39, 44–48, 52–53, 90, 106, 109, 118, 189
   U.S. invasion plans, 40

Turner, RAdm Richmond K. (Kelly), 84, 90, 93, 100, 103–104, 166
Turzai, Pvt George, 137–138, 142–143
Twibell, CMM Murell D., 309

United States Congress, 4, 5
United States Army Air Forces (USAAF)
   V Bomber Command, 82, 108, 116, 162
   11th Heavy Bombardment Group, 115, 176, 223–224, 285, 292, 314, 327, 329
   19th Heavy Bombardment Group, 82–83, 100, 108, 116, 156
   22d Medium Bombardment Group, 82
   67th Fighter Squadron, 156–157, 187–189
United States Marine Corps
   1st Engineer Battalion, 104, 115, 143
   1st Marine Division, 40, 103, 117–118, 135, 136, 143
   1st Marine Regiment (1st Marines), 135, 141
      1st Battalion, 143
         Company A, 134, 144
         Company B, 145
         Company C, 144
      2d Battalion, 135, 139, 141, 143
         Company E, 137
         Company G, 139, 141–142
   1st Pioneer Battalion, 104
   1st Special Weapons Battalion, 135, 140, 142
      Battery B, 139

3d Defense Battalion, 10
  Battery E, 188
11th Marine Regiment (11th
  Marines)
  3d Battalion, 135, 141
Marine Air Group 23 (MAG-23),
  109–110, 130, 133, 187
Marine Fighter Squadron 212
  (VMF-212), 109, 114, 151, 152,
  190
Marine Fighter Squadron 223
  (VMF-223), 109, 114, 130, 145–
  146, 164, 187–188, 190–191,
  324
Marine Observation Squadron 251
  (VMO-251), 111
Marine Scout-Bomber Squadron
  232 (VMSB-232), 109, 130–131,
  164, 323–325
United States Navy
  advanced carrier training groups
    (ACTG), 23–24
  Aviation Cadet program, 21
  Bombing Squadron 3 (Bombing-3,
    VB-3), 41, 44, 49, 164, 165, 170,
    210, 212–216, 219, 221, 229,
    233, 291, 306, 312
  Bombing Squadron 6 (Bombing-6,
    VB-6), 41, 107, 182, 204, 206–
    207, 220, 234, 281, 291, 303,
    305, 317
  Construction Unit, Base, 1 (CUB-1),
    111–112, 115
  Enterprise Air Group, 41, 44, 69,
    74, 90–91, 160–161, 167, 174–
    175, 180–184, 204, 207, 234–
    235, 257, 287, 302, 312, 318,
    322

Enterprise Flight 300, 234, 315,
  317, 318, 323–324, 326–327
Fighter Direction School, 227
Fighting Squadron 5 (Fighting-5,
  VF-5), 41, 43–46, 48–49, 55–56,
  59, 66, 85–86, 88, 91, 93–94,
  149, 180, 182, 184, 227, 229,
  232, 236–238, 239, 243, 244,
  246–248, 269–272, 274, 279–
  280, 285, 287, 293, 301–302
Fighting Squadron 6 (Fighting-6,
  VF-6), 44–45, 49, 55–56, 71,
  73–74, 84, 87–89, 91, 93–94,
  97, 154, 182, 203, 227, 232,
  237–238, 240–243, 246, 248–
  250, 261, 268–269, 271–272,
  275, 278, 281–282, 286–287,
  293, 301, 305–307, 328
Fighting Squadron 8 (Fighting-8,
  VF-8), 44
Fighting Squadron 71 (Fighting-71,
  VF-71), 41, 44, 47, 49, 56, 78,
  88, 93, 94, 129
Fleet Carrier Air Group 10, 24
Pacific Fleet, 107, 154
  intelligence section, 90, 158
    159, 166–167, 174
Pacific Fleet headquarters, 54
Patrol Squadron 11 (Patrol-121,
  VP-11), 332
Patrol Squadron 23 (Patrol-23,
  VP-23), 150, 161, 175–181, 183,
  193, 205, 227, 324
Saratoga Air Group, 41, 45, 48–49,
  90, 91, 93, 154, 156, 160–161,
  163, 164–170, 174, 179–181,
  183–184, 193, 210–222, 233–
  234, 291, 292–294, 305, 322,
  328

Scouting Squadron 3 (Scouting-3, VS-3), 41, 44, 46, 49, 51, 128, 155, 165, 168, 209–213, 216, 219, 221, 292, 329

Scouting Squadron 5 (Scouting-5, VS-5), 41, 44, 47, 161, 163, 177, 182, 200, 234, 281, 287–288, 317, 327

Scouting Squadron 71 (Scouting-71, VS-71), 41, 44, 47, 49, 67, 95–96, 129, 147, 328

Scouting Squadron 72 (Scouting-72, VS-72), 41, 91, 149

Task Force 11, 229, 256, 288, 323, 328, 329

Task Force 16, 158, 163, 245, 250, 255–257, 269, 274, 276, 279, 281, 285, 287, 291, 295, 301, 306, 316, 318, 322, 323, 328

Task Force 17, 107

Task Force 18, 158, 181, 320, 323, 328–329

Task Force 44, 150

Task Force 61, 40, 54–55, 84, 94, 99, 106, 108–111, 114–115, 122, 133, 147–150, 154, 157–162, 166–167, 175–178, 180–183, 193, 202–203, 205, 207–208, 221, 226–228, 232–233, 237–238, 245, 285–288, 292, 303, 307, 310–312, 315, 320

Task Force 62, 40, 54–56, 71, 84, 99–100, 110

Task Force 63, 108 *see also* South Pacific Force

Torpedo Squadron 3 (Torpedo-3, VT-3), 30, 34–35, 41, 155, 182, 193–200, 234–235, 237, 243, 251, 281, 283, 288, 290, 304–305, 315–317, 332

Torpedo Squadron 7 (Torpedo-7, VT-7), 41

Torpedo Squadron 8 (Torpedo-8, VT-8), 41, 156, 160, 164, 210, 217–220, 229, 233–234, 304, 312–313, 332

United States Fleet, 3, 4

Wasp Air Group, 41, 67, 90–91, 131, 160, 167, 181, 323, 328

USS *Alhena*, 153, 155

USS *Astoria*, 99, 106, 114

USS *Atlanta*, 255–256, 259, 268, 328

USS *Balch*, 250, 256, 272, 305–306, 309

USS *Barnett*, 96

USS *Benham*, 256

USS *Blue*, 153, 166

USS *Chicago*, 62, 99, 106, 110, 114

USS *Curtiss*, 332

USS *Dewey*, 86–87

USS *Ellet*, 256

USS *George F. Elliott*, 96, 98–99

USS *Enterprise*, 4, 33, 40–41, 45, 89, 107, 128–129, 154–155, 157, 160, 163, 175, 181–182, 193, 198–200, 202–203, 207, 226–228, 231–233, 236–237, 240, 244–278, 280, 286, 288, 290–292, 296–304, 306–310, 316–317, 319, 322–323, 327–328

USS *Essex*, 5

USS *Farragut*, 303

USS *Fomalhaut*, 153, 155

USS *Grayson*, 248, 256, 275–278, 302

USS *Henley*, 153, 166

USS *Hornet*, 5, 41, 44, 107

USS *Jarvis*, 96, 98
USS *Langley*, 3–6
USS *Lexington*, 3–4, 6–7, 41
USS *Long Island*, 5, 109, 114, 129–130, 132–133
USS *Mackinac*, 148, 161, 175, 177, 228, 233
USS *Maury*, 256
USS *Minneapolis*, 303
USS *Monssen*, 251, 256, 258, 262, 265, 278
USS *Mugford*, 85, 88
USS *North Carolina*, 235, 248, 256–257, 259, 268–269, 272–275, 277–278, 287, 328
USS *Platte*, 128
USS *Portland*, 157, 158, 256
USS *Quincy*, 99, 106, 114
USS *Ranger*, 4, 6–7
USS *San Juan*, 95–96
USS *Saratoga*, 3–4, 40–41, 45–46, 51, 55, 66, 89, 90, 94, 154, 156, 160–161, 170, 177, 179, 181, 183–184, 192, 202, 207, 209, 228–229, 231–233, 237–239, 244–245, 256, 270–272, 285–286, 288, 295, 301–305, 307, 312, 314, 317, 319, 323, 328
USS *Vincennes*, 99, 106, 114
USS *Wasp*, 5, 40, 90, 94, 128, 158, 160, 166–167, 303, 320, 323, 328
USS *Yorktown*, 4, 6, 7, 41, 288

Vandegrift, MajGen Alexander A. (Archer), 131, 146, 147, 164, 323–324

Velasquez, ARM3 Edward, 314
Visto, F3 Ernest R., 309–310
Vorse, Lt Albert O., Jr. (Scoop), 84, 88, 154–155, 227, 237, 241–243, 301
Vouza, SgtMaj Jacob, 135–136
Vunakanau Airdrome, Rabaul, 54, 79, 82–83, 92, 100, 156

Wadsworth, Pvt Joe, 140
Warden, Mach William H., 74–78
Ware, Lt Robert M., 149
Washington Naval Disarmament Treaty of 1922, 5, 6
Weis, RE Werner I., 305, 315
Weissenborn, Lt(jg) D. E. (Weasel), 237, 259, 290
Wendt, AOM1 Ervin F., 222
Weymouth, Lt Ralph, 99, 212, 293, 295
Wiley, ARM3 Delmer D., 199, 332
Wilger, ARM2 Harold J., 287–288
Williamson, Lt John, 264–265
Wilson, Cpl Dean, 140
Woodhull, Lt Rodger B., 177
World War I, 3
Wright, RAdm Carleton H., 150
Wyrick, Ens James W., 298–299

Yamada, RAdm Sadayoshi, 52–53, 81–83, 92, 98, 104, 119
Yamamoto, Adm Isoroku, 22, 41–42, 119–120, 124–125, 133, 157, 162, 167–168, 191, 329
Yoshida, PO1 Mototsuna, 77
Yoshimoto, Lt Kazuo, 293–294